P9-ASK-939

Transcendental Resistance

RE-MAPPING THE TRANSNATIONAL
A Dartmouth Series in American Studies

SERIES EDITOR
Donald E. Pease
Avalon Foundation Chair of Humanities
Founding Director of the Futures of American Studies Institute
Dartmouth College

The emergence of Transnational American Studies in the wake of the Cold War marks the most significant reconfiguration of American Studies since its inception. The shock waves generated by a newly globalized world order demanded an understanding of America's embeddedness within global and local processes rather than scholarly reaffirmations of its splendid isolation. The series Re-Mapping the Transnational seeks to foster the cross-national dialogues needed to sustain the vitality of this emergent field. To advance a truly comparativist understanding of this scholarly endeavor, Dartmouth College Press welcomes monographs from scholars both inside and outside the United States.

JOHANNES VOELZ

Transcendental Resistance

The New Americanists and Emerson's Challenge

DARTMOUTH COLLEGE PRESS
HANOVER, NEW HAMPSHIRE

Published by
University Press of New England
Hanover and London

Dartmouth College Press
Published by University Press of New England
www.upne.com
© 2010 Trustees of Dartmouth College
All rights reserved
Manufactured in the United States of America
Designed by Katherine B. Kimball
Typeset in Sabon by Integrated Publishing Solutions

University Press of New England is a member of the Green Press Initiative. The paper used in this book meets their minimum requirement for recycled paper.

For permission to reproduce any of the material in this book, contact Permissions, University Press of New England, One Court Street, Suite 250, Lebanon NH 03766; or visit www.upne.com

Library of Congress Cataloging-in-Publication Data
Voelz, Johannes.
   Transcendental resistance : the new Americanists and Emerson's challenge / Johannes Voelz.
      p.   cm. — (Re-mapping the transnational)
   Includes bibliographical references and index.
   ISBN 978-1-58465-936-5 (cloth : alk. paper) — ISBN 978-1-58465-937-2 (pbk. : alk. paper) — ISBN 978-1-58465-948-8 (electronic)
   1. Emerson, Ralph Waldo, 1803–1882 — Criticism and interpretation.   2. Transcendentalism.   3. National characteristics, American, in literature.   4. Transnationalism.   I. Title.
   PS1638.V64 2010
   814'.3—dc22   2010021335

5 4 3 2 1

For my teachers

CONTENTS

III EMERSON AND THE NATION

ACKNOWLEDGMENTS

INDEBTEDNESS IS DIFFICULT to measure. Perhaps as scholars we are what we write. In that sense those who have enabled me to begin and finish this book have allowed me to come into being. A deep debt, indeed.

First and foremost, I want to thank Winfried Fluck. His presence in this study is noticeable even in the very conception of the New Americanists as an object of study. His resistance to Emersonian enthusiasm was a healthy check whenever I was tempted to "understand all and forgive all." Ultimately even more important is the intellectual inspiration he has offered me in the nearly ten years that I have considered him a mentor. Many of my central ideas I owe to him. During my time as a Visiting Fellow at Harvard in 2006–2007, Larry Buell most immediately watched the individual chapters emerge, and was immensely helpful in sharpening my readings of Emerson. A truly Emersonian teacher, he consistently upheld a posture of reciprocity in our meetings, even when a disproportion of expertise was obvious to both of us. I am also particularly grateful to Don Pease, who continually demonstrates that even in the cool endeavors of abstraction, there is no mastery outside of passion. Not once did he take my project of critiquing the premises exemplified by the New Americanists personally. On the contrary, he has encouraged me intellectually with all his might and has offered vital help for this book.

Ulla Haselstein, Heinz Ickstadt, Leo Marx, Herwig Friedl, Ross Posnock, Thomas Claviez, Susanne Rohr, Elisa New, and Harald Wenzel read and commented on individual chapters; Homi Bhabha and Louis Menand discussed contemporary criticism with me. Several friends went through large parts of the manuscript and gave me meticulously detailed feedback, among them Michael Boyden, Julian Hanich, Jeff Hole, Maria Slowinska, and Ulrike Wagner. Were it not for Erin Hart's support and contagious self-discipline, I could not have written the largest part of this book in one year. In 2006 and 2007, the participants of the Futures of American Studies Summer Institute at Dartmouth, where I presented early versions of chapters 2 and 6, made many helpful suggestions, as did the members of the doctoral colloquium in American literature at Harvard, where, in 2007, I presented chapter 4. My students in Berlin, particularly a 2006 seminar on Transcendentalism, collaborated with me in trying out many ideas that ended up in these chapters. Richard Ellis, former editor of *Comparative American Studies*, and Paul Kane, guest editor at *Religion & Literature*, helped improve the portions that were published in those journals: A different version of chapter 1, including some material from chapter 2, appeared as "Representation, Emerson, and the New Americanists" in *Comparative American Studies* 6, no. 1 (2008): 37–54 and is reprinted by permission of Maney Publishing (www .maney.co.uk/journals/cas). A different version of chapter 2 was published as "Emerson and the Sociality of Inspiration" in *Religion & Literature* 41, no. 1 (Spring 2009): 83–109 and reprint permission has been granted by the University of Notre Dame.

In its final steps toward publication, the book has greatly benefited from the work of Richard Pult, Ann Brash, and the other staff members at the University Press of New England, as well as the copyediting of David Chu. Financially, my leave from teaching—essential for completing the manuscript within the duration of my contract at the Freie Universität Berlin— was made possible by a dissertation stipend from the German Academic Exchange Service (DAAD). Of my friends and former colleagues at the Kennedy Institute of the Freie Universität, to all of whom I am grateful for creating a stimulating environment of ritualized discussion, I am especially indebted to Laura Bieger and Andy Gross. In their own way, both clarify to me why it makes sense to pursue this career despite its hazards to the self. My parents—all four of them—and my sister have given me a strong sense of backing me up, come what may. Gratitude of its own kind goes to Magda Majewska. She makes the mind matter in ways I had not known.

AW   *Emerson's Antislavery Writings*, ed. Len Gougeon and Joel Myerson (New Haven, CT: Yale University Press, 1995).

CP   *Collected Papers of Charles Sanders Peirce*, ed. Charles Hartsthorne, Paul Weiss, and Arthur W. Burks, 8 vols. (Cambridge, MA: Harvard University Press, 1960–1966).

CS   *The Complete Sermons of Ralph Waldo Emerson*, ed. Albert J. von Frank et al., 4 vols. (Columbia: University of Missouri Press, 1989–1992).

CW   *The Collected Works of Ralph Waldo Emerson*, ed. Alfred R. Ferguson et al., 7 vols. to date (Cambridge, MA: Belknap Press of Harvard University Press, 1971–).

E   Locke, John. *Essay Concerning Human Understanding*, ed. Peter H. Nidditch (Oxford: Oxford University Press, 1975).

EL   *The Early Lectures of Ralph Waldo Emerson*, ed. Stephen E. Whicher, Robert E. Spiller, and Wallace Williams, 3 vols. (Cambridge, MA: Harvard University Press, 1959–1971).

JMN *The Journals and Miscellaneous Notebooks of Ralph Waldo Emerson*, ed. William H. Gilman et al., 16 vols. (Cambridge, MA: Belknap Press of Harvard University Press, 1960–1982).

L   *The Letters of Ralph Waldo Emerson*, ed. Ralph L. Rusk and Eleanor Tilton, 10 vols. (New York: Columbia University Press; 1939, 1990–1995).

LL   *The Later Lectures of Ralph Waldo Emerson, 1843–1871*, ed. Ronald A. Bosco and Joel Myerson, 2 vols. (Athens: University of Georgia Press, 2001).

TN   *The Topical Notebooks of Ralph Waldo Emerson*, ed. Ralph H. Orth et al., 3 vols. (Columbia: University of Missouri Press, 1990–1994).

W   *The Complete Works of Ralph Waldo Emerson*, ed. Edward W. Emerson, 12 vols. Centenary edition (Boston: Houghton Mifflin, 1903–1904).

Transcendental Resistance

THROUGHOUT THE LAST four decades, the field of American Studies has been reshaped by various forms of revisionism. In the late 1960s, the intellectual history synthesis of the Myth and Symbol school became increasingly untenable as the academic landscape began to reflect the social, political, and cultural transformations brought about by various social movements, including the civil rights and student movements. Since then, American Studies has adopted social scientific methods, ventured into ideology critique, and increasingly focused on race, class, and gender studies, as well as on a host of other minority discourses such as queer studies and disability studies. Most recently, the field has tried to challenge intellectual frameworks based on the category of the nation by proclaiming a "transnational turn." In light of these developments, American Studies is frequently described as having undergone a process of diversification and pluralization. Yet these varied forms of revisionism, different as they may be, are held together by a consensus concerning a set of underlying premises. To this day, these premises have remained largely unchallenged and even unacknowledged.

My study formulates a critique of these theoretical assumptions. I thus intervene in how Americanists have approached their material in recent decades, whether their work is concerned with colonial America or the most recent past. To unfold my critique, I give my study a dual focus. First, I narrow down the revisionism under scrutiny to the New Americanists. A loosely organized group of scholars, the New Americanists have engaged in revisionist criticism with the greatest vigor and have radicalized the logic of revisionist arguments. Having emerged around the end of the Cold War, the New Americanists originally caused a stir by criticizing with particular severity older Americanists as well as the canonical authors venerated by the latter. Above all, New Americanists attacked their precursors for reiterating an ideology of American exceptionalism. Soon this critique developed into an elaborate agenda of empire criticism. American culture, from this vantage point, had to be seen as fully permeated by imperialism. Lately, empire criticism has been fused with the "transnational turn." Since this latest turn has been fully embraced by established American Studies scholars, the term New Americanists has begun to lose some of its currency. Yet the critical assumptions exemplified by New Americanist scholarship have not therefore lost their influence; on the contrary, they have become even more widespread.

I further sharpen the focus of my critical intervention by taking Ralph Waldo Emerson as my exemplary interpretive object. Concentrating on Emerson allows me to pursue two goals. By analyzing New Americanist interpretations of Emerson, I dissect and critique their reading practices. But just as central to my project is the second step: Taking up "Emerson's challenge," I develop a series of alternative interpretations based on a set of premises that I take to be more plausible than those used by New Americanists and other revisionists. Emerson is particularly conducive to my project for several reasons. In trying to set themselves apart from earlier Americanists, New Americanists have relied on reinterpreting canonical American authors, particularly those associated with the American Renaissance. While New Americanists have been active in the extension and revision of the literary canon, Emerson, Herman Melville, and Nathaniel Hawthorne have remained among the authors most widely debated in American Studies. Of these three, Emerson stands out as the most polarizing figure. As Philip Gura has recently shown, the controversies over Emerson go back to his own time; even within Transcendentalist circles he was far from uncontested.[1] As early as the 1840s, his audiences and acquaintances were divided on a central ambiguity of his work: Because of his insistence on what he once called "the infinitude of the private man," he has appeared at once radical and reactionary.[2] His individualism, however complex it may be, has seemed to many critics to be radically nonconformist. Yet his emphasis on the individual also led Emerson to a habitual reluctance concerning collective action. Although the image of Emerson as solitary and withdrawn has been corrected in the last two decades by scholars who have revealed his deep engagement in reform movements, particularly abolitionism,[3] it remains true nonetheless that Emerson's idea of radical change ultimately looked to the individual rather than the group. Thus what made Emerson politically suspect is precisely what made him radical.

The continuing interest in Emerson clearly has to do with this ambiguity that is internal to his thought, writings, and public action. Many New Americanists have attempted to correct an uncritical stance toward Emerson putatively maintained by earlier critics. They have thus aimed to reveal that his idealist individualism was not nearly as liberating as claimed by those who have celebrated him as a hero of democracy. Indeed, there has been a strong tendency by New Americanists to demonstrate Emerson's ideological complicity. This position repeats critical pronouncements from earlier periods of Emerson's reception, though with the vocabulary and theoretical assumptions characteristic of the recent revisionism.[4]

Emerson is also particularly useful for developing an alternative to New Americanist reading practices. As a poet-philosopher, he addressed many of the New Americanists' concerns more explicitly than the novelists of the American Renaissance. This makes it possible to take up some of the terms that inform New Americanist interpretations, dislodge them from their underlying assumptions, and redeploy them for a very different interpretation. The three terms that I consider most important for New Americanist scholarship and that I will therefore appropriate for my alternative interpretation of Emerson are representation, identity, and the nation. The centrality of representation and identity stems from the fact that the various branches of revisionism in American Studies emerged along with the theory boom of the 1970s and 1980s. Theories associated with post-structuralism and related schools of thought have been predominantly concerned with the connection between the subject and language. Identity and representation therefore became key categories of a theoretically informed revisionism. The category of the nation has been crucial for New Americanists because Americanists, by carrying the nation's name in their field identity, have always had to position themselves vis-à-vis the nation, whether implicitly or explicitly.[5] As already indicated, New Americanists first gained visibility by distancing themselves from the ways older Americanists had supposedly supported the liberal ideology of American exceptionalism. In order to arrive at such an argument, it was necessary to interrogate the role of the nation-state in general, as well as the relationship between American Studies and the United States.

As my analysis of the three organizing terms in New Americanist scholarship will show, these critics have predominantly tied themselves to the debate over whether Emerson brought about radical change or enforced the status quo. I argue that this dichotomous structure is the result of the New Americanists' own premises. The relationship between resistance and co-optation becomes figured as a matter of either-or because New Americanists generally assume an all-pervasive scope of cultural power. As Winfried Fluck has argued, this assumption is widely shared among revisionists. Fluck writes that although

the dominant approaches of the last fifteen years, ranging from poststructuralism and deconstruction, new historicism, and cultural materialism to the various versions of race, class, and gender studies differ widely in many of their arguments, premises, and procedures[, what] unites them is a new form of radicalism that I would like to call, in contrast to older forms of political radicalism, *cultural radicalism* because the central source of political domination is no longer attributed to the level of political institutions and economic structures but to culture. . . . Thus recent critical theories, different as they may be in many respects, nevertheless have one basic premise in common . . . : they all take their point of departure from the assumption of an all-pervasive, underlying systemic element that constitutes the system's power in an invisible but highly effective way.[6]

Resistance, from this perspective, must be capable of opening up a space that is wholly uncorrupted by systemic cultural power. My title, "Transcendental Resistance," is an attempt to capture this very polarity arising from revisionist assumptions. Both the grip of power and the scope of resistance become, at least in tendency, totalized. As I will explain, this totalization reintroduces a form of idealism, despite the fact that revisionist critics set out to do away with any kind of idealism.

By contradistinction, I aim to show that such a dichotomous view stands in the way of understanding the role that representation, identity, and the nation play in Emerson's work. Emerson is more fruitfully seen, in Richard Teichgraeber's phrase, as a "connected critic," which is to say that his thought and action evolved immanently out of the society in which he lived—sometimes critically and sometimes less so.[7] Emerson was thus "complicit" or "co-opted," both because he chose the stance of immanent critique as a strategy, and, more importantly, because cultural criticism necessarily involves a degree of complicity. This also means that the scope of resistance I see at work in Emerson's writings is much more limited than that identified by some New Americanists. Resistance in my framework amounts to no more than employing the given for creating momentary experiences of excess. This understanding of resistance emphasizes spaces of in-betweenness that emerge within the order of language and culture. Order, from this perspective, is less a prohibitive, oppressive, or disciplinary structure than a condition that forces the individual to act. In sum, my approach most fundamentally differs from that developed by the New Americanists by shifting the perspective from systemic structures back to the individual. Rather than understanding the modern individual as increasingly shaped by various regimes of power, I see the modern individual as increasingly burdened with having to shape a place in the world. Such shaping comes up against constantly changing conditions, which are themselves in part the result of the individual's acts. In this situation, cultural artifacts and aesthetic activity play a role in helping the individual fulfill his or her task.[8]

In offering an alternative to those readings whose main aim is to reveal Emerson's complicity in various ruling ideologies, I am not trying to "save Emerson." I freely admit, however, that it is at times a rhetorical challenge to avoid this impression. Demonstrating the limitations of arguments that make him out to be a perpetuator of various ideologies necessarily involves showing that he was not only the reinforcing agent of these ideologies, be they imperialism, racism, patriarchy, or others. But what is driving my critique is not the wish to rehabilitate some fallen hero (given the unabated productivity of the "Emerson industry," this would indeed seem superfluous) but rather to reflect on the theoretical plausibility of the assumptions that underlie such arguments. And the fact of the matter is that Emerson, by our standards, did entertain imperialist, racist, and sexist attitudes. Measured by the standards of his own time, and taking into account his (in)famous inconsistency, he must at times be placed squarely with reactionaries, at times with progressive radicals. And at times, ideology critique is absolutely necessary to show that what seems to be progressive about Emerson was in fact reactionary. So again, saving Emerson cannot be the goal. In fact, it is one of my points to argue that the attempt to produce a sanitized Emerson—a figure who effectively fought for the common good and explored possibilities for resisting cultural hegemonies—is very often driven by the same assumptions that are at work in studies emphasizing his complicity.

Emersonian Revisionisms and the Hope for Transcendental Resistance

As this study revolves around the three critical terms representation, identity, and nation, I devote two chapters to each of them: First I develop my critique of how the recent critical consensus has employed each term for reading Emerson. (Chapter 1 is concerned with representation, chapter 3 with identity, and chapter 5 with the nation.) Following each of these chapters, I propose an alternative interpretation of the role the respective term plays in Emerson's work (chapters 2, 4, and 6).

As I argue in chapter 1, representation becomes the most fundamental problem for New Americanists. If power is wielded through culture, the way that culture wields power is through representation. In Stuart Hall's summary of this view, "Representation connects meaning and language to culture."[9] I am not concerned with problems of political representation, then, but rather with the accounts of how cultural signifying systems operate, the most central one being language. New Americanists have taken a special interest in the concept of representation in Emerson's work for an additional reason: Emerson himself was centrally concerned with language theory, whether in *Nature*, "The Poet," or in *Representative Men*.

Negotiating structuralist concepts of representation with various strains of humanist Marxism, Emerson's revisionist critics generally come to the conclusion that his idealist accounts of language served to secure the social status quo and to induce a contemplative passivity in the language user. Engaging in close readings of a select number of critics—Carolyn Porter, John Carlos Rowe, Christopher Newfield, and Donald Pease—I detect in most of their arguments a fear of what I call "empty signification," which is the flip side of the assumption that ideology has the capacity to performatively produce (and thus impose) ideological effects via representation. As most of these critics suggest, empty signification is the most harmful side of Emerson's representational idealism. In their view, he tacitly propagates an understanding of language in which the subject, though being encouraged to use language as much and as creatively as it wants, is incapable of representational acts that will have an effect on the world; they will never exceed the world of aesthetics. In the New Americanists' dual assumption of the power of language to work performatively in the service of ideology, and of the complete loss of representational agency of the Emersonian poet, we encounter a tendency of totalization that, I argue, is characteristic of New Americanist work in general. In the case of representation, this tendency faces the problem of creating an ideal use of language that is next to impossible to put into practice: Unless representation directly and palpably transforms the social world, it becomes denigrated as empty and contemplative. Thus, ironic as it may be, much New Americanist criticism, having heaved representation onto the pedestal of the prime category of cultural criticism, is in fact deeply suspicious of representation. Indeed, the suggestion to put representation (and this also tends to mean literature) aside altogether and to move on to political action always lurks around the corner. The critical impetus to move representation from "a world elsewhere" into the realm of the political tends to totalize the politicization of representation in such a way that representation becomes relegated to a world elsewhere yet again.[10]

If the work of representation is crucial to culturalist assumptions because in representation we see the symbolic and cultural order at work, this also suggests the exceptional importance of the question of identity for the recent revisionism. As I discuss in chapter 3, identity is generally seen by these critics as the result of an ideological process that is commonly called, following Louis Althusser, *interpellation*. Since, in this view, ideology *interpellates* the individual into a subject (that is, ideology turns the individual into a subject by subjecting the individual to its "call"), we can see that representation has the capacity to shape identities. In making this argument, New Americanists take up a specific position in the larger debate (carried out in moral philosophy, the social sciences, and the humanities) over how to negotiate the recognition claims of diverse identities with the centripetal forces inherent in the structure of society. The New Americanist position, which I call "deconstructive-pluralist," is the direct outcome of their conceptualization of identity. "Deconstructive pluralism" suggests the double strategy of calling for the recognition of excluded identities and urging the marginalized to disidentify from these newly recognized identities. What the call for disidentification implies is that recognition is an imposition, rather than an intersubjective process. Understanding identity formation as a unilateral process, New Americanists see subjects as needing to constantly resist identity. By the same token, almost any alteration of an identity becomes legible as a subversive act.

Applying these premises to Emerson has led critics to focus on his idea of self-reliance as well as his thoughts on friendship, which are interpreted as sanctioning hierarchical power relations. Self-reliance here generally takes the place of what other critics in the debate over identity decry as "possessive individualism" or "the unencumbered self." Indeed, in regard to identity, the critique of Emerson often reads like a test case of a more general critique of liberalism. In the view of critics such as Russ Castronovo, Christopher Newfield, Julie Ellison, and Susan Ryan, Emersonian self-reliance and friendship have the joint effect of making palatable a life based on hierarchy, exclusion, and lack of solidarity. Nonetheless, I claim that there are individualist and even transcendental overtones in the New Americanist revisions of self-reliance. Most crucially, the widely shared idea that disidentification is the only way to dodge the impositions of identity formation suggests that the aim of New Americanists, too, lies in setting free the individual. New Americanists, especially if associated with the political project of "radical democracy," like to emphasize that their egalitarian concept of freedom relies on notions of process (as exemplified by social movements) and on blurring the distinction between the self and the other. What remains to be addressed, however, is that this description resembles some dominant features in Emerson's thought. The ideas of process and of a transitory merging of the individual in a larger body are the cornerstones of Emerson's transcendentalist concept of freedom. Indeed, if there are unacknowledged similarities between Emerson's critics and Emersonian transcendentalism regarding their normative horizon, this has far-reaching implications for assessing the New Americanists' politics, which claims to valorize difference and the particular over universalism.

Along with representation and identity, the concept of the nation is the third core category organizing the New Americanists' critical assumptions;

to it I dedicate chapter 5. On one level, the nation is merely a specification of the logic that drives revisionist identity theory. As a result of multiple inter-pellations, individuals take on various identities or subject positions, which include national as well as race and gender identifications. In this sense, nationalism structures the dominant worldview because cultural power is wielded through representations that divide the world into a national "us" and "them." But for the New Americanists, the nation is a category that occupies a privileged position. By definition, the nation remains essential to Americanist scholarship. This is not to say that Americanists are doomed to reiterate nationalism. But whether they attack the United States for its imperialism or urge replacement of the national framework with one that is transnational or cosmopolitan, Americanists, whether old or new, cannot treat the nation as a simple nonissue. This analysis is borne out by the New Americanists' insistence on critically linking studies of race and gender with the imperial demeanor of the United States. In this view, the category of the nation is not situated on the same axis as race and gender; rather, the per-petuation of race and gender hierarchies becomes the mode in which impe-rialism operates, at home and abroad.

In the last decade, Americanist scholarship has shifted its emphasis from focusing on U.S. imperialism to adopting a transnational perspective. This shift bespeaks the codependence of the seemingly incompatible assumptions of a nearly all-pervasive hegemonic power wielded in culture and the pos-sibility of liberating resistance. This same codependence also informs the revisionists' approaches to representation and identity: Just as the subver-sion of an all-pervasive representational regime is hoped to bring about im-mediate change in the social world, and just as resisting the impositions of identity is understood to lead the way to freedom through disidentification, so transnational resistance to the imperial nation is suddenly discovered to harbor a truly liberating potential.

This dual perspective has led to widely divergent interpretations of Emer-son, which seem less at odds with each other if the logical codependence (not to say the dialectic) of empire criticism and transnationalism is kept in mind. In fact, depending on the critic, Emerson is represented either as per-petuating the force of U.S. imperialism or as leading the way to transnational resistance, although the former interpretation is the dominant one. Critics such as Myra Jehlen, Jenine Abboushi Dallal, Malini Johar Schueller, Eric Cheyfitz, John Carlos Rowe, and Jonathan Arac all argue that Emerson's idealism denies truly "punctuating difference" (Jonathan Arac's phrase, ad-opted from Edward Said). Although Emerson's idealism is energized by an-tagonism, these critics claim, such antagonisms are in the end overruled and superseded by universal sameness. Emerson's philosophy seems to articulate the essence of the imperial ideology with which the United States has attempted to expand its power and suppress difference. The blind spot in this analysis, however, concerns the question of whether a culturalist approach is well suited at all to explain U.S. imperialism. Before even entering the debate over whether these critics are correct in regarding Emerson as a propagator of sameness, one needs to reconsider whether the cultural dimension of imperialism really relies on the suppression of difference. In other words, is the contention that Emerson endorses sameness not merely a logical consequence of exaggerating culture's function for imperialism?

If the goal is to find out something about U.S. imperialism rather than just to offer an original literary interpretation, reconsidering culture's imperial role is all the more urgent precisely because it is far from clear whether Emerson can be described as the perpetuator of sameness. Suppose Emerson is not: where does this leave the New Americanists' analysis of Emerson's relationship to U.S. imperialism? The answer is suggested by the recent reappraisals of Emerson by Wai Chee Dimock.[11] According to Dimock, Emerson interrupts the temporal and spatial boundaries of the nation-state. Following the culturalist interpretation of U.S. imperialism, agreement with Dimock's analysis leaves no other logical conclusion than catapulting Emerson from the ranks of imperialists to those of radical resistance.

Such sudden switches from oppression to radical resistance are typical of how New Americanists treat all three key categories that inform their work. As already indicated, these swift changes become possible because of the New Americanists' theoretical totalization of both power and resistance. Looking at potential remedies for what is treated as a systemic power, it becomes clear that this totalization reintroduces a form of idealism. Every system, in this view, has a constitutive outside, and it is this outside that comes to play the lead role in a politicized cultural criticism interested in the arts of resistance. Thus, what is located at the margins of the system, or, even better, on the outside, allows for the articulation of a whole new system or order uncontaminated by the old. Real change—cultural or political— becomes increasingly imagined as a form of total change because partial change would be a sign of having been co-opted.

This suggests why the emphasis on the pervasiveness of power implies an understanding of resistance that is idealist and, ironically, approaches the transcendental: The change to be brought about by resistance is not conceptualized as resulting in and from reformed institutions, amendments to the legal structure, or the gradual reform of cultural rituals. Rather, the change brought about by resistance must bring forth a whole new cultural order. Sometimes it is the new order itself that is invested with millennial hopes of life without oppression, life that is radically egalitarian. Other critics realize that any order has the tendency of reification; for them, it is therefore the transition from one order to the next—a state of emergence—that becomes invested with the hope for life in which a particular kind of freedom unfolds. In both cases, this ideal of freedom is idealist in that it is, in Pheng Cheah's words, a "freedom from," rather than a freedom that requires and enables the individual to engage with the given.[12]

The Fractured Idealism of a Public Lecturer

My alternative approach to the role that "representation," "identity," and "the nation" play in Emerson's work begins by replacing idealist totalization with a view of the subject that can, indeed must, find dynamic responses to the given. This brings to light a very different Emerson: neither a reactionary nor a revolutionary, the Emerson I reconstruct is placed in the midst of the transformations of modernity that the United States was undergoing in his time. Subject to the pressures of the market, both of ideas and audiences, Emerson develops not only a rhetorical style but, more centrally for my project, a way of thinking (though hardly a consistent philosophical system) well suited for a "culture of eloquence."[13]

Having quit his position as the minister of Boston's Second Church in 1832, Emerson carved out his new profession as a public lecturer at the very moment the institution of the lyceum spread throughout New England. R. Jackson Wilson does not go too far when he writes, "More than any other major writer of what came to be called the American Renaissance, he was a creature of the Lyceum."[14] Originally designed as a network of local institutions that allowed community members to engage in mutual education and self-culture, within two decades the lyceum evolved into a lecture system stretching far into what is now the midwestern United States. By the 1850s, Emerson was one of the star lecturers, performing roughly seventy times a year in fifty different towns.[15] As early as the 1830s, the lyceum became Emerson's main source of income (he also relied on an inheritance from his first wife). Virtually all his books of essays consist of revised lectures. Though most other lecturers who enjoyed name recognition had a home base in more traditional professions, whether medicine, the law, or the pulpit, they shared with Emerson the challenge, as Donald Scott puts it, of "how to create or improvise a career."[16] This became necessary because of the transformations that most professions and trades underwent during the period of Emerson's career: having lost the coherence they had had in the eighteenth century, most professions had not yet taken the steps toward rationalization that would mark the end of the century.

As a public lecturer in a professional system still in flux, Emerson had to be particularly responsive to the requirements of reaching and securing an audience. As I argue at the outset of chapter 2, Emerson, standing at the lectern, did so by transforming a catalogue of middle-class virtues such as character and sincerity into a listening experience. Underlying my interpretations of Emerson is the contention that the lecture system allowed him to turn his lack of philosophical systematicness into an asset. He developed a style of thinking conducive to the needs of success in the public lecture hall, but to do so he did not have to make a choice between philosophical rigor and effectiveness with the audience. Rather, the demands of the lecture system amplified the philosophical eclecticism that marks even his earliest journals. As this study is designed to focus on textual and philosophical explication rather than historicist and archival scholarship, I adopt Emerson's professional and personal situation in an emerging modern public as a backdrop and starting point for bringing to light the *engagement* (in its two shades of meaning) of his way of thinking.

Emerson's preoccupation with what we today call identity is the best way of entry into this approach of reading Emerson. Underlying his concern with self-reliance and friendship is the idea that the self is the product of social relations. Put in Hegelian terms, Emerson is an early expounder of the view that identity is the result of reciprocal recognition. Emerson's approach to this idea stresses two points that are not commonly addressed by his contemporaries. First, he considers what being recognized would actually mean. Recognition, it turns out, is less a state one can achieve than the entryway to a process in which the individual gains access to what Emerson calls a "higher self"; this process exceeds the economy of recognition altogether. Thus, successful recognition points beyond itself, yet needs to remain reciprocal so as not to lose momentum. Emerson also explores another aspect of reciprocal recognition. In chapter 4, I examine how Emerson's ideas of friendship and self-reliance are shaped by an anxiety over the scarcity, or even lack, of recognition. Although disapprobation and shame already concerned Scottish common sense philosophers, the lack of recognition becomes an increasingly anxiety-provoking challenge during the Jacksonian era because it is at this time that the need to secure one's own recognition in a democratic society becomes felt more sharply than before. Significantly, when Emerson addresses this problem in discussions of friendship, he frequently switches the subject to ruminate on the lecturer's delicate relation to his audiences. Self-reliance, friendship, and the new profession of lecturer are all centrally concerned with the fragility of recognition.

In this reading, Emersonian misrecognition becomes understandable as a breakdown of interpersonal relations, the prospect of which every individual faces. Across his journals, lectures, and essays, one finds passages in which Emerson tries to formulate a response to the problem of misrecognition. He develops a concept of what I call "immanent patience," with the help of which the individual is to adapt to the permanent scarcity of recognition. The key to this form of patience lies in revising the sense of linear time, not by reaching for transcendental timelessness, but by "weakening" its linear push. This requires a heroic effort of abnegating the narcissistic wish for full recognition. But while Emerson tries to find a path to becoming less vulnerable to the scarcity of recognition, he does so by letting the drama of recognition continue to play out in his texts. As I demonstrate in a close reading of his essay "Friendship," the essay's meandering rumination on the possibility or impossibility of true friendship creates an implied reader or listener who comes to experience the intellectual problem of "friendship" as his or her own encounter with the uncertainty of recognition.

The dynamic of reciprocal but fragile recognition is closely linked with Emerson's theory of representation, which I explore in chapter 2. Beginning with his "language of nature," I reconstruct Emerson's account of language as driven by a relay and fissure between "reception" and "expression." Focusing on *Nature*, "The Poet," and "Experience," I explore this rift between reception and expression, making use of Charles S. Peirce's concepts of "Firstness," "Secondness," and "Thirdness" (without thereby claiming that Peirce and Emerson say the same thing in different terms) to show that this rift marks the difference between two modes of being. Integral to every signifying process but varying in depth, the rift sets in place a process of constant linguistic transformation. Reception (or "inspiration," or "abandonment," to use two of Emerson's roughly synonymous terms) is not a moment of obedience to an authoritarian figure called Spirit, but rather a moment in which the language user gets a glimpse of previously unseen relations, or—to put it less mystically—in which the reader has the *feeling* of being able to see relations between previously unconnected entities of thought. I describe Emerson's idea of reception not as an extrarepresentational domain, but as a specific kind of signification, which has to be imagined as limitless and thus cannot carry over into expression in its full scope. What Emerson calls "the highest truth" cannot be spoken, yet it is what drives speech. But not only is expression motivated by the urge to put into words the limitless signification of reception; expression, in all its limitation, also provides the source and occasion for the receptive moment of abandonment, in which a socially embedded language creates its own excess.

Emerson's theory of representation can also be redescribed from the perspective of eloquence. The speaker's words must assume the power to reach the audience by a technique one might call "stimulation" or "inspiration":

the speaker must produce a moment of representational reception that exceeds the necessary limits of expression. From my perspective, Emerson's theory of representation appears to be closely modeled after his own concerns as a professional public speaker. The requirement to create and maintain an audience goes a long way in explaining Emerson's preoccupation with the fissure between reception and expression, because what happens at this fissure directly affects what he sees as the relay between speaker and audience. And although Emerson's representational theory is not to be confused with his representational acts, his discourse does in fact tend to go after an effect of stimulation, in which moments of excessive insight quickly alternate with the contraction of meaning.

My chapters on the centrality of representation and identity in Emerson's work aim to show that his thinking is energized by breakdowns of philosophical idealism. Instead of merely celebrating friendship as a relationship that will propel friends to a union of the mind, Emerson explores the brittleness of that very relationship and devises strategies to amend the failure of mutual idealist enlargement. And instead of praising the poet for expressing "the highest truth," it is the failure to give words to spiritual insight that becomes the driving force in his model of representation. In my sixth and final chapter, I argue that in speaking of the nation, Emerson employs an idealist and Romantic figure of thought—man is to embody his nation's "idea"—and from there is catapulted to a whole series of incompatible political positions that range from endorsing the British Empire to sharply rejecting it, from celebrating cosmopolitanism to criticizing it as limited to the understanding, and from calling for U.S. expansionism to decrying it as belonging to the "party of force." At times seeming subject to the unexpected directions in which his positions might take him, in a key moment after the Compromise Bill of 1850, Emerson attempts to take control by politicizing abstraction in order to affirm the principles of his idealist nationalism and at the same time to distance himself from its political ramifications. The occasion is Emerson's address of welcome at Concord to the Hungarian revolutionary Lajos Kossuth. Although Kossuth was celebrated in most of the United States as a hero reminiscent of the American Founding Fathers, Emerson greets Kossuth with pointed reserve. While affirming the idealist principles of Kossuth's achievement, Emerson implicitly turns down his calls for help in order to reject the use to which Kossuth and his American supporters put these principles. In fact, Emerson comes to regard with skepticism the very claim that Kossuth (or anyone else, for that matter) managed to incarnate the ideal. Again, Emerson's idealism becomes fractured.

As Sacvan Bercovitch has explained, the "American ideology" has been so successful because any criticism that points out the failure of actualizing the American Dream renews the promise that the dream will come true. But in his engagement with the public, Emerson does something slightly different: He promises the achievement of the ideal while also declaring the futility of the promise. Emerson's fractured idealism is idealist despite itself: it undermines its own utopianism and thrives on its internal dynamics thus mobilized. Having virtually no consistent position on any single issue, and not worrying too much about formulating a systematic philosophy, Emerson profits from the sheer mobility of his thinking by giving his readership and audiences an imaginary and affective insight best described as inspiration. Emerson's chief modern invention (or, differently put, the sign of his modern, nonlinear personality structure) is that he works at replacing substance for effect—within the very medium of thought. To comprehend the historical and philosophical significance of *this* Emerson effect requires one to think of "effect" beyond the limited scope of the mechanics of ideology.

A few final words are necessary to address a methodological consequence of my critique of the reading practices exemplified by the New Americanists, namely the "resurgence" in my own interpretations of sometimes more, sometimes less explicit appeals to authorial intention. As my positioning of Emerson within the transformations of modernity makes clear, I am not engaging in an intentionalism that would claim to understand Emerson by some autonomous, metaphysical, and ahistorical authorial intention alone. But proposing an alternative to the culturalist logic pervading much of recent scholarship also requires reconsidering the now common assumption that authorial intention is a categorical mistake. It is, in fact, less than clear what it would actually mean to conduct scholarship that is radically anti-intentionalist. Walter Benn Michaels has gone the furthest in exploring this question in recent years, and one of his provocative claims is that anti-intentionalism and identitarianism are in fact the same. Behind this claim stands the larger argument that theories of subject positioning—or identitarianism—are in fact always essentialisms. If intention doesn't explain the meaning of the text because it is all a matter of point of view (or perspective or subject position), then perspective becomes both the sole authority and source for meaning or truth: "difference without disagreement [that is, difference that arises merely from different perspectives] makes the subject-position essential (since to differ without disagreement is nothing more than to occupy a different subject-position)."[17]

I am not concerned here with Michaels's polemical point that anti-essentialist thinkers are in fact employing essentialist arguments themselves. But what is important for my purposes is the argument that when the intention of the author is deemed irrelevant, the subject position takes up the logical position previously occupied by intention. While the old intentionalism was indefensibly metaphysical, the new anti-intentionalism creates a reductive cultural determinism. In sum, the now common anti-intentionalism is just as dissatisfying as the cultural determinism I criticize in the work of the New Americanists. Therefore, opting for premises according to which the subject is capable of responding to its cultural surrounding brings appeals to intentionalism back to the table. This does not mean, however, that my appeals to authorial language take Emerson to be in control of every utterance he makes; nor does it imply that his contradictions can ultimately be resolved because they must have all made sense to him. Rather, my appeals to authorial language address an irreducible nonidentity between determining forces acting upon the self, and the self's reactions and utterances.

Although I distance myself from the metaphysics of older forms of intentionalism, I argue that the constitutive nonidentity at the heart of the subject can only be addressed in the language of authorial intention. To explain this with George Herbert Mead's terminology of "I" and "Me" as two aspects of the self, the acts of the "I," which are nonidentity at work, can never be observed while in progress. We can only ever account for the "I" retroactively, looking back onto it, seeing a "Me" (and this concerns both ourselves and others). If texts are the product neither of a metaphysical author, nor of a narrowly determining discourse, but of a nonidentical subject (who intervenes in discourse without being able to fully control his or her meaning), we are condemned to attribute the textual nonidentity of the "I" to the graspable part of the self, which is the "Me." Thus, the language of the self, along with the appeal to authorial intention, is the result of replacing cultural determinism with a view of the subject based on nonidentity.

However, the return to the vocabulary of authorial intention does not constitute a sufficient interpretive legitimation in itself. Otherwise such a return would have to result in attempts to do away with theory. For instance, I legitimate my own interpretive differences from the New Americanists not by claiming to have a better understanding of Emerson's true intentions. Rather, I argue that my theoretical premises, which highlight the increasing urgency of the problem of intersubjective recognition for a lecturer in the emerging modern public, are more plausible than those employed by the New Americanists. The language of authorial intention remains relevant on top of such a theoretically grounded interpretation. Thus, demonstrating the plausibility of theoretical premises in an actual reading involves accounting for how the nonidentical author interacts with the realities posited by one's theory. In my case, this requires the demonstration that the modern problem of recognition permeates Emerson's thought, whether the focus is on representation, identity, or the nation.

[I]

EMERSON AND REPRESENTATION

1

THE NEW AMERICANISTS AND REPRESENTATION:
BETWEEN INTERPELLATION AND REIFICATION

The New Americanists and Postparadigmatic American Studies

BEFORE I BEGIN my analysis of revisionist assumptions about representation, the New Americanists need to be placed within the history of American Studies. This will explain why the term remains difficult to define. I will show that the New Americanists entered the field at a moment in which there had emerged the need for a label that balances coherence with elusiveness. The term New Americanists had a critical impact neither because it systematically resisted any ascription of meaning nor because it narrowly defined a program of inquiry, but because it took up the position of a paradigmatic signifier and then refuted its paradigmatic status. This balancing act became necessary as a result of the field's transformation, which had begun in the late 1960s and early 1970s with the mounting critique of the Myth and Symbol school.[1] I want to describe this change as the transition from paradigmatic to postparadigmatic American Studies. I use the term *paradigm* in a narrow sense, derived from Thomas S. Kuhn's 1962 study *The Structure of Scientific Revolutions*. In this limited sense, the postparadigmatic is not to be confused with any kind of liberation. In fact, my use of the term starts from the assumption that it is not at all clear that literary or cultural studies in the majority of cases is aptly described as paradigmatic.

According to Thomas Kuhn's study, paradigms are functions of "normal science." For Kuhn, these are the natural sciences. In his words, paradigms are "universally recognized scientific achievements that for a time provide model problems and solutions to a community of practitioners."[2] One can thus describe a paradigm as a set of agreements regarding (1) what is to be observed, (2) what kinds of questions are to be asked, (3) how these questions are to be structured, and (4) how the results are to be interpreted. Although Kuhn limited the notion of the paradigm to the natural sciences in order to differentiate between "normal sciences" and those parts of academia (such as the social sciences) in which there are "overt disagreements . . .

about the nature of legitimate scientific problems and methods" (Kuhn, *Structure*, x), one may well argue that Myth and Symbol American Studies was united by a paradigm. It was agreed that one should (1) look at cultural products, preferably high literature, (2) ask which myth(s) or symbol(s) of America these texts give expression to, (3) structure such inquiry by mixing New Critical close reading methods with historical analysis, and (4) interpret the findings in ways that reaffirm the contention that these texts provide access to the nation's (subversive) myths and symbols.[3] As Kuhn suggests, this kind of paradigm was generative of ever finer elaborations within its parameters. Working like "a promise of success discoverable in selected and still incomplete examples," the paradigm provided an incentive to keep accumulating more and more paradigm-conforming scholarship (Kuhn, *Structure*, 23–24).

But if Myth and Symbol American Studies resembled a paradigm-based science, the crisis that American Studies entered in the 1960s cannot be accurately described as a *scientific* revolution because it cannot be separated from *social* turmoil. (The two are distinct in Kuhn's model.) For Kuhn, a scientific revolution occurs when a paradigm repeatedly comes up against a problem it cannot solve. Because a paradigm is expansive in the breadth of material to be explained by it, as well as in its increasing inner differentiation, it carries the seeds of its own destruction. In the phase of having come upon a problem that cannot be explained with the ruling paradigm (although it is this very paradigm that has led scholars to the problem), normal science shifts to "extraordinary science," which can include "the proliferation of competing articulations, the willingness to try anything, . . . [and] the recourse to philosophy and to debate over fundamentals" (Kuhn, *Structure*, 90). After this phase of extraordinary research, a new paradigm, incompatible with the old one, will win acceptance (compare Kuhn, *Structure*, 91) and thus continue the course of paradigm-guided scholarship.

What happened in American Studies, however, was clearly not that the Myth and Symbol scholars came up against a problem they could not solve. (There is nothing inherent in the material to have prevented them from myth-and-symbolizing happily ever after.) Rather, scholars from a younger generation uttered political discontent with the existing paradigm, in large part because of its very paradigmatic nature, which was interpreted as restrictive and exclusionary. This is why the critique of the Myth and Symbol school was not containable by developing an alternative paradigm but rather led American Studies into its postparadigmatic phase.

However, American Studies did not just diversify and pluralize. While refraining from installing a full-fledged new paradigm, over time American Studies nevertheless created a consensus about underlying assumptions that allowed a pluralized field, which now encompassed such new, autonomous disciplines as women's studies, black studies, and others, to gather and communicate. The very fact that American Studies acted as an institutional host to a wide range of these disciplines during its conventions and in its publications suggests that there was still something at work beyond the plural and the particular. Postparadigmatic scholarship does not mean, then, that scholars have learned to listen to the voice of the street instead of following the inner logic of academia. Nor does it mean that Americanists have entered a state of disciplinary hybridity in which the regulations that normally come along with disciplines are suspended. Postparadigmatic American Studies merely means that what guides scholarship is no longer as encompassing and pervasive as a paradigm. Most importantly, it is possible in postparadigmatic American Studies to suspend the need to agree on a particular overarching object of study (what used to be called "the American mind"). Instead, the range of objects to be studied has proliferated (race, gender, and so forth), and the frame of reference is no longer necessarily the United States.[4] Thus postparadigmatic American Studies has developed a mode of scholarship that is highly effective under the conditions of social and disciplinary pluralism.

Stories of an Epochal Break

Americanists' self-reflexive accounts of their field's history have long emphasized an epochal break that purportedly took place in the late 1960s and early 1970s. The problem with these historicizations lies in their understanding of what I term the postparadigmatic. In general, the field's inner pluralization and difference are presented as if American Studies were no longer organized by inner norms. Depending on the critic's view, the postparadigmatic stage describes either the liberation of American Studies from restrictive protocols or the discipline's plunge into chaos.

In the first influential critical history of American Studies, written by Gene Wise in 1979, the epochal change is turned into a drama that organizes the entire text. Wise's aim was to present the history of American Studies in a historically sophisticated way. Instead of employing a "'climate of opinion' mode of explanation," he wanted to delineate the history of American Studies as a series of "paradigm dramas"—hence the article's title, "'Paradigm Dramas' in American Studies: A Cultural and Institutional History of the Movement." By "paradigm dramas" he meant "a sequence of representative acts . . . which crystallize possibilities for integrated American Studies in each stage of the movement's history."[5] Here Wise seemed indebted more to Victor Turner's anthropological theory of "social drama" than to Thomas

Kuhn's theory of scientific revolutions through paradigm shifts. As a result, Wise's story of American Studies from Vernon Parrington's pioneering work *Main Currents in American Thought* of 1927 through 1930 to the publication of Alan Trachtenberg's *Brooklyn Bridge: Fact and Symbol* of 1965 implies that there were in fact no major paradigmatic shifts as far as the intellectual history of American Studies is concerned. From Parrington's *Main Currents in American Thought* to the mid-1960s, the Myth and Symbol approach to American Studies, in Wise's account, reigned largely unchallenged and unchanged.[6] Wise's paradigm dramas instead emphasized an institutional story of ambivalent progress (a sequence of *social* dramas), which described the journey of American Studies from an unrecognized activity of impassioned outsiders such as Parrington to an incorporated stage, in which American Studies became a discipline firmly entrenched in academia and well supported by financially powerful foundations.[7]

Wise's emphasis on institutional development instead of intellectual change up to the 1960s reflects what we have largely come to accept as the history of the discipline. But it is important to recognize that this emphasis was built into his model. After all, his sequence of paradigm dramas relied on "possibilities for *integrated* American Studies in each stage of the movement's history."[8] In the 1960s and 1970s, practicing integrated American Studies was precisely what came under attack, and so did the Myth and Symbol approach, which was geared toward achieving an intellectual synthesis, or integration, through a nationalist idealism of sorts (the "American Mind," the "national character").[9] It is little more than tautological that with the breakdown of integrationist Myth-and-Symbolism, Wise could make out no further representative act that qualified for a paradigm drama, since, for him, such a drama relied on the possibility of intellectual integration. Thus, although Wise aspired to provide the intellectual and institutional history of American Studies, his model only allowed for true drama on the institutional side.

While Wise's history of American Studies is divided into paradigmatic and postparadigmatic stages, this transition from one to the other amounts to a shift from integrated to nonintegrated American Studies. Because he could not see what held the field together in its postparadigmatic stage, Wise issued a warning call prophesying the discipline's impending death. What has happened to American Studies since the mid-1960s "makes for a depressing story" (Wise, "'Paradigm Dramas,'" 317), because American Studies has intellectually never recovered from the "earthquake-like jolts" brought on by the '60s (Wise, "'Paradigm Dramas,'" 314). Although many Americanists disagree with Wise for various reasons, his division of American Studies into two phases has remained extremely influential.

Wise's impact can be seen, for instance, in Donald Pease and Robyn Wiegman's reply to him, published in 2002. Pease and Wiegman criticize Wise's account because of what they argue is a "future fear" inherent in his argument.[10] But in claiming that the "futures of American studies" could not be pinned down to a single paradigm or a set of competing paradigms,[11] they affirmed the thesis of the epochal break between paradigmatic and postparadigmatic American Studies. For them, the Cold War version of American Studies before the breakdown was marked by a unifying narrowness that was so restrictive that in the 1960s, just before the break, American Studies was positioned toward scholars linked with the new social movements in a "negative reciprocity": "scholars in emergent identity-based (inter)disciplines defined themselves and their projects against those of establishment American studies and vice versa" (Pease and Wiegman, "Futures," 17).[12]

Shortly after Pease's and Wiegman's reaffirmation of the field's irreducible openness in its postparadigmatic stage, Leo Marx, from a very different perspective, came to reiterate the thesis of an epochal break yet again. Speaking as a member of the founding generation, and displaying a sense of alienation from the field he had helped to establish as an academic discipline, he divided the history of American Studies into a phase "before the divide" (B.D.) and "after the divide" (A.D.). Initially, he offered the narrative of this stark separation as a caricature of the revisionist accounts of the field's history. His article seemed to be driven by the question, why do they (the A.D.'s) hate us (the B.D.'s) so? However, Marx also ended up reaffirming the divide: he argued that the principal investment of Americanists of his generation in America itself (what he called the "Ur Theory of American studies") was no longer shared by the younger generation. Thus, B.D. Americanists "believed in America," whereas A.D. Americanists had "apparently" come to hate it (Marx, "On Recovering the 'Ur' Theory," 130). Marx argued that revisionists were holding on to the same egalitarian Enlightenment ideals that had guided earlier Americanists, but they had disconnected them from America as a whole and attached them to various subordinate groups of Americans. He thus pointed to a degree of continuity, "a quotient of persistent if disappointed idealism," which had to be repressed by revisionists and thus turned into an unbridgeable split (Marx, "On Recovering the 'Ur' Theory," 130). But while his explanation of the split had recourse to the revisionists' collective psyche, this split was nonetheless very real in his account. The A.D. radicals' loss of belief in America had resulted in the "conviction that the US as a whole—the nation-state itself—no longer is a worthy subject of teaching and research" (Marx, "On Recovering the 'Ur' Theory," 130). In other words, because a plurality of irreducible subjects had come to replace the nation-state, the A.D.'s had once and for all rejected integrationist American Studies.

The Function of Theory

What is addressed neither by Wise, Wiegman and Pease nor by Marx is how the field has been operating since the epochal break that they all perceive. I have already noted that postparadigmatic American Studies has developed a mode of scholarship that is highly effective under the conditions of social and disciplinary pluralism. The import of European (mostly French) critical theory at this particular point in history served a function that can be explained against this background of the postparadigmatic turn. It is essential that we broaden the perspective from American Studies to the humanities more generally. After all, American Studies was not the only academic discipline that came under pressure from the changes called for by the new social movements. What the import of theory provided was a set of grounding assumptions that allowed disciplines to diversify, even to break apart, and yet ensured the survival of the academic system (and, indeed, led it to a new flourishing). Theory became something of a lingua franca that allowed for diversification and collaboration.[13]

Of course, French theory is far too diverse for blanket statements about it. Nor do I argue that American scholars across the humanities had the same understanding of what theory was and how it was to be employed. But the theory boom nevertheless provided a set of terms that could be turned into a widespread consensus between the 1970s and 1990s, a consensus general enough to allow for competing theoretical schools and approaches as well as for contradictory aims and analyses. French theory was particularly useful in this regard because it grew out of the French student movement, or, in some cases, at least experienced a boost from the events now associated with "May '68."[14] French theory was thus politically allied with the new North American social movements from the start. Since many theorists in Europe and the United States were actively engaged in the social upheavals of the '60s, theory could be interpreted as growing organically out of the various social and academic transformations.[15]

In my introduction I have drawn on Winfried Fluck's work to describe the substance of this consensus. Fluck speaks of "cultural radicalism," that is, "the assumption of an all-pervasive, underlying systemic element that constitutes the system's power in an invisible but highly effective way" (Fluck, "Humanities," 216). While American Studies was hard pressed to negotiate the imperatives of pluralization and diversification with its own integrationist design, the cultural radicalist premise of an all-pervasive cultural power allowed American Studies to continue to function, in close cooperation with the newer fields and disciplines. It is in this situation that the term New Americanists could gain immediate cachet.

In the next section, I will look more closely at how this term emerged. Here I only note that Frederick Crews introduced the term in a review article in *The New York Review of Books* in 1988, in which he critiqued a number of revisionist studies from the mid-1980s. In calling the revisionists New Americanists, he reiterated the idea of an epochal break. Yet for him, what followed the break was neither chaos nor liberation. Rather, the term New Americanists designated something of a new paradigm. Two years later, Donald Pease (one of the scholars critiqued by Crews) appropriated the term and turned it from a derogatory epithet into a positive and marketable label. It was Pease's dilemma that as a full-fledged paradigm, the term would have undermined the postparadigmatic revolution that had enabled revisionist approaches in the first place. As a consequence, Pease's various introductions to, and further theorizations of, the term emphasized the impossibility of narrowly defining it.[16] Indeed, from the beginning Pease was adamant in distinguishing the New Americanists from those developments in the scholarship of the 1980s that took the general concern with ideology in a direction that questioned the open plurality of American Studies (and of the United States). Thus, a certain version of ideology critique, while principally allied with the New Americanist project, actually threatened to undermine its foundational condition, that is, the openness of postparadigmatic American Studies.[17]

At first glance, then, the term New Americanists seemed to be doing nothing but defending and reaffirming what had by then become the pluralized status quo. But of course, coining and appropriating the term at the particular moment of the end of the Cold War was an act of considerable ingenuity on both Crews's and Pease's part. In retrospect, it even seems as if the end of the Cold War called for a term sounding like a new paradigm. Although assuming an immediate trickle-down effect from world-historical events to the academic system is very risky (especially if one takes into account the considerable delays in academic publishing cycles and the fact that Crews's article had already appeared by 1988), it seems safe to say that the time directly following the fall of Communism was an attractive one for calling for a new kind of American Studies, as it was for all kinds of epochal pronouncements, from the "end of history" to the "clash of civilizations" that supposedly replaced the contest of ideologies.

Pease's use of the term "New Americanists" in fact competed with Philip Fisher's coinage "New American Studies," which Fisher (who, like Pease, had been labeled a New Americanist by Crews) used in order to collect some well-received articles from the journal *Representations* from the mid- to late 1980s, written by critics who were more or less closely associated with the new historicism. The "New Americanists" and the "New American Studies" differed drastically in their programmatic aims: while Pease resisted the paradigmatic pull of his term in order to keep post-1965 pluralism in place, Fisher decided to give his term the force of paradigmatic closure, although the heterogeneity of the collected articles could hardly bear this out. In his introduction, Fisher presented the cultural diversity celebrated since the '60s as a new wave of "regionalism." This allowed him to contain the politics of difference in what he claimed was a perennially swinging pendulum "between a diversity of sectional voices and an ever-new project of unity" that constituted "cultural life in America."[18] Fisher even went so far as to conclude that the new American Studies marked the end of the latest phase of diversity, "that the new American studies has grown up alongside but also as an alternative or aftermath to this regionalism that tore apart the various unifying and singular myths of America" (Fisher, "New American Studies," xiv).

One can't quite help reading Fisher's new American Studies as the conservative twin of the New Americanists, especially in light of Fisher's pronouncement that "we [Americans] have no ideology because we lack the apparatus of ideology" (Fisher, "New American Studies," xxii). But maybe Pease was simply more clever than Fisher in crafting a term that managed to link up the diversity-consensus with the category of the nation (if only negatively, via the critique of U.S. imperialism and exceptionalism) at the moment that the role of the United States in the world needed to be redefined. The term New Americanists also gained currency with the taking of a stand in the entrenched culture wars at the very moment of the rise of neoconservatism, the final collapse of the remaining New Deal coalition, and thus the total transformation of national politics, a situation in which an assertive label could at least suggest that the volatile gains of the 1960s were not going to be given up without a fight.[19] This also in part explains the ideological ferocity and polemical tone of the early programmatic pronouncements of the New Americanists: the term became a weapon for Americanists against the attempts of neoconservatives such as Francis Fukuyama to triumph in the culture wars with appeals to a liberal-sounding, end-of-ideology rhetoric, although, being labeled with an academic referent, the New Americanists could never effectively counter the effects of the mass dissemination enjoyed by Fukuyama's end-of-history thesis.

The placeholder of a paradigm, the New Americanists provided a way to repackage post-1965 pluralism, place it in rhetorical proximity to American Studies, and thus give the field new urgency. In a way, Pease accomplished what seemed like an impossible feat: he made American Studies relevant on the basis of the pluralism that had until then threatened to undermine its relevance.[20] And he did so by giving a name to what the pluralism had already been doing, which was not simply to undermine but also to effectively reorganize American Studies.

The Crews-Pease Debate

I will now turn to the founding moment of the New Americanists, namely Donald Pease's appropriation of Frederick Crews's epithet. My interest from here forward is no longer primarily historical. Rather, the debate between Crews and Pease is a welcome starting point for an analysis of the New Americanists' underlying theory of representation. I begin my critique of the New Americanists with the concept of representation because over the course of the last thirty years, the humanities have turned it into a purloined letter: placed prominently in our critical thought, it is yet, as it were, continually overlooked. Having gained its high standing in the wake of the linguistic turn, the concept of representation has proven particularly useful for literary and cultural scholars because representation, in Stuart Hall's phrase, "connects meaning and language to culture" (Hall, "Work of Representation," 15). This connection of meaning, language, and culture, it is widely agreed, is a key site from which power operates. Thus, in order to analyze power relations at work, the academic left has paid close attention to cultural representations. Yet over the years the concept has become so thoroughly integrated into our critical craft that the way in which representation works has been increasingly taken for granted. As a result, theoretical debates about representation have been largely absent in recent years. This is a worrying development because what is at stake in such a debate is not some scholastic question. Rather, if the connection of meaning, language, and culture is related to power, then the theories of representation that frame the political projects pursued by academic critics have immediate relevance for how these critics understand the political itself. Scrutinizing the underlying theories of representation of recent revisionist criticism may call into question whether these critics have been conceptualizing political power and the means of engaging with it in plausible ways.

Frederick Crews coined the term New Americanists in an omnibus review article in *The New York Review of Books* in 1988 titled "Whose American Renaissance?" Crews grouped together two essay collections and five monograph studies from the early and mid-1980s that marked, in his view, a way of conducting American Studies that differed from the established paradigms. The methodology Crews detected in the books under consideration was built on ideological analyses and could be aligned with a broader critical movement across literary studies as a delayed result of the 1960s.[21] Crews elaborated several specific concerns about the New Americanists that, taken together, led him to dismiss the movement, while he also prophesied that it would wield a heavy influence in academia in the years to come.

Two years later, Donald Pease, whose works of criticism Crews had discussed extensively in his article, edited a special issue of *boundary 2* entitled "New Americanists: Revisionist Interventions into the Canon." In his introductory essay of the same title, Pease undertook a close reading of Crews's text and analyzed Crews's own ideological investments. These aligned Crews, in Pease's view, with the very disciplinary problems the New Americanists aimed to tackle. Rather than defending himself against Crews's accusations and criticisms, Pease took them as the occasion for calling into being a critical Americanist project that defined itself against the establishment of American Studies. Pease's appropriation of Crews's label constituted a founding gesture that gained its urgency from a dual focus. On the one hand, Pease's proposal was enormous in scope, offering a theory of academic fields and disciplines, as well as a broadly refined research agenda based on the belief that ideological critique can lead to political and social change. On the other hand, Pease insisted on a very narrow focus that ruled out comprehending the New Americanists within the context evoked by Crews, that is, the post-1960s, post-structuralist ideological revisionism visible across literary studies. More specifically, Pease attempted to describe the New Americanists' emergence as resulting from a battle with established Americanists. It is this narrow perspective that made Crews appear to be deeply engaged in that struggle himself. To understand better how Pease turned Crews's critique around, it is necessary first to reconstruct Crews's argument.

Frederick Crews: The Politics of Books
versus the Politics of Readers

Crews began his article with a general consideration of paradigm shifts in literary studies in light of the then-impending publication of *The Cambridge History of American Literature*, edited by Sacvan Bercovitch, which, in Crews's estimation, would soon replace Robert Spiller's *Literary History of the United States* of 1948 as a standard reference guide. But rather than immediately side with the older paradigm, he went on to approvingly sketch the history of American literary studies through the eyes of Bercovitch, arguing that "the study of American literature has never lacked a ruling ideological mood."[22] He described the history of the discipline as moving from the stage of a "gentleman's club," to Vernon L. Parrington's "chauvinistic celebration of such sturdy-looking realists and democrats as Walt Whitman, Mark Twain, Theodore Dreiser, and Sinclair Lewis," on to the "New Critical or modernist era" (Crews, "Whose American Renaissance?" 68) made up of "post-war liberal critics," who, "for all their rejection of simplistic myths of progress, acquiesced in a literary nationalism that went largely unchallenged until the New Americanists began their assault on it" (Crews, "Whose American Renaissance?" 70).

Up to this point he constructed his position as in agreement with, and even grateful for, the ideology critique undertaken by the New Americanists. This allowed Crews to reverse the blame that revisionists had heaped on establishment Americanists due to their alleged ideological blindness. Suddenly it was the New Americanists whom Crews could reveal to "claim to belong to the first scholarly cohort that does *not* consist of ideologues" but merely unmasks ideology. From here it was only a small step to one of Crews's major points: the New Americanists could be exposed as ideological themselves. One example concerned an article in which Donald Pease discussed F. O. Matthiessen. Crews criticized Pease for denying that Matthiessen was a Communist fellow traveler and that the shock Matthiessen felt when confronted with Soviet Realpolitik contributed as much to his decision to commit suicide as did McCarthyism. For Pease, Crews suggested, the designation of fellow traveler was no more than a sign of American postwar hysteria; it had no basis in reality whatsoever: "Pease's failure to register these well-established facts would seem to make up a textbook illustration of partisan myopia, and more generally to cast some doubt on the New Americanists' belief that they have put ideology behind them" (Crews, "Whose American Renaissance?" 74).

By claiming that any attempt to speak from a position uncontaminated by ideology is futile, Crews could consider the strengths and weaknesses of what he saw as the New Americanist paradigm without having to address his own methods accordingly. Presumably, it was sufficient to admit that one always speaks from an ideological position. What is more, this admission, properly understood, should keep the critic from taking a judgmental attitude: if we are indeed all ideologically tainted, Crews seemed to say, we should not build our academic careers on blaming canonical authors for their moral and ideological shortcomings.

Another recurring objection in Crews's text was the New Americanists' treatment of "literary quality" as an ideological tool. Crews accused the New Americanists of subsuming all questions of quality under the issue of ideology: "[T]his pretense that great art must be decoupled from the struggle for social dominance makes no sense to the New Americanists. Or rather, it makes sense to them as a repressive strategy, a means of keeping the lid on divisive differences of interest" (Crews, "Whose American Renaissance?" 74). There are really two different objections behind this observation. First, Crews considered it a danger to declare the issue of quality to be a mere ideological tool because it opened the canon to any text that could be usefully read, and "usefully read" must mean either showing how ideology becomes visible in the text, or showing how ideology is subverted by it. Crews's second objection concerned what the work of the academic critic should be. Here Crews seemed unwilling to differentiate between his job as a reviewer for *The New York Review of Books* and his work as an academic critic, who, as a result of the thorough professionalization of academia, does not have to legitimate the artistic merit of the works he analyzes. Crews's main concern, then, was both that the canon would no longer be determined by literary quality and that the academic critic would no longer take part in judging literary quality.

Behind the issue of assessing the quality of a work to delimit the canon and legitimate the critic's work stands the question of aesthetics, which, according to Crews, could not be analyzed in any detailed way by the New Americanists' single-issue focus on ideology. This was especially evident to Crews when it came to humor: "Wary of being taken in by an establishment author's rhetorical charm, a New Americanist will maintain a clinically humorless position toward, say, the extravagant experimentalism of Melville or the whimsical irony of Hawthorne or Thoreau" (Crews, "Whose American Renaissance?" 75).

Finally, Crews raised two methodological objections. First, New Americanists in his view were susceptible to circular reasoning, which resulted from deciding on the ideological meaning of the text on the basis of extratextual criteria. In Crews's words, "What New Americanists discover in a standard work is usually a defect of consciousness that they had posited from the outset" (Crews, "Whose American Renaissance?" 75). Crews also voiced another version of this objection: considering that ideology in the New Americanists' view was disguised in literary works, for instance through the mechanisms of repression or transference, Crews questioned the critics' efforts to return the repressed to the manifest level. In his view, such attempts propelled the critics to rewrite the original texts rather than interpret them. To Crews, such a rewriting tended toward pure invention on the part of the critic. In his second methodological objection, Crews claimed that "New Americanists are unwilling to establish methodological ground rules that would cover both the works they promote and the works they resent" (Crews, "Whose American Renaissance?" 81). His example was that New Americanists granted authorial intention only to artists writing from the margins, not to establishment writers. Marginalized authors, in this view, could be celebrated for willfully subverting ideology; mainstream writers, on the other hand, merely reproduced the system. Such inconsistencies, Crews argued, frequently occurred within a single scholarly text.

In sum, Crews claimed to be in favor of the New Americanists' dismantling of the liberal nationalism at the core of the New Critics' version of American Studies, yet he had several reservations that ended up putting in question whether there were in fact any level of agreement. He saw the New Americanists themselves trapped in an ideology that tended to lead them to partisan myopia; he bemoaned their unwillingness to measure literary quality on its own terms and to maintain the old canon, or to construct a new one, on the criterion of literary quality; he balked at what he referred to as the "aprioriness" of New Americanist criticism, which ideologically predetermined its results from the outset; and he demurred at the lack of methodological consistency. Crews himself offered a summary of his qualms that is not entirely representative of his text but begins to suggest his vision of the ideal critic:

> All the liabilities of the New Americanist enterprise that I have touched upon—its self-righteousness, its tendency to conceive of American history only as a highlight film of outrages, its impatience with artistic purposes other than "redefining the social order," and its choice of critical principles according to the partisan cause at hand—suggest that there may yet be a role for other styles of reading American literature. It ought to be possible for critics who are politically unembarrassed by ambiguity and irony to leave "cold war" rationalizations behind, branch out from the canon, yet continue to affirm what radicals sometimes forget, that there is no simple correlation between political correctness and artistic power. (Crews, "Whose American Renaissance?" 79)

One must ask whether Crews's ideal critic, positioned between being critical of Cold War ideology and insisting on aesthetic mastery independent of ideology, corresponded with his claims to a principal alliance with the New Americanists, or whether this ideal in the final instance aligned him with the liberal consensus attacked by the New Americanists. The question, in other words, is whether Crews could back up his rhetorical stance of creating a compromise position. From this point on, Crews seemed to explore that question himself by assessing the suitability of several critics for proving the actual existence of his ideal. First he singled out David S. Reynolds as one New Americanist who could differentiate between literary greatness and the politics inherent in a work. Here, it seemed, was a candidate who could bring together the best of old and new Americanists. A few sentences further on, however, Crews discarded Reynolds because he had defined aesthetic criteria for great art in the manner of the New Critics and thus, strictly speaking, turned out not to be a New Americanist at all: "Reynolds, unconstrained by left politics, can freely acknowledge, as Matthiessen did, that the political elusiveness of already canonical 'Renaissance' texts is intimately connected with their durability, but he turns that elusiveness into a universally valid test for entry to the pantheon, a nonnegotiable demand that would freeze the canon where it is" (Crews, "Whose American Renaissance?" 81). Criticizing Reynolds in this way, Crews positioned himself as a critic who could appreciate Reynolds's drawing a line between aesthetics and politics while declaring that line ideological. The most obvious candidate at this point, then, was not Reynolds but Crews himself. Needless to say, he couldn't quite let matters rest there.

Crews next considered Philip Fisher, but finding him similarly unfit, he suddenly came upon Edmund Wilson, who "[a]lready in 1962 . . . found *Uncle Tom's Cabin* 'a much more impressive work than one has ever been allowed to suspect'" (Crews, "Whose American Renaissance?" 80–81). Wilson—something of a deus ex machina in Crews's text—was the one American critic Crews could come up with who appreciated the power of a work independent of its politics, and who was sensitive to the ideologies that inform any all too doctrinal attempts to judge aesthetics on its own terms: "In Wilson we had a model of the critic who can appreciate the historical reasons for a novel's power without needing to convert its politics into his own" (Crews, "Whose American Renaissance?" 81). Settling on Wilson may be considered a shrewd move on Crews's part. For Crews didn't need to mention in his article that Wilson had entertained strong links to Marxism and later, during the Cold War, became a famous dissenter who criticized the government for using the threat of Communism as a pretense for weakening civil liberties.[23] It would be a real challenge, in other words, to include Wilson in what Pease called the "cold war consensus." What also made Wilson attractive for Crews was Wilson's self-image as a journalist rather than as an academic. From Wilson, Crews could draw support for his wish to retain the responsibility of aesthetic judgment, although this point goes unmentioned in Crews's text.[24] Thus, Wilson became the solution in the search for the golden mean. He seemed to separate politics and aesthetics without falling into the trap of the Cold War consensus.

Donald Pease: The Disciplinary Unconscious and the Idea of Privileged Exclusion

If Crews believed he had found a strategy to bypass the ideological naïveté of earlier critics as well as the shortcomings he found in the work of the

New Americanists, he certainly did not convince Donald Pease, who in his reply two years later constructed Crews as the personification of the liberal Cold War consensus. To make a cogent argument, it should have been Pease's challenge to show that Crews's Wilsonian solution amounted to a reiteration of the Cold War consensus. But Pease did not engage with Crews's arguments and propositions in a comprehensive fashion; rather, he tried to unmask Crews at a point early in the essay at which Crews signaled his general alliance with the approach of ideology critique. Here, Crews argued against "the complacent liberal consensus" of "former or chastened leftists [who] arrived at the postwar era at once alarmed by the exposure of Stalinist barbarity and exhilarated by America's new preeminence and guardianship of democratic values." For Crews, Lionel Trilling was the exemplary figure of those complacent liberals (Crews, "Whose American Renaissance?" 70). Pease, however, claimed that Crews was in no way in agreement with the New Americanists concerning the liberal tradition and its ideological interestedness: "As if he had only mechanically repeated [the New Americanists'] words, rather than understood their meaning, Crews, throughout the remainder of the review, responds to the ideological critique of the New Americanists with remarks revealing the tacit assumptions of the liberal consensus."[25]

Pease set out to uncover these tacit assumptions, not by showing how Crews's vision of the ideal critic might reveal the liberal consensus, but by reshuffling Crews's professed allegiances. As evidence for Crews's alleged support of Trilling's end-of-ideology view, Pease noted that Crews had cited Trilling instead of the much more politicized Matthiessen as the "key shaper of Americanness." Pease further claimed that Crews had omitted from his paraphrase of Trilling the latter's explicit claim for the nonideological stance of American canonical writers. Pease intimated, in other words, that Crews had kept Trilling's claim that "[true American artists] do not submit to serve the ends of any one ideological group or tendency" (quoted in Pease, "New Americanists," 5) out of his text because Crews had wanted to convey the false impression that he shared with the New Americanists a concern about the general impossibility of ideologically neutral criticism, while tacitly trying to hold on to the ideology of the "end of ideology." But Pease's claim of exposing Crews is crucially undermined by Crews's critique of Trilling for precisely his blindness to ideology. Crews related that Trilling had proposed that the great American artists were nonideological because their minds internally encompassed the dialectical contradictions of society. Contrary to Pease's claims, Crews did not subscribe to Trilling's view that great artists had "'dialectically' capacious minds" (Crews's paraphrase of Trilling, "Whose American Renaissance?" 72) and were therefore nonideological. In fact, Crews made his opposition to Trilling clear by quoting a "justly cele-brated article" (Crews, "Whose American Renaissance?" 72) from 1980 by Nina Baym titled "Melodramas of Beset Manhood," in which she had pointed out that the artists who complied with Trilling's criterion all hap-pened to be white males. Crews's criticism could hardly have been more direct: "The likelihood that Trilling and his followers would find the right stuff in a female author was scarcely greater than that of seeing Miss Wat-son board up her house and light out for the territory" (Crews, "Whose American Renaissance?" 72).

Pease's strategy to expose Crews resembled quite accurately what Crews had described as the New Americanists' tendency to reveal the political "re-pressed" of a given text at the price of rewriting that text. Pease, for in-stance, claimed that when Crews "fails to quote Trilling's critique of Mat-thiessen in 'Reality in America,' [he] silently uses *The Liberal Imagination* to displace *American Renaissance* as the master text with which to discrimi-nate among Americanists" (Pease, "New Americanists," 9–10). While Pease may have been right that Crews succumbed to the consensus of the liberal imagination, which maintains the separability of aesthetics and politics, he did not convincingly substantiate his claim of Crews's "tacit" vindication of Trilling, since this would have required showing that Crews's criticism of Trilling was somehow no real criticism at all. Reading Crews's text selec-tively, Pease in fact mentioned neither Crews's criticism of Trilling nor—what would have been the real challenge for establishing his point—Crews's use of Reynolds, Fisher, and Wilson.

From a different perspective, however, Pease's claim and his manner of conducting his argument make absolute sense, and it is this perspective that reveals some fundamental insights into the New Americanists' underlying theory of representation and ideology. Through this lens, Pease's argument can be reconstructed as follows: Because Crews in the end can be under-stood as insisting on the possibility of severing the appreciation of a literary text from the ideology that works through the text—or, as Crews put it, to "appreciate the historical reasons for a novel's power without needing to convert its politics into [one's] own" (Crews, "Whose American Renais-sance?" 81)—he is de facto subscribing to Trilling's consensus. In other words, Pease constructs an overruling meaning of Crews's text through which it carries out its ideological work. Any other facet of the text (Crews's criticism of Trilling or his professed sympathy with the perspective of ideol-ogy critique) must be subordinated to this meaning, not so much as a con-tradiction, but as a function of the text's ideological effect. While Pease at-tacks Crews as an author who is responsible for his reactionary politics, he thus also argues that what is at work in Crews is an ideology beyond authorial intention or control. In this light, those statements of Crews that seem to conflict with the ideological master text either function to disguise the ideology or are symptoms of repression.

Pease fittingly works with a vocabulary derived from psychoanalysis and the Marxist appropriations of Sigmund Freud and Jacques Lacan (for instance, Fredric Jameson's *The Political Unconscious*) to argue that Crews betrays both a "disciplinary unconscious" and a "field-Imaginary":[26]

> By the term field-Imaginary I mean to designate a location for the disciplinary unconscious mentioned earlier. Here abides the field's fundamental syntax— its tacit assumptions, convictions, primal words, and the charged relations binding them together. . . . Once constructed out of this syntax, the primal identity can neither reflect upon its terms nor subject them to critical scrutiny. The syntactic elements of the field-Imaginary subsist instead as self-evident principles. (Pease, "New Americanists," 11–12)

In other words, both terms, the "disciplinary unconscious" and the "field-Imaginary," are built on the premise that belonging to the field requires the practitioner's identification with an established representation of the field. In the Cold War consensus, according to Pease, the liberal imagination as exemplified by Trilling provides this identificatory representation. Thus, Crews must be seen as ensnared by his own (field) imaginary, which explains why at times Pease, rather than accusing him of aggressively promoting Trilling's ideological stance with an overbearing will to power, analyzes Crews as "misread[ing] the ideology of his own critical attitude" (Pease, "New Americanists," 9).

But if the identification with the field supposedly leaves no room whatsoever for critical scrutiny of the premises that make up the field imaginary, the term "disciplinary unconscious" signals that, as in psychoanalytic models of subject formation, the imaginary identification with the field requires the repression of all that contradicts the identification. Thus, in the disciplinary unconscious of a consensus Americanist resides the repressed awareness that what is taken to be separated from the political, that is, the aesthetic that is intelligible to a universal subject, is actually bound up with specific political interests. The New Americanists, one could say, reside in the consensus Americanists' disciplinary unconscious.

Thus, according to Pease, Crews is thrown into a crisis by confronting the New Americanists' insistence on the ideological permeations of the aesthetic; he faces what his Americanist identification required him to repress. In Pease's view, Crews's only defense mechanism in this moment of crisis is to declare the work of the New Americanists as not belonging to his field: "Crews comes to terms with this self-division by constructing and then policing an institutional boundary line that distinguishes true laborers within the field of American Studies from ideologists, activists, and academic special interest groups represented by New Americanists" (Pease, "New Americanists," 11). As one might expect, the repressed, according to Pease, must uncannily return. Pease's privileged example of this occurs in the very last paragraph of Crews's text, in which Crews writes: "And the New Americanists themselves seem destined to become the next establishment in their field" (Crews, "Whose American Renaissance?" 81). Pease emphasizes the fact that Crews writes "*their* field," arguing that here we see clearly Crews's inner constitutive division at work: only the return of the repressed can account for Crews's sudden recognition of the New Americanists, which, according to Pease, finds support nowhere else in the review. And even this recognition must still calm down the crisis in Crews's imaginary by separating their field from his. Pease's reading of Crews is a revealing showcase of his own premises precisely because it contradicts the evidence of Crews's text. The "recognition" of the New Americanists at the end of Crews's essay is less a return of the repressed than a reprise of the topic of paradigm shifts, with which he began his review.

What Pease's reading demonstrates is that underlying his account of Crews is Louis Althusser's theory of ideological subject formation as interpellation. As is well known, Althusser writes that ideology interpellates the concrete individual as a subject. This scene is famously figured by the police officer's hailing a pedestrian by saying, "Hey, you there." Once the pedestrian turns around, he has identified with the "you" and turned it into an "I." Accordingly, he has then become a constitutively ideological subject.[27] This theory implies that representation itself produces whatever makes up our imaginary. The policeman's hailing with "Hey, you there" is a representation insofar as it produces for us an image with which we identify willy-nilly in the act of interpellation: we recognize "You" as a representation of "I." But rather than mimetically reproducing the "I" in the "You," this kind of representation works performatively: it produces the "You" as an image of the "I," which is to say that it performatively produces the "I" as a subject.

In Althusser's structuralist account, it is necessary to remember the interplay of the structural and the concrete. While the actual power speaking and interpellating is nothing less than the (economic) structure, phenomenologically speaking we experience interpellation on the level of individual subjects: "[T]here is no ideology except by the subject and for the subject. Meaning, there is no ideology except for concrete subjects, and this destination for ideology is only made possible by the subject: meaning, *by the category of the subject* and its functioning" (emphasis in original).[28] This disparity between the concrete and the structural is connected in Althusser's Lacanian-tinged thought with the concepts of misrecognition and the imaginary. Through the act of interpellation, the subject *misrecognizes* himself or herself. This misrecognition is rooted in the fact that only through the act of interpellation does the subject recognize itself as subject; but as this recognition entails a belief to be speaking as an autonomous subject, the recognition that results from interpellation is a misrecognition. As Althusser writes, "But to recognize that we are subjects and that we function in the practical ritual of the most elementary everyday life . . . this recognition only gives us a 'consciousness' of our incessant (eternal) practice of ideological recognition . . . but in no sense does it give us the (scientific) *knowledge* of the mechanism of this recognition" (Althusser, *Lenin and Philosophy*, 173, emphasis in original). Instead of scientific knowledge, ideology provides us with an imaginary of ourselves as subjects, or as *the Subject*, as Althusser puts it to distinguish between our imaginary of the empowered self as a universal and absolute subject, and the scientific reality of the self as entirely subjected to power.

Althusser, then, uses the term *imaginary* in a specifically Lacanian context: "We observe that the structure of all ideology, interpellating individuals as subjects in the name of a Unique and Absolute Subject is *speculary*, i.e. a mirror-structure" (Althusser, *Lenin and Philosophy*, 180, emphasis in original). Thus, in an attempt to create an omnipotent ideology that works through representation, Althusser conflates Lacan's categories of the *imaginary* and the *symbolic order*—for Lacan, the two remain ultimately irreducible to each other, even if they work simultaneously—for a maximized power effect.

In the example at hand, the Althusserian perspective suggests that Crews is interpellated as an Americanist subject by the Cold War consensus ruling within American Studies. From this starting premise, Crews cannot help producing an ideological text that reproduces the Cold War consensus. In other words, the representation that the field imaginary offers and that enables Crews to achieve an identity through identification with this imaginary is a priori binding. Analyzing Crews's text then becomes a practical example of ideology critique because it allows Pease to trace the charades that ideology performs in Crews's text, with resulting contradictions and crises that in the end cannot unsettle the initial interpellation.

If Pease comprehends representation as interpellation, this of course does not mean that any speech act has the power to interpellate. When Crews excludes the New Americanists, his speech acts wield interpellative power. His manifest statements about Trilling, on the other hand, apparently have no interpellative or performative power. In other words, individual speech acts only interpellate their listener insofar as the ruling ideology speaks through them. Otherwise speech acts are mere examples of the "artistry" of ideology that tries to conceal itself through its evasiveness. One problem of this assumption is that in order to analyze such interpellative acts, one must determine in advance what the content of the ruling ideology is. Otherwise it becomes impossible to differentiate between real interpellative acts and ideological self-concealments. Pease must already know that it is the liberal consensus that Crews's ideological speech acts are trying to foster before he begins his analysis.

Another problem with this interpellative theory of representation lies in the fact that it makes it almost impossible to account for political activism on the level of representation. This leads to a theoretical contradiction that can also be read as a missed opportunity. After analyzing Crews in the terms suggested by Althusser, Pease notes the New Americanists' strong belief in the possibility of change through activism. He does so by referring to Antonio Gramsci's concepts of *hegemony*, *counter-hegemony*, and the *war of position*. Pease attempts to avoid any appearance of contradiction by incorporating Gramsci into his theoretical framework derived chiefly from Althusser and Lacan, as this somewhat lengthy quotation shows:

> A war of position takes place . . . during periods of organic crisis, when the collective will organized according to one interpretation of reality gives way, after years of struggle, to alternative interpretations. Gramsci locates the origin of organic crisis in moments of drastic cultural change which illuminate the incurable contradiction at work within prevailing organizing principles. Gramsci is as interested 'to research into how precisely permanent collective wills are formed' out of a 'concrete fantasy' as he is to study where 'there exists in society the necessary and sufficient conditions for its transformation.' . . . Throughout this discussion of the New Americanists, I have argued the relationship between their emergence and the change in what Gramsci calls the 'concrete fantasy' (what I have described as a crisis in the field-Imaginary) of American Studies. (Pease, "New Americanists," 29–30; quotations are from Gramsci's *The Modern Prince*)

Two aspects of this quotation are especially striking. First, while Pease accurately describes Gramsci's idea of the war of position as taking place within the field of culture, he does not spell out what model of representation Gramsci assumes in order for this war to take place. It turns out that Gramsci's model of representation, spread out in fragments across his *Prison Notebooks*, is incommensurable with Althusser's notion of interpellation. This is not the place to pursue a detailed reading of Gramsci, and I will restrict myself here to presenting the results of Renate Holub's illuminating analysis of Gramsci's theory of representation. In her 1992 study *Antonio Gramsci: Beyond Marxism and Postmodernism*, she develops two dimensions of his theory of representation by reading his notes on Dante's Canto 10 and his notes on linguistics, which were the result of his final research efforts in prison (Notebook 29).[29] The first dimension suggests Gramsci's emphasis on the active role of the reader in filling in the gaps left by Dante. (Here, Holub points to similarities between Gramsci's thought and Barthes' *The Pleasure of the Text*.) In the second dimension, Holub reads Gramsci as having worked toward a communicative model of interaction that exceeds the structuralist division of *langue* and *parole* and puts *langue* and *parole* into a dialectical relationship with each other.[30] Here, Holub points to the similarities to Valentin Vološinov's linguistics (now sometimes ascribed to Mikhail Bakhtin), but one could have gone even further and pointed out similarities between Gramsci and both Charles S. Peirce and William James.[31]

In any case, Gramsci could only fashion his model of the war of position abreast a model of representation that encompassed a notion of consciousness beyond an ideological effect and that allowed speech from within, but importantly, beyond ideological determination. For Pease, this position is difficult to take up because of his subscribing to Althusser. Consequently—and this is the second noticeable element of his quotation about Gramsci above—Pease attempts to appropriate Gramsci by stressing his rhetoric of fantasy and by immediately interpreting this within a Lacanian and Althusserian framework. Thus, the "concrete fantasy" becomes the field-Imaginary. Pease makes it sound as if hegemony meant exchanging one interpellative force for another, neglecting Gramsci's interest in what could be located at once inside and outside interpellation.

While Pease does not consider the possibility of linguistic agency to a degree that would question the entire model of interpellation in its stricter application, he himself, in his criticism, uses language in a way that can hardly be grasped with the interpellative model. In fact, it becomes clear that his critique of Crews is underwritten not only by certain theoretical assumptions but also by a keen sense of how to engage in arguments strategically.[32] By characterizing Crews as the embodiment of the Cold War consensus, he manages to use the attention stirred up by Crews most effectively: he emphasizes the difference of the New Americanists not only to the American Studies establishment in general but to the public voice of that establishment.

This becomes readily visible in hindsight. In one of his latest statements on the New Americanists—the 2006 article "9/11: When was 'American Studies after the New Americanists'?"—Pease repeats the origin story of the New Americanists and summarizes Crews's article from 1988, reproducing his earlier, productive misreading that claimed to reveal Crews's "tacit" support for Trilling. But later on in the same article, Pease takes a more balanced view and thus becomes entangled in a theoretical contradiction. He now points to Trilling's "imagination of disaster" as a critical step, similar to the New Americanists' attention to the supplementary knowledge of "colonial violence," thus calling Trilling's move "a New Americanist intervention avant la lettre" (Pease, "9/11," 84). Second, he also reconsiders Crews's stance toward the end-of-ideology ideology. Pointing to Crews's December 2005 review of Andrew Delbanco's *Melville: His World and Work* in *The New York Review of Books*, in which Crews criticizes Delbanco's belief in the possibility of disinterested criticism, Pease claims that Crews has "repeated the supplemental operations of the New Americanists" (Pease, "9/11," 100). In other words, Pease now finds Crews's position toward the impossibility of ideological neutrality credible, whereas he dismissed it as mechanical, mindless repetition in the 1988 article.[33] Considering that Crews has not changed his viewpoint since 1988 on the basic impossibility of disinterested criticism, there is little support for Pease's reassessment.[34]

But even if Pease were right and Crews had changed his opinion in this specific matter, how could this be harmonized with Pease's earlier explanation that Crews was unable to call seriously for a partial acceptance of New Americanist insights because of his binding interpellation as a Cold War–consensus Americanist? According to Pease, scrutinizing the tacit assumptions of the Cold War consensus had become impossible from Crews's field-Imaginary. But according to Pease's more recent view, Crews *was* capable of providing such scrutiny when it came to Delbanco's book. (Like Crews, Delbanco may be described as a liberal, mainstream Americanist, and like Crews, he has openly criticized revisionist approaches, although Delbanco concerned himself with the field of "Melville studies" rather than with the New Americanists).[35]

Pease attempts to solve the apparent inconsistency and also tries to arrive at a theory of agency from within the model of interpellation (thereby making the appropriation of Gramsci seem less contradictory) by arguing that Crews could only offer this criticism by making use of the New Americanist logic of the supplement "to materialize a social injustice to which the Liberal Imagination turned a blind eye" (Pease, "9/11," 100). The "contradictory logic of the supplement," in the context of the New Americanists, designates the addition of alternative knowledge to the received consensus, which then opens up a gap within this very consensus and shows its constructedness and democratic shortcomings.[36] But the reason why the New Americanists could deploy this logic, according to Pease, is not based on their critical will or disposition, but on their own specific, multiple interpellations. As he explained in 1992, ideological unmasking is possible for the

New Americanists because, unlike "other American identities, New Americanists subsist at the intersection between interpellation and exclusion. At this divide, they are able to recognize as their disciplinary practice the sheer constructedness of every one of the givens of the national narrative."[37] Pease, then, constructs a privileged space of "in-betweenness" that emerges from multiple interpellations, and, more specifically, from a partial disinterpellation (exclusion). This allows the New Americanists a level of insight that is at once within the limits of ideological subject formation and outside it. Crews, according to this theory, could never claim this position of partial exclusion. For him, interpellation had to lead to a coherent identification, which resulted in his internalizing exclusions by way of repression. Hence, Pease argues in 2006 that if Crews was able to criticize his own tacit assumptions, he did not do so consciously, because he had no access to the epistemologically privileged position of partial exclusion: "In aspiring to invent the terms that would represent the social wrongs that the neoliberal imagination disallowed representation, Crews *uncannily* reanimated the New Americanists' initiatives at the very moment in which he was banishing them from the field of American studies" (Pease, "9/11," 100–101, emphasis added). But even this argumentative detour does not explain why Crews should have been "aspiring to invent the terms that would represent the social wrongs that the neoliberal imagination disallowed representation," or why he could have deployed "the contradictory logic of the supplement." Virtually the only explanation Pease can offer for Crews's allegedly changed stance from "mechanical repetition" of New Americanist beliefs to a serious demurral of the "liberal imagination" is something akin to a Freudian slip.

Yet it is clear throughout Pease's formulations that his recognition of Crews's more nuanced view cannot be fully explained by his psychoanalytically informed theory of interpellation. Indeed, Pease cannot help using a vocabulary that allows for a level of representational agency, self-conscious reflection, authorial intention, and even rational argumentation that outstrips his theoretical model and leads him back to what he could have gotten from Gramsci all along. Pease characterizes Crews as "arguing," "attempting to do interpretive justice," "finding himself under an obligation to respond," "deploy[ing] the logic of the supplement," "aspir[ing] to invent terms," and "invok[ing] the New Americanist specter" (Pease, "9/11," 100–101). In other words, Pease's repeated engagement with Crews suffers from the attempt to turn him into both a subject spoken by ideology and an agent whose contradictory self-positioning at times consciously seems to banish the New Americanists and at times seems to agree with them. In Althusserian theory, agency is founded on being subjected in the scene of interpellation, with the result that this agency can never encompass that which had to be excluded as a constitutive condition of the interpellation or identification. But the agency that Pease is at times forced to ascribe to Crews to explain the latter's maneuvers does in fact encompass that very realm of the inaccessibly excluded. For Pease, the trouble with Crews becomes a struggle with his own theory of representation. What is more, Pease's own argumentative steps require a degree of epistemological mobility that is likewise difficult to accommodate within his theoretical framework. In light of his own critical agency, he can only precariously secure his theoretical assumptions by creating a privileged space of in-betweenness that ushers in something like an untainted clairvoyance in which the tacit assumptions that are usually blocked from self-knowledge become surprisingly transparent.

The New Americanist Emerson:
Empty Signification and the In-Between

I have so far focused on Donald Pease's theory of representation in his debate with Frederick Crews as a way of entering the premises underlying much of the New Americanists' scholarship. The mapping of those theoretical assumptions becomes more variegated when New Americanists are reading literature rather than their detractors. Emerson is a revealing example in this respect, partially because many of his essays are themselves preoccupied with the issues of representation, language, and signification. This has enabled his New Americanist readers to attack the issue directly.

Notable in these readings is the emergence of a further theoretical key concept, Georg Lukács's term "reification," which New Americanists sometimes refer to explicitly and sometimes only evoke. Although the concept is sometimes deployed as a complement to interpellation, it inevitably leads to theoretical tensions. In the remainder of this chapter, I will look at four representative New Americanist readings of Emerson's theory of language and representation in order to uncover underlying New Americanist theories of representation. All four of these positions, articulated by Carolyn Porter, John Carlos Rowe, Christopher Newfield, and Donald Pease, in different ways attempt to negotiate a structuralist model of representation with elements of humanism that bespeak the New Americanists' progressive agenda. In theoretical terms, this plays out in varying dynamics between interpellation and reification. The case is complicated by the fact that arguments based on reification are sometimes accompanied by a third concept of hegemony, which, while related to reification in its underlying humanism, comes into conflict with reification because, as I have just argued, the model of representation typical of hegemony allows for considerably greater agency.

Georg Lukács and the Immediacy of Mediation

First, it is helpful to take a brief look at Lukács's theory of reification and its implied model of representation. In his classic 1923 article "Reification and the Consciousness of the Proletariat," Lukács understands reification to designate a thorough deformation of human beings in their relations to the objective world, their fellows, and themselves as a result of capitalist commodity relations. All aspects of life, including individuals' understanding of their minds and selves, are treated as commodities, that is, as autonomous, objectified things. Because the reified "objects" they encounter everywhere cannot be grasped as the result of their own productive participation in social relations, individuals are condemned to adopt a passive, contemplative stance toward the world. As Lukács writes:

> Neither objectively nor in his relation to his work does man appear as the authentic master of the process; on the contrary, he is a mechanical part incorporated into a mechanical system. He finds it already pre-existing and self-sufficient, it functions independently of him and he has to conform to its laws whether he likes it or not. As labour is progressively rationalised and mechanised his lack of will is reinforced by the way in which his activity becomes less and less active and more and more contemplative.[38]

For Lukács, reification is the process that best explains the commonly described malaises of modernity: rationalization, fragmentation, division of labor, intellectual specialization, and the general loss of an organic relationship to the world. For him this also includes the attempts by German idealists to philosophically overcome the divide between the individual and the reified world—between thought and thing. According to his argument, idealism recognized the ultimate gap between the thing as constructed by the laws of the mind and the thing as part of brute nature. As a consequence, idealists redefined the latter as the unknowable "thing-in-itself" and thus began to offer theoretical, abstract accounts of the contemplative attitude. But unwittingly, idealists thereby merely solidified the attitude of contemplation typical of reification by presenting the thing-in-itself as completely separate from human subjects and by specifying the laws of the mind. Thus they separated the objective form of the mind (Kant's categories and so forth) from subjective content:

> The critical elucidation of contemplation puts more and more energy into its efforts to weed out ruthlessly from its own outlook every subjective and irrational element and every anthropomorphic tendency; it strives with ever increasing vigour to drive a wedge between the subject of knowledge and 'man',

and to transform the knower into a pure and purely formal subject. (Lukács, "Reification," 128)

To make Lukács useful for my purposes here, it is necessary to specify the theory of representation that informs his theory of reification. Lukács speaks repeatedly of the need for mediation in order to overcome reification. To him, mediation is a form of representation that differs from theories of reflection.[39] Reflection keeps things and thoughts apart dualistically and is thus a symptom of reification, while mediation, for Lukács, refers to the way human beings contribute to the production of their world. His essay is thus also a call for replacing the dominant view of representation as reflection with one modeled on mediation. Hence his critique of the model of representation at work in art and idealist philosophy (what he also calls "bourgeois thought"), which in his view ossifies reification. Bourgeois thought poses an obstacle to mediation because it suggests a false immediacy, thereby hiding its own processes of mediation:

> Bourgeois thought entered into an unmediated relationship with reality as it was given. . . . In this way the very thing that should be understood and deduced with the aid of mediation becomes the accepted principle by which to explain all phenomena and is even elevated to the status of a value: namely the unexplained and inexplicable facticity of bourgeois existence as it is here and now acquires the patina of an eternal law of nature or a cultural value enduring for all time. (Lukács, "Reification," 156–57)

But if bourgeois thought functions to hinder mediation by prescribing passive contemplation, Lukács also implies what true mediation would look like: the creation of a unity between thing and thought, theory and praxis, the material and the ideational, initiated in the moment the reified worker discovers a class consciousness. Nearly replicating Fichte's identity philosophy, Lukács comes to claim that true mediation leads to the identity of subject and object in the form of class consciousness:

> We can already see here more clearly and concretely the factors that create a dialectic between the social existence of the worker and the forms of his consciousness and force them out of their pure immediacy. Above all the worker can only become conscious of his existence in society when he becomes aware of himself as a commodity. . . .
> [W]hen the worker knows himself as a commodity his knowledge is practical. That is to say, this knowledge brings about an objective structural change in the object of knowledge. (Lukács, "Reification," 167–68)

Perhaps ironically, what can be inferred from Lukács's text is that this ideal process of mediation itself allows us to enter a state in which mediation turns into a fully organic *immediacy*. He hints at this when he contrasts the false immediacy of landscapes (as an aesthetic representation—always bourgeois—of nature) with the "peasant's unconscious living within nature" (Lukács, "Reification," 157). In other words, Lukács's idea of representation as mediation is implicated in a dialectical process that strives toward a state of the absolute in which representation has become obsolete. The tendency to demand a more advanced model of representation, that is, mediation instead of reflection, then, turns out to be underwritten by a secret wish not only to render a frozen dualism more dynamic and mutually productive but, ultimately, to dissolve it once and for all.[40] But insofar as this ideal of immediacy as the end result of mediation proper unites thing and thought, it is important to see that, as a consequence of Lukács's leaning on Fichte's idealism, this unity must be understood as the *product* of the class subject. In other words, Lukács developed a theory of representation that assumes a telos of self-produced unity in which otherness has no place whatsoever.[41]

Carolyn Porter: Emerson's Contemplative Idealism

Lukács's concept of reification holds considerable appeal for New Americanist readers of Emerson. Considering Emerson's frequent lament about the effects of society on the individual, it has been tempting to argue that Lukács provided not only a useful paradigm for late-twentieth-century scholarship but also one that is intimately related to (although not identical with) Emerson's cultural critique as well. One of the most obvious of these Lukácsian moments may be found in "The American Scholar," where Emerson complains about the division of labor, stating that "Man is not a farmer, or a professor, or an engineer, but he is all. Man is priest, and scholar, and statesman, and producer, and soldier. In the divided or social state, these functions are parcelled out to individuals, each of whom aims to do his stint of the joint work, whilst each other performs his" (CW, vol. 1, 53). Though not including Marxist remedies for the effects of industrialization and the division of labor, Emerson's Romantic ideal of "being all" is closely connected to Lukács's goal of overcoming reification. Restoring man's wholeness remains the normative, ultimately idealist horizon of Lukács's analysis of the effects of modern capitalism, according to which a pervasive commodity structure comes to include the self's relation to itself: "[T]he worker, too, must present himself as the 'owner' of his labour-power, as if it were a commodity" (Lukács, "Reification," 92). Carolyn Porter was the first revisionist

Americanist to apply Lukács's concept to Emerson (and other canonical American authors) in a comprehensive manner in her *Seeing and Being: The Plight of the Participant Observer in Emerson, James, Adams, and Faulkner*, from 1981.[42] She pointed to the common ground between Emerson and Lukács and, more crucially, undertook a Lukácsian critique of Emerson.

In Porter's reading of Emerson's major texts, her Lukácsian perspective leads to a somewhat predictable result: Emerson, like those proponents of bourgeois thought critiqued by Lukács himself, turns out to promote an attitude of passive contemplation while, on the surface, he tries to wed thing and thought, or, in Emerson's Fichtean terms, Me and Not-Me. Interestingly, though, according to Porter, Emerson's attempt to overcome reification commends signification as the means to do so. Thus, the "use of nature" at the core of Emerson's *Nature* is itself signification. "The relationship between words and natural facts, and between natural and spiritual facts, represents a fundamental 'use of the world,' because it establishes a model for transcendence which can operate endlessly. 'Nothing in nature is exhausted in its first use,' because the signifier-signified model can always be invoked again, using the signifier to focus on the signified."[43] This process of endless (re-)signification, however, exacerbates the problem inherent in idealism, in which the individual must face what Emerson famously calls his "noble doubt": does the external world actually exist? In other words, the idealist self has only aggravated the original split between Me and Not-Me. In a world consisting of our own significations, brute nature seems further removed than ever before. In Porter's view, Emerson attempts to solve the problem of the noble doubt by the introduction of the Spirit. To her, this solution is flawed and ends up creating new problems. The Spirit, she claims, takes on a dual function in *Nature*: it provides a teleological goal for the process of signification, whereby the individual is encouraged to keep signifying, assured that the Spirit is in fact to be found in signification, and it ontologically grounds the world of the mind in nature, supplying the missing link that had led to the painful, if "noble," doubt in the first place. In Porter's reading, this dual function of the Spirit turns out to have devastating results. While the self keeps on signifying forever, it will get no closer to an understanding of how it is productively related to the world around it. All the introduction of the Spirit does is to add an authority figure that the self has to trust and submit to. "[T]he authority derived from Spirit exacts its price, for it results in a new form of imprisonment; man is in effect endowed with the freedom of a sentient thrown stone; he can see what throws him, but he has no power to resist being thrown" (Porter, *Seeing and Being*, 106). In other words, Porter's Emerson proposes to take up the position of a passive spectator who can only marvel at the prowess of the Spirit.

Porter's criticism of Emerson's advocacy of submission to the authority figure of the Spirit—however counterintuitive this may seem for this major advocate of self-reliance—has proven to be very influential on Emerson's New Americanist readers. But at the core of Porter's result lie two critical suppositions. First, she declines to consider how the submission to authority is to be figured if the Spirit is an agency that is neither identical to nor different from the self. What if we take seriously Emerson's basic point that the Spirit, as the *impersonal*, can only be thought of as intimately related to (though not congruent with) the personal?[44] This premise would undermine the dualistic framework of activity and passivity on which Porter's argument is built.

Thinking of representation in terms of activity and passivity also structures her second supposition, a Lukácsian fear that the process of endless signification does no more than reproduce the social order, with all its existing exclusions. In this model of representation, which I will call "empty signification," speakers have no linguistic agency precisely because ideological representation is presumed to work seamlessly, as immediacy. But how plausible is the assumption that representation is so successful that we never begin to doubt its false immediacy and are doomed to failure in our attempts to represent the relationship between word and thing? In other words, if "bourgeois" thought offers us a falsely coherent worldview at the price of condemning us to passivity within signification, is it likely that the possibility of endless resignification leaves this immediacy untouched and keeps us tied up in passivity? I argue that this nightmare of an empty signification is the inverse of Lukács's idealist dream, in which representation, via mediation, finally becomes immediate. In the first case, representation cannot touch upon the real processes of mediation and thus appears as an immediate relation of thing and thought. In the second, representation is congruent with the processes of mediation, which results in a real, immediate relation of thing and thought, which really is a nonrelation, a union. Porter writes that she does "not pretend to address the many issues it [the concept of reification] has raised for Marxist theorists, particularly those generated by Lukács's identity theory."[45] However, as long as she uses Lukács's assumptions to arrive at a verdict that proposes the failure of a writer like Emerson to get beyond contemplation, she unwittingly subscribes to this identity theory, because it serves as the implied ideal of representation and structures the analysis of the Emersonian representational malaise. To deploy the concept of reification without its idealist ramifications would require an alternative explication of how the split in reification is to be healed.[46]

Porter's disclaimer is eloquent, however, in that it points to a contradiction in her text. This becomes more obvious when she refers to the concept of hegemony, quoting from various chapters of Raymond Williams's *Marxism and Literature*. She writes, "The dominant culture can never completely incorporate all human experience; there is an active residual element which persists, often in the realms which the dominant culture excludes from its 'ruling definition of the social.' Such is art itself, so that it is not surprising that the most radical resistance during this period comes from men like Melville, Thoreau, and Emerson" (Porter, *Seeing and Being*, 90). What this suggests is not merely that incorporation has its limits, outside of which the residual is located. Rather, the limits of incorporation lie inside the incorporated itself. Here resides the ambiguity of hegemony. On the one hand, as Williams writes, "all or nearly all initiatives and contributions, even when they take on manifestly alternative or oppositional forms, are in practice tied to the hegemonic: that the dominant culture, so to say, at once produces and limits its own forms of counter-culture" (Williams, *Marxism and Literature*, 114). Porter adopts this formulation (Porter, *Seeing and Being*, 90), yet she elides Williams's turn to the other, more productive, side of the ambiguity. It "would be wrong," Williams writes, "to overlook the importance of works and ideas which, while clearly affected by hegemonic limits and pressures, are at least in part significant breaks beyond them, which may again in part be neutralized, reduced, or incorporated, but which in their most active elements nevertheless come through as independent and original" (Williams, *Marxism and Literature*, 114). This aspect is missing from Porter's account.

It is as if Porter omitted this latter portion of Williams's thought because it would conflict with her ensuing close reading of Emerson, which, as we have seen, aims to demonstrate that he falls short of his promise of "radical resistance" because of his endorsement of the Spirit, and, thus, of passive contemplation. Thinking through the ramifications of Williams's reformulation of Gramsci's concept of hegemony would call into question both the fear of empty signification and the ideal of idealist immediacy as the full disclosure of mediation. Porter would have to face the fact that while the social process creates appearances of immediacy through signification, this process of creation is anything but seamless. The endless signification she diagnoses in Emerson, in this view, would counter the fear of a complete submission to the Spirit. The "passive stance" of contemplation would turn out to be more involved in a "lived hegemony," which is, according to Williams, "always a process. . . . It is a realized complex of experiences, relationships, and activities, with specific and changing pressures and limits" (Williams, *Marxism and Literature*, 112). In other words, confronting the full implications of the promise of radical resistance might suggest that Emerson does not empty out endless signification because of his introduction of the Spirit, but rather uses the Spirit for the purposes of resisting within representation.

Ultimately, this raises a question that also lurks in Gramsci's writings, namely, is this activity really adequately described as "resistance"? Resistance implies a power relation in which the hierarchy is settled and then shattered by the subordinate subject. When Gramsci speaks of a "war of positions" that takes place in civil society, however, this assumption of a fixed hierarchy is replaced with the image of entrenched warfare:

> The superstructures of civil society are like the trench-systems of modern warfare. In a war it would sometimes happen that a fierce artillery attack seemed to have destroyed the enemy's entire defensive system, whereas in fact it had only destroyed the outer perimeter; . . . Of course, things remain not exactly as they were; but it is certain that one will not find the element of speed, of accelerated time, of the definitive forward march. (Gramsci, *Prison Notebooks*, 489–90)

If civil society is characterized by a war of positions, both its potential and its dangers may be missed if all hope is placed in some form of radical resistance—what Gramsci calls a "definitive forward march"—that promises greater gains than can be achieved from the back-and-forth of entrenched fighting.

Although Lukács's humanist (Hegelian) Marxism contradicts Althusser's structuralist Marxism, we see in Porter's work how an engagement with the Lukácsian approach is nevertheless often informed by notions that border on the totality of Althusserian structuralism. Instead of facing this theoretical tension openly, Porter deploys it in a rhetoric of dramatic disillusionment: the hopes built up by her humanist strain are crushed by the force of her structuralist totalizations. John Carlos Rowe's work on Emerson exploits a similar inner tension, yet he tips the balance toward structuralist thought.

John Carlos Rowe: Contemplation as the Result of Interpellation

Rowe has repeatedly pointed to Porter's work on reification. While Porter arrived at her initial hope for radical resistance via Williams, her partial quotation from Williams already indicated her uneasiness with his analysis of the ambiguity of hegemony, which includes aspects of the incorporation of resisting energies by the dominant culture, along with the possibility of the emergence of "independent and original" elements. Rowe radicalizes this uneasiness as a strict repudiation of the latter possibility. Thus, in "Deconstructing America: Recent Approaches to Nineteenth-Century Literature and

Culture," a review essay from 1985, he approvingly quotes Porter's adoption of Williams's argument that "the dominant culture can produce and limit its counterculture," yet he goes on to criticize her because she "too quickly and easily grants genuinely subversive and critical authority to the literary strategies of Emerson [et al.]"[47]

Rowe here rehearses an argument that he developed in a series of articles throughout the 1980s. In these articles he criticizes deconstruction from a Marxist perspective, seeing it as resulting in a politically crippling formalism that adds up to a repetition of the conservative formalism of the New Critics.[48] The upshot of this argument is that aesthetic dissent is a hopeless, ultimately reactionary endeavor and that all we can learn from looking at aesthetics is how artfully ideology itself operates. This conviction also underlies his 1997 study *At Emerson's Tomb*, in which he criticizes Emerson as the founder of the tradition of classic American literature, a tradition that in Rowe's view includes deconstructionist readers of the twentieth century.[49] Thus, Rowe does not criticize Emerson for having too long evaded social injustices like slavery. Rather, he blames Emerson for the conservative ramifications that he sees in Emerson's taking up of abolitionism within a transcendentalist framework. To Rowe, this framework made it impossible per se to reach effectively into the political: "In short, the classic American literature founded on Emersonian values would be an explicit instance of an 'aesthetic ideology' working to support the very social forces it overtly criticizes."[50]

We find in Rowe's argument an assumption that resembles Porter's: the world is represented to us through language in a manner fully in agreement with the dominant ideology, and the use of language, however subversive it may seem, can only reaffirm this representation. Despite this similarity, Rowe's theoretical cornerstone differs significantly from Porter's. He arrives at his grim result via Althusser's theory of interpellation, according to which the individual is hailed by an ideological voice and is transformed into a subject. There are by now many different applications of Althusser's theory; some of them have tried to lessen Althusser's fatalistic undertones, for instance by arguing that interpellation is inherently unstable because it requires constant reiteration.[51] Yet Rowe's understanding of interpellation surely ranks among the sternest ones. This becomes visible in two ways.

First, in Rowe's eyes, the positioning of the subject through interpellation seems almost entirely to predetermine the ideological import of a given author's or tradition's texts. He writes, "Given the fact that Emersonianism has so profoundly shaped our traditional understanding of classic American literature, then that same American literature would appear to be profoundly implicated in the ideology of American commercialism that stretches from

Jacksonian America to the present" (Rowe, *At Emerson's Tomb*, 22). Rowe here reduces ideological criticism to a syllogism of the following kind: American society has been plagued by an ideology of commercialism; Emerson may have been the most influential figure in American literature; hence, Emerson has supported the ideology of American commercialism.

Second, because (in this argument) aesthetic dissent is doomed to remain locked up in the prison of language, true dissent can only come about by transcending representation and rising to action. This can only be achieved by those who are not from the beginning interpellated into the center. Thus, writers who belong to disempowered groups can help build up solidarity through their literature, by providing "fictional experiences of sympathetic identification" (Rowe, *At Emerson's Tomb*, 12). To avoid the pitfalls of aesthetic dissent, however, such identifications need to be "linked with specific political practices" (Rowe, *At Emerson's Tomb*, 12). Rowe may just be stating the obvious by observing that literary texts that are not deployed directly by political movements cannot be said to tangibly help those movements. The problem is that his interpellation clause does not let him look at what else these texts—and, in fact, representation in general—may be doing, because this question seems already to have been answered: if they do not measurably contribute to political movements, they must support the status quo. Surely it has been Rowe's intention to warn us about those representational acts that claim action to be unnecessary. Ironically, though, Rowe himself runs the risk of partitioning off language or representation into a world elsewhere. He conceptualizes representation and action as separate, implicitly repudiating Emerson's idea in his essay "The Poet" that "Words are also actions, and actions are a kind of words" (*CW*, vol. 3, 6), a formulation in which Emerson suggests the mutually constitutive character of representation and action rather than either their congruity or their categorical difference.

Indeed, it remains unclear how to account for the relationship between action and representation within Rowe's model. And because he renders absolute the distinction between the center and the margin (except when the center co-opts the energies of the margin), it is also unclear how to describe the dynamic processes between margin and center. The political analysis that emerges from Rowe's theory of representation thus has limits in its ability to explain what happens to the input (the actions) from the margins, once they find their addressees. What is implicit in Emerson's idea that "words are also actions, and actions are a kind of words" is that these actions undergo a process of reception that is similar to that of words. Upholding the distinction between margin and center at that moment becomes detrimental to understanding the receptive as a crucial part of the political.

Christopher Newfield: Reconstructing Individual Agency against Emersonian Submission

The notion of passivity induced by empty signification, which is at the heart of Porter's and Rowe's analyses of Emerson's works, and specifically Emerson's thoughts on language, also resonates throughout Christopher Newfield's influential study from 1996 titled *The Emerson Effect*.[52] More acutely than most of Emerson's readers, Newfield focuses on Emerson's undeniable attempts to procure a dimension of freedom out of imposed strictures, a move that for Emerson, as Newfield shows convincingly, leads to a valorization of such strictures. Thus, Newfield focuses on Emerson's fascination with such figures as the moral law and the Spirit, which Newfield calls "authoritarian." In his unwillingness to grant the possibility of agency's emergence from strictures of any kind, Newfield's reading can be understood as a radicalization of that of Carolyn Porter, who, as we have seen, interpreted Emerson's treatment of the Spirit in *Nature* as a source of imprisonment. Newfield radicalizes both Porter and Rowe insofar as he tries to show, not how the Emersonian tradition concealed submission behind an appearance of freedom, but how this tradition managed openly and unabashedly to vindicate submission as a necessary precondition to freedom. In Newfield's argument, this ideology finds its equivalent in the emergence of the corporation: "*Corporate individualism* is the term I'll use to describe the desired outcome of Emerson's liberalism: the enhancement of freedom through the loss of both private and public control."[53]

The force of Newfield's argument arises from his radical repudiation of the liberal consensus among Emerson readers. Thus, his book also functions as a continuous dismantling of liberal attempts to accommodate submission with freedom. For Emerson's liberal readers, Newfield writes, "oppositional structures work roughly but symbiotically, hence universal and particular individuality or imitation and invention or Cratylian realism and possessive individualism coexist in mutual support" (Newfield, *Emerson Effect*, 45).[54] Newfield's argument is compelling to the degree that his analysis of the liberal tradition of Emersonian criticism is correct. Indeed, most influential Emerson readers in recent decades (with the exception of most New Americanists), whether Sacvan Bercovitch, Lawrence Buell, Stanley Cavell, Barbara Packer, or Richard Poirier, have insisted on Emerson's productive use of restrictions as enabling forces.

The actual challenge Newfield sets himself, however, lies in proving that Emersonian attempts to use restrictions in the name of creating possibilities for agency actually end in individual and collective submission. To show this, Newfield cannot resort to the circularity that structures Rowe's argument. He does not construe the indisputable fact of the rise of the corporation as *proof* of Emerson's complicity, but rather in meticulous readings tries to show how Emerson comes to establish a tradition of corporate individualism that has become dominant in American culture. In other words, we do not find a sweeping theory of interpellation underlying Newfield's study. Rather, Newfield's political hope is to awaken the individual and collective in order to break with a *habit* of consenting to submission. This is possible because this habit has not yet become fully systemic. Accordingly, Newfield insistently calls for a vindication of individual agency, which, from a Marxist perspective, would seem not only naive but retrograde.[55]

According to Newfield, it is in Emerson's treatment of language that his call for submission becomes especially apparent: "[The] problem with the Emersonian notion of self-determination becomes particularly acute around the question of poetic language. Here Emerson denies the power of meaning to the free poet by siding with Neoplatonic realism against nominalism" (Newfield, *Emerson Effect*, 44). In my next chapter, I will demonstrate that Newfield misinterprets the internal necessity of a submissive moment in Emerson's thought as resulting in total submission. Newfield's answer to this would certainly be that this proves, rather than challenges, his point, and that such a critique merely replicates the established, liberal common sense. As he says, "Most influential commentaries have this dual form, melding freedom with determinism and metamorphosis with permanence. In such accounts, the poet restores tarnished language through a dialectic between perception and creation" (Newfield, *Emerson Effect*, 49). But to make his point, it is not enough to criticize the assumption of a "dialectical presence of invention and imitation" (Newfield, *Emerson Effect*, 49) for its hurtful political effects. Newfield must also prove these critics wrong, showing that Emerson's understanding of language is thoroughly misunderstood by them. To do this, he contends that "at no point in 'Language' [the fourth chapter of *Nature*] does Emerson describe this kind of active yet 'embedded' invention. His language chapter has the most impossible time trying to maintain any kind of dialectic between nature and independent mind" (Newfield, *Emerson Effect*, 49).

Regarding Newfield's various models of representational theories, he repeatedly comes back to Cratylus and Friedrich Schlegel as two figures who stand for the opposite poles of imitation and invention, or realism and nominalism. "The realist view," Newfield writes, "does not encourage invention but demands imitation. . . . Invention, to the contrary, depends on something like the nominalist's view, which Emerson repudiates in 'Language'" (Newfield, *Emerson Effect*, 45). Therefore, in order to promote a sustainable notion of invention, an invention that can stand its ground even in the face of concomitant imitation, those "dialectical" liberal theories that claim to make imitation and invention coexist mutually would have to reject realism in favor of nominalism: "The dialectical poet, that is, the liberal sage, must act as a 'lawgiver' in Friedrich Schlegel's sense rather than simply in that of Cratylus, who traced the legislating of the first poet to a power of imitation" (Newfield, *Emerson Effect*, 49). Listing Schlegel, Rousseau, Wordsworth, Shelley, and Hazlitt on the side of the nominalists and thus underlining the reprehensibility of Emerson's views, even—in fact, especially—by Romantic standards, Newfield points out: "The bond within a language of thoughts, things, and spirit on which [Emerson] insists was believed by these kindred authors to be fatal to thought" (Newfield, *Emerson Effect*, 57). As we can see with Schlegel, this is an overstatement.[56] But as I will also show in my next chapter, the idea that realism cannot issue in "embedded invention" is not convincing either, as the philosophy of Charles S. Peirce amply demonstrates. Rather, Newfield's equation of realism and nominalism with imitation and invention bespeaks a dualism in his own thought. This dualism calls for an individual agency so unconditional ("unburdened") that it is probably impossible to fulfill, and it assumes that all modes of representation that fall short of this demand for agency lead to passivity or what Lukács would have called contemplation. Because the criteria for agency and invention are almost insuperably high, Newfield in effect comes to support a view of representation in which Emerson, as a proponent of passivity, is not the exception but the sad norm. In other words, those kinds of models of representation that argue for invention on the basis of imitation must fail Newfield's test, while, on the other hand, those theories that he holds up (for example, Schlegel's) tend to require his misreading in order to qualify. Thus, in the end, Newfield's reading resembles Porter's in its Lukácsian refusal to acknowledge the possibility that the dominant Emersonian tradition of representation might break out of the passive attitude of contemplation; even more basically, it shares the belief, attributable to both Althusser and Lukács, that representation fosters and replicates submission. While Newfield seems to be saying that all that is necessary is the replacement of passivity-inducing representation with its opposite, this opposite has, in his critical imagination, become strangely inaccessible, at least within the realm of representation. It is remarkable that when later, in 2002, he specifies his ideal as "contact," exemplified by sexual relations, he searches for a bodily immediacy that can promise a degree of fluidity *because* it is located beyond representation.

Donald Pease: Moving the Space-In-Between
from Speech to the System

Donald Pease's writings on Emerson, which focus on signification and representation throughout, operate with theoretical ingredients similar to Porter's, Rowe's, and even Newfield's. Pease, however, does so with the clear intention of showing under which conditions representation opens up possibilities for transformation. In his view, this focus on transformation is a defining trait of much New Americanist work: "Whereas, for [Sacvan] Bercovitch, there was no way outside oppositional containment, for many New Americanists at work in his Cambridge History project (and elsewhere), there exists the possibility of countering the hegemony" (Pease, "New Americanists," 29).[57]

Pease has produced three major statements on Emerson, which have spanned almost his entire career as a scholar. In 1980, he published "Emerson, *Nature*, and the Sovereignty of Influence," a close reading of *Nature*. Several years later, this article became the backbone of "Emerson and the Law of Nature," a chapter from his book-length study of 1987, *Visionary Compacts*. Finally, in 2007, he published "'Experience,' Antislavery, and the Crisis of Emersonianism," which, although it shifts its focus from *Nature* (1836) to "Experience" (1844), can be understood as a rereading of his own prior interpretation. At no point does Pease directly base his thoughts on Lukács's theory of reification. However, in his first two texts, he pays close attention to the remedy Emerson suggested for the modern separation of man from himself and his social relations. To this end, Pease argues, Emerson, like other American Renaissance authors, devised a "visionary compact." In Emerson's case, the visionary compact replaced a sense of wholeness based on the individual with one that serves, to use Emerson's phrase, "the commonwealth."

Pease argues that Emerson's concept of self-reliance must be understood to work in the service of this very visionary compact. Accordingly, "the faculty of self-reliance" tries to restore the self to wholeness by discriminating "the person's transitory interests from the unchanging principles upon which this person relies."[58] If the restored self relies on the discovery of principles that are bound neither to himself nor to any "great man," "hero," or "representative man" but that in fact underlie "all Americans," then self-reliance is in the end also responsible for Emerson's political awakening to the abolitionist cause: "An individual could then put those principles into practice, as Emerson did when he opposed the Fugitive Slave Law" (Pease, *Visionary Compacts*, 204). This is a crucial moment in Pease's text, because, as we will see, it is Emerson's initiation into the political that stirs Pease's interest both in 1987 and 2007. Crucially, his accounts of this event differ in precisely the way his theory of representation changes: while in his earlier account representation can still lead to restored humanity, later on representation is understood along the lines of interpellation, doing away with a notion of humanity that might be restored.

A closer look at Pease's earlier account of Emerson's theory of representation helps us trace this negotiation of humanist restoration and structuralist interpellation. Pease's reading of *Nature* reveals two contradictory figures, which, in the drama Emerson stages in his book, are at odds with and complementary to each other. One is the figure of the idealist, who tries to master, that is, to represent, nature through his abstract concepts. The other figure is the child, who demands an "original relation" to nature and the universe, a position Pease calls materialist. Finally, Pease introduces the figure of the Spirit as a third term that evolves in the space between those two figures. This space-in-between will become the central focus of his analysis. According to Pease, *Nature* shows that the "only adequate representation" of nature resides in that which cannot be captured by the idealist's abstract concepts and that which cannot be represented in the child's "precognitive relation to nature" (Pease, *Visionary Compacts*, 220).

Representation proper only evolves when we include the site in between a direct relation to nature and the idealist's abstractions of nature as a constitutive element of representation. This representational model is what Pease's Emerson means by nature's law. "Nature works best when all the things that can be realized from thought, and all the thoughts that can be inferred from things, are simultaneously achieved. Nature's law might best be described as the relation, the ever-enlivened relation, between thought and things" (Pease, *Visionary Compacts*, 216). Without trying to foster an unnecessarily close link between Pease's reading and Lukács's model of reification and mediation, we ought to keep in mind that both are looking for a remedy to a comparable ailment (the loss of wholeness) and that both find it in a model of representation in which thought and thing are brought into constant exchange. The difference is that Lukács envisions an idealist unity, while Pease singles out the space-in-between, which bars mediation from turning into unity.

But if Pease here is indebted to a humanist Marxism, his space-in-between is anticipatory of a privileged space that he later develops from a principally structuralist account of interpellation. In this later account, a space-in-between emerges from negative interpellation, that is, from a position between being excluded and being part of a social order that has not yet fully emerged. These two spaces-in-between are not identical, although it is at times difficult to tell them apart. In the earlier texts, the space-in-between must be understood in the context of a logical, formal process of representation, although what this means is itself embattled in Pease's text. This battle is in full swing in Pease's interpretation of Emerson's famous image of the "transparent eye-ball." Pease writes:

> The eyeball . . . is itself a gap, a transition between what can be written and what can be 'grasped' as meaningful. It literally surprises us out of our propriety and breaks us free of the closed circle of the discourse of idealism and its language authorized by its fathers. Not a meaningful expression but the imaged interval between words, the unthinkable transformative power or the genius of language that makes all significance possible, the 'transparent eyeball' traverses the common sense of all words. (Pease, *Visionary Compacts*, 226)

This quotation is oddly separated into two halves. In the first half (the first two sentences), the space of the in-between seems to be literally external to a habitual idealist discourse, which is figured as a circle. Pease, in other words, describes the gap as disruptive of the idealist discourse of the fathers. In the second half, however, the gap seems to reside within all discourse, even inside the idealist discourse of the fathers. The question then is whether inhabiting the space-in-between is a moment of every act of signification, or whether this space is a (possibly temporary) subject position.

Pease does seem to lean toward the latter answer when he singles out the orphic poet as the fulfillment of his Emersonian vision. The orphic poet teaches us that we have to seek the in-between by finding a way of being spoken by discourse: "In [the orphic poet], neither Emerson nor the reader speaks, yet both are spoken by him" (Pease, *Visionary Compacts*, 234). Rather than integrating the moment of transition in a circular structure of representation, Pease here privileges a model in which we first have to be passive (spoken by the orphic poet, by discourse) in order to then, as the next step, appropriate the power of the orphic poet from this space. The space-in-between, which was originally introduced as a "separative connection" between idealist and materialist, thus tends to become severed from what it supposedly connects. Within Pease's early argument, then, representation slides toward valorizing the position of the excluded, not as a transitional moment within representation, but as an effect of representation. This position is best described as "exceptional," as belonging to the order of representation through its exclusion. And only through this exclusion, Pease implies, can the circle of the idealist discourse be broken up and self-reliant power be assumed.

This sliding marks an ambiguity in Pease's text between a model of representation that is close to Lukács's idea of mediation (but that does not attempt to steer mediation toward immediacy) and that of Althusserian interpellation. Twenty years after *Visionary Compacts*, it has become clear in which direction Pease would resolve this ambiguity. In "'Experience,' Antislavery, and the Crisis of Emersonianism," Pease attempts to describe anew how Emerson came to protest against slavery. Pease tells an uncommonly sophisticated version of the familiar story of Emerson's transformation from a transcendental enthusiast elevated by his Genius into a skeptic who, in "Experience," suffers from the impossibility of grieving his son's death and who thereby experiences the failure to access his Genius.

Pease's interest lies in showing how this transformation makes visible one aspect of the reception of Genius that Emerson had not confronted openly in his early essays such as "Self-Reliance." He argues that in "Self-Reliance," Emerson had, without acknowledging it, associated the moment of inspiration with the social death of slavery, because in Emerson's text the moment of being called by Genius depends on the condition of kinlessness. As Emerson writes in "Self-Reliance," "I shun father and mother and wife and brother, when my genius calls me" (*CW*, vol. 2, 30). Referring to Orlando Patterson's concept of "social death," developed in his 1982 study *Slavery and Social Death*, Pease points out that "Natal alienation, or the social condition of radical kinlessness, constituted . . . the communal fiction through which slave societies rationalized slavery as a form of social death."[59] Pease further argues that, in accordance with this unspoken parallel between the call of Genius and the social death of slaves in Emerson's thinking, in "Self-Reliance" Emerson calls on abolitionists to divest themselves of their affection for the slaves of Barbados and to reinvest it in their kin and local community (while he also calls for voluntary kinlessness). Thus, the unspoken parallel between inspiration and slavery is formulated in the context of Emerson's turning against the project of abolitionism. At least as problematically, in leaving the parallel unspoken, Emerson cannot differentiate between the individual who consciously withdraws from society in order to perceive the call of Genius and thus achieve his emancipation, and the situation of the slave, who neither wills his kinlessness nor can use it for the sake of emancipation. In short, "the metaphorical usage to which Emerson had . . . put slavery in his articulation of 'Self-Reliance'" is informed by a "racist logic" (Pease, "'Experience,'" 103).

It is only later, in "Experience," that the failure to receive the call of Genius makes Emerson realize that the position of social death, of kinlessness, does not open the gate to creativity and the receptivity of Genius at all. Pease argues that Emerson's failure to receive the call of Genius and to mourn the death of his son Waldo in "Experience" forces him to acknowledge historical slavery, an institution on which his concept of inspiration and provocation silently depended all along. As he explains, the essays from the period of "Self-Reliance" were based on an "order of provocation," but this order now becomes replaced with an "order of trauma." The order of provocation allowed the individual speaker to remove himself from the social world, and, in receiving the "provocative" call of Genius, to create (or performatively provoke) an entirely new world. This has become impossible in the order of trauma: instead of being able to call forth a new world, the individual is stuck in a realm in which the social world has been literally removed (as expressed in the death of his son), yet no new world of spiritual insight becomes graspable.[60]

Pease calls the entry of Emerson's speaker into the order of trauma his "crisis of witnessing": confronted with his son's death, he can no longer use the social death of slaves to call forth an alternative order. This crisis of witnessing is itself witnessed and ultimately enabled by a figure Pease calls the "Anti-Slave." (Pease here takes up a phrase Emerson uses at the climax of his lecture on the emancipation in the British West Indies, given in the same year, 1844, in which "Experience" was published.) Like Pease's Emerson of the order of trauma, this figure of witness "whom the speaker desired to engender . . . did not belong either to the preexisting social order or to the Emersonian alternative" (Pease, "'Experience,'" 103). The crisis of witnessing that Pease diagnoses in Emerson's "Experience," then, turns Emerson into a writer openly concerned with slavery and abolition, because Emerson now experiences the faltering of his old mechanism of averting his attention from slavery in order to arrive at the creation of an alternative world.

Pease's reading showcases an Emerson who is politically more progressive than the Emerson who negates and even exploits slavery to arrive at spiritual emancipation through the reception of Genius's calling. Traumatic Emersonianism abandons the old protocols of creating a new world by renouncing the old. But if the Emerson Pease presents here begins to have at least a rudimentary awareness of the position of the slave, who is stuck between being desymbolized and being incapable of creating a compensatory and emancipating order, Pease's theoretical move (ascribed to Emerson) also produces a problem. For when Pease claims that the order of provocation is replaced with an order of trauma, he implies a commensurability of both orders. Without such commensurability, the replacement would be impossible. Pease not only reconstructs a shift within Emerson's world of thought but devises it himself by depicting the process of Emersonian spiritual insight (the call of Genius) as based on an exceptional position in relationship to the symbolic order, rather than as explicable by the inner workings of signification and representation.

Thus, to come back to his transformation of the space-in-between, the replacement that Pease enacts shifts the space-in-between from one inherent in the process of signification to one in the realm of subject positions. This replacement becomes possible because Pease here redefines the first meaning of the space-in-between: even the moment of receiving Genius's call in the order of provocation is now recast in terms of subject positions. It is the self-reliant speaker who removes himself to a position of desymbolization, only to then create an emancipating alternative order. In *Visionary Compacts*, this very step was described more ambiguously, and part of Pease's explanation treated self-reliance as deriving from the Emersonian structure of representational acts themselves. It is because of this redefinition of the space-in-between undertaken by Pease that Emerson can then, in "Experience," move ahead and realize the traumatic dimension of being in a subject position, in between the current order and an emerging alternative. Pease thereby reduces the complexity of representation itself: he now describes the in-between (understood as a subject position) as an effect of representation, rather than as a constitutive component of the act of representation. Hence, Pease now presents the order of provocation and the order of trauma as equally beyond signification (or, more precisely, related to it by the logic of exception): "Emerson replaced the order of social signification with the order that Emersonian provocations would call forth" (Pease, "'Experience,'" 79) and "Emerson underwent a crisis of witnessing in the interspace between the order of signification and the death of his son" (Pease, "'Experience,'" 103). The last clause makes it particularly clear that signification and representation have now become located as one of the sides that border the space-in-between, whereas before representation and signification were structured by the space-in-between. As a result, representation or signification becomes unavailable for the subject once it has positioned the subject in the interspace of the traumatic order. This focus on the traumatic, and the claim that the traumatic is an in-between bordered by the order of signification and an (unavailable) alternative order, necessarily loses sight of, and reduces the relevance of, the more flexible dynamics of representation within the symbolic order, which Pease had illuminated in his earlier writings.

I have focused here at considerable length on Pease's work, not only because it is intellectually the most challenging contribution to New Americanist scholarship on Emerson, but also because it representatively reveals a problem that all critics discussed in this chapter run into in one way or another. The New Americanists' theories of representation operate within frameworks of totalization, in which representational transformation is figured as the succession of symbolic orders (although such succession can be stalled by trauma) or as the transcendence of representation toward a unity of thought and action. New Americanists have always looked for political change through literature, and they have leaned on Gramsci's notion of counterhegemony to express that hope. But while Gramsci's theory indeed offers a dynamic model of constant struggle through the means of representation, New Americanists have chosen a different route. When the humanist implications inherent in Gramsci's idea of counterhegemony are usurped by a theory of reification, attempts to free readers from false immediacy through literature seem to endlessly repeat the failure diagnosed by Lukács in the German idealists. And when representational change is limited to the site of symbolic exclusion, it must be conceptualized, at least normatively, as a full-blown emergence of new orders. These theories are in danger of underestimating the instability both of what seems to be fixed by ideology and of what emerges as democratic achievement from the margins. As a result, a deeply utopian strain runs through New Americanist models of representation, a utopianism that is presented as a viable route to resistance.

In the next chapter, I will show that an account of representation that eschews these totalizations offers up an Emerson who would be barely recognizable to the New Americanists. Rather than promoting an understanding of language and representation that enforces submission, contemplation, or traumatic repetition, this Emerson ponders excesses of representation that result from the failure to transcribe the Spirit's message—an "embedded invention" spun out of control.

2

REPRESENTING POTENTIALITY

"TO UNDERSTAND EMERSON'S writings, one must first see him at work as
a lecturer," the editors of the *Later Lectures* have stated with just conviction
(*LL*, vol. 1, xx). My intent in this study is not to provide a historical study
of Emerson's role as a lecturer, nor am I claiming privileged status for those
of his texts that come to us as addresses and lectures rather than as essays.
My claim is a more indirect one, though perhaps that makes it all the more
bold: my interpretations of Emerson's writings, largely carried out in the
mode of philosophical explication, are based on the historical awareness that
the overwhelming majority of these texts were written for lecture audiences.
I am claiming, in other words, a direct link between Emerson's philosophy
and his engagement as a public lecturer. Many of those who followed Emerson have left us their testimony of the listening experience peculiar to his
lectures. Those who were not repelled by his typical lack of structure tend
to point out the "uplifting" and "inspiring" effect his lectures had on them.
It is, indeed, safe to argue that his career as a lecturer depended on just such
effects. Few scholars, however, have attempted to connect these audience
responses with his style of thinking. As a result, those scholars who have
read Emerson as a philosopher have generally shown little interest in placing
him in the lecture hall; those who approach him historically tend to shy
away from the intricacies of his thought, implying that his audiences could
not have cared for, or even been capable of following, overly fine distinctions. To be sure, the practice of reading philosophical texts differs from
listening to a lecture, especially if that lecture was given in the U.S. lecture
system of the mid-nineteenth century, and thus was situated, in the expectation of the listeners, somewhere on a continuum between instruction and
entertainment. However, in Emerson's philosophical style, distinctions, even
overly fine ones, are rarely scholastic (or, as he would have put it, "pedantic") ends in themselves: they frequently produce contradictions as well as
unexpected analogies, the operations chiefly responsible for creating the effects so often reported by his listeners. As I will argue, Emerson's manner of

producing these effects cannot be sufficiently accounted for by describing disjunctions, contradictions, analogies, and the like as if they were mere ornaments to ideas that can be neatly summarized and traced back to various intellectual traditions. But if, following Stanley Cavell, Emerson's style *is* his substance, then the "Emerson Effect" cannot be reconstructed without following him on his path of dramatizing the ambiguities of moral and philosophical idioms.[1] Exploring Emerson's theory of representation as an act of philosophical stylization conducive to the needs of the lecture hall is the main goal of this chapter; to get there, I will first contextualize Emerson in the institution of the public lecture.

Emerson as Lecturer

In an influential account of Emerson's career as a lecturer in the Midwest, Mary Kupiec Cayton has argued that Emerson's audiences of the 1850s to the 1870s—bourgeois, business oriented, and interested in a narrowly mercantile version of self-culture—created a simplified Emerson that neatly fit their class interests. Comparing news reports of Emerson's lectures to the versions authored or authorized by Emerson, Cayton comes to the conclusion that midwestern audiences ignored or dismissed the essentially unchanged idealist backbone of Emerson's message: "By applying [the laws of nature that transcended social convention, tradition, or proscriptive statute] to subjects that were ostensibly nonpolitical and nonreligious, Emerson seemed to his listeners to be merely passing along practical advice on practical subjects—the epitome of self-culture."[2] By providing such opportunities for misunderstanding, Emerson, probably against his intentions, helped reduce self-culture, understood in its fullest sense as the "active expansion of one's faculties and the promotion of self-awareness," to a narrower version of "culture," that is, "the conspicuous consumption of people who were nationally and internationally defined as important intellectuals" (Cayton, "American Prophet," 618). In effect, Cayton portrays Emerson as a hegemonic figure who ended up reaffirming the power of his own class by deceiving himself and his audiences: "He represented the paradox of a dominant culture that *claimed* to be dedicated to self-improvement but that increasingly took self-improvement to mean adherence to an ever-more-clearly defined body of standards and behaviors sanctioned by the mercantile and professional groups who sponsored him" (Cayton, "American Prophet," 619, emphasis added).[3]

Cayton's conclusions rest on at least two assumptions that are problematic. First, she suggests that real self-culture can be distinguished from its corrupted version, mere culture. She thereby begins to mourn the disappearance of an unadulterated self-culture (meaning, to her, "active expansion of one's faculties and the promotion of self-awareness"), although in her study this concept of self-culture initially seemed no more than the historical product of a particular social constellation that in fact dims the glow emanating from the self-culture she embraces. Second, it is not clear why audiences of the later Emerson should have engaged only in conspicuous consumption. Even if it became fashionable to hear Emerson (and I grant that for some, this gain in status may have been the chief gratification), this does not mean that his performances suddenly became incapable of eliciting the effects of his earlier lectures.

Thomas Augst has recently provided an alternative analysis of the reception of Emerson's lectures. In his 2003 study *The Clerk's Tale*, he describes Emerson's appearance on the lecture platform as an occasion for young men of the emerging middle class to engage in "literary practices of character."[4] Similarly to Cayton, he makes Emerson a promoter of a liberal individualism that came to replace the humanist ideal of republican virtue.[5] But while for Cayton this replacement signifies a decline from a spiritually imbued self-culture to a shallow materialism of culture, for Augst liberal individualism is quite different from the materialism Cayton decries. In his account, conceptualized in part as a response to Cayton, "character" is a virtue of the "new sort of moral personality" (Augst, *Clerk's Tale*, 7) of liberal individualism. Character becomes necessary in the emerging market culture as it responds to the crisis of moral authority that accompanies the new, liberal, individualistic market society. As Augst describes it, character is a method of developing the self and a "standard for social presentation," that is, for demonstrating to others that one shares values such as autonomy, independence, and self-reliance (Augst, *Clerk's Tale*, 4). Thus, the new culture of liberal individualism at once espouses an economic individualism and equips the new order with a moral dimension to be realized by the self. In Augst's phrase, the lecture—along with other acts of literacy, such as the diary— becomes "a medium of spiritual exercise" (Augst, *Clerk's Tale*, 13) and the "privileged arena for the acquisition of moral conviction in nineteenth-century America" (Augst, *Clerk's Tale*, 119).

For Cayton, moral, and ultimately, spiritual life and the social order of liberal individualism are radically at odds with each other. For Augst, the two go together hand in glove. While providing a much-needed demonstration of how the literary and communal activity of the lecture fulfilled individuals' needs that emerged out of the transformation of the social order from republican to democratic, Augst's interpretation also runs into a serious problem. He is so intent on throwing light on the moral dimension of liberal individualism, in particular, on "the means with which people give their lives moral consequence" (Augst, *Clerk's Tale*, 15), that he can no longer sufficiently account for the tensions between the spiritual and material sides of life as they were experienced in paradigmatic fashion by Emerson's listeners. As even a cursory glance at Emerson's essays and lectures on the economy and wealth makes clear, the central drama of these texts is the ambiguity with which at one moment he celebrates laissez-faire capitalism and at another he questions that order's maxim of material acquisition. To give just one example, in his lecture on "Wealth," Emerson praises laissez-faire capitalism, not only as a metaphysical principle but also in its lower form of everyday, material life. Property, he tells his audience in (fairly) unmistakable words, should not be redistributed to the needy, and prices should not be determined by laws, even if "flour dealers hoard their flour for high prices" (*LL*, vol. 1, 235). Yet he begins the lecture with a generalized broadside against American property owners: "Our rich men are not rich, nor our powerful men truly strong. . . . They have their wealth as substitute for manhood" (*LL*, vol. 1, 231). Here, manhood and character, virtues that Augst so astutely puts at the center of his analysis, appear to be fundamentally at odds with the pursuit of wealth.

In Augst's reading, such tensions must disappear because, for the young clerks he examines, Emerson's lectures provide "practical guidance on the conduct of life" in the uncertain world of the market (Augst, *Clerk's Tale*, 119). Thus, diary and lecture hall become "tools for casting off despair over what was beyond one's control, in order to realize moral conviction, a hope for the future" (Augst, *Clerk's Tale*, 152). Augst gives the experience of the lecture a utilitarian function. Attempting to show the groundedness of Emerson's performances in his listeners' everyday lives, he reduces the "spiritual exercise" of his clerks to concrete advice in life management. According to him, nothing in the clerks' listening experience exceeds direct applicability to the coping requirements of everyday life.

Reports on the Limits of Language

By looking at some of the responses to Emerson's lectures, it becomes clear, however, that part of the attraction of the listening experience lay in its incommensurability with the quotidian. More precisely, what Emerson made available to his listeners was an experience that lasted only for the duration of the lecture and that could not be captured in words. Franklin Benjamin Sanborn, who was a follower of Emerson's and reported on him in his journalistic work, says it quite explicitly: "The truth is, in listening one perceives a coherence of thought lying back of the isolated statements—like a vast encircling dome where lamps hang; in Mr. Emerson's presence one feels the great dim curve which surrounds all—but afterwards it is only the separate glancing lights one recalls" (quoted in *LL*, vol. 1, xxix). Another follower, John Albee, in his *Remembrances of Emerson*, from 1901, describes a similar characteristic of the listening experience: "The enchantment of his voice and presence moved all auditors to a state of exaltation like fine music, and like the effect of music it was a mood hard to retain. It needed a frequent repetition, and those who heard him oftenest, at length became imbued with the spirit of his teachings and could appropriate as much as belonged to them."[6] The key here is that for Albee, the teachings and the spirit are not quite identical. Spirit would describe the feeling, artfully created by Emerson, that isolated and disjoint statements are united by what Sanborn calls "coherence of thought," a feeling that is not reproducible by reciting individual teachings.

Taking this experience seriously allows us to understand a common structure in the newspaper reporting that emerged concerning Emerson's lectures. The journalistic output spawned by Emerson is enormous and demonstrates how closely the performance culture of the lecture hall intersected with the growing importance of print media. Newspapers announced and reported on his public lectures. They mentioned how many people came to hear him and assured their readers of the audience's conformity with codes of conduct (by default, the audience was described as "highly respectable.")[7] The newspapers described Emerson's voice, appearance, and comportment, summarized his lectures (ranging from a few paragraphs to several columns), collected unconnected sound bites, or printed entire transcriptions. (Emerson repeatedly intervened against the latter practice, since he depended on repeating the same lectures in town after town.)[8]

To be sure, what journalists published in newspapers cannot be taken as direct evidence of how audience members experienced Emerson's lectures. Whatever these writers observed was molded by the journalistic conventions of the day. Yet journalists covering Emerson's speaking engagements developed a peculiar formula for their reports (which was certainly applied to other speakers as well), and this formula does provide us with a glimpse into the dynamics of an Emerson lecture. In its purest form, this journalistic standard consisted of a short account of the audience, a short description of Emerson's demeanor, a disclaimer that Emerson's lecture could not be properly summarized, and finally—the main part—a summary of the lecture of varying length. A look at a few of these disclaimers about the impossibility of summarizing Emerson reveals how deeply concerned newspaper reporters were with the effect Emerson had on his audiences.

One reporter, writing about Emerson's lecture "The Young American" at Boston's Mercantile Library Association in February 1844, described it as "a discourse so full of interest, so extended in its views, and so abounding in beautiful illustration, that, whilst we paused on one idea forcibly represented, another not less vigorous appeared, and the endeavor to retain the freshness of each became ineffectual." It was thus "by no means an easy task to convey, in newspaper limits, any just idea of [Emerson's] lecture."[9] While in this reporter's view, "vigorous" ideas were so abundant in Emerson's prose that they cancelled each other out (they lost their "freshness"), other writers tried to capture an aesthetic excess erupting from Emerson's lectures. On February 9, 1843, a reporter for the *New York Evening Post* described "an atmosphere of serenity [emanating from Emerson's performance] that expands and exhilarates while it purifies."[10] Another journalist, reporting on a lecture from the same tour along the East Coast,[11] described Emerson's effect as resulting in a surplus of oratory: "No man can listen to him attentively without being led into new trains of thought, and feeling, so that he has heard much more than has orally been delivered."[12] While reporters usually took the description of aesthetic effect no further than this and went on to summarize his main points, some reporters decided to devote a substantial part of their articles to Emerson's effects of uplift. Since summing up his ideas in accessible language was not helpful toward this goal, these writers had to adopt a poetic tone, which could result in overblown orphisms that were eagerly satirized by other reporters. How to write about Emerson's lectures could thus turn into the topic of discussions and satirical exchanges in and between newspapers—a secondary discourse so concerned with the effect of Emerson's lectures that Emerson himself all but disappeared from it.

In one such instance, on January 25, 1849, a journalist writing for the *Boston Post* pushed the limits of acceptable journalistic language, to the point that the *New York Tribune* ridiculed his piece by reprinting the text with added illustrations that took his verbal imagery literally. Emerson, in these caricatures, looks like a fantastic, even jesterlike figure from an esoteric children's book. He stands on top of a face-shaped globe, chipping out splinters with an axe; he balances on one leg, emanating rays of electricity from his head and fingers; he is hurled through the air by a gnomelike comet; and he swings on an inverted rainbow, dropping hat and shoes in infantile bliss. The *New York Tribune's* satire garnered so much attention that another Boston newspaper, the *Evening Transcript*, decided to reprint the *Tribune*'s article, along with a short introduction that included the explanation that there had been "considerable inquiry for it [the reprint] among the curious."[13] In the original piece in the *Boston Post*, the reporter had asserted,

"Yet it is quite out of character to say Mr Emerson lectures—he does no such thing." This statement merely sounded the habitual disclaimer that Emerson's lectures were impossible to summarize because they were so much more than lectures. But instead of continuing with an account of the lecture, the reporter for the *Boston Post* began to wax poetic about what Emerson did instead of lecturing:

> He drops nectar—HE CHIPS OUT SPARKS—he exhales odors—he lets off mental skyrockets and fireworks—he spouts fire, and, conjurer-like, draws ribbons out of his mouth. He smokes, he sparkles, he improvises, he shouts, he sings— HE EXPLODES LIKE A BUNDLE OF CRACKERS—he goes off in fiery eruptions like a volcano, but he does not *lecture*.[14]

In most images of this metaphorical fluster, Emerson's enunciations are figured as blazing spectacles, performed by nature's forces or figures with supernatural powers. The hints of violence contained in this imagery are emphasized in the illustrations for comical effect: Emerson's hair seems to have caught fire, and the globe's face is carved with an axe like a pumpkin. Clearly, the author tries to echo Emerson himself, especially his trademark imagery from his early texts, in which ecstasy is described as corporeal metamorphosis bordering on disembodiment. (One cannot help thinking here of the "transparent eyeball," which was itself subjected to a well-known caricature by fellow Transcendentalist Christopher P. Cranch.)[15] From this perspective, both the language and the illustrations can be placed in a tradition of speaking about Emerson, even if the *Tribune* published the drawings to demonstrate the report's absurdity. In fact, recurring metaphors of fireworks are contemporary clichés for descriptions of oratory.[16]

Fireworks, along with the equally popular metaphor of energy, not only evokes the Transcendentalist ideal of the speaker's unity with nature or spirit but also addresses the collective character of the public lecture. In his essay "Emerson the Lecturer," compiled from review articles for his 1871 book *My Study Windows*, James Russell Lowell reminisced: "I watched . . . how the quick sympathy ran flashing from face to face down the long tables, like an electric spark thrilling as it went, and then explodes in a thunder of plaudits."[17] Lowell is instructive in describing how Emerson's characteristic lecture style helped create this communal character. While most speakers attempted to present their lectures in a dramatic and fluid manner, and some excelled at extemporaneous speech, Emerson at first glance appeared to be an oratorical failure: he got lost in his manuscript pages, continuously shuffled his unbound sheets, and thus delivered his texts with frequent interruptions. In fact, however, these pauses created moments of anticipation—gaps in the flow of delivery—and the impression of spontaneity in both speaker and audience: "[H]ow artfully (for Emerson is a long-studied artist in these things) does the deliberate utterance, that seems waiting for the fit word, appear to admit us partners in the labor of thought and make us feel as if the glance of humor were a sudden suggestion, as if the perfect phrase lying written there on the desk were as unexpected to him as to us!" (Lowell, "Emerson the Lecturer," 383).[18]

The exaggerated description of Emerson's lecture in the *Boston Post* therefore can be interpreted not only as an attempt to convey what were considered to be the elusive yet heavily corporeal qualities of Emerson's performance. In line with the dialogic character of Emerson's appearances, the journalist's strained description becomes a performance itself, designed to attest to the *effect* of Emerson's lecture. In beginning to speak like a poet, the journalist enacts the "new trains of thought, and feeling" that Emerson aimed to provoke in his audiences, as if he had taken to heart Emerson's encouragements to trust his own genius.[19] This writer thus dramatizes the excessive effect most journalists described in Emerson's lectures. While these journalists have little to say about how exactly Emerson swayed his audiences, they agree that what sets Emerson apart resides in that which cannot be summarized.[20] In fact, if one takes the disclaimers seriously, it is not only that there is more to the lecture than what can be summarized, but that the summaries themselves are inept even as far as they go. In other words, Emersonian excess involves the level of ideas, which makes it difficult to isolate any coherent thought from the overall effect.

The Genre of Elevation

Whether they adhere to accepted formulas or transgress into the poetic, the newspaper reports on Emerson's lectures indicate how deeply the demands of succeeding as a public speaker permeate Emerson's writings and performances. If the reporters come back over and over again to the inspiring effects that his lectures purportedly had on the audience, this is quite simply because Emerson aimed to achieve just such an effect of uplift. In fact, this is precisely what was expected of the public lecture in general, and of literary lectures like Emerson's in particular.

Several historians have given us detailed accounts of the lyceum and the public lecture in the nineteenth-century United States.[21] Crucial for my purposes is a tension between the goals of instruction and entertainment that accompanied the lyceum throughout its entire history, from the late 1820s until it petered out in the late 1870s. Though the balance between the two terms progressively tipped toward entertainment, the public lecture continued to negotiate both poles. As devised and promoted by Josiah Holbrook, the lyceum was originally a local association, spreading first through Massachusetts and geared to mutual self-improvement. Members of each local branch shared their specialized knowledge with fellow members, taking turns in lecturing to each other. Holbrook's model had been the British "mechanics' institutes," and like its model, the American lyceum was designed for artisans and farmers, teaching them the "practical application of science— which would result in better workmen and more efficient farmers."[22] Lectures constituted no more than a portion of the original lyceum's activities. Members also met to debate specific questions pertaining to contemporary politics as well as values, organized classes, and schooled children and youth. (In 1833, the Concord lyceum debated, among other questions, "Does the Pulpit or the Bar afford the greatest field for Eloquence?")[23] By the early 1850s, however, debates and local lectures had mostly given way to invited lecturers and the establishment, particularly in the Midwest, of a lecture circuit. The lyceum had entered its second phase. Among the prominent lecturers, Emerson was a forerunner. As Angela Ray points out, his offering whole series of lectures as early as the mid-1830s "was the exception rather than the rule" (Ray, *Lyceum and Public Culture*, 29).

What had begun as an outgrowth of Federalist culture, driven by the republican, Enlightenment goal of instilling virtue in the community's members through education and self-culture, developed into a commercialized enterprise increasingly dependent on the celebrity lecturer. One of the conditions for this development was the "transportation revolution," which enabled speakers to travel more easily from one lyceum to the next.[24] The so-called "Buffalo Trail," a string of local lyceums in upstate New York along the Erie Canal, can be seen as a direct outcome of this "revolution." R. Jackson Wilson notes that while Emerson regularly went on the Buffalo Trail, his lecture engagements were spread out widely across the United States: besides speaking along the East Coast, New England, and the Erie Canal, at the height of his career Emerson also made extended tours of the Midwest and even California. All in all, in the 1850s Emerson gave about seventy lectures per year, visiting fifty different towns (Wilson, "Emerson as Lecturer," 78).[25]

Of equal importance were the effects transportation had on communication. With the establishment of a lecture circuit and the spread of the newspaper, the print media established a whole discourse on the public lecture. Besides reporting on well-known lecturers, the press undertook a further step in establishing the celebrity system: in the 1850s, the *New York Tribune* began publishing yearly lists of available lecturers that were widely reprinted in local papers. Making it onto this list amounted to having crossed a threshold level of name recognition.[26] Yet, while Emerson had depended on the lyceum stage for most of his income since the 1830s (in addition, he relied on an inheritance from his first wife), many of those on the list were not full-time lecturers but remained active in their home professions, whether medicine, the law, or the pulpit.[27] As Donald Scott notes, the challenge lecturers faced, no matter the profession in which they had received their training, was "how to create or improvise a career" (Scott, "Popular Lecture," 795). This was a predicament peculiar to the second and third quarters of the nineteenth century (the period of Emerson's career): "The coherence and organization that had marked most trades and professions in the eighteenth century had eroded, and the rationalized and bureaucratic professional structures of the last decades of the nineteenth century had not yet emerged" (Scott, "Popular Lecture," 795). Steps toward such rationalized and bureaucratic professional structures included the founding of the Associated Western Literary Societies (AWLS) in 1864, which allowed local lecture sponsors in smaller towns to attract well-known lecturers by offering them a whole set of speaking engagements in the region. In 1868, James Redpath took professionalization to the next level, creating Redpath's Boston Lyceum Bureau, which was the first management agency to plan entire lecture tours (including the negotiation of fees) for individual speakers (compare Ray, *Lyceum and Public Culture*, 36–46).

But even if the lyceum shifted its emphasis between 1830 and 1860 from education to a commercialized entertainment culture, lecturers continued to be expected to comply with a strict set of norms. Until shortly before the Civil War, lyceum propriety demanded lecturers to refrain from addressing partisan politics and religious conflict. The Concord Lyceum, for instance, considered officially prohibiting the topic of slavery and abolition when Wendell Phillips announced his intention to lecture on slavery in 1842. (It did not follow through with this plan and voted to invite Phillips back.) Phillips was one of the stars, yet his most popular lecture, "The Lost Arts," did not touch on abolition. As Bode reports, "When the time came that lecturers were paid fees, he offered local lyceums these alternatives. If they would listen to him on abolitionism, there would be no charge; if they wanted a noncontroversial subject, he would have to be paid for it" (Bode, *American Lyceum*, 206). Similarly, when Emerson presented his lectures on "Human Life" at the Franklin Lyceum, half way through the series local organizers asked him not to talk about religion in the remaining lectures (compare Ray, *Lyceum and Public Culture*, 29). These restrictions had directly to do with the idea that the public lecturer should enlarge the audience's view by offering a generalized perspective. Generalization and abstraction were considered guarantors of wholesome instruction. Direct engagement in politics, by contrast, was often denigrated as a form of sensationalism inappropriate for the lyceum stage. As Donald Scott writes, "no matter how specific the topic, a lecture was expected to be broad and expansive in its implications rather than pedantic and esoteric. . . . The large category of lectures that sought to explicate life in contemporary America . . . both illuminated the present situation and reinforced a sense of the existence and applicability of commonly held moral precepts" (Scott, "Public Lecture," 797, 804).

What I wish to emphasize here, however, is that literary lecturers like Emerson did not just affirm the existence and applicability of moral precepts. Rather, they redefined essential moral concepts of the period such as "sincerity" and "character," transforming them from precepts to be followed in conduct into experiences to be had by the individual listener in the act of giving oneself over to the lecturer. This shift toward individual experience accompanies the transformations of eloquence taking place in the mid-nineteenth century. While neoclassical orators such as Edward Everett had attempted to persuade listeners with the help of arguments and learned prose, thereby relying on codes of respectability that reigned largely unchallenged among Federalist elites, lecturers at mid-century, and particularly those working in the lecture system, had to gain the audience's acceptance through their personal performance. Edward T. Channing, formerly Emerson's rhetoric professor at Harvard, summarized this transformation in his *Lectures Read to the Seniors at Harvard College*, from 1856:

> It is his virtues, his consistency, his unquestioned sincerity that must get the orator attention and confidence now. He must not rely too much upon the zeal or even the soundness with which he treats a question under immediate discussion. His hearers must believe that his life is steadily influenced by the sentiments he is trying to impress on them,—that he is willing to abide by principle at any hazard, and gives his opinions and professions the full authority of his actions.[28]

At first glance, the sincerity Channing invokes is a simple concept: it consists of the congruence between being true to oneself and being true to others. It is, however, difficult to pin down how exactly the lecturer was to *make* his listeners *believe* that the sentiments preached were those that steadily influenced the lecturer, and how making the audience believe in one's sincerity could be distinguished from the make-believe of insincerity. Lionel Trilling, in his landmark 1971 study *Sincerity and Authenticity*, phrases the problem this way: "If one is true to one's own self for the purpose of avoiding falsehood to others, is one being truly true to one's own self?"[29] This difficulty begins to suggest the contradictions that made the virtue of sincerity so pressing and that continued to trouble it. Sincerity has been interpreted as a kind of defense mechanism against the loosening of social structure, which was the outcome of processes like urbanization and industrialization and resulted in the new experience of living in a world of strangers. Sincerity was the weapon for battling the increasing possibility and profitability of becoming a "confidence man," being someone who one was not, or, engaging in acts of what could be called "social passing."[30] Yet if increased social mobility made the confidence man possible and the virtue of sincerity necessary, it also called into question the very attempt to reinstate, through rules of conduct, the hierarchical order of preindustrial society. The reason is that sincerity is a double-edged concept. On the one hand, it aligns the self, through a code of sincerity, with the self's assigned position within the social order. This is what Trilling identified as the English version of sincerity (in contrast to the French): "The English ask of the sincere man that he communicate without deceiving or misleading. Beyond this what is required is only a single-minded commitment to whatever dutiful enterprise he may have in hand" (Trilling, *Sincerity and Authenticity*, 58). On the other hand, sincerity has begun to reflect the distinction between self and society, thus posing the question whether society with its rules of conduct and hierarchies is not in fact a block to the true self. Emerson's discontent with the norms of society and his simultaneous espousal of the Victorian virtues of sincerity, culture, and character inhabits this very ambiguity.

According to Trilling, this tension inherent in sincerity was eventually resolved by its replacement with authenticity (in Trilling's view, with ultimately debilitating consequences). Whereas sincerity had struggled to combine being true to oneself with one's social role, authenticity came to regard the social role as a mere mask. Discovering the authentic self required its unmasking, eventually ennobling society's outcasts as models of authenticity (thereby giving rise to the artist's dream triumvirate of the criminal, the insane, and, well, the artist).

Emerson and his fellow lecturers did not go as far as embracing authenticity. They instead focused on the individual experience enabled by their lectures as a partial resolution of the tension of sincerity. At the moment at which "the rhetorical theory taught at colleges turned away from the public knowledge of the community and inward toward the experience of the individual as the locus of moral authority,"[31] the rhetorical practice of the public lecture elevated the immediate experience of inspiration as a foolproof sign of a sincerity that was as true to oneself as it was to others. Intriguingly, while Emerson depended on the audience's approval and was happy to acknowledge this, he also stepped in front of his listeners with the professed conviction that he was bound to them only by ideas, not by a social bond. Thus, despite partaking in a literary culture that was self-consciously public, Emerson also fit the transformation of the artist from one who pleases the audience to one whose "reference is to himself only, or to some transcendent power which—or who—has decreed his enterprise and alone is worthy to judge it" (Trilling, *Sincerity and Authenticity*, 97).[32] This in turn contributed to the elevation of the lecturer as one providing an experience that is inspirational: "This devotion [now given to art] takes the form of an extreme demand: now that art is no longer required to please, it is expected to provide the spiritual substance of life" (Trilling, *Sincerity and Authenticity*, 98). While inspiration had to be seen as a new function of art—and at least from this angle, Emerson left behind the Federalist values espoused by his forefathers—this function was cast in the residual terminology of moral virtue. Virtue turned into inspiration was the public lecture's midway habitat between sincerity and authenticity.

Emerson filled this role perfectly. He excelled in a cultural institution that required a complicated balance: he was to avoid showmanship and sensationalized stage antics, keep up the decorous manners of an earlier age, abstain from populist rhetoric, and yet gear his entire performance toward creating an effect for his audience. By all accounts, Emerson refrained from any hint of pathos or sentiment on stage.[33] Delivering his lectures in a sonorous and even baritone, he achieved the desired effects with the help of the very shape of his thought.

But how exactly did he create those inspiring moments that became intelligible as the moral experience of sincerity and character? In brief, Emerson used a simple reception-aesthetical trick: by activating his listeners' minds—suggesting to them connections between things entirely disparate, without ever spelling them out—his audiences began to attribute to him the enlargement of their minds they felt they were experiencing. Their activation warranted his *and* their sincerity. His necessarily hazy suggestions of the interconnectedness of the universe corresponded directly to the lecture's generic expectations of elevating a given topic to a generalized and abstract level. Here Emerson's particular form of idealism, which was certainly not adopted for the purposes of the lecture, but rather was the result of his New England intellectual environment mixed with his disposition toward eclecticism, proved particularly effective. Rather than simply setting up dichotomous value judgments—for example, your wealth is only material, true wealth is spiritual—his "fractured idealism" rendered the distinctions between the ideal and the actual ambiguous and allowed him to switch back and forth between addressing particulars and abstractions. In one moment he suggested to his audiences that they were on the brink of actualizing their universal potential, in the next moment this potential was declared unreachable, and in the moment following the actual turned out to have been identical with the ideal all along. This constant interplay between the particular and the general, and between the actual and the ideal, allowed Emerson to alternate between insulting and reassuring his listeners, and to authorize his doing so with the promise of broadening their minds.[34]

In a limited sense, Emerson's performances perpetuated the ideological tenets underwriting the lecture system, particularly the ideology of self-culture. But a narrowly ideological reading of Emerson's cultural work at the lectern misses what is most remarkable: the experiences he enabled and encouraged his audiences to have must be described as aesthetic experiences. Though cast in moral terms, if successful, they outran social and indeed moral categories, opening into an imaginary dimension in which the self merged with a larger sphere of interconnectivity. The function of such an imaginary experience arose from the same transformations in the social structure that also led to the blossoming of the virtues of sincerity and self-culture, with all their ideological ramifications. But the distinction is crucial: while the ideological function of self-culture is located in power struggles that pushed and responded to social transformations—on this level, the mercantile elite tried to solidify its power after the old hierarchical order of Federalism had been toppled—the dimension of the aesthetic experience of sincerity and self-culture addresses the individual's need to adapt to these transformations. These individual needs of imaginary self-affirmation, filled by experiences that cultural institutions such as the public lecture provided, play out on a different level, and in that sense, exceed the ideological struggle. If, however, individualized aesthetic experience and ideology are set on different levels, this also means that the exhilarating effect of an Emerson lecture should not be equated with an act of ideological subversion. For the remainder of this chapter, I will reconstruct Emerson's theory of representation against the backdrop of his career as a professional public speaker as I have laid it out so far. From this theory will emerge a philosophical style, geared toward a particular experience, which poses an alternative to New Americanist readings that see in his theory of representation largely an ideological promotion of submission and passivity.

Emerson's Theory of Representation

In his first book, *Nature*, from 1836, Emerson famously treats language as an essential stage in developing his Transcendentalist philosophy. Although Emerson at times seems to suggest that the aim of finding correspondences between nature and the Spirit requires a set of symbols that is fixed as well as imitative ("the book of nature"), a closer look reveals this to be a misreading of his thought. Even the early Emerson of *Nature* is centrally concerned with formulating a transformative theory of language. By the time of *Essays, Second Series*, in 1844, which includes "The Poet," "Experience," and "Nominalist and Realist," he has sharpened this interest into a set of reflections focusing on the rift between reception and expression—a communicative dimension that focuses on the sheer potentiality experienced in inspiration, and the limits of expressing it. This critical relay between reception and expression is precisely what concerned him as a public speaker as well, which becomes clear when his reflections on language are tied to "eloquence," another topos frequently discussed by Emerson and particularly popular with his audiences. Emerson's figure of the poet—seer and sayer—can in fact never be fully distinguished from the eloquent lecturer.

But it is not only that Emerson's theory of representation *describes* the work of the lecturer. His thinking on representation is also functional for enabling an inspirational effect for his audiences and readers. Emerson's writing and thinking stage a sequence of dramatic encounters with limitlessness and limitation. Each moment of overcoming limitation holds the potential for the reader and listener to imaginarily experience it as an expansive moment of the mind. But it is also here that his theory of representation comes into conflict with the reception aesthetics of his thought. As I will argue, any prolonged meditation of failure and stagnation runs the risk of having to be denied by his poetics. In other words, even when he describes stagnation, he must enable his readers and listeners to carry the day. I will begin this section with a rereading of his language of nature and then proceed to the conflicts between reception and expression as he theorizes them in his mature essays.

Borrowing from Locke

Emerson's most famous tract on language, the fourth chapter of *Nature*, begins by listing the "threefold degree" in which language helps turn nature into a "vehicle" (*CW*, vol. 1, 18). In a tone that sounds deceptively matter-of-fact, Emerson states:

    1. Words are signs of natural facts.
    2. Particular natural facts are symbols of particular spiritual facts.
    3. Nature is the symbol of spirit. (*CW*, vol. 1, 18)

While one might expect these three statements to add up to a syllogism so that the third line would read, "Words are symbols of particular spiritual facts," Emerson instead creates a lot of confusion out of three misleadingly simple sentences. First, there is an abundance of semantic differentiation, the significance of which remains unclear. For instance, "natural facts," "particular natural facts," and "nature" all seem to address different levels of specificity. It is as if Emerson were loosely troping on the deductive step of the syllogism, in which the general rule of the first sentence is brought into conjunction with the particular case of the second sentence in order to arrive at a conclusion (All humans are mortal—Socrates is human—Hence Socrates is mortal.) Since Emerson strays so far from any meaningful syllogism, however, it is anything but evident what his point is. If he aims to convey that nature is the symbol of the spirit (the bottom line of his list), then what does this have to do with language? In fact, the first line, which alone addresses language (supposedly the entire chapter's topic), is oddly disconnected from the second and third lines. To complete the confusion, Emerson's distinction between "signs" and "symbols" seems to differentiate linguistic from non-linguistic signs. While this makes sense in itself, one wonders how he understands signs to work if they operate differently from symbols.

Considering the role of language in Emerson's thought, this last point is particularly crucial. To explain what he means by his first line, "Words are signs of natural facts," Emerson offers a list of examples taken, in part, from John Locke's *Essay Concerning Human Understanding*: "*Right* originally means *straight*, *wrong* means *twisted*; *Spirit* primarily means *wind*. . . . We say the *heart* to express emotion, the *head* to denote thought; and *thought* and *emotion* are words borrowed from sensible things, and now appropriated to the spiritual nature" (*CW*, vol. 1, 18).[35] As Christopher Newfield has rightly pointed out, Emerson here lumps together different classes of examples. In some cases an intellectual (abstract) word is connected to a signifier of nature through etymology (*spirit* means *wind*), which is a connection that ratifies, in Newfield's words, "inner resemblance" (Newfield, *Emerson Effect*, 54). Other examples rely purely on figuration—*heart* means emotion—without any kind of "innate, preexisting alignment" (Newfield, *Emerson Effect*, 54). Newfield argues that in juxtaposing these different kinds of examples, Emerson ends up subjugating the creative work of figuration under the authoritative process of imitation at work in the examples that depend on "inner resemblance." In other words, Newfield's Emerson yokes the creative dimension of "borrowing" to imitation. The point of this claim is to show that Emerson's language theory endorses an imitative and thus passive role for the speaker.

However, in Emerson's mix of examples it is not the etymological but the figurative link that comes to stand for the master mechanism. Emerson introduces his examples with the statement, "Every word which is used to express a moral or intellectual fact, if traced to its root, is found to be borrowed from some material essence" (*CW*, vol. 1, 18). This sentence, again a riff on Locke, references the etymological link ("to its root") along with the figurative process of borrowing. But after he lists five examples, among them actual etymological cases, he uses his final example to make clear which of the two mechanisms—borrowing or etymology—is dominant: "We say the *heart* to express emotion, the *head* to denote thought; and *thought* and *emotion* are words borrowed from sensible things, and now appropriated to spiritual nature." In this final example, Emerson stresses the figurative dimension, particularly through his confounding wordiness. What one would expect after the semicolon is something like this: "*thought* and *emotion* are borrowed from head and heart, two sensible things that are now appropriated to spiritual nature." But in Emerson's phrasing, it becomes somewhat unclear whether the sensible things that *thought* and *emotion* are borrowed from are actually *head* and *heart*. Emerson's lack of directness highlights the difficulty in pinning down the figurative connection. And because his examples are framed by references to the mechanism of "borrowing," he is not burying borrowing beneath imitation. Instead, Emerson's real interest in "language" lies in the function of "borrowing," a concept he develops by creating a contrast to Locke's use of "borrowing" in his *Essay Concerning Human Understanding*.

In the third book of the *Essay*, Locke's sense impression theory is extended into a philosophy of language, according to which words act as arbitrary signs of ideas. Locke distinguishes between simple and complex ideas. Simple ideas are directly caused by sense impressions of the outer world. All other ideas ("complex ideas") are combinations of simple ideas. These complex ideas are products of the mind and are therefore not directly caused by nature, that is, by a natural sense impression. Thus for Locke, simple ideas stand in a direct relationship to their natural cause, while complex ideas are, as he likes to put it, "the workmanship of the understanding." No matter whether one deals with simple or complex ideas, however, words (or "names") are *arbitrarily* "annexed" to the ideas.[36]

It is important to remember that for Locke signification involves three levels: object, idea, and word. Generally speaking, objects are represented by ideas, and ideas in turn are signified by words.[37] Locke's theory of language must be understood as a definite repudiation of any sort of Adamic approach to language. Adamic theories of language assume that there is a "language of nature" in which words have an inner tie to their natural referent (a language supposedly spoken by Adam before the Fall).[38] Emerson, confusingly, appropriates Locke by mixing Adamic assumptions into Locke's theory. When he says that "Every word which is used to express a moral or intellectual fact . . . is found to be borrowed from some material essence," he leaves out the level of ideas, and instead connects the word directly to its material referent: in its original state, the word is tied to "some material essence," and borrowed from there. He thus suggests an original, nonarbitrary language at the basis of language, which expresses moral and intellectual facts. Emerson's sneaking of Adamic notions back into Locke must be seen in the context of the critiques of Locke current in the New England of his time. He particularly builds on Sampson Reed's and James Marsh's attacks on Locke. Both noted that the Lockean progression from simple to complex ideas was founded on the belief that the operations of the mind could be reduced to rules such as the law of cause and effect.[39] Extending Reed and Marsh, Emerson rejects Locke's notion of arbitrary signification because it implies an impoverished mind bereft of access to divine inspiration and the divine origination of meaning. Ironically, he develops this critique by construing Locke's very theory of sense impression as a theory of an original, nonarbitrary link between words and objects. It is this move that is operating behind his revision of Locke's concept of "borrowing."

Locke wants to explain how the earliest language users found ways to express complex ideas. His answer is that they "borrowed" words annexed to sensible ideas. This goes back to Locke's argument that simple ideas are the same for different people because they stem directly from sense impressions of the outer world. In Locke's view, these words can then be used to reach a consensus about words for complex ideas, that is, for ideas that are not necessarily the same among different speakers:

> [W]hilst, to give Names, that might make known to others any Operations they felt in themselves, or any other Ideas, that came not under their Senses, they were fain to borrow Words from ordinary known Ideas of Sensation, by that means to make others the more easily to conceive those Operations they experimented in themselves, which made no outward sensible appearances; and then when they had got known and agreed Names, to signify those internal Operations of their own Minds, they were sufficiently furnished to make known by Words, all their other Ideas. (*E*, bk. III, ch. i, para. 5, 403–4, emphases in original)

Locke's understanding of "borrowing" is very much in line with our everyday understanding of the word. Something is borrowed for a limited time; thereafter it is no longer needed. Thus, words are borrowed from sensible ideas to be used for communicating about complex ideas. This enables language users to settle on how to signify complex ideas: "they were sufficiently furnished to make known by Words, all their other Ideas."

In Emerson's hands, "borrowing" takes on a very different meaning that cannot be reduced to his analytical elimination of the role played by ideas. Borrowing no longer stands for the transition from simple to complex, but for a model of signification in which borrowing turns into appropriation. As we have seen, Emerson uses the verb "to borrow" twice to frame his list of examples. It is his second use ("We say the *heart* to express emotion, the *head* to denote thought; and *thought* and *emotion* are words borrowed from sensible things, and now appropriated to the spiritual nature") that signals the difference from Locke (again, the theoretical absence of ideas notwithstanding). Emerson stresses that the word that originally belonged to a sensible thing remains active in the derivative word for the spiritual fact through the process of appropriation.

Emerson adds yet another twist: strictly speaking, he does not describe a transition from an original tie (which Locke posited for simple ideas via sense impression and which Emerson seems to transfer to the linkage of word and natural fact) to one that is conventional (for Locke, in the linkage of several simple ideas, and for Emerson, in the linkage of word and spiritual fact). In Emerson's elusive formulation, the initial connection between the word *heart* and the physical thing, heart, remains a blank, something unaccounted for. Instead, borrowing describes a relation in which what is borrowed is already transformed in the act of borrowing. Borrowing, in Locke's sense, would mean that the word annexed to the simple idea, which in turn is connected to a natural fact through sense impression, is used to give expression to a complex idea. For Emerson, on the other hand, the word borrowed is not that which is linked to the natural fact; instead, the word borrowed already relies on the transformation of the coupling of word and natural fact, so that what is borrowed is the word *emotion*, instead of *heart*. The upshot of this semiotics is that borrowing turns out to be a process in which that which is borrowed is no longer what it used to be. But if it is already transformed in the act of borrowing, it cannot be discarded once the transformation is achieved. Emerson thus constructs borrowing as a continuous act. Consequently, it cannot be relegated to the age of the first language users. While Emerson concedes that "Most of the process by which this transformation [from the sensible to the spiritual] is made, is hidden from us in the remote time when language was framed," he insists that "the same tendency may be daily observed in children" (*CW*, vol. 1, 18).

The important implication of this revision is that borrowing as a mechanism does more than enable the transition from the sensible to the complex (or intellectual, or spiritual). The link between the sensible and the complex is more properly described as a relationship of creativity: it becomes imaginable only after the fact, when it has produced a new signification (the metaphorical sign of heart or emotion). Emerson says as much in his essay on Plato from *Representative Men*: "But the inventor only knows how to borrow" (*CW*, vol. 4, 24), a phrase that goes back to a quotation ascribed to Napoleon and used by Emerson in his lecture on Michelangelo from the year after the publication of *Nature*: "Only an inventor can use the inventions of others" (*EL*, vol. 1, 114). This suggests more strongly than we have seen so far that there must be an agent behind Emerson's phrase "words are borrowed." Although in his account the connection of word and thing is natural, it must be *put to use* by individual language users and thereby continuously transformed.

Picturesque Correspondence

But how can this be reconciled with the common assumption that in *Nature* Emerson subscribed to a strict kind of correspondence theory that he later criticized, most famously in "The Poet," from 1841, and "Swedenborg," from 1850?[40] Emerson introduces the second section, summarized as "Particular natural facts are symbols of particular spiritual facts," by aligning the language of words with the language of nature: "It is not only words that are emblematic. It is things that are emblematic" (*CW*, vol. 1, 18). But in the rest of the second section he shifts his interest to the nuanced differences between the two: While both are emblematic, they are so in quite different ways. Thus, when we try to resolve the tension between his theory of language centered on borrowing and transformation and his alleged faith in strict correspondence, it is important to note that Emerson does not once use the word *correspondence* in the first section on "Words are signs of spiritual facts." Correspondence is rather the subject of the second and third sections of "Language." In fact, the connection between words and things is only related to the entire issue of correspondence insofar as words that refer to the spiritual, through the process of borrowing and transformation, relate back to nature.

A closer look at his theory of correspondence shows that it is not nearly as fixed as sometimes claimed.[41] In fact, the correspondence of natural and spiritual facts turns out to be as dynamic as the language of words. The difference is that these dynamics inhabit different media. At first, Emerson's examples of correspondence seem indeed terribly fixed: "Every natural fact is a symbol of some spiritual fact. . . . An enraged man is a lion, a cunning man is a fox. . . . A lamb is innocence; a snake is subtle spite" (*CW*, vol. 1, 18). Not only does Emerson take some of his examples directly from Swedenborg; he puts them to much more rigid use than Swedenborg himself. Swedenborg, in fact, admits that:

> [N]o one at this day can know the spiritual things which are in heaven, to which the natural things which are in the world, correspond, except from heaven; since the science of correspondence at this day is entirely lost. But

what the correspondence of spiritual things with natural things is, I will illustrate by some examples. The animals of the earth, in general, correspond to affections; the great and useful to good affections, the fierce and useless to evil affections.[42]

With the science of correspondence "entirely lost," the examples he goes on to suggest are intended to designate not actual correspondences, but only hypothetical ones (taken from common speech) that demonstrate the kind of correspondence he has in mind. Therefore, he can afford to offer *two* correspondents for each character trait without diluting his argument: "Man is also similar to them [animals], as to his natural man; wherefore also he is compared to them in common discourse; as, if he be gentle, he is called a sheep or a lamb; if fierce, he is called a bear or a wolf; if cunning, he is called a fox or a serpent, and so forth" (Swedenborg, *Concerning Heaven*, 66).

However, although Emerson's examples seem to render Swedenborg's more rigid by treating them as the actual correspondents (which Swedenborg claims to be unknowable presently), the answer to how representation works in Emerson's examples is not as evident as it may seem. "Every appearance in nature corresponds to some state of mind, and that state of mind can only be described by presenting that natural appearance as its picture," he writes immediately before listing his examples (*CW*, vol. 1, 18). The symbol, significantly, becomes in this section a *picture*, a word that he repeats later on, when he talks about "picturesque language," and that he implies when he mentions "the radical correspondence between visual things and thoughts" (*CW*, vol. 1, 20, 19). Why should the description be possible in a picture, and *only* in a picture? If we know the two elements of the correspondence, why can't it be described in language? And what happens when Emerson lists his examples that clearly do not make use of pictures, but instead, metaphors? If he is serious about the function of pictures as something relating to the visual, then clearly Emerson is not enacting the actual correspondences in his examples.

The difference between presenting the lion as a picture and presenting the lion as an element of discourse is that the visual produces a level of engagement that cannot be grasped by discursive language. But wherein does this difference lie? The most obvious solution would be that pictures differ from words in that only they afford a relationship that is mimetic, or, to use Peirce's term, iconic. But why should the picture of a lion be an iconic sign of a certain state of mind when the state of mind does not even exist in the realm of the visual and thus makes necessary the visual *correspondent* in the first place?

A more accurate solution, then, lies in the aesthetic specificity or individuality that the *picture* of the lion holds. Describing a state of mind *only* in a picture would require taking an aesthetic attitude toward the correspondent picture, for it would mean regarding those specifics that cannot be captured in any other medium. Looking at a picture, not in order to decode its message, but in order to look at that which cannot be readily decoded, means taking an aesthetic attitude toward it. "Description" thereby is turned into aesthetic experience, which is indeed a task verbal description can only perform if it relies on a poetic use of language itself (and even then it will be a different aesthetic experience). In this context, it is crucial that aesthetic experience for Emerson is strongest, or "affects us" most, as he likes to put it, whenever it makes us aware of the manifold relations and analogies between nature, spirit, and ourselves. "[T]he most trivial of these facts . . . applied to the illustration of a fact in intellectual philosophy, or in any way associated to human nature, affects us in the most lively and agreeable manner," he writes in the second section (*CW*, vol. 1, 19).

Tying this back to his theory of correspondence, we begin to see that even in "Language," Emerson does not exactly propose the fixed symbolic order that his examples and much of the literature on Emerson suggest. If the terms corresponding to mental states can only be described as pictures, if what sets these pictures apart from a discursive use of language is the possibility of engaging with them in an aesthetic experience, and if, finally, the aesthetic experience for Emerson is affective because it reveals our manifold connections to the world of nature and spirit, then the very reception of the "strict" correspondence pushes this form of signification onto the slippery ground of excess and sliding. The picture that was supposed to represent a state of mind represents something so amorphous that it cannot be captured by language, and likewise, the individual picture calls a succession of different pictures onto the scene as it makes the viewer begin to see that "a ray of relation passes from every other being to him" (*CW*, vol. 1, 19). Looking at the picture of a state of mind, in fact, shows us the world of things to be in flux: "Who looks upon a meditative river and is not reminded of the flux of all things?" (*CW*, vol. 1, 18).

Thus, the assumption of a one-to-one correspondence between, say, a lion and an enraged man proves to be no more than a heuristic starting point for a process of semiosis that revises the assumption of a fixed correspondence. This is why "Language" gives us both those phrases that sound hyper-Swedenborgian and those that sound like the flux-oriented approach to correspondence that characterizes Emerson's works from his mature and later phases, for instance "The Poet" or "Poetry and Imagination."[43] "Strict correspondence" emerges as a necessary fiction that makes us see and feel how the perception of correspondence really works, as an aesthetic experience of pictures, in which we are moved to call forth a whole series of states of mind as well as other pictures. It is essential that this strict correspondence is claimed, as Emerson demonstrates in his own text, in language. Discursive language must enter the process of the semiosis of pictures at the point when it requires a fresh jolt for further proliferations.

The result so far is that "Language" differentiates between two kinds of languages, both of which seem open to a process of semiosis that takes place in different senses and media but that works along nearly parallel lines. First, the language of words is a language that is originally grounded in nature. And although this grounding cannot be accounted for (it is elided from the process of "borrowing"), it makes possible the creative process of borrowing and appropriation. Words thus not only fulfill the requirements of rational communication; they can and must be transformed, not through a consensual settlement of new meanings, but through poetic use. To refresh the possibility of this transformation, the grounding of language needs to be continually reinvoked. Thus, language users must retain an awareness that the transformation happens *in time*, which is to suggest both a moment of origin at a point in time, and the transformation's continuing existence through time.

Second, besides the order of linguistic language, there is the language of nature that plays out in the realm of the visual (with the possibility, actualized in Emerson's more mature work and famously also in the writings of Henry David Thoreau, of extending it to the other senses, specifically to the aural). Signification in this order takes a very similar route: it assumes a foundational beginning (constitutive for triggering a process of signification), in which a mental state finds its corresponding term in a picture. Since the actual signification takes place in an aesthetic experience in which analogies and relations proliferate, the coupling of the corresponding terms becomes loosened. To refuel this moment of proliferation, it then becomes necessary to claim anew the original moment of correspondence, and these claims are made in language. In fact, one could say that the return to a "picturesque language" that Emerson calls for has the dual function of refreshing the process of borrowing or appropriation in verbal language and the pictorial experience in the language of nature.

Thus, while Emerson attempts to keep the two orders of language apart for analytic purposes, he switches back and forth frequently. A large portion of the second section of "Language" in fact concerns itself with the language of words: language has become degraded by the "prevalence of secondary desires"; hence now the goal must be "to pierce this rotten diction and fasten words again to visible things" (*CW*, vol. 1, 20). By reinjecting the first section into the second, Emerson, in my view, is not just neglecting his own structure (although there may have been little that was more tedious for him than the rigid structure of a philosophical system). He is combining the two orders of language because the language of words must propel both kinds of signification.

Receptivity and Expression

In "Language," Emerson gestured toward the aesthetic value of the picture that exceeds description in verbal language. As we have seen, the excess of the aesthetic experience of the picture sets the very coupling of picture and idea in motion. The flip side of this excess is—and this is where the order of language as words and the order of language as pictures come together— that the aesthetic experience of the picture must be reactivated through a confirmation in language. "The Poet" explores not only why this might be so, but also what this means for representation in language. To anticipate the result, I will say as a first approximation that only verbal language, whether speech or writing, can lead us to the experience of correspondence (understood here as a fluxional relation, exemplified by the pictorial experience in "Language," rather than by a strict, one-to-one match of natural and spiritual fact), although that experience takes place in a realm not identical with our language. This in turn necessitates translating the experience back into verbal language. From this, a further point evolves: because language is fundamental for triggering the aesthetic experience, it struggles with its own shortcomings because it is nonidentical with that experience. The Poet is "the representative man," as Emerson says in "The Poet," but he is representative only insofar as he is capable of reducing the degree of the failure of language. By the same token, his meliorated use of language facilitates the experience that takes place outside of language.

But is there really such a thing as an experience "outside of language" for Emerson? He frequently distinguishes between two powers, that of reception and that of expression. Reception is also figured as thought in "The Poet,"[44] which implies that "thinking is not inhabitation but abandonment," as Barbara Packer writes.[45] The link between reception and abandonment describes the centrifugal pull of the experience of the spirit. As Emerson says:

> It is a secret which every intellectual man quickly learns, that, beyond the energy of his possessed and conscious intellect, he is capable of a new energy (as of an intellect doubled on itself), by abandonment to the nature of things;

that, beside his privacy of power as an individual man, there is a great public power, on which he can draw, by unlocking, at all risks, his human doors, and suffering the ethereal tides to roll and circulate through him: then he is caught up into the life of the Universe, his speech is thunder, his thought is law, and his words are universally intelligible as the plants and animals. (CW, vol. 3, 15–16)

The subdivision of the powers of reception and expression reaffirms the distinction between the language of words and the language of nature from "Language." In fact, Emerson describes those who have no access to the Poet's power of expression as "minors . . . or mutes who cannot report the conversation they have had with nature" (CW, vol. 3, 16). And Poet or no Poet, "nature offers all her creatures to him as a picture-language" (CW, vol. 3, 8). The Poet differs from less poetic individuals by being able to make use of that offer by expressing a second image behind the first: "Being used as a type, a second wonderful value appears in the object, far better than its old value" (CW, vol. 3, 8). In other words, although Emerson distinguishes between the power of reception and the power of expression, both are already part of orders of signification, albeit of different ones. On the side of reception, this would, in fact, force us to see "abandonment" as a sort of signification, and even as dialogue. The inverse would also be true: a certain kind of dialogue and signification must be understood as abandonment.

At this point we may conclude that the Poet is capable of conversing with nature in its own language (what Emerson also describes as the picture-language of nature) and of then translating that into verbal language. In the next moment, however, Emerson overthrows this idea, saying that the Poet writes "what must be written" and that "poetry was all written before time was" (CW, vol. 3, 5). I take it that here, what is received or perceived does not have to be translated into verbal language, as it is already presented in it (rather than in a visual language). So the Poet has to express or utter what is already there in his "own" language. Even more confusingly, when attempting to do this, poets habitually do a sloppy job, but they are not really to blame, because what was just presented as verbal language now somehow occurs in a different medium after all: "[W]henever we are so finely organized that we can penetrate into that region where the air is music, we hear those primal warblings, and attempt to write them down, but we lose ever and anon a word, or a verse, and substitute something of our own, and thus miswrite the poem" (CW, vol. 3, 5–6). Emerson here all but explodes the distinction between a heavenly language of nature and our verbal language. On the one hand, there seem to be different media at play (music and primal warblings versus the language of the Poet), which contradicts the implication of the sentence that "poetry was all written before time was." On the other hand, the Poet runs into problems not because he cannot find the proper words for the primal warbling, but because he loses a word or a verse and substitutes it with a word of his own. What the Poet is doing here is reminiscent of a recitation of a given text: when he cannot remember a word or a verse, he replaces it with an *Ersatz* made up by himself. But even this swerve from translation to recitation is undermined and reversed, because Emerson speaks of "loss." The concept of loss makes sense most clearly in a translational model in which meanings, contexts, or connotations are lost because translation can at best match near-equivalents that are situated in different semiotic systems. The problem that "The Poet" poses, then, is how to account for what happens in and between reception and expression, or thinking (understood in the Emersonian sense as abandonment) and speech. "Translation" does not seem to be the proper model, and neither does mere recitation or copying. I will use the remainder of this chapter to reconstruct how Emerson solves this problem.

The Seriality of Experience

First, there is an additional thought to be considered, namely the relevance of "experience," which has a central position in the essay. The issue is raised from the beginning, when Emerson criticizes current poets for not grounding their verses in experience: they "are contented with a civil and conformed manner of living, and to write poems from the fancy, at a safe distance from their own experience" (CW, vol. 3, 3). Compare this to the importance of experience in the ideal poet: "The poet has . . . a whole new experience to unfold; he will tell us how it was with him, and all men will be the richer in his fortune" (CW, vol. 3, 7). What does Emerson mean by "experience" here? Is it what happens to us out there, in the real world, rather than in a world of "fancy"? Is it the opposite—is experience that which happens to us when we receive and perceive the language of nature in a moment of inspiration? Are world and spirit really the same, just as "to think is to act," as Emerson says in "Spiritual Laws" (CW, vol. 2, 94)? Or, finally, does he speak of "experience" in the moment when both world and spirit are *made* to touch? Most likely this last option is the case, as Emerson sees the principal strength of the poet in his power to reconnect the banal (railways, for instance) with the spiritual.

Speaking of "experience," how does the reference in "The Poet" to the beginning of the essay "Experience" (the next essay in the series) play into the problem of representation? "Experience" famously begins with the question "Where do we find ourselves?" and continues, "In a series, of which we do not know the extremes, and believe that it has none" (CW, vol. 3, 27). In "The Poet," Emerson finds us far elsewhere: "Here we find ourselves, suddenly, not in critical speculation, but in a holy place, and should go very warily and reverently. We stand before the secret of the world, there where Being passes into Appearance, and Unity into Variety" (CW, vol. 3, 9). This holy place, brought to life in so different a tone and with such different imagery from the scene in "Experience," is apparently the very place of experience that Emerson wants to send his poet to; it is the place where we can watch the secret of the world in the making. It is the meeting ground that grounds divine "fancy" (or imagination) in experience: Oneness becomes enfleshed in the individual, the spiritual is embodied in the natural. And somehow this site, where the transformation of the spiritual into the natural originates (close to, but not identical with Plotinus's idea of *emanation*, which is a moment of efflux from the One into the apparent rather than a point of differentiation), is the locus of perfect intelligibility and legibility. "Things admit of being used as symbols, because nature is a symbol, in the whole, and in every part" (CW, vol. 3, 8), Emerson writes by way of recalling the second and third sections of "Language." And although he does not dare try to list here the correspondences that fill the symbols with content, we must assume that they can be experienced at this moment and site where the correspondences are produced or articulated. The Poet, then, is witnessing the origin of meaning. And the effect that this witnessing has on him individualizes the holy place into his experience. Witnessing is thus turned into "how it was with him." This is the experience he will unfold. Thus, in its visionary ecstasy, "The Poet" does not merely differ from "Experience" but does so specifically regarding *experience*.

What I am suggesting in drawing attention to "Experience" is the possibility that the series in which we find ourselves in that essay is connected to "The Poet" through the series of the essays, and through "finding ourselves" in the seriality of that very phrase. This would retroactively also redefine finding ourselves in "The Poet," and this retroactive dimension is crucial for "finding," which comes after lacking or searching. Thus finding ourselves in "Experience" relates back to our place in "The Poet"; and likewise, "finding ourselves" in "The Poet" suggests that the holy place itself is only a transitional place that depends on its prior place ("critical speculation") in order to enable our finding ourselves. This is a process of infinite regress. Reading "The Poet" with "Experience" deflates the holiness of the place by aligning it in a series, injecting it into metonymy, as it were. This also confirms the feeling that Emerson works as a master of irony, undermining his moments of greatest ecstasy without reducing them to sheer mockery.[46]

But aligning "The Poet" with "Experience" also raises the questions of why the holy place should differ from critical speculation and whether both are not subject to all kinds of limitations and mishaps as laid out in "Experience." Emerson's distinction between the holy place and critical speculation goes back to the very beginning of the essay, where he criticizes both current poets and critics—"the umpires of taste"—for not living up to the potential of the true poet and for being materialistic, superficial, and fanciful instead of connected to experience. But considering that the ideal poet is then shown to have his poetic insight in the form of "new thoughts," and that the authorial voice of the essay, as Julie Ellison has shown in her *Emerson's Romantic Style*, continuously hovers between the role of the critic and that of the poet, the difference between the holy place and critical speculation crumbles (Ellison, *Emerson's Romantic Style*, 114–40). In fact, I suspect that the holy place in which we do not critically speculate is the place where we are speculating so successfully that we have entered our speculative world as the real. It is thus the moment in which thinking as abandonment (claimed to be different from critical speculation) has fully succeeded in giving us access to the real *through representation*. But again, the seriality of experience calls into question this very success.

What makes the holy place even more ironic is the fact that this passage is advertised as a less "vain" though still hopeful cure from the preceding passage that is just as overblown. In that earlier passage, Emerson waxes reminiscent of the "transparent eyeball" passage, stating "I shall mount above these clouds and opaque airs in which I live,—opaque, though they may seem transparent,—and from the heaven of truth I shall see and comprehend my relation. . . . now I am invited into the science of the real," a vision that is soon exposed as fancy: "Such is the hope, but the fruition is postponed" (*CW*, vol. 3, 8). This fruition is postponed indefinitely, it seems, as one vain hope is followed by the next. The excessive visions of this "miniseries" outdo each other rather than deflate each other ironically, although that is how Emerson advertises them. But this seriality of excess is only a further level of relational contrast to the disillusioning series of "Experience." Thus, with the help of the seriality of "The Poet" (a seriality that must be denied, seriality being per se antithetical to the sublime of the unique and timeless moment of ecstasy), the holy place becomes an ideal representation, which, through its placement in a series with "Experience," is *found* to be what could have been known even in "The Poet" (and which seems, in fact, to have been lost there): just another chain in the series, and hence just another mood, just another step on the ladder, just another colored lens through which we look (to use three images of contiguity from the later essay). And to inject the lesson of "Experience" into "The Poet" becomes possible only because of the immense difference between the two spaces "where we find ourselves," that is, between the two accounts of experience. The dual function of this difference is that, although seriality deflates holiness, holiness also relies on the series. Thus, while seriality enables our finding ourselves and the representation thereof, it does not contain the fleeting uniqueness and unique fleetingness of the moment of inspired vision. And neither does it overcome the obstacles to inspiration in "Experience."

To come back to our problem, with the seriality of "Experience" in mind, how does "The Poet" account for that space in and between reception and expression, if it is regarded neither as translation nor as copying or reciting? To reiterate the previous steps of my argument: If critical speculation and being a witness in the holy place are not essentially different, if both witnessing and telling "how it was with him" make up the experience of the poet (and potentially of us), and if experience cannot be separated from the metonymic seriality addressed in "Experience," then reception and expression must share an overarching framework of belonging to signification, a framework that allows for an inner differentiation into different kinds of signification.

Peirce's Firstness, Emerson's Infinite Regress

To make this more precise and plausible, it is useful to connect this train of thought with Peirce's pragmaticist phenomenology in order to elucidate where Emerson is going and also in order to show, with the help of Peirce's terminology, where Emerson differs from Peirce. Peirce's elaborate system of the sciences, which, in its high degree of structure, appears to be so completely un-Emersonian, places phenomenology in the rubric of philosophy, and philosophy in the rubric of "science of discovery," in contrast to "science of review" and "practical science." Phenomenology, as a subcategory within philosophy, is grouped alongside "normative science" and "metaphysics." The task of phenomenology is described by Peirce as follows: "Phenomenology ascertains and studies the kinds of elements universally present in the *phenomenon*; meaning by the phenomenon, whatever is present at any time to the mind in any way" (*CP*, vol. 1, para. 186). Although Peirce tends to want to convey the impression that his system of the sciences is rigidly structured, as soon as he explains it, he points out manifold interconnections. Thus, phenomenology, the science of that which is present to the mind at any time, turns out to be related, among many other things, to "Logic," which is a subcategory of "normative science" (which in turn belongs to "philosophy"). Logic is more precisely "the theory of self-controlled, or deliberate, thought; and as such, must appeal to ethics for its principles. It also depends upon phenomenology and upon mathematics. All thought being performed by means of signs, logic may be regarded as the science of the general laws of signs" (*CP*, vol. 1, para. 191). It is important that phenomenology is related to the study of signs, because phenomenology, as the study of the elements present in the phenomenon (and thus of what is present in the mind), must be related to thought (although, as we will see, not everything present to the mind is "thought"), and all thought is "performed by means of signs."

The connection between phenomenology and signs becomes clearer when we enter the field of phenomenology, which identifies three modes of being, *Firstness*, *Secondness*, and *Thirdness*. In other words, the elements present in the mind take these three forms of being. Firstness is described as a quality that exists without having any actuality; it is pure potentiality. "Redness" is one of Peirce's favorite examples. Redness exists, but it exists completely independent of anything that is red. In Peirce's words, "The mode of being a *redness*, before anything in the universe was yet red, was nevertheless a possible qualitative possibility" (*CP*, vol. 1, para. 25, emphasis in original). Peirce sometimes tries to describe how this Firstness would feel in the mind by suggesting "to make and in a slumberous condition to have a vague, unobjectified, still less unsubjectified, sense of redness" (*CP*, vol. 1, para. 303).

In Secondness we encounter more than mere potentiality: we encounter a thing. This thing possesses actuality, but independently of any other thing. How is this unrelated thing present to our minds? Although we encounter it, we cannot define it yet, for that would require more "things." Thus, the only way our relationship to that "brute" existence (*CP*, vol. 1, para. 24) can be described is to say that "we have a two-sided consciousness of effort and resistance." Again, Peirce has a favorite example: "I instance putting your shoulder against a door and trying to force it open against an unseen, silent, and unknown resistance" (*CP*, vol. 1, para. 24).

Finally, there is Thirdness: in this realm, we connect the element of Firstness to the element of Secondness and end up with a Third. Peirce describes the sign as a genuine Third. The sign consists of three poles: the *representamen* (here Peirce means what Ferdinand de Saussure calls *signifier* and what Peirce sometimes also calls, confusingly, *sign*), which belongs to Firstness; the *object*, which belongs to Secondness; and finally the *interpretant*, which could best be described as the interpreting consciousness, or more generally, the mediator that connects Firstness and Secondness. Peirce describes the sign as follows:

A *Sign*, or *Representamen*, is a First which stands in such a genuine triadic relation to a Second, called its *Object*, as to be capable of determining a Third, called its *Interpretant*, to assume the same triadic relation to its Object in which stands itself to the same Object. (*CP*, vol. 2, para. 274)

This explains why Peirce says all thinking is done by means of using signs. He conceptualizes all thought as the interplay between the pure quality as potentiality, the thing as actuality, and the consciousness that adds them together as relationality. Consciousness must be used with care here, because, as seen in the previous quotation, Thirdness as a state of consciousness is something determined by Firstness and Secondness. Peirce's account of thinking, which, despite the determining force of Firstness and Secondness, is still conceptualized as "deliberate," also means that Firstness alone, or Firstness and Secondness without Thirdness, do not qualify as thought. Likewise, thinking never consists of Thirdness in some isolated sense. According to its definition, Thirdness involves Firstness and Secondness.

Another aspect is vital here and is captured in Peirce's obscure formulation, "to assume the same triadic relation to its Object in which stands itself to the same Object." What this means is that every sign belongs to a sign chain. The reason is quite simply that the interpretant adds together Firstness and Secondness as an *interpreting* consciousness. While the interpreting consciousness (not to be confused with a human individual as "interpreter") completes the sign and produces meaning, this very first meaning is no more than an interpretation that needs further interpretation. Eventually, Peirce thinks, interpretation will come to a stop when meaning and truth coincide. But until then we must keep extending the sign chain. The way this is done is through what Peirce calls "self-control": it is the interplay of belief and surprise, followed by a phase of intelligent adjustment, that leads to a new belief. This phase of adjustment is where logic as self-control is most interesting and most creative, because it is here that Peirce introduces *abduction* as a way of finding a new hypothesis, which becomes a new belief if it passes the tests of deduction and induction. This is also the point at which the intersubjective foundation of Peirce's thought comes into view: the verification of a new hypothesis in deduction and induction takes place in a scientific community. To the extent that a new hypothesis does not come out of the blue but is itself based on prior intersubjective findings, even the creative element of abduction must be seen to evolve from an intersubjective situatedness. Peirce conceptualizes the entire process of belief, surprise, and reconstruction (which is *the* archpragmatist thought) as experimentalism, "understood as covering all rational life, so that an experiment shall be an operation of thought" (*CP*, vol. 5, para. 420). Essentially, however, what

Peirce conceives of as rational and scientific experimentalism is nothing but the continuous chain of interpretations that lead from meaning to meaning; and each meaning consists of the combination of Firstness and Secondness in Thirdness.[47]

I have introduced Peirce's terminology of Firstness, Secondness, Thirdness, and the sign in order to think about how this might help us in the discussion of Emerson's theory of representation. To be able to do so will require focusing on Peirce's Firstness, which will appear as related to (but not identical with) what Emerson describes as inspiration. To avoid confusion, Emerson's and Peirce's notions of thought must be kept clearly separate. Emerson, as we saw, thinks of thinking as abandonment, which is another term for the state of inspiration. Peirce also knows this state, and his term of Firstness comes close to it. But as we have seen, what is present to the mind in the state of Firstness is, in Peirce's terms, not the same as thinking.

Throughout his works, Peirce describes states in which Firstness is "predominant." The concept of predominance is important here, because it shows that in reality there is no such thing as isolated Firstness in the mind; or at least, we cannot talk about it from a phenomenological perspective. When Firstness is predominant, Secondness and Thirdness move to the background, but they are not entirely absent.

Firstness is predominant in the "ideas of freshness, life, freedom" (CP, vol. 1, para. 302), as well as "in feeling, as distinct from objective perception, will, and thought" (CP, vol. 1, para. 302). The link of Firstness to feeling is interesting for our purposes. This interest, however, forces us to address a terminological problem that will come back to us later: Peirce associates both "feeling" and "quality of feeling" with Firstness. While the terms differ, it is not entirely clear how their respective relationships to Firstness differ. By "quality of feeling," Peirce "does not mean the sense of actually experiencing these feelings, whether primarily or in any memory or imagination. That is something that involves these qualities as an element of it. But I mean the qualities themselves which, in themselves, are mere maybes, not necessarily realized" (CP, vol. 1, para. 304). Quality of feeling differs from the experience of the feeling because feeling would already imply a situation in which the feeling is actualized. It is necessary then for the "quality of feeling" to remain a pure possibility, which means that it cannot be called something that exists in the mind as an occurrence or event: "That mere *quality*, or suchness, is not in itself an occurrence, as seeing a red object is; it is a mere may-be" (CP, vol. 1, para. 304). However, the "suchness" would at least have to be felt as a suchness (rather than as an object), otherwise it would not even be a part of phenomenology.

While Peirce differentiates "quality of feeling" from "feeling" in this section, in the next chapter of his *Phenomenology* the term "feeling" itself takes on many of the meanings that the "quality of feeling" was invested with to differentiate it from "feeling":

> By a feeling, I mean an instance of that kind of consciousness which involves no analysis, comparison or any process whatsoever, nor consists in whole or in part of any act by which one stretch of consciousness is distinguished from another, which has its own positive quality which consists in nothing else, and which is of itself all that it is, however it may have been brought about. (*CP*, vol. 1, para. 306)

Although feeling differs from the quality of feeling because it can be remembered, or as Peirce states, "it must be admitted that a feeling experienced in an outward sensation may be reproduced in memory" (*CP*, vol. 1, para. 308), feeling nevertheless qualifies as Firstness, just as the quality of feeling does, but not as Secondness, as one might expect. Thus, although feeling has entered a state of existence in the mind, as a state of pure consciousness that cannot be defined, it is still clearly marked by the idea of Firstness: it is "not an event," but rather "simply a *quality* of immediate consciousness" (*CP*, vol. 1, para. 308, my emphasis). If we cannot define or talk about the experience of a quality of feeling because it is mere "may-be," feeling, though it may be one step nearer to actuality, has the same effect on consciousness: we cannot "gain knowledge of any feeling by introspection, the feeling being completely veiled from introspection, for the very reason that it is our immediate consciousness" (*CP*, vol. 1, para. 310).[48]

This haziness in Peirce's thought about quality of feeling and feeling in relation to Firstness would not concern us if it were not a point that Emerson can be said to clear up in "The Poet"; thus Emerson's move will become intelligible by using Peirce as a foil. Before this can happen, though, Peirce's feeling must be tied to Emerson's thinking. Feeling, as immediate consciousness, cannot be grasped in language. And yet, as *immediate* consciousness, feeling has a privileged status for Peirce, despite his turn away from phenomenology in "What Pragmatism Means," which led to the statement, "Pragmaticism does not intend to define the phenomenal equivalents of words and general ideas, but, on the contrary, eliminates their sential element, and endeavors to define the rational purport, and this it finds in the purposive bearing of the word or proposition in question" (*CP*, vol. 5, para. 428).

Peirce repeatedly associates Firstness with poetry, as in his second lecture on "Pragmatism and Pragmaticism," where he makes the point that the "poetic mood approaches the state in which the present appears as it is present" (*CP*, vol. 5, para. 44), and in *Phenomenology*, where he exclaims in his most Transcendentalist mood, "Bad poetry is false, I grant; but nothing is truer than true poetry. And let me tell the scientific men that the artists are much finer and more accurate observers than they are, except of the special minutiae that the scientific man is looking for" (*CP*, vol. 1, para. 315).[49]

The point made by Peirce that is useful to the discussion of "The Poet" is his view that Firstness is a *distinct mode of being* that differs from the mode of being in which we find signification (the category of Thirdness). And yet, as a constituent element of signification, Firstness is also within signification. If we conceptualize Firstness as Emerson's abandonment or reception for a moment—and indeed, the passivity of receptiveness is precisely at work in Firstness, which thereby differs from the deliberateness of Thirdness—we get a model of how reception and expression are related to each other in a way that differs both from translation and from copying or recitation. In fact, I believe that this is the most advantageous model for redescribing what Emerson is after in "The Poet." The poet's state of inspiration is a keen awareness of Firstness; expression, "our other half," becomes necessary because our "first half" (or should we say, "our first third") is a constituent element of expression or signification. Firstness is tied into expression for the reason, then, that it is unintelligible in itself. Thus, when we approach it "in a poetic mood," Firstness may be "predominant," but it in fact always coexists with Secondness and Thirdness. We can only approach Firstness through means such as poetry that take place in Thirdness. Moreover, even when we imagine experiencing the state of Firstness, that experience also includes Secondness and Thirdness, though they are pushed into the background.

In other words, reading "The Poet" with Peirce highlights two things. First (and this point is not new), our moment of inspiration—what Peirce calls "pure consciousness"—cannot be captured by language because language always lags behind. Emerson says so explicitly in "Self-Reliance": "And now at last the highest truth on this subject remains unsaid; probably cannot be said; for all that we say is the far off remembering of the intuition" (*CW*, vol. 2, 39). But connected with that is the second, more surprising point: although the highest truth must remain unsaid, it is not absent from what is said; it enters it as Firstness, one of the constituent parts of Thirdness.

But Emerson is not merely explained by Peirce; he also challenges Peirce on the very point of how feeling and quality of feeling relate to Firstness. As we have seen, even in "Language," and certainly in "The Poet," Emerson conceptualizes the moment of inspiration not as pure consciousness in which we see a pure quality. While Emerson shares Peirce's ascription of potentiality to Firstness, he does conceive of it as a moment of signification, usually expressed by some belief in the language of nature. Thus, we are affected by such a state when we see how the entire world relates to us, or when, in the holy place, we see how signification is "framed," how Unity passes into appearance. Emersonian Firstness has its own signification, and this signification differs from signification in verbal language in that it is located on a different level. This means that language doubles on itself in Firstness, which is another way of saying that in abandonment we are capable of an energy "as of an intellect doubled on itself" (*CW*, vol. 3, 15): Firstness, which makes up signification, is itself made up of the interplay of Firstness, Secondness, Thirdness. What we see here is a microcosmic structure (common in much of Emerson's thought) of multiplication on ever-smaller levels.

In other words, our spiritual and poetic experience is the experience of language on a smaller level. Just as Peirce suggests, our poetic feeling or intuition is thus not some direct self-introspection where we know what is in our state of pure consciousness, but what Peirce describes as pure consciousness, for Emerson is still microcosmic signification: when we are inspired, we envisage signification, and this envisaging becomes, as Firstness, a constituent element of signification. This is a modification of Peirce, who describes the proliferation of the sign chain through Thirdness; Emerson, as an expert on the poetic mood, shows that the endless proliferation of the sign chain does not happen only through the process of abduction, deduction, and induction on the level of Thirdness. Even on the level of Firstness, we see a chain of signs unfold infinitely.[50] Another way of saying this is that feeling relates to Firstness as an intuited interplay of Firstness, Secondness, and Thirdness. The quality of feeling references merely the *function* of Firstness. Thus, when we redescribe Peirce's Firstness with Emerson, feeling is the interplay of Firstness, Secondness, and Thirdness within the realm of Firstness, and the quality of feeling is a reference to just the Firstness within Firstness; but as soon as that second-order Firstness is looked at, it becomes transformed from a quality of feeling to a feeling, and thus produces a third level of signification.

This conception of the interplay between reception and expression accounts for Emerson's insistence on the symbolic structure of divine nature, which he is never willing to pin down but instead couples with feeling and intuition. It explains why Emerson can swing back and forth between a conceptualization of inspiration as the power of the individual to create and subdue the world through symbolic mastery (this is Emerson the idealist) and a conceptualization of inspiration as our reception of nature as a flux that "names itself" and subdues us. Rather than partitioning the two approaches into two different phases of his career, as is still common practice among Emerson's critics, reading Emersonian inspiration as an endless regress of Firstness suggests that inspiration makes us feel empowered through a vision of endless potentiality in representation and also subjects us to the continuous succession of signification that makes infinite control impossible. Ulla Haselstein has succinctly explained that "In *Nature* as well as in many of Emerson's essays, the two positions of Romantic philosophy, namely idealist self-assertion (the egotistical sublime) and a philosophy of nature are being put forward: again and again Emerson alternates between them without ever settling for one of them or reconciling them in a dialectical model."[51] Instead of using a dialectical model, Emerson arranges expression and reception, or idealist self-assertion and the philosophy of nature, in an endless series. The picture-language in the vision of infinite potentiality, and the verbal language of expression, are experienced as constant alternations.[52] But although we experience the two modes of signification as an alternating series, both modes maintain their reality as different modes of being. Seriality, for this reason, can also be conceptualized as circularity. It is this circularity that allows us to place Emerson's version of the interplay of Firstness, Secondness, and Thirdness in an intersubjective framework: although what gets envisioned as the sheer potentiality of signification in Firstness always exceeds that which can be expressed in signs and thus what gets injected into the symbolic social, this vision of potentiality itself is fed by the intersubjective manifestation of the sign chain that is located on the level of Thirdness. Reception and expression depend on each other without turning into a dialectic of progress.

"Nominalist and Realist": The Representation of Concealment

Emerson's model of serial experience is reformulated and clarified in his essay "Nominalist and Realist," the penultimate piece in *Essays, Second Series*. This essay also provides a further link between Emerson and Peirce. Peirce's model of Firstness, Secondness, and Thirdness should be read as an intervention into the age-old philosophical debate between nominalists and realists, that is, the debate about the status of generals or universals. While nominalists maintain that generals (for instance, redness) have no real existence but are mere abstractions of the mind to which we have given arbitrary names, realists believe that such generals possess real being. For Peirce, the debate is skewed because both nominalists and realists do not quite get it right. While nominalists only believe in one mode of being (the category Peirce calls Secondness, or "brute existence"), realists believe in two modes of being. As an example Peirce enlists Aristotle, who believed not only in the existence of Seconds but also in "an embryonic kind of being, like the being of a tree in its seed" (*CP*, vol. 1, para. 22). This would fall under Peirce's category of Firstness. Peirce's addition to the realist position is the reality of Thirdness, which he also describes as the reality of "prediction" (after all, abduction is a hypothesis). The prediction of Thirds is real because it takes on the form of a law: "To say that a prediction has a decided tendency to be fulfilled, is to say that the future events are to a measure really governed by law" (*CP*, vol. 1, para. 26).

Thus, Peirce's realism makes him the defender of the truth of a law both physical and divine. This position is at odds with the antifoundationalism and immanence for which pragmatism has come to stand. Peirce is a thinker of immanence only insofar as truth can only be discovered within experimentalism. Thus, when we move from one belief to the next, we also move from one truth to the next. But there is nevertheless an outside to this process that determines where the experimentalist discovery of truths must go. It is probably Peirce's realism that explains why the link between Peirce and Emerson has received relatively little attention in the stream of publications of the last twenty years that has read Emerson as a protopragmatist. And although the difference between a Peircean and a Jamesian Emerson is smaller than one might think—after all, most Jamesian readers of Emerson (for example, Poirier and Levin) emphasize the dimension of transition and constant flux in Emerson's thought, which is compatible with Peirce as well[53]—this gulf between pragmatism and Peircean "pragmaticism" should not be underestimated. For Emerson's model of representation takes on its distinctive shape only if his realist leanings are taken into account. As I have argued, what is perceived in the moment of Emersonian intuition is a vision (recall the *picture*-language of "Language") and feeling of a signifying order of sheer potentiality. But importantly, what is intuited thereby is indeed a higher truth, although this higher truth may never materialize and not even be signified. Moreover, this truth achieves its "height" only through its bond with the commonness of the social signifying process. The point here is that it is only by taking seriously Emerson's realism that we can claim that his model of representation is structured by different modes of being.

"Nominalist and Realist" may not be all too seriously concerned with the philosophical debate of the Middle Ages, since Emerson discusses the matter in terms of a seemingly undecidable race for priority between the particular and the universal. Throughout the essay, Emerson performs the difficulties of making up his mind on the question of which horse he should bet on, and thus, at one point, comes to doubt the existence of particulars: "Human life and its persons are poor empirical pretensions" (*CW*, vol. 3, 135). In the end, however, Emerson does take up a realist position by affirming that both the universal and the particular constitute modes of being. These do not become resolvable in a synthesis but rather produce an aporia: both ways of viewing life are plausible and in fact right, and yet they are incompatible with each other. Emerson writes:

> All the universe over, there is but one thing, this old Two-Face, creator-creature, mind-matter, right-wrong, of which any proposition may be affirmed or denied. Very fitly, therefore, I assert, that every man is a partialist . . . ; and now I add, that every man is a universalist also, and, as our earth, whilst it spins on its own axis, spins all the time around the sun through the celestial spaces, so the least of its rational children, the most dedicated to his private affair, works out, though as it were under a disguise, the universal problem. (CW, vol. 3, 144)

As Laura Dassow Walls aptly writes about this passage, "The upshot is that every man is both part and whole, contributing his fragmented individuality to the great circle, and working out on his own single pulse the universal problem."[54] But there is more in Emerson's invocation of the earth that turns both on its own axis and around the sun, something relevant for his theory of representation as it relates to the following question: if both the particular and the universal are real modes of being that are nevertheless incommensurable with each other, how does representation relate one mode to the other? In other words, if intuition provides us with a vision of potentiality in the field of signification (potentiality is here redescribed as the existence of universals), and if signification itself narrows down and limits the potentiality to the existence of a particular, how do we as individuals perceive the transition from one mode of being to the other? The last part of the above quotation leads to the answer provided in "Nominalist and Realist": the universal problem is treated by the individual, but it is treated "under a disguise." The transition from one mode to the other is not experienced at all because the mode of potentiality remains hidden from us. Images of disguise and hiding abound in the essay and lead to the idea of representation as concealment:

> Nature keeps herself whole, and her representation complete in the experience of each mind. She suffers no seat to be vacant in her college. It is the secret of the world that all things subsist, and do not die, but only retire a little from sight, and afterwards return again. Whatever does not concern us, is concealed from us. As soon as a person is no longer related to our present well-being, he is concealed, or *dies*, as we say. Really, all things and persons are related to us, but according to our nature, they act on us not at once, but in succession, and we are made aware of their presence one at a time. (CW, vol. 3, 142, emphasis in original)

While all things are related to us in a field that can be called potentiality, Emersonian Firstness, or intuition, this field no longer coincides with our field of vision. Concealment is the result of the aporetic simultaneity between potentiality and actual signification, universality and particularity. When the tension between these sides becomes too severe, the individual can no longer jump back and forth from one to the other; instead, concealment comes to level out the alternation. The mood here resembles the end of "Experience," in which the paucity of excessive insight is grudgingly turned into practical power.[55] In "Nominalist and Realist," the consequence of concealment is a prudent contentment with the limitations of the particular, and thus with the limited range of expression: "If we cannot make voluntary and conscious steps in the admirable science of universals, let us see the parts wisely, and infer the genius of nature from the best particulars with a becoming charity" (CW, vol. 3, 143). But in contrast to the end of "Experience," limiting oneself to the particular nevertheless holds out the promise that the universal will again become accessible, if only by inference and not by direct insight. Furthermore, Emerson implies that the fact that the field of potentiality is concealed from the individual does not mean that it loses any of its reality, nor does it mean that the individual is not still at work in this realm. In fact, Emerson comes close to arguing that our experiences of abandonment have not ceased but that we have merely become anesthetized by the aporetic structure of representation. Our abandonment has thus become concealed from us. As a consequence, Emerson's representation of concealment forces us to engage in potentiality without knowing what we are doing.

This is perhaps the ultimate challenge of Emerson's theory of representation: we are to understand our language use as energized by something we no longer know, and in using language, we rely on feeding back into this concealed realm of our own future experiences. Certainly, this model of representation is a far cry from any notion of linguistic freedom. It understands the use of language to result from an excess that we no longer witness and that we fail to live up to in our representative acts. Nevertheless, even in his disillusioned moods, Emerson keeps intact the basic structure I have worked out throughout most of this chapter: representation is the dynamic between incongruent and overlapping modes of being. These different modes constitute, yet do not strictly determine, each other: without Firstness, there could be no symbolic signification, and without the social process of signification, there could be no Firstness.

This understanding of representation is at odds with the assumptions of and the readings by Emerson's New Americanist critics. As I argued in the previous chapter, their interpretations tend to assume a seamless efficacy of representation when representation is in the service of a ruling ideology, or the futility of representation when representation is employed by the individual language user; the only way for representation to effect change is to crack open the symbolic system at its borders. Because Emerson can only be interpreted as inhabiting this border space when he is read through the lens of trauma, most New Americanists propose that his writings on representation endorse passivity and enforce the status quo. In my interpretation, however, Emerson's thinking about representation is not geared toward reinforcing the grip of the ideological because he emphasizes the transitions that disturb the totalizing reach of ideology. But as I have just shown, neither does his model of representation celebrate some sort of linguistic freedom. What he offers is no more than an aporia that produces moments of ecstatic and excessive abandonment. This is what it means, then, to build a theory of representation on the rift between reception and expression.

The Power of Eloquence

A New Americanist reader would probably object that an ideological rupture based on the rift between reception and expression would be much too mechanical an account, one that is blind to actual power relations. However, it is not Emerson's aim in the essays under consideration here to consider questions of fixed hierarchies of power, although power itself is of the highest importance for his thought on representation. Power in Emerson's thought is closely linked to eloquence, which brings us to the implied context that has driven my articulation of Emerson's theory of representation. The inner connections to the topics of eloquence and power demonstrate how closely Emerson's theory of representation is linked to his professional engagement as a public lecturer.

I want to note briefly here that for Emerson, power and eloquence, like representation, are built on the rift between reception and expression. The problem of power concerns the question, can we work that rift? In "Shakspeare," from *Representative Men*, which was published in 1850, Emerson locates power first at the pole of reception and then at the point of expression: "Great genial power, one would almost say, consists in not being original at all; in being altogether receptive; in letting the world do all, and suffering the spirit of the hour to pass unobstructed through the mind" (*CW*, vol. 4, 110). And some pages later, he writes: "This power of expression, or of transferring the inmost truth of things into music and verse, makes him the type of the poet, and has added a new problem to metaphysics" (*CW*, vol. 4, 122). To have a calculated effect on the world, it is not enough to trust the dispersing effects of the rift between reception and expression; it is up to the individual's power to make use of this rift by simultaneously being "altogether receptive" and "transferring . . . truth . . . into music and verse." Of course, this does not explain at all what such a transfer could look like—it is merely suggested once again that the relationship between reception and expression is not imitative but transformative.

Emerson's thought on eloquence begins to take steps to render the transformative performative. In this context, the rift between reception and expression is addressed with an audience in mind.[56] As Emerson writes in a late essay on "Eloquence," assembled by his friend and literary executor James E. Cabot and based on a lecture first given in 1867, "Eloquence is *the power to translate a truth into language perfectly intelligible to the person to whom you speak.* He who would convince the worthy Mr. Dunderhead of any truth which Dunderhead does not see, must be a master of his art" (*W*, vol. 8, 130, italics in original). If, in "Shakspeare," the power of expression consisted of "transferring the inmost truth of things into music and verse," eloquence merely looks at the same act from a different perspective, emphasizing that the way the "inmost truth" is transferred must be "perfectly intelligible" to the audience.

What eloquence adds to the discussion of power is the concern with the speaker's craft and will: "The special ingredients of this force are clear perceptions; memory; power of statement; logic; imagination, or the skill to clothe your thought in natural images; passion, which is the *heat*; and then a grand will, which, when legitimate and abiding, we call *character*, the height of manhood" (*W*, vol. 8, 117, italics in original). As I understand it, the source of character, of the individual's will, is not located in transcendence, but precisely in the fissure between reception and expression. When Emerson speaks of eloquence and power, it turns out, he hopes to minimize the gap between reception and expression in the speaker's act through the performative effect of that act. "In perfect eloquence," he writes in his journal in August 1838, "the hearer would lose the sense of dualism; of hearing from another; would cease to distinguish between the orator & himself; would have the sense only of high activity and progress" (*JMN*, vol. 7, 52). In this ideal speaking situation the orator would thus use craft and will to create the effect in the listener of having entered the mode of impersonal abandonment from which the orator's speech came forth. The ideal transfer from reception to expression is thus figured as a communicative circle: when expression, derived from reception, is presented with perfect skill and will, it will set the listener into a stage of abandonment that makes her forget that the words that got her there ever had to make the transfer from reception to expression.

This brings me to the final point of my chapter. I argue that Emerson's dream of perfect eloquence and the reception aesthetics he builds into his texts to approach that ideal delimit the range of his topical explorations of failure, stagnation, and concealment. Emerson's literary strategies, because they evolve out of the requirements of the public lecture, generally privilege the moment of abandonment. On the levels of both theory and aesthetic effect, such moments only become possible through the limitations experienced in the act of expression. This precludes Emerson's engagement with failure from becoming dominant in any given text. It is perhaps no coincidence that "Experience," generally taken to be his darkest piece of writing, is one of the few essays that did not directly derive from a lecture.

A quick, self-reflexive turn may illustrate my point: I have tried in this chapter to read Emerson *on his own terms* in order to realize some of the venues he opens up. These terms—*witnessing, the holy place, the passing of being into appearance, experience, the series, finding,* to name a few— enable a form of receptive creativity insofar as their conjoining opens up fields and chains of association. This informal relatedness is achieved by the variety of characteristics and registers of tone among his terms, which range from (often metaphysical) spatial designations ("the holy place") to activities that waver between the concrete and the abstract ("being passes into appearance"), formal descriptors ("series"), and terms that hover between everyday language and more specialized discourses, whether philosophical, scientific, or criminal ("experience," "finding," "witnessing"). Each term carries a whole semantic field that begins to resonate with a surprising degree of literalness through its unlikely but suggestive combination with the other terms. This readerly effect, which can hardly be distinguished from an "audience effect" in Emerson's case, is dependent to a large degree on the literalness with which each term can be read and cannot fully be captured by analyses of his use of metaphor and allegory. This associative style is better described as metonymic, as a transporting from one field of association to another along a chain of representative suggestions.[57]

The terms on which I have focused here stem from "The Poet" and "Experience," two texts that, at first glance, express opposite moods, enthusiastic insight and nearly hopeless stagnation. Yet despite the difference in mood, both essays perform the associative chain that rescues language from ossification and allows the reader to switch from the mode of imprisonment to the mode of receptive insight. What I want to suggest, then, is that Emerson's thought on stagnation and failure, so central to the logical reconstruction of his theory of representation, must be kept in check by his writing. In the final implication of his retroactive introjection of the seriality of experience into "The Poet," we now see that the Poet has also been intro-jected into "Experience." If Emerson's poetic project is that of a celebrity lecturer in the nineteenth-century U.S. lecture system, his poetic contain-ment of failure and stagnation marks the limit of this project. The lecture hall requires a reception aesthetics that transforms failure into excessive abandonment. This requirement must be met even when Emerson laments the failure to reach abandonment.

II

EMERSON AND IDENTITY

[3]

THE NEW AMERICANISTS AND THE VIOLENCE
OF IDENTITY

The New Americanists and the Debate over Identity

IN CHAPTER 1, I showed that the New Americanists' understanding of representation is influenced most importantly by Louis Althusser's theory of interpellation. According to Althusser, the individual becomes a subject in the act of being hailed, or interpellated, by ideology. Representation itself is thus modeled after a performative speech act. These performative acts are conducted by what Althusser calls "Ideological State Apparatuses" (such as the church and the school), each of which contributes to the continuous interpellation of the subject. While performative speech acts may be seen as the model for the act of interpellation, ideological hailing is conducted not only through language but also through various kinds of material practices. While interpellation ushers in the individual's mistaken sense of being an autonomous being, a proper understanding of interpellation, so the argument goes, highlights the fact that language and other means of representation create and form the subject. Thus, interpellation is more than a theory of representation; it is first and foremost a theory of the subject. In other words, interpellation gives us an important clue as to what the New Americanists' understanding of identity is.

In this chapter, I will demonstrate that the New Americanists' constructions of Emerson are prefigured by their theory of identity. As the theory of interpellation was first formulated in response to both Marxist and liberal humanisms, it is hardly surprising that it has moved New Americanists to criticize Emerson for being a major architect of American liberalism, or, to put it the other way around, that it has served New Americanists well in the formulation of a critique of liberalism. By the same logic, those of the New Americanists who have defended Emerson have interpreted him as undermining the hegemony of the liberal order. As I will argue, however, the way in which New Americanists have appropriated the idea of identity construction from Althusserian theory has led them to make implicit, normative

claims that are themselves ultimately liberal. One might be perturbed or relieved by this insight, depending on one's view of liberalism. The problem
arises from the fact that the New Americanists' liberal norms remain disavowed. This results in blind spots in their work—incongruities between
what their tacit liberal norms require and what their theoretical assumptions
provide. The particular blind spot on which I will focus in this chapter concerns the way in which New Americanists conceptualize recognition.

Recognition is a term that attempts to account for the social genesis of
identity. Liberal theory has worked out the intricacies of the process of recognition, which, from Hegel onward, has most often been described as a
struggle. Yet the New Americanists, informed by Althusser's theory of interpellation, have not sufficiently grappled with the processual and unstable
character of recognition. They tend to assume that the individual either is or
is not recognized. This absolutist view explains why they deem problematic
both being and not being recognized. Coming to terms with the unstable
dynamic that marks the process of recognition would require them to move
beyond a theory of identity based on the idea of the unilateral construction
of identities by cultural practices and discourses. Moreover, as I will show in
chapter 4, a more nuanced perspective on identity formation through recognition would allow New Americanists to address a dimension in Emerson's
work that has largely escaped them because of their theoretical framework.
As I will argue, Emerson's notion of self-reliance was concerned with recognition much more centrally than has hitherto been noted.

To understand the New Americanists' theory of identity more fully, it is
helpful to place it within the larger debate on identity that evolved in the
context of feminism, postcolonialism, and multiculturalism across the humanities beginning in the 1980s. Most New Americanists, especially those
who openly identify themselves with the label, tend to eschew this contextualization when providing a genealogy of their movement. Most of them
describe their emergence by emphasizing differences with prior paradigms
within American Studies.[1] They typically point to their differences with the
Myth and Symbol school, which they portray as complicit with the Cold
War consensus. Moreover, they usually distance themselves from the more
recent ideology critique presented by Sacvan Bercovitch, who describes the
co-optation of dissent by a national consensus.

There are obvious reasons why this intradisciplinary lineage is emphasized. From an institutional perspective, an important reason lies in the necessity of securing the relevance of one's revisionist work by keeping the
discipline intact. This in part explains why most New Americanists, despite
their advocacy of canon revision, have spent a good part of their careers on
interpreting the canonical authors of the American Renaissance.[2] A further

reason for the dominance of the intradisciplinary genealogy can be found in the flip side of this logic: in order to keep the discipline intact, it seems necessary to revitalize it through continuous injections of revisionism.[3] But precisely because these *intra*disciplinary differences provide the legitimation of the New Americanists—as I showed in chapter 1, according to their own "founding myth," the New Americanists emerged from an outsiders' position imposed on them by the Americanist establishment—the *inter*disciplinary context in which the New Americanist paradigm evolved has, at least in its theoretical delineation, received less acknowledgment.

In order to shed light on this broader context, I want to begin by showing that New Americanists base the claims of their political efficacy as a formation in the academy on theoretical arguments that have been significantly influenced by developments in other disciplines. In their original context, these arguments served specific intradisciplinary purposes, but they also contributed to a larger debate over multiculturalism and feminism. I will briefly reconstruct this debate in order to place the New Americanists within it.

Four Positions on Identity

I will subdivide the wide range of positions in the debate on identity into four groups, fully aware of the necessarily schematic shape of this outline. Positions tend to overlap, and proponents of one group sometimes share some of the views of a very different group. Nevertheless, the theoretical grid I am about to unfold helps to structure the debate. I call the positions' proponents: (1) liberals, (2) communitarian liberals, (3) hard pluralists, and (4) deconstructive pluralists. At stake in the discussion is the question of how a morally just society should be organized in an age of multiculturalism. In other words, this debate is concerned with an understanding of identity and recognition that highlights less the process of the formation of individual identities than the political negotiation of recognition claims of groups endowed with collective identities. My chapter will move from a consideration of the discussion of a politics of recognition to a debate over how the process of recognition is to be described philosophically and psychologically. The point is that the two dimensions—the debate over how to negotiate recognition claims politically, and the debate over how to theorize identity formation—are interdependent. The politics of recognition involves struggles over the definition of moral justice, which in turn is contingent on the assumptions one makes about the individual and identity. The debate over the politics of recognition has been concerned with the problem of whether in a pluralistic society one should perceive of justice as an issue of individual rights, of group rights, of some combination of the two, or whether the logic of rights itself must be enriched by nonformalized concerns.

1. Liberals typically give the highest priority to the rights of the individual, and, indeed, they look at moral and political questions from the perspective of the individual. Making this distinction between a perspective focused on the individual and one that is focused on the group already implies that the individual cannot be accurately described by membership in groups. This does not mean that, for most liberals engaged in this debate, individual identity is antithetical to social identity (that is, they usually do not argue from the vantage point of the "unencumbered self"),[4] but they do differentiate between the individual's capacities, agency, and moral responsibility, and the social components of individual identity. In the debate over multiculturalism, liberals typically oppose the valorization of diversity as an end in itself, arguing that cultures are dynamic and that the individual should not be tied to any static notion of culture. In other words, cultures need to be understood as highly flexible, and individuals are never intrinsically wedded to a culture. Among the most prominent proponents of this liberal position are political philosopher Anthony Appiah and economist Amartya Sen. As my understanding of the liberal position differs from a purely Lockean, rights-based formalism in which society provides an arena for private persons to interact according to market principles, I include Jürgen Habermas's position of discourse theory in this category, although, according to Habermas's self-description, he offers a "third way" that reaches beyond the binary made up of liberalism and communitarianism.[5]

2. Communitarian liberals also conceive of justice from the perspective of the individual. However, they differ from liberals in their assumption that cultural belonging is an essential component of individuality and should thus be understood as an individual right. They typically seek to promote cultural survival and cohesiveness—in short, cultural diversity. But the reason they do so is not to elevate the group over the individual. On the contrary, the dimension of cultural belonging is highlighted in order to grant the individual the fullest possibilities of self-realization. As Anthony Appiah writes, "In soft, or liberal, pluralism, the individual remains both the terminus a quo and the terminus ad quem: its concern for identity groups is not only motivated by but ultimately subordinated to the well-being of the individual and the bundle of rights and protections that traditional liberalism would accord her."[6] Of course, the inherent problem of this position lies in the possible conflicts between two groups' rights or one group's rights and those of other individuals. The pragmatic solution has been to argue that group rights can only be granted—and institutionalized—as long as they do not violate another person's individual rights. The advantage of this position,

according to its proponents, lies in its greater sensitivity to the social nature of individual identity. The "politics of recognition" is seen as largely compatible with this approach. Because individual identity is the result of intersubjective recognition, and because individual identity itself consists of the internalization of how others see one's social group, the individual and the individual's social identity have a right to be respected. If the image of one's social identity is negative, the argument goes, this image will be internalized and will damage the individual. As Charles Taylor writes: "Nonrecognition or misrecognition can inflict harm, can be a form of oppression, imprisoning someone in a false, distorted, and reduced mode of being."[7] But this position also draws a boundary line regarding which cultures deserve recognition: a culture must itself support the individual's self-realization in order to deserve recognition. Otherwise it comes into conflict with the overarching goal of liberal communitarianism, which is precisely to allow for the flowering of a socially embedded self. Besides Charles Taylor, the main proponents of this liberal communitarianism are Will Kymlicka, Michael Sandel, and Michael Walzer.[8]

3. Hard pluralists take the pluralism of liberal communitarians much further (within the American context, they sometimes refer back to Horace Kallen's earlier concept of pluralism as a multiethnic federation).[9] In their opinion, the problem with the liberal communitarians lies in their focus on the individual. This prevents them from doing what hard pluralists urge us to do: to valorize diversity itself. Thus, hard pluralists attack what they see as the liberal ideology of individualism even in the liberal communitarian's contention that the self is "encumbered." In their view, the basis of diversity should not be the individual but the group. Otherwise, pluralism remains hypocritical, only allowing for the kind of difference that is not different from liberal individualism at all. While hard pluralists sometimes uphold the possibility of intercultural mixing, and, to some extent, intracultural heterogeneity, they typically do promote the institutionalization of group rights when it comes to legislative measures. In order to do legal justice to groups, they affirm the necessity of fixing group identities in law. Both within legal frameworks and in more informal arenas of culture, they argue for an egalitarian politics of recognition in which all excluded groups are granted recognition, independently of the question of whether they conform to the moral standards of liberal society.[10] This also requires that the individual member of a group be legally bound to conform to what is defined as the group's cultural identity. To mention a famous example, hard pluralists defend Quebec's Bill 101, which, in framing the province's language rights, grants the right to send children to English language public schools only to those parents who have gained an English language education themselves.

In feminist and postcolonial theory, some scholars have formulated calls for "strategic essentialism"—a term introduced by Gayatri Chakravorty Spivak. The idea is that invoking essentialism strategically is a valid step in order to gain recognition for a subordinate group, even if the essentialism that often accompanies calling for recognition is principally rejected. The starting assumption is that culturally specific differences need to be defended against efforts to subordinate or eradicate them. Hard pluralism here comes to refer to the egalitarian recognition of subaltern groups, even if this may mean that these groups only come into existence as formal entities through the act of recognition. Thus, this branch of hard pluralism distinguishes between cultural differences (they do exist) and cultural identities (they are not naturally or essentially given, but must be produced) and for practical reasons temporarily eclipses this difference. Among the proponents of hard pluralism are the political philosophers Susan Mendus and Bhikhu Parekh, as well as the cultural and feminist theorists Spivak (who has sharply distanced herself from the uses to which the term "strategic essentialism" has been put, and who, as a deconstructionist, has strong alliances with the thinkers of my fourth category), Luce Irigaray, and Diana Fuss.

4. Finally, deconstructive pluralists are often closely allied with hard pluralists, yet they shy away from what they perceive as the reification of identity that comes about as an unintended side effect of the politics of recognition. In other words, deconstructive pluralists pursue the dual aim of rescuing marginalized and suppressed identities from invisibility or demeaning images, while at the same time trying to avoid a close identification of individual subjects with these rescued identities. Subaltern identities are understood here as the products of liberal discourse—they are the "constitutive outside" of the liberal subject, whom liberal ideology describes as neutral, but who in reality is assumed to be male, white, and heterosexual. While these subaltern identities need to be brought to public awareness because they are most harmful when they are disavowed by the liberal norms of the neutral subject, emancipation from them requires a step beyond bringing them to light, namely disidentification (an idea formulated by Michel Pêcheux and used by Foucault in the final phase of his work).[11]

The strategy of deconstructive pluralists is thus to keep the entire discursive matrix in flow, that is, to make the diversity of identities visible and to transform their boundaries. The assumption is that the subject is the result of discourses and culturally instituted practices, which means that the only way to escape the prison of language and culture is to keep significations and practices constantly in flux, or, in the language of postcolonial theory, to maintain a level of hybridization against the binding force of binary divisions through which power operates.

Spivak's "strategic essentialism" caused discontent mainly among deconstructive pluralists (she herself, as the translator and disseminator of the work of Jacques Derrida, is generally taken to belong to that group) because it diverged from the very imperative of disidentification. Disidentification is seen as the only solution to the threat of identities' deployment by disciplinary power. The subject implied in this view is understood not to be unitary, but a conglomerate of multiple subject positions. The governing paradigm of this approach thus insists on the dividedness of the subject. This dividedness—itself the result of multiple subjections—comes to stand for the basis of hope, insofar as the multiple subject has internalized the very heterogeneity that can undermine the binaries of power. The ranks of deconstructive pluralists include many of the theorists who dominated the debate on gender, postcolonialism, sexuality, and race in the humanities in the 1990s. They specifically include political philosophers who have identified with the project of "radical democracy," among them Wendy Brown, Chantal Mouffe, Ernesto Laclau, and William E. Connolly. It is also this group of theorists that has had an especially noteworthy influence on the identity theory prevalent among New Americanists. In fact, several New Americanists, among them Russ Castronovo, Dana Nelson, and Christopher Newfield, have themselves been actively engaged in formulating possibilities of radical democracy.[12]

As I will be arguing, deconstructive pluralists who differ from hard pluralists in their anxiety over the reification of identity shift their focus from group identity back to the individual subject, although, as I have said, this subject is no longer described as unitary.[13] What is striking, especially about the New Americanist version of this position, is that, while it upholds the hard pluralists' attack on liberal individualism as well as the affirmation of the importance of rescuing marginalized identities from eclipse by liberal, "neutral" conformity, the liberal aim of emancipating the individual is revived and even radicalized: emancipation must now include those informal and as yet unrecognized aspects of the individual that rights-based liberalism could not capture. The demand to escape the violence of identity can be interpreted as a redefinition of emancipation from a one-time act of liberation to a ceaseless process of emancipating.

Emerson and His Emersonian Critics

In the next section, I will analyze the New Americanists' portrayal of Emerson with regard to identity. It will become obvious how their allegiance to deconstructive pluralist identity theory shapes their analyses. Their main target is Emerson's concept of self-reliance, because it is here that his liberal individualism most centrally informs his thought. Self-reliance, from this perspective, is seen as an ideology of the unencumbered self that promotes the establishment and reinforcement of hierarchies, the exclusion of anyone who differs from the implicit norms of the liberal subject, and the passivity of the individual. By way of these three charges—hierarchization, exclusion, passivity—New Americanists rehearse the central components of the deconstructive pluralists' critique of liberalism and apply them to Emerson. Their fundamental critique seems to set these critics radically apart from Emerson. Indeed, in their calls for political action they differ from Emerson, who, despite his eventual engagement in reform movements, preferred to begin political reform by turning inward. Yet, I argue, Emerson's recent critics stand much closer to him than is commonly admitted. To the degree that the final, normative horizon of this criticism lies in the emancipation of the individual from the impositions and exclusions of liberalism, at least some versions of the New Americanists' critique of Emerson can be reinterpreted as an update of the avowed goals of Emerson's individualism. While the respective means to achieve the normative goals of the individual's emancipation differ, the normative goals themselves are clearly related.

Emerson as Representative Subject

The starting hypothesis of most New Americanist scholarship assumes that whatever Emerson promoted and proclaimed was itself determined and overdetermined by his own interpellation as a subject. In 2003's *Reconstituting the American Renaissance*, Jay Grossman makes the point most explicitly: "[By] invoking Althusser's formulations, I seek to shift our perspective sufficiently to examine the ways in which Emerson and Whitman might themselves be considered 'representative' subjects, particularly with regard to the cultural institutions and practices of social class" (Grossman, *Reconstituting the American Renaissance*, 120).[14] Grossman's interest lies in demonstrating the continuity between Emerson, at least in his younger years, and his father's social position, which Grossman presents as elitist Federalism:

> American criticism at least since Matthiessen has widely disseminated an Emerson who is a rebel and a democrat, but the Emerson who emerges from his early writings is not clearly either of these; he seems rather the spokesman of political axioms . . . inherited from his father's social position in which "to be termed a 'democrat' was a reproach." (Grossman, *Reconstituting the American Renaissance*, 121)[15]

Grossman's larger point, shared by Dana Nelson,[16] is that the constitutional debate continued to organize ideological positions in the nineteenth century. In Grossman's characterization, this debate was carried out between "radically" inclined, democratic Anti-Federalists, who questioned the legitimacy of federal delegates to represent the people and favored representation on the state level instead (where the ratio of voters per delegate was much smaller), and the Federalists, whose democratic convictions are portrayed by Grossman as limited by their endorsement of a national representative body. In his view, the Federalist idea of representative democracy, because it drastically diverges from the ideal of one-to-one correspondence, is deeply tied to "virtual representation" and is thus a betrayal of the initial revolutionary impetus for democratic representation. From here, Grossman claims that "the story of American literature in the United States is the story of gradually, over the course of the nineteenth century, making this virtuality into a 'literary' value" (Grossman, *Reconstituting the American Renaissance*, 73).

Independently of the question of whether this argument is historically tenable—and the problems begin by tying the Federalist position to "virtual representation"—it is noteworthy that Grossman does not merely argue that members of the two generations (that is, the revolutionary generation and that of Emerson) came to hold ideologically congruent viewpoints.[17] Rather, because he bases his argument on Althusser's theory of interpellation, Grossman lends the democratic deficiencies he detects in Emerson an air of necessity. Thus, he argues that Emerson's dependence on his father's ideological position begins with the materiality of his writings.

Grossman points out that four of Emerson's notebooks were originally used by his father, and that Emerson sometimes rebound his father's covers to different spines. He interprets this technique as an example of the material practices that constitute what Althusser calls interpellation: "I take as my point of departure the startling material *continuity* between the writings of this father and his son. . . . Ralph Waldo Emerson's writings bound within the covers of texts provided by his father thus reveal themselves a fitting emblem of the Althusserian binding(s)/boundaries of subjectivity" (Grossman, *Reconstituting the American Renaissance*, 121). In other words, the binding of his father's notebook helped bind Emerson's subjectivity and serves as one instance in a complex network of transmissions between his father's and his own ideological stance. This premise of Emerson's own interpellation—perhaps expressed nowhere else as explicitly as in Grossman's book, but widely shared by implication—persists in the subsequent New Americanist work on Emerson, particularly in the examination of how he established and reinforced an ideology of American liberalism.

The Dying Citizen

The critique that Emerson's individualism is politically quietistic is anything but new. According to Philip Gura's recent history of Transcendentalism, the young Emerson's allegedly apolitical stance was a bone of contention among the Transcendentalists themselves. Moreover, throughout the reception history of his work, Emerson's writings have been critiqued for their privatism.[18] From this perspective, the New Americanists are merely extending a reaction to Emerson that has accompanied his voice from the very beginning and that may thus be seen as an integral (counter)part of his thought. Just as Grossman's aim in aligning Emerson with the Federalists was to point out his lack of democratic commitment, many revisionist critics have argued that the emancipatory potential of self-reliance is stifled by its privatizing, depoliticizing logic. Among these critics are Russ Castronovo, Christopher Newfield, John Carlos Rowe, and Wai Chee Dimock (whose allegiance to the New Americanists was much stronger in the 1980s and early 1990s than it is now), along with the scholars Julie Ellison, Anita Haya Patterson, and Susan Ryan, who are not directly affiliated with the New Americanists but whose views overlap in some areas.[19] The difference from earlier criticisms of this kind lies in the alleged source of this quietism. It is essential to the New Americanist argument that the problem is not so much Emerson's personal lack of commitment to democracy, but rather that his writings are expressive of an ideology that fundamentally organizes American liberalism.

Russ Castronovo's 2001 book *Necro Citizenship* is a good example of this claim, and I will discuss it here as a paradigmatic case. According to Castronovo, Emerson's privatizing of cultural critique helped to reinforce an ideology of the citizen as an abstract category, which urged on the disembodiment of particular subjects to the point where the ideal of the liberal citizen became the corpse: "Dead bodies . . . imply a type of democratic subject produced in the nineteenth-century public sphere. Guaranteed formal equality and cultural autonomy, the citizen encounters politics as a near-death experience: he or she thus prefers privacy to public life, passivity to active engagement, and forgetting to memory."[20] There are two components to Castronovo's argument. On the one hand, he criticizes liberalism's abstract or neutral conception of citizenship. This conception, he claims, becomes manifest in a widely held definition of freedom as disembodiment, which is epitomized by Emerson's fascination with the Spirit. On the other hand, he argues that this disembodiment of liberalism privatizes politics and thus returns it to the private body. His example is a specific pedagogical and physiological reform discourse of the nineteenth century that resulted in hysteria over masturbation. This antimasturbation discourse, which focused on the body, he claims, is mirrored in Emerson's ideology. He notes that the antimasturbation literature diagnosed an ill that was described as a form of enslavement and that could only be overcome by the self:

> The "body in subjection," as *The Library of Health* put it in 1842, "must be self-emancipated." Emerson staked out this democratic doctrine in which all must reform themselves a year later in "Self-Reliance" and later used this stance to critique the Fugitive Slave Law. (Castronovo, *Necro Citizenship*, 79)

In other words, Emerson's self-reliance worked in ways analogous to the antimasturbation crusade in claiming that reforms, and politics in general, had to be undertaken by the individual, not in public, but in private. This focus on the self served as a distraction from problems that could only be solved by scrutinizing the community. The argument is that the depoliticization at work in Emerson's writings shares with the antimasturbation campaign a replacement of the body politic with the individual's body.

But how, one may ask, does the focus on the private body work with the abstraction of citizenship as disembodiment? Castronovo's answer follows the argument common among hard pluralists and deconstructive pluralists in pointing out that abstraction is the result of universalizing one specific kind of subjectivity—white, male, heterosexual—which is thereby silently redefined as the neutral standard. By defining the privileged body as the standard, the ideological process of deflecting attention from particular bodies, which Castronovo calls disembodiment, can begin. Castronovo chooses a Baudrillardian vocabulary to make this claim: he describes the elevation of the white, male body to the universal standard as "hyper-embodiment" (Castronovo, *Necro Citizenship*, 17, 74, 95). One particular body becomes eroticized so thoroughly that it comes to stand for the body per se. But hyper-embodiment, according to Castronovo, always runs the risks of displaying its particularity and tearing the veil of disembodiment. That is why liberal ideology, which had to avoid the appearance of the particularity of the hyper-embodied white male, needed spokespersons like Emerson and the leaders of the antimasturbation discourse to push white men and the danger of exposing their partiality out of the public sphere and into the space of the private: "the hyper-embodied subject that stays at home and shuns social intercourse is an identity reserved for white men who know better than to seek republican pleasures in the public sphere" (Castronovo, *Necro Citizenship*, 95).

Ultimately, Castronovo's argument is far less extravagant than his rhetoric of death and disembodiment may suggest. It is underwritten by a concern about the eroding effects of negative liberty, and it suggests that Emerson was one of the chief contributors to this erosion.[21] In his normative claims,

Castronovo is divided between endorsing a restricted, communitarian notion of the common good (Castronovo, *Necro Citizenship*, 80), and calling for radical democracy, in which all particularities can participate in public representation. In his introduction it becomes apparent that he does not want to seem to differentiate between republican (and, although he does not acknowledge this, republican means restricted) and egalitarian modes of recognition as long as there is contestation instead of liberal abstraction:

> [Legacies of radical democratic action] fade when citizenship is reduced to a formal game where the stakes of recognition and exclusion are as absolute and final as death. But at the edges of legal incorporation and political dispossession, the dead walk, too: citizens are reanimated by republican, feminist, and Africanist senses of subjectivity that materialize in the seams of abstract personhood. . . . *Necro Citizenship* looks at bodies who exercise histories that work to the opposite effect, making the public a bumpy terrain of contestation. Not all subjects lie in democracy's graveyard. (Castronovo, *Necro Citizenship*, 3)

Several aspects of this passage deserve further examination. First, while republican, feminist, and Africanist senses of subjectivity may or may not exclude each other—depending on the boundaries of the common good of the specific republic—their invocation in a single, dehierarchized enumeration is strictly speaking incompatible with republicanism because republicanism must ensure that the common good itself rests on a higher level than those elements that constitute it. This is true even if the content of the common good itself is understood to be the object of an ongoing contestation. Inside this processual understanding of republicanism, one cannot proclaim a number of particular subjectivities as given and also claim that nothing is given apart from the collectively negotiated common good.[22] Castronovo's argument is not communitarian or republican but pluralist, and inside this pluralism, strong republican voices may be heard, but they must not prevail. In this sense, his pluralism radically differs from what I have called, following Appiah, "hard pluralism." Hard pluralism could also be described, in Amartya Sen's term, as "plural monoculturalism." In that model, a society is made up of several distinctive cultural groups, each of which must be allowed to follow its own common good.[23] Hence there is little room for the contestation among various senses of citizenship envisaged by Castronovo.

Castronovo supports a pluralism of a deconstructive bent. Elsewhere he points out, quoting Wendy Brown, that while particular identities must be represented in public space, this representation itself becomes susceptible to disciplinary power. But by the same token, the body's materiality exceeds attempts at total disciplinary control. While the body is inscribed by liberal disciplinary power, its materiality remains specific and thus potentially undermines this disciplinarity.[24] In a manner typical of deconstructive pluralists, Castronovo thus affirms the necessity both of representing partialities and of using the inherent excess of materiality in order to flee from the prison that builds up around these newly recognized identities. This dual goal is best achieved in the "bumpy terrain of contestation," which in one form or another provides the ideal for all of the literature on radical democracy.

The reason why this "antagonistic democracy," to use Chantal Mouffe's term, is so appealing is its individualist capabilities. It is so individualistic that it even makes room for nonindividualist forms of citizenship, but because these nonindividualist forms are themselves contested, they do not endanger the self-realization of their members. Nevertheless, this individualistic aim, which carries differentiation into the individual self, is generally disavowed by deconstructive pluralists. Both Castronovo and Chantal Mouffe, for instance, make the implicit argument that a validation of the notion of the common good is commensurable with the emancipation of particularities once one overcomes the false distinction between the individual and the group. To make this argument, both refer back to interpellation theory, claiming that the individual is not a unitary subject but an assemblage of different subject positions. Thus, according to Castronovo, his book questions the duality of self and other. But this argument merely reaffirms my contention that an account of subject formation based on Althusserianism comes into conflict with the progressive aims of the New Americanists. If subjects are mere assemblages of diverse subject positions, each of which is the result of interpellative acts, why should one take any political initiative toward a radically democratic activation of the citizen? Indeed, the insistence on the tension between the particular and the abstract universal amounts to a redescription of the old tension between the individual and society in a different vocabulary. The reason why the New Americanists defend the partial is precisely that, despite all interpellation, the partial remains normatively tied to the individual in need of emancipation from social pressures.

This brings us to a further point. Castronovo's disdain for liberal democracy—the claim that its formalization is linked to death, and not merely metaphorically so—relies on a particular assumption about recognition in liberal democracy. When Castronovo claims, in the quotation discussed above, that "the stakes of recognition and exclusion are as absolute and final as death," what he is implying is not only that this finality is comparable to death, but that recognition and its opposite (he calls it "exclusion," but he might also speak of nonrecognition) are indeed responsible for the (political) death of the democratic citizen. But what is the basis of this claim that recognition and exclusion are totalized in liberal democracies? The only answer he provides is formalization itself, as if the institutionalization of citizens' rights and liberties (negative freedom) were a death sentence.

I would argue that this premise is problematic in two ways. First, it assumes that rights and the law in general are beyond the reach of democratic review. Here it is helpful to remember Habermas's point that the citizen of liberal democracy needs to be understood, at least ideally, not only as subject to the law but also as its author.[25] Second, Castronovo's premise is problematic because it claims that once a legal conception of citizenship is in place, the legal and institutional scope of citizenship settles any question of recognition. Note that in order to connect recognition and exclusion to death (either literally or metaphorically), Castronovo uses a rich concept of recognition that exceeds the legal realm to include the entire scope of the individual's sense of self. Castronovo ascribes to the formal, legal status of inclusion and exclusion the power to settle the question of recognition in toto.

However, even in liberal democracies, recognition, understood as an intersubjective process, relies on those informal domains of personal and public relationships that Castronovo claims liberal democracy has put in the grave. They remain open to contestation even in rights-based liberalism. I contend that the totalization of recognition is not so much a property of liberal democracy as a conceptual decision on the part of liberalism's critics. In short, Castronovo's founding assumption that the formalized character of liberal democracy totalizes the stakes of recognition and exclusion is hardly the indisputable fact that he presents. This does not mean that liberal democracy is as inclusive and neutral as some would like to argue. My point is, rather, that the way in which exclusions are theorized by critics like Castronovo suggests an abridgment of the mechanism of recognition and misrecognition. Legal exclusion does not necessarily result in full-scale misrecognition, and likewise, legal inclusion does not equal recognition in the richest sense. Even in "formalized" liberal democracies, the informal domain of one's identity (and this includes both personal and social identity) remains open-ended.

If this point suggests the limited scope of formalized recognition, one must also turn this point around and reconsider the political costs that would be incurred if formal and institutional kinds of recognition were replaced with a vitalized, face-to-face struggle. I here question whether radical democracy's suspicion of formal inclusion makes a political order based on the principles of radical democracy sufficiently protected against the tendency of state power to transgress its legally defined limits. I understand radical democracy as an ideal conception of the social order in which partial subjectivities can equally participate in public representation. This participation, however, is not primarily geared toward input for the political decision-making process, but rather toward input for a process of continuous, face-to-face contestations. The focus of this vision does not lie on the democratic legitimation of decisions and laws, but on the antagonisms that are located beyond the reach of the law and that require making room for nonformalized domains.[26] What I am suggesting is that radical democracy's tendency to pit legal formalism against political vitality runs the risk of ushering in not a more radically democratic, but rather a less democratic society. The flight from formalism puts the individual's protection from the state in danger.[27]

But questioning the New Americanists' assumptions about liberalism's totalization of recognition also has more direct ramifications for literary studies. Since literature itself does not make direct decisions about who is legally recognized, the struggle over individual and cultural recognition, as it is enacted in literature and in the aesthetic experience of reading literature, must be distinguished from legal inclusion and exclusion in liberal democracies. While recently Gregg Crane has convincingly shown that literary appeals to a higher law in nineteenth-century America influenced legal discourse and contributed to the abolition of slavery,[28] the reverse assumption that it has been one function and result of literature to ideologically ground legal exclusion by reduplicating this exclusion through a lack of recognition in literature is problematic. For the claim behind that assumption is not just that certain subjects are portrayed as excluded or that their exclusion is advocated (for many texts, including some remarks by Emerson on race and gender, this is certainly true) but that the reading process itself enacts the totalization of recognition and exclusion.

As scholars working on reception aesthetics have argued, however, the literary reading process itself must be understood as an encounter between the reader and the text that does not work by mere indoctrination but by an imaginary transfer (I will come back to this point at the end of this chapter). In this sense, as I will argue in chapter 4, reading can be conceptualized as a struggle for recognition that is far from totalized. This late-twentieth-century conception of reading is indebted to the hermeneutical theories of reading shared by Emerson and his contemporaries—theories that in large part resulted from theological discussions about the status of the Bible and that were, as Robert Richardson has shown, chiefly influenced by Schleiermacher.[29] As Emerson writes in "The American Scholar," "There is then creative reading as well as creative writing" (CW, vol. 1, 58), a statement that still holds true today and that is incommensurable with the assumptions made about the ideological effect of the writings of the liberal tradition regarding the crippling of the individual's engagement in political causes. In short, both on the political and on the literary level, Castronovo displays a problematic fear of the totality of recognition, believing that the perceived definitiveness of the law translates into issues of recognition in all nonlegal realms.[30]

Before resuming this argument in this chapter's final pages, I want to turn to a few more New Americanists' positions on identity and liberalism. Like Castronovo, these critics ground their studies on the assumption that Emerson contributed to the formation of American liberalism by fostering exclusion, hierarchization, and political passivity.

The Submissive Friend

In Christopher Newfield's influential 1996 study *The Emerson Effect*, Emerson, as a key builder of American liberalism, contributes to hierarchization, political passivity, and marginalization by rendering his individualism private instead of public. While Castronovo suggests that the public sphere of nineteenth-century America was fertile ground merely for those discourses that promoted depoliticization by pushing political subjects into the private sphere, in Newfield's view a perverted form of the public retains a central function for Emerson's private individualism. This is captured by what Newfield calls "corporate individualism." Corporate individualism is a surrogate democracy, in which submission to the privatized, unappeasable laws of an undemocratic collective body (the corporation) replaces democracy's collective agency. Emerson is centrally involved in this process of replacement; in fact, he becomes something like its founding father:

> Emerson's double legacy, then, is this: freedom means endless flexibility, and freedom means loss of control. Both sides of his thought are in continual operation. The tension is obvious in a concept like liberal authoritarianism, and suppressed when it appears as corporate individualism. (Newfield, *Emerson Effect*, 26)

The collective, semipublic body of the corporation thus ensures the submissiveness of every one of its members. To this privatization of the public in the corporation, Newfield connects Emerson's treatment of personal relationships, more precisely male friendship and heterosexual love. Male friendship affords a certain, regulated amount of equality between friends. Indeed, Newfield writes, "Where democracy is really like male friendship, it is not only bearable [for Emerson] but necessary to the existence of free subjectivity" (Newfield, *Emerson Effect*, 121). But this equality depends on two conditions. First, it must be removed from the public into the realm of the private: "Fearful sodomy depends in Emerson less on the male/female difference in object-choice than on the difference between the couple and the crowd. He seeks not to suppress homoerotic intimacies but to privatize them" (Newfield, *Emerson Effect*, 99). Second, the object of the shared and equal eroticization in private ends up being submission itself. This requires an explanation: Newfield argues that Emerson's modeling of democracy after male friendship is not conducive to democracy at all. Because Emerson conceptualizes personal identity as the result of friendship, the boundaries between male friends tend to dissolve. Emerson's ideal democratic relationship thus rests on a loss of the self in the other. This, however, becomes an impossibility when a single friendship joins a wider network of social relationships in a democratic public. Such a democratic public, if modeled after friendship, would require engaging with multiple others in a cross-boundary fusion. Such multiple fusions would either divide the self or require the individual to make a choice of person with whom to engage in a union. Thus, Newfield concludes, "The problem with association appears not when it forces a monolithic identity on a complex and unique character, but when it fails to do this" (Newfield, *Emerson Effect*, 123). Therefore, the goal of "equality" in friendship is not a reciprocal exchange between equals but the individual's submission to exactly one friend. This requires one to accord the friend a higher position than one inhabits oneself: "But this individual wants union with those who are above him, associated with Spirit, guidance, mastery, or force of some kind. The brother Emerson seeks is a big brother, he who can be imagined as a father. . . . Individuality means not reciprocity with but submission to the other" (Newfield, *Emerson Effect*, 124).

I will address Emerson's thought on friendship at length in the next chapter. For now I want to note that Newfield's reading is, on one level, very acute: Emerson indeed conceptualizes individual identity as the result of personal relations, and he does face the problem of having to translate this one-on-one relationship into the sphere of the public. As I will show, Emerson typically envisions the public as his audience, and he treats the audience as if it were a singular friend—in fact, he sometimes abruptly switches from talking about his audience to talking about "a friend." What Newfield neglects to consider is that submission in Emerson's model is not an end but only a means of growth and thus a transitory state. In other words, Newfield falsely substantializes Emerson's ideal of unity—as if Emerson had proclaimed that unity could be achieved once and for all—and thus passes over the processual character of personal relations as envisaged by Emerson. This suggests Newfield's own assumption about recognition (here he is close to Castronovo): in contrast to Emerson, and in fact to the philosophical tradition since Hegel, he conceives of recognition as a state, not as a movement.

The Subject of Hierarchies

While Newfield shares with Castronovo a common emphasis on liberalism's effects of passivity, depoliticization, and submissiveness, the focus on hierarchization in personal relations also plays a central role in the work of Julie Ellison and Susan Ryan, two critics whom I do not directly associate with the New Americanists, but whose work displays similar concerns.[31] In Ellison's 1992 essay "The Gender of Transparency: Masculinity and the Conduct of Life," Emerson's texts on social manners are read alongside the rich popular literature of conduct-of-life manuals from his time. The emphasis of her essentially Foucauldian reading is not so much on depoliticization, but rather on the way Emerson's texts help shape the nineteenth-century American subject of hierarchized mannerliness. In Ellison's reading, both conduct-of-life literature and essays by Emerson such as "Domestic Life," "Behavior," and "Friendship" do more than describe in sentimental terms how one should foster intimate social relationships. They also produce a specific identity along the lines of race, gender, and class.

According to Ellison, Emerson claims that the intimate, sincere encounter provides access to the other's interior so that all layers of identity (race, gender, and class) appear as transparent clothes around the other's core. Yet this transparency merely veils the fact that intimacy itself is structured around the reaffirmation of hierarchies. After all, only where there are hierarchies is it possible to see through them: "The knowledge of subjectivity, another's or one's own, requires the plunge through the surface constituted by status and economic position."[32] Even worse, however, once one has plunged through these hierarchies to arrive at classless, transparent subjectivity in the other, one finds quite the opposite: "But the social surface . . . is actually doubled at the level of 'deep identity,' where rank is also the issue" (Ellison, "Gender of Transparency," 593–94). These class divisions not only have the function of creating order in society but also play a specific role in masculinity, which tends to be challenged by too much intimacy among male friends: "Class distinctions intervene in order to assert the masculinity of Emersonian tenderness" (Ellison, "Gender of Transparency," 596).

In her 2003 book *The Grammar of Good Intentions*, Susan Ryan tells a related story. Rather than following Ellison by focusing on the sentimental import of mannerly intimacy, she studies the nineteenth-century discourse of benevolence, which tended to be more rationalized and professionalized than sentimentalism:

> Benevolent discourse shared with sentimentalism an emphasis on such familial bonds of responsibility and affection, through which other kinds of social

responsibility might be understood. But the culture of benevolence also accommodated a distinctly and deliberately antisentimental strain that emphasized bureaucratic and rationalized processes for determining whom to aid and to what extent. These elements, early instances of professionalizing social work, rejected sympathetic identification altogether as untrustworthy, espousing instead a set of investigative strategies fueled more by suspicion than by sentiment.[33]

To be sure, Ryan's reconstruction of this early phase of the professionalization of social work is a fascinating and impressive achievement. However, the epistemological horizon before which she conducts this work is both familiar, and, I argue, problematic: "The field changes considerably, though, if benevolence is understood as a central paradigm in antebellum culture, one that provided Americans with ways of understanding, describing, and constructing their racial and national identities" (Ryan, *Grammar of Good Intentions*, 5). Predictably enough, she draws support for her interpretation of Emerson from both Newfield and Ellison. While she argues that Emerson's concept of self-reliance amounts to a disavowal of neediness—he only cares for relations between self-possessed men who can be benefactors to each other without being dependent on each other—she supports Newfield's and Ellison's emphasis on the hierarchizations effected by Emerson's writings:

> Such explorations [as Newfield's and Ellison's] are more compatible than they might seem with my portrayal of Emersonian friendship as free of benevolent dependencies and responsibilities. The perfect mutual needlessness I have described is not identical to equality, in that the absence of a hierarchy structured by and articulated through benevolence does not guarantee, or even suggest, that there is no ascendancy, no submission, no power, no fear. Hierarchy, and the self-positioning and competition it engenders, inheres in even the most apparently equal relations. (Ryan, *Grammar of Good Intentions*, 84–85)

Ryan is correct: even in what seems like equality, there will be space for subtle hierarchies. But on second thought, her reminder of the imperfections of the "apparent equality" that the discourse of benevolence promotes reveals a blind spot in her assumptions. Her unspoken normative conviction, stated with more clarity by Newfield, is that equality must and should be possible; otherwise the whole point of showing how subtle hierarchies are produced and maintained even in benevolence would have significantly less of a critical edge. But whether the absence of any form of hierarchy is actually desirable—politically and ethically—is a question that Ryan evades. One should note that even the radical democracy approach cannot do entirely without inequality: its ideal of face-to-face contestation is much more of a throwing of congealed power relations into the vitalizing maelstrom of politicization. But with perfect equality there would be little to contest. Proponents of radical democracy rarely spell this out; in fact they seem to deny the dependence of their alternative democracy on swiftly shifting power ratios, and they thus come to see any form of hierarchy as antithetical to their political ideal. In a similar way, Ryan equates any kind of hierarchy with submission, neglecting possible spaces of contestation within hierarchies, spaces that themselves rely on alterable forms of inequality.

This brings us to the question of why it is problematic, in my view, to hinge studies of benevolence or sentimentalism on the function of identity formation. While it is without doubt true that identities are the result of social processes, the way in which both Ryan and Ellison imply that identity construction works betrays their dependence on Foucauldian and especially Althusserian identity theories. The process of negotiation and recognition of identity is replaced with its performative production in utterances imbibed with power. This makes an analysis of "major authors" such as Emerson attractive in the first place: every word he says can be taken as an identity-shaping utterance of power, especially if one can find similarities between his writings and broader discourses either against masturbation or pertaining to the conduct of life, benevolence, or other concerns. While the avowed goal of reading literary works alongside such discourses is typically said to lie in putting literature back into dialogue with the cultural materials from which it emerged, the way many of these studies proceed is to enlist these discourses as evidence of literature's interpellative capabilities. In this way, the assumption of interpellative identity becomes circular: broader discourses shape literary works (as highlighted by Grossman), and they also prove the formative power of literary texts themselves. Illogical entanglements notwithstanding, one problematic consequence of this understanding of identity as the hierarchical imposition of power is that it produces a normative assumption of what identity should be. The ideal identity that emerges from this thinking is the undoing of identity that results from disidentification, just as it is formulated by the proponents of what I call deconstructive pluralism. It is the only identity that can be accommodated by the egalitarian normative framework employed by these critics.

Denials of Reciprocity

I said earlier that Emerson's recent critics, against their own intentions, share many of the normative goals that inform Emerson's doctrine of self-reliance.

What I mean by this is that the normative horizon of New Americanist criticism lies in the simultaneous celebration of diversity and radically democratic openness in the contestation of identity ascription. Deconstructive pluralism houses seemingly incompatible notions from the two liberal positions in the debate over identity. Like liberal communitarianism, it holds that personal identity cannot be described without its constitutive cultural components. But like liberal individualism, it is also anxious about the communitarians' fixation on group identity. From the perspective of the individual who is seen as irreducible to any one group, such a fixation is regarded as a lack of freedom. Thus, I view the New Americanists' deconstructive-pluralist position as an attempt to strike a balance between two liberal positions, a balance that has become necessary because the concern for the subject's emancipation (itself deeply liberal) silently structures their work. It is in this sense that I consider the New Americanist project to follow Emerson's ideas of nonconformity and individual agency rather than to oppose them. The difference is that Emerson, from the New Americanist perspective, is not individualistic enough. For while he espouses individual nonconformity, his writings center on the limits of individual autonomy, whether formulated through what Stanley Cavell calls an "epistemology of moods," the necessity of grounding one's genius in the language and thought of one's time, or the aspiration to abandon oneself to the impersonal soul.

In a sense, then, the New Americanist critique of Emerson is based on an unwillingness to accept that an espousal of individual freedom (or agency) may have to accommodate freedom's limits (for Christopher Newfield, for instance, propagating such a compromise is itself symptomatic of liberalism's tendency to diminish the power of both the individual and the collective).[34] This anxiety over limitation as a condition for agency gives New Americanist criticism a certain paranoid twist because identity itself, in their account, is first and foremost an imposition.

It is this perspective that creates a clash between a deeply liberal normative horizon and critical premises that must condemn liberalism as the source of the political malaise of the last two hundred years. I do not quarrel with their analysis that the liberal order relies on exclusions, although I do think that liberal democracy is capable of addressing and reversing these exclusions more effectively than other political orders. More importantly, however, I have argued that the reason why liberalism must seem like a harmful idea to these critics lies in their particular conception of recognition as it structures identity formation. New Americanists display a fear of recognition because it is seen to impose imprisoning identities. Their alternative vision, captured by the term radical democracy, does not suggest a more reciprocal version of identity formation, but instead a more antagonistic model, in which identities are resisted through disidentification. The way to handle the process of recognition democratically, in this view, is to undo it.

I want to suggest that a more plausible model of recognition is available once one questions the premise of interpellative, unilateral subject-formation through power-laden discourses and practices. In order to conceptualize recognition in a less totalizing, more reciprocal fashion, it is necessary to ascribe to the individual a greater capacity to respond to ideological ascriptions, without assuming a presocial, metaphysically grounded subject.

George Herbert Mead's Theory of Intersubjective Identity Formation

I will linger for a moment on George Herbert Mead's pragmatist account of identity formation, which has been all but absent from the deconstructive pluralists' camp,[35] although it has received some marginal attention from liberal communitarians arguing for the necessity of a politics of recognition.[36] Mead's theory offers an alternative to the totalizing unilateralism that underlies New Americanist analyses. Although he himself displayed no extended interest in aesthetic analysis, he provides an alternative foundation for thinking about literature and identity by interpreting the social genesis of identity as a reciprocal process.

In his most famous work of social psychology, Mead conceptualizes the individual and the social sides of identity as two different aspects that, borrowing from William James, he calls the "I" and the "Me." First of all, the interesting thing is what this distinction between "I" and "Me" does not do. It does not pose the "I" as an individual, presocial, or in any way unencumbered identity, which is balanced, or dialectically entangled with, a socialized aspect of identity. Rather, both the "I" and the "Me" are at work together in the individuation and socialization of the self.

Mead understands identity to be a social product, but this does not mean that the self is limited to the roles or images society has in store for it. On the other hand, without the individual's adoption of society's attitude or point of view, it would be impossible to have any sense of self, not to mention to go beyond what the social provides. By the same token, only by exceeding the adopted norms is it possible to take in these norms.

In Mead's terms, the self can only gain self-understanding and thus have a sense of individual identity if it becomes an object to itself. In order to do so, it needs to adopt the perspective of the other in regarding itself. What the individual sees from the perspective of the other is a "Me." But even at this point, there is more than just the "Me," that is, the adopted perspective of the other. In taking the other's role, the self really takes two roles—its own as well as the other's. Without the self's act or contribution, there would be nothing regarding which the self could take the other's role. The point here is that the understanding of one's own act is only possible once one has taken the role of the other. But this does not mean that one is merely present to oneself from the perspective of the other. One is also an actor.

In Mead's theory of socialization and individuation, the individual undergoes a learning process in which he or she gradually abstracts from individual others and creates the fiction of what Mead calls a "generalized other." This is a necessary step in functionally differentiated societies: in order to coordinate a complex society, it is necessary to mentally construct how collaboration is to work; this requires an understanding of the general rules and the parts played by others. Thus, Mead's favorite example for explaining the generalized other is a ball game in which every player must know the rules, although no one plays the same position. But whether the other is singular or generalized, the self sees itself from the perspective of that other, as a "Me."

This generalized other ought not to be understood as the totality of objectively existing society. The objectively existing society, with its norms, rules, laws, and institutions, is not given in advance but is itself the result of the social process, in which selves continuously reconstruct themselves and their world through reciprocal role-playing. From the perspective of the individual, the generalized other is thus rather something like a map on which the individual charts his or her path.[37] To draw this map, the self relies on input from two sides. On the one hand, it is forced to take in ever-new viewpoints from the other. Thus, the individual's construction of the generalized other is more than a solipsistic vision of society: it is grounded in the individual's interaction with the world, and this interaction consists of continuous acts in which the other's attitude is adopted. The other input comes from the "I"—a faculty Mead takes to be spontaneous and impossible to observe when at work. The "I" reacts to the image that makes up the "Me." What follows is something like a discussion between "I" and "Me," which Mead, in the essay "The Social Self," calls the "forum and workshop of thought."[38] This discussion transforms the "Me." However, the "I" is only ever capable of being reconstructed retrospectively, once it has altered the "Me" into a different self. And it is at this point that Mead's account becomes most interesting. After the dialogue between the "Me" and the "I" has produced a new self, this self is perceived, by the self and by others, to be at odds with the norms of the generalized other. But as a result, Mead does not suggest that the self recoils from that difference and aims to readjust the self to the prevailing norms. Instead, it aims to *adjust the norms to the self* by anticipating a social order that would accommodate the self. This is how Mead explains creativity, social change, and individual agency: as a result of the conflict between "I" and "Me," the self clashes with the generalized other, and by anticipating a different generalized other, it influences actual society.[39]

This process can also be rephrased in the language of recognition. The aberrant self that results from the difference between the "Me" and the "I" anticipates its recognition and thus makes claims for recognition. Because the other members of the group rely on taking the other's role (that is, the role of the self in question) as much as the self relies on taking their role, the newly formulated self will ideally become recognized. However, this is only possible if the individual's new contribution can be integrated into the existing generalized other. In Mead's words, the requirement for the possibility of integration of this new self is "reason." Mead certainly does not want this reason to be understood in a metaphysical sense. Rather, reason itself describes the social reciprocity and the dialectic of adopting the role of the other, in addition to making input for the generalized other. Mead writes:

> A person may reach the point of going against the whole world about him; he may stand out by himself over against it. But to do that he has to speak with the voice of reason to himself. He has to comprehend the voices of the past and of the future. That is the only way in which the self can get a voice which is more than the voice of the community. . . . We can reform the order of things; we can insist on making the community standards better standards. We are not simply bound by the community. We are engaged in a conversation in which what we say is listened to by the community and its response is one which is affected by what we have to say.[40]

There is little doubt that Mead's theory is a highly idealistic account, which at least in part is the expression of how a Chicago reformer from the first third of the twentieth century wanted democracy to work. But although his account brackets such questions as institutionalized inequalities of access to the conversation that shapes the self and that is shaped by the self, there is much to be said for his basic model of the mechanics of identity formation. I find a most important insight in his conceptualization of recognition. While New Americanists try to run away from recognition (and also subscribe to a politics of recognition to some extent) because any recognized identity seems like a prison, Mead posits that not only is recognition not to be feared, it is indispensable and unavoidable. We cannot have any sense of self without recognition. At the same time, he does not succumb to the idea that the telos of recognition is the perfection of recognition. No one is ever fully recognized, and the dialogue between "I" and "Me" will not come to an end. The self is in a constant state of nonidentity, understood not as disidentification but as reciprocal negotiation. Mead does believe that the continuous reconstruction of the generalized other through the input of the "I," along with taking the role of the generalized other, will lead to progress in morality and justice. He calls this process universalization, and he assumes that it can lead to a world society in which the individual will eventually be able to take on the role of a generalized other who consists of common elements shared by humanity. However, even at this utopian point, the reciprocal movement between "I" and "Me," between taking the role of the other and injecting novelty into the intersubjective exchange, will not come to an end.

In this regard, Mead diverges from the contemporary philosopher of recognition Axel Honneth, although Honneth enlists Mead (and Hegel) for his normative model. Honneth builds his theory of justice on the idea that society should guarantee every individual recognition in the domains of (1) emotional affection in social relations of intimacy; (2) legal recognition; and (3) appreciation of the individual's achievements and skills.[41] Honneth's goal is the institutionalization of social guarantees (as far as possible) on all three levels. By contrast, for Mead, recognition remains an ungrounded— by this I mean it is based purely on relations—and interminable dynamic, which of course does not mean that certain claims for recognition will not or should not be fixed in the law. While Honneth wants to create a society in which every individual feels recognized in terms of love, the law, and solidarity, Mead's account is more open-ended. Although his theory does pave the way for increasing levels of socialization and individuation (thus, a growing number of people and facets of each self become part of the interplay between the generalized other and the self), Mead's theory does not envisage an end point at which universal recognition is achieved. Recognition is always already achieved, so far as it goes at any given moment.

Mead allows for a distinction between the individual and social aspects of identity, not by thinking in terms of separate identities, one individual and one social, from which one may choose, but rather by positing a non-identity that keeps the intersubjective process of identity formation moving. More recently, a related theoretical effort has included conceptualizing the social and individual dimensions of identity through the interplay between particular life scripts and the ways in which these scripts are narrated or authored by the individual. In the image of the script, one can see a similarity to my understanding of Mead's generalized other as a map that allows us to determine our way, although a script seems to leave much less room than a map, which does not even prescribe where one is headed. I want to present one example of the script theory of identity to again underline how the self's social character can be understood as something other than a straitjacket.

Identity of Scripts and Stories

In his reply to Charles Taylor's essay "The Politics of Recognition," and more recently in his 2005 study *The Ethics of Identity*, Kwame Anthony Appiah has suggested that both the social and personal dimensions of identity are necessary for the formation of the self. He argues that an identity requires a story or narrative. Social identities provide the conventions and scripts for that narrative:

> One thing that matters to people across many different societies is a certain narrative unity, the ability to tell a story of one's life that hangs together. . . . It is not just that, say, gender identities give shape to one's life; it is also that ethnic and national identities fit a personal narrative into a larger narrative. For modern people, the narrative form entails seeing one's life as having a certain arc, as making sense through a life story that expresses who one is through one's own project of self-making. That narrative arc is yet another way in which an individual's life depends deeply on something socially created and transmitted. (Appiah, *Ethics of Identity*, 23)

Appiah fully subscribes to the view held by many across various positions in the debate on identity: identities are the result of dialogical and socially embedded processes. Like Taylor, he also assumes that the lack of respect paid to one's ascribed social identity can harm the individual, and that it can make sense to invest this very painful identity with self-affirmation in order to overcome that injury. Like many New Americanists, and like deconstructive pluralists more broadly, he warns of getting too attached to these newly valorized identities and turning them into a new tyranny. Whether used by the oppressor or by the proponent of a radical politics of recognition, identities do pose a threat of limitation. Appiah refers to this problem as the Medusa Syndrome:

> We know that acts of recognition, and the civil apparatus of such recognition, can sometimes ossify the identities that are their object. Because here a gaze can turn to stone, we can call this the Medusa Syndrome. The politics of recognition, if pursued with excessive zeal, can seem to require that one's skin color, one's sexual body, should be politically acknowledged in ways that make it hard for those who want to treat their skin and their sexual body as personal dimensions of the self. And personal, here, does not mean secret or (*per impossible*) wholly unscripted or innocent of social meanings; it means, rather, something that is not too tightly scripted, not too resistant to our individual vagaries. (Appiah, *Ethics of Identity*, 110)

I said that his notion of the Medusa Syndrome—or as he has stated elsewhere, the fact that "in the realm of identity there is no bright line between recognition and imposition" (Appiah, *Ethics of Identity*, 110)—brings his position close to that of the New Americanists, who fear recognition, as I argue, precisely because they understand it mainly as imposition. I take the fear of the Medusa Syndrome to be the main reason why the norms that underlie New Americanist criticism are ultimately liberal. But while this surprising commonality between the New Americanist position and Appiah's view is noteworthy, the difference between them is even more interesting.

I see this difference as located in the assumed danger of the Medusa Syndrome. New Americanists reject the imposition of identity because it is through constructions of identity that disciplinary power works. That is why the only real counterstrategy against identity is continuous disidentification, and the means of doing this is face-to-face contestation. Appiah, on the other hand, fears the Medusa Syndrome because it limits the space for the individual's personal identity. This personal identity is located in the space between the script and the possible stories that can be made of it. Appiah's concept of identity thus comprises both a notion of Meadian role-taking—the script is related to a generalized other—and room for individual maneuvering inside the script. He goes as far as calling this capacity for maneuvering autonomy. In other words, while his theory of recognition sees the possible threat of reification, recognition is not necessarily a reifying imposition. Inside recognition, as it were, the self becomes an author who writes one's "own" life story, following the conventions of scripts, but not blindly following conformist norms.

Now, why do theories like Mead's and Appiah's matter for an analysis of New Americanist criticism? Because, as I have shown in this chapter, the way in which New Americanists have shaped their critical agenda is fundamentally organized in accordance with their beliefs that (1) identity, via interpellation, is an imposition; (2) the marginalization of identity is harmful to individuals and cultures; and (3) after initially being affirmed to get back a sense of validity, fixed identities must be avoided. Because these three steps seem to have been written in stone, much New Americanist criticism is mainly interested in whether an author complies with this program or not. And even in the case of critics not directly affiliated with the New Americanists, the core of these assumptions is still maintained: their predominant interest is in the question of how a certain author uses a certain discourse to foster or undermine hierarchies and identities.

I see two problems here. First, too often the unspoken motivation for making the construction of identities the chief concern lies in the conviction that identities must be overcome or undone because the very fact of the construction of identities, qua imposition, contains the seeds of injustice. But besides the fact that the literary construction of identity becomes implicitly equated with an unjust imposition, New Americanist identity theory leads to a second problem. Because recognition is not seen as a reciprocal process but rather as a unilateral imposition, New Americanists do not have adequate tools to conceptualize how identities in texts are actually constructed. (The word "construction" itself, from an intersubjectivist position, is already misleading.) This problem has two levels. One level concerns the thematic, the other the effect of literature on its readers. On the first level, New Americanists are in danger of underestimating the intricacies in the texts' struggles with recognition. As I will show in the next chapter, this applies in exemplary fashion to their readings of Emerson. I will focus on Emerson's theory of friendship to show that what several critics understand as a thinly veiled ideology of hierarchization is actually better described as a struggle for recognition. In my story, Emerson comes to suffer from a felt lack of recognition on the interpersonal level, and he tries out different methods of alleviating this lack. What he thereby comes to question is the possibility of feeling fully recognized. Thus, in Emerson's concept of recognition, gaining recognition means giving up hope of its direct achievement and looking instead for a less pleasing but ultimately more rewarding kind of recognition in friendship. Of course, Emerson's friendship theory itself is not the answer to the problem of recognition and identity. He has, for instance, little patience for considering how individual and social identities might work together. But unless one allows for the possibility of a more reciprocal and intersubjective process of identity formation than the theory of imposition suggests, his venture into the dynamics of identity and recognition remains opaque.

On the level of the aesthetic effect of literature, New Americanists face the problem of having rejected most effective tools of analysis as a consequence of their suspicions of the ideological import of the aesthetic as universalizing, dehistoricizing, and depoliticizing. Aesthetics has thus increasingly turned into a blind spot, often been fully subsumed into ideology, or, when evoked as a means of resistance, often been described simply as "powerful." As I discussed in chapter 1, aesthetic representation is thereby assumed to work along the lines of interpellation. Once this view is rejected, however, a more promising avenue opens up. Aesthetic reception can be described, in Winfried Fluck's terms, as a process of imaginary transfer between the reader and the text,[42] and this transfer itself shares many elements of an intersubjectively conceptualized process of recognition. In the next chapter I will describe how Emerson, in his essay titled "Friendship," develops a reception aesthetics that short-circuits the theme of interpersonal recognition between friends with a reading experience in which the reader faces a constant push and pull from the text—an oscillation between the promise and withholding of recognition. In the end, the processes of reading and the problem of interpersonal recognition remain different due to the relatively greater control the reader has over the text. But this difference between interpersonal and textual recognition only makes it more apparent that accounts of identity construction through literary texts must move beyond the binary of imposition and disidentification.

[4]

IDENTITY AND THE PARSIMONIOUS RECOGNITION
OF "FRIENDSHIP"

Identity, Recognition, and Approbation

"WE HAVE A GREAT DEAL more kindness than is ever spoken," Emerson assures his readers at the very beginning of his essay "Friendship" (*CW*, vol. 2,
113). How that which exceeds what is spoken relates to what can be expressed was the central question I asked about Emerson's theory of representation in chapter 2. I argued that, although what is received in the moment of reception (for Emerson, the social and spiritual elements of reception
cannot be neatly differentiated) cannot be directly expressed in language, it
nevertheless belongs to expression as one of its constituent parts. Expression
differs from reception and yet is of it. This disjunction between reception and
expression gives Emerson's theory of representation both its edge and its
ambivalence: it saves the speaker from becoming programmed by ideology,
but it also disables the speaker's ability to exert full control in undermining
or subverting it. Emerson envisions a high level of linguistic agency, which
is nevertheless incapable of being employed for the purposes of resistance.
Emersonian representation, in other words, is the result of a subjective dynamic between visions of potentiality and their limiting materialization,
which cannot take place outside of sociality but which cannot be limited to
the mechanics of social and cultural force. Thus, in Emerson's thought the
internal disjunction within representation (expression differing from reception, yet being of it) displaces the bipolar constellation of representational
domination and resistance.

What I could only cursorily touch upon in chapter 2—the question of
sociality, of the interpersonal—is what Emerson addresses by stating that
not only do visions of representation exceed expression, but so do feelings of
kindness toward others, toward ourselves, and toward that which exceeds
all of us. Emerson's thought on friendship displays a tension between potentiality and actuality that is similar to his texts on representation, and at
some points friendship and representation directly touch. Thus, early on in

"Friendship," from 1841, it is the friend, our thinking about her,[1] that allows us to represent: "The scholar sits down to write, and all his years of meditation do not furnish him with one good thought or happy expression; but it is necessary to write a letter to a friend,—and forthwith, troops of gentle thoughts invest themselves, on every hand, with chosen words" (CW, vol. 2, 113). Thus, when we write to a friend it is as if our thoughts emancipated themselves, not exactly to create their own expression, but to find those words that are right—chosen—for them. How does the friend achieve this? Or is it us? Or (our) thoughts?

It is striking that these questions give friendship a utilitarian hue. Emerson is often said to idealize friendship. In many ways this is true, but in one sense it is not: he does not consider friendship an end in itself, as, for instance, Aristotle does when in the *Nicomachean Ethics* he distinguishes the highest form of friendship—in which people "wish goods to each other for each other's own sake"[2]—from those lower forms of friendship in which people love each other for utility or pleasure. To Emerson, friendship must be of use, for us, for our achieving self-reliance. Friendship, in other words, is a relationship from which we want to extract identity. Friendship is a relationship from which we seek recognition.

Identity and *recognition*—these are key terms for today's politicized literary criticism, as discussed in the previous chapter. I use these terms for a moment without qualification to make two points: First, they are indeed helpful lenses for reading Emerson. But, second, it is necessary to rethink them, to dislodge them from today's usage, in order to capture the problem Emerson is most concerned with. Emerson, I will argue in this chapter, uses friendship as a model for the formation of identity. The dynamics that structure Emerson's model of friendship can be accurately described as a process of individual recognition. Yet by reading friendship as recognition, it becomes apparent that recognition is subject to the same frustrations that befall Emerson's concept of friendship. For Emerson, the friend oscillates between proximity and distance, between holding out fascination and boredom. Thus, on the one hand, "A new person is to me a great event, and hinders me from sleep" (CW, vol. 2, 115). On the other hand, "as soon as the stranger begins to intrude his partialities, his definitions, his defects, into the conversation, it is all over" (CW, vol. 2, 114). Recognition in like manner wavers between moments of euphoric success and painful withholding of growth. As I will show, Emerson reacts in different ways to this drama of recognition. At times he revels in the lack of recognition, dubbing it, in a pseudocompensatory gesture, self-reliance. In extreme moments, this mood leads him to the verge of masochism. At other times he aims to control the vagaries of recognition by lowering the expectations of friendship, by leveling out the peak moments of euphoria and the low points of rejection. His device for achieving this—transforming the scarcity of recognition into a self-controlled parsimony—is a revised understanding of linear time that comes to fruition in the context of patience.

Emerson develops an ethics of patience, which he associates with the "law of friendship." This law of friendship valorizes the immanence of being patient over the future-directed reward of patience. Whenever Emerson speaks of laws, it is usually a reliable warning sign that he is indulging in an idealist moment. But the law of friendship, I argue, is more precisely understood as an instance in which his idealism becomes fractured. Rather than providing entry to the higher self located in the domain of reason, the law of friendship insists on the potential destructiveness of such idealist striving. Heeding the law of friendship holds out the promise of coming to terms with the inaccessibility of the ideal, despite the fact that the ideal's appeal can never be vanquished entirely.

As I will show in the concluding section of this chapter, Emerson structures the reception aesthetics of his essay "Friendship" around this revised concept of recognition and his ethics of patience, suggesting that the model of parsimonious recognition is itself derived from the reading experience of literature. This also marks the limit of Emerson's original analysis of the challenges to successful recognition: while both reading and interpersonal relationships can be described as interactive experiences, they nevertheless differ too much to model the solution to the interpersonal problem of recognition after the experience of reading. Moreover, theorizing an ethics of patience in order to grasp the scarcity of recognition conflicts with the demands Emerson puts on the literary. Emerson's reception aesthetics ends up rubbing against the ethics of patience by creating a drama that thrives on a continuously renewed hope for recognition. In the end, the tension between the law of friendship and Emerson's literary performance cannot be smoothed out.

Emerson's joining of personal relations and reading must be understood from the perspective of his professional engagement. For when Emerson considers the reader of his essays, this reader is also a listener. The essay "Friendship," like so many others, is the result of a series of literary exercises in the form of lectures, and, prior to that, sermons. (I will delineate this evolution later on.) Emerson's reception aesthetics is thus immediately linked with his professional situatedness in the emerging institution of the public lecture as I have sketched it out in chapter 2. Indeed, Emerson tends to equate relationships of friendship with the public speaker's relationship to the audience. Throughout his journals, these topics are treated contiguously and often even interchangeably. Thus, Emerson's thought on friendship has ramifications for his reception aesthetics because friendship is the principal mode in which Emerson addresses the problem of recognition as it concerns him in the emerging modern public.

In order to read Emerson's thought on friendship in this manner, it is necessary to move beyond the assumptions regarding identity and recognition that underlie the influential criticism of the New Americanists and their new establishment offspring. As I argued in chapter 3, the New Americanists tend to conceptualize recognition as a violent imposition rather than as an intersubjective process. The normative ideal of these critics thus demands that literature undo identities and bypass recognition or loosen up its reifying effects, in order to promote a radically egalitarian world free of unjust ascriptions. Emerson, from their perspective, usually fails to live up to these normative ideals because of his putative racism, sexism, capitalism, and imperialism. To be sure, Emerson, even during his political activism beginning in 1844, is not free of these ideological limitations. Yet he does something that runs counter to the organizational pattern of New Americanist thought. While they assume that recognition indeed can impose identities on subjects, they rarely inquire about the actual process through which these imprisoning effects of recognition come about. Because they are fearful of recognition, they tend to take the possibility of "successful" recognition for granted: for identities to be violent, they must have the power to really fix the individual. But seen from my perspective, Emerson puts into question the very possibility of being recognized. His writings gesture not toward the violence of recognition, but toward the violence of its lack.

Recognition and Approbation:
Two Paths to Individual Growth

To make this argument, I need to point out that recognition and identity for Emerson have meanings quite different from those that are common today. *Identity* is not used by Emerson in the sense of individual self-definition; rather, Emersonian identity has a strong platonic ring and describes that which connects the individual with everything else—that which makes us identical with everyone and everything else. Thus, his understanding of identity seems to denote almost the opposite of what we mean today by identity (which I take to be, roughly, the unique coming together of various social identity components in one person, and their being taken up by that person). But of course, even this contrast is a tricky one, considering that Emerson, unwilling to tie himself to the language of the bounded self, would claim that what exceeds our individuality is precisely what the fullest individual self-definition should encompass. In the fourth lecture of his series called "Natural Method of Mental Philosophy," given in 1858, he writes,

"All difference is quantitative: quality one. However we may conceive of the wonderful little bricks of which the world is builded, we must suppose similarity, and fitting, in their make" (*LL*, vol. 2, 89).[3] Identity, for Emerson, is just this: the sameness in quality despite all difference in quantity. The term *recognition* is closely related to this transindividual field of identity:

> Wonderful pranks this identity plays with us. It is because of this, that nothing comes quite strange to us: As we knew our friends, before we were introduced to them, and, at first sight distinguished them as ours; so to know, is to re-know, or to recognize. We hail each discovery of science as the most natural thing in the world. (*LL*, vol. 2, 89)

Recognition, or re-knowing, touches on memory, on that which we have not exactly forgotten, but which has become unavailable to us, and which now is being re-presented. It requires our receptivity, which is enabled by the other, and which results, ideally, in discoveries coming to us. It is telling that Emerson uses the example of friends in this passage: in the interpersonal dimension, filled with affect and affection, we gain access to that which is ours but which also transcends both ours and our friends'. This kind of recognition is a rather standard moment in Emerson's thought. We find a more famous formulation of it in "Self-Reliance": "In every work of genius we *recognize* our own rejected thoughts: they come back to us with a certain alienated majesty" (*CW*, vol. 2, 27, my emphasis). Or, similarly, from a 1831 journal entry: "In the wisdom or fancy (which is oft wisdom) of Bacon & Shakspear we do not admire an arbitrary, alien creation, but we have surprize at finding ourselves, at recognizing our own truth in that wild unacquainted field" (*JMN*, vol. 3, 240).

To provide a fuller view of the dynamic of identity and recognition, we need to be aware of another Emersonian term that is very similar to recognition and likewise often linked to friends and society. This term is *approbation*, and a good example to show the contrast with *recognition* is found in "Circles":

> We thirst for approbation, yet cannot forgive the approver. The sweet of nature is love; yet, if I have a friend, I am tormented by my imperfections. The love of me accuses the other party. If he were high enough to slight me, then could I love him, and rise by my affection to new heights. A man's growth is seen in the successive choirs of his friends. For every friend whom he loses for truth, he gains a better. (*CW*, vol. 2, 182)

While recognition seems to be a function of our own cognition, albeit activated by the presence of the friend, approbation is more like a gift: something given to us by another. (It is not accidental that in Emerson's essay

"Gifts" we find a parallel sentence: "We do not quite forgive a giver," *CW*, vol. 3, 94.) Because we do not have an equal share in the act of being approved, Emerson is much less comfortable with approbation than with recognition. Approbation tends to limit us and to bring to a halt our growth, unless the friend is our superior and approves of us by slighting us. If this is the case, friends risk ceasing to be friends as soon as we have reached their height. Hence the merciless succession of friends, which is really a devouring: in order to quench our thirst for approbation, we must suck our friends' lifeblood. (We will see in this chapter's final pages that, in the essay "Friendship," "sucking" is something of a key Emersonian image for this problematic of *using up* our friend.)[4]

Despite this difference in regard to activity and passivity, recognition and approbation describe processes that share the goal of the individual's growth. For Emerson, the process of growth itself is part of the individual's identity. In other words, he conceptualizes what we think of as identity as the tension between a moment of fixity and transformation, or, self-possession and growth. As in the Hegelian tradition of recognition theories, he sees identity as dependent on recognition, except that for him recognition must be a relation that enables transformation, whereas for Hegel the process of recognition must strive toward the absolute, at which point full recognition is achieved and identity comes to rest. This is also the difference between Emerson's concepts of identity and recognition and those of today: when critics and activists demand recognition of an identity—or, in the case of the New Americanists, demand and fear it—they assume that recognized identity is a stable entity, whereas for Emerson recognition has to enable and affirm the transformation of that identity.

Emerson's emphasis on continuous transformation puts a heavy burden on friendship. As the above passage implies, we grow with another's help, which can only avoid the rapid casting away of our friends if the process is reciprocal and friends are equal. While I can profit from a friend who is superior to me, this friend cannot profit from me. Lasting friendship thus requires mutual profit, that is, equality. But can this be practiced? Both friends would need to grow along parallel lines. But because growth for Emerson is directed toward the impersonal, this kind of friendship would move into a sphere where friends become so celestial that they do not any longer touch as sensuous human beings. The problem is, of course, that even if one finds an ideal friend, it is impossible to leave behind one's needs as a sensuous and bodily being. Emerson often insists on the central element of affection in friendship, but by the same token he seems to deny affection its place.[5]

It is this parallel upward movement that has led critics to characterize Emerson's theory of friendship as idealistic and impossible to put into practice.

Both Emerson and his circle of friends were aware that this aspect of his philosophy put an impossibly high demand on friendship. But then again, the ideal is no more than an ideal; it differs from actual friendships and yet has a function for those actual friendships: it keeps them moving, striving for more. In Emerson's life experience, he did not implement the merciless disposal of friends that his theory seems to prescribe in the face of the near impossibility of growing reciprocally toward the impersonal. As Lawrence Buell has recently pointed out, Emerson's friendships tended to last for decades. The friendship of Emerson and Thoreau, to take the most prominent example, may have been marked by ebb and flow. Both men may have become increasingly distant from each other; yet to the very end, both also acknowledged their continuing mutual appeal.[6] The point I will be driving at throughout this chapter extends this important corrective: not only did Emerson's life experience differ from his theory but the theory itself is much more complex than the passage quoted above suggests. Friendship in Emerson's thought is not simply caught between striving for an impossible ideal and disposing of imperfect friends. If Kuisma Korhonen is correct in stating that "[t]he history of essayistic reflection on friendship is the history of weighting the ideal of friendship and balancing it with the praxis of human relationships,"[7] then Emerson radicalizes this tradition, both in his essay "Friendship" and, to a lesser degree, in the various sermons, lectures, letters, and journal passages that paved the way for that essay, by attempting to incorporate the act of balancing into the weighting of the ideal, without ever fully letting go of the ideal. This is what I mean when I call Emerson's idealism fractured.

The complication begins with the fact that we are dependent on recognition; we are much too dependent to carelessly throw away our friends whenever we feel that we cannot gain any more from them. To speak of our "thirst for approbation" may be another way of expressing what contemporary recognition theorists like Charles Taylor and Axel Honneth now take for granted: as social beings, we have an anthropologically grounded need for recognition. The entire project of self-reliance may be regarded as growing out of the problem of the need for recognition. Thirsting for approbation, we feel that the approbation that society grants us is insufficient: "Every man supposes himself not to be fully understood or appreciated," Emerson writes in his journal in May 1840 (*JMN*, vol. 7, 347). Something always exceeds recognition: "[T]here is always a residuum unknown, unanalysable" (*JMN*, vol. 7, 347). What is more, society always misrecognizes true greatness. As he writes in a sermon in 1832, "[The genuine man should] raise up a great counterbalance to the engrossing riches of popularity & make him feel that all these ought to be his servants & not masters" (*CS*, vol. 4, 412).

In this state of perpetual misrecognition, we are forced to look for alternative sources of recognition. But while Emerson often strives to convey the impression that this alternative source will be found on the inside, his imagery tends to concede that even this inwardness cannot be severed from a social dynamic, as in the lecture "Private Life," from January 1840: "Time receives into its faithful bosom the true and just deed . . . and *choirs of witnesses* shall certify the Eternal approbation" (*EL*, vol. 3, 352, my emphasis).

Recognition in the Jacksonian Era

The urgency that this question takes on in Emerson's thought suggests that he is responding not only to an anthropological need but also to the historical exigencies of the Jacksonian period, in which it became more and more apparent that the nominal equality of democracy put an enormous demand on the individual to secure his—and increasingly, her—recognition. Here Emerson clearly speaks as a contemporary of Tocqueville, whose second volume of *Democracy in America*, from 1840, is organized around the observation that equality burdens the individual with demonstrating distinctiveness.[8] I have already noted that the problem of recognition has direct ramifications for Emerson's career as a public lecturer who has to create and secure an audience. But he reflects on recognition from a more encompassing perspective as well. In a journal entry from April 13, 1841, he considers how the problem is woven into the fabric of a modern, democratic society:

> In the unwelcome great snowstorm of this day I must blot a line to acknowledge the value of those social tests to which we all are brought in turn to be approved or damned. Precisely as the chemist submits the new substance to the action of oxygen, hydrogen, electricity, vegetable blue, &c. each soul in our little Massachusetts coterie is passed through the ordinary series of social reagents, the market, the church, the parlour, the literary circle, writing, speaking, the ball, the reforms, &c to ascertain his distinctive powers. Those tests which call out our latent powers & give us leave to shine, we love & applaud; those which detect our deficiencies we hate & malign. The poet who is paralysed in the company of the young & beautiful, where he would so gladly shine, revenges himself by satire and taxing that with emptiness & display. It is but fair that they for whose friendship we are candidates, and they who are candidates for ours,—and such are all men & all women,—should have the opportunity of putting & of being put into all the crucibles. (*JMN*, vol. 7, 426–27)

Emerson begins by acknowledging the very mechanism of what we would now refer to as social recognition: "I must blot a line to acknowledge those social tests." By way of this metarecognition, he can zoom in on the various institutions and practices of recognition. How far the logic of recognition and social contest has, in Emerson's opinion, infiltrated American life becomes clear from his remarkable list. While one may have expected the appearance of such highlights of conspicuousness as the market and the ball, Emerson deliberately includes those areas that might be deemed too spiritual (the church) or too genteel (the literary circle) to be part of the logic of the social mechanisms of testing and condemning; and his inclusion of "the reforms" can be said to show how a politics that tends to oppose these mechanisms is itself structured by them. At least as surprising is his abrupt connection of these scenes with democratic friendship. All men and all women are candidates of our friendship, and because of this inclusiveness, we must pass the test in a plurality of social fields. The reverse is also true: in a democratic society, we must at least believe in the possibility of engaging in any social field, which means that anyone may be a candidate to become our friend. This is not to be misunderstood as liberal blindness to hierarchies and de facto boundaries. Emerson does not state that all candidates are equally likely to pass the test. The point is rather that the nominal equality of democracy multiplies the scenes of recognition in which we become involuntarily involved.

Emerson here distinguishes between approbation as what we call recognition, and damnation as what is now called misrecognition. This raises the question, what exactly does misrecognition mean for Emerson? Generally, today's recognition theorists distinguish between two kinds of misrecognition. On the one hand, we feel misrecognized when we receive negative feedback. Here we are confronted with a negative image of our self, which we are in danger of integrating into our attitude toward our self. The second form of misrecognition can be called nonrecognition, and it is typically described as invisibility. Here we do not even feel acknowledged, which seemingly constitutes an even more fundamental case of misrecognition.[9] Considering Emerson's transformation-centered idea of recognition, we have to come up with yet another definition of misrecognition: according to his logic, we feel misrecognized whenever we feel that a social relationship by which we have grown has collapsed. In the journal passage above, what is so painful about tests "which detect our deficiencies" is that they do not "call out our latent powers." Emersonian misrecognition, then, does not exist primarily in an internalized, demeaning image or in the feeling of being an invisible nobody, but in stagnation. Yet Emerson's brand of misrecognition does not exist independently of invisibility and condemnation. Both of these standard forms of misrecognition can lead to stagnation. This is noteworthy: for condemnation to turn into stagnation, Emerson would have to diverge from his own

understanding of self-reliance. After all, in "Self-Reliance" he famously describes self-reliance as the "aversion" to conformity, and thus as a movement of growth that relies precisely on condemnation—a condemnation of
the self by society, and along with that, a condemnation of society and the
conforming self by the self.

The Masochism of the Double Standard

I will argue in this section that Emerson indeed tends to react to condemnation in ways that directly contradict a model of self-reliance that gains its
impetus from condemnation. Although this argument presents an Emerson
who is virtually absent from the critical literature, one of his reactions to
misrecognition as condemnation leads to an embrace of stagnation as his
own unalterable failure. In these instances, he comes to explicitly rule out self-
reliance as a remedy for misrecognition, exposing it as no more than a psychological defense mechanism that cannot reactivate the growth of the self.

To bring this Emerson to light requires a bit of biographical criticism,
which can reveal another layer of the above journal passage. When looking
at the list, "the market, the church, the parlour, the literary circle, writing,
speaking, the ball, the reforms," it becomes apparent that Emerson is describing his own social circles. Moreover, when he speaks of friendship here,
he in all likelihood refers to his own friends. For instance, "the ball" most
likely refers to his socialite friends Anna Barker and Samuel Gray Ward,
both of whom Emerson met through Margaret Fuller. As Caleb Crain has
shown in the greatest detail, Emerson was smitten not only with Barker but
also with Ward. It is highly likely that Barker and Ward provide not only the
journal entry's reference to "the ball," but also the reference in the sentence,
"The poet who is paralysed in the company of the young & beautiful, where
he would so gladly shine, revenges himself by satire and taxing that with
emptiness & display."

In the fall of 1839, it became common knowledge among Emerson's
friends that Ward was courting Barker, and initially it was Margaret Fuller
who could not conceal her disappointment.[10] In the ensuing months, Ward
and Barker tightened their emotional bonds, but in the spring of 1840
Barker rejected Ward's proposal. Ward had told her that, while he had a
career in finance awaiting him, he preferred to lead the life of a scholar, and
Barker had just been informed by her father that she could not expect any
family fortune and needed to look for a husband with a steady job.[11] Finally, in August 1840, Barker told Emerson that she and Ward had just
become engaged after all. Emerson's reaction to the news comes close to his

characterization in the journal passage from April 1841. In a letter to Caroline Sturgis, another friend he met through Fuller, he made little effort to see the marriage as the kind of idealized union he advocated and instead came close to taxing it "with emptiness & display":

> The news which Anna told me at Cambridge affected me at first with a certain terror. I thought that the whole spirit of our intercourse at Concord implied another resolution. I thought she had looked the world through for a man as universal as herself & finding none, had said, "I will compensate myself for my great renunciation as a woman by establishing ideal relations: Not only Raphael [Ward's nickname] shall be my brother, but the Puritan at Concord who is reputed at some time to have seen the mighty Gods, I will elect him also." . . . Of course it seemed when I heard the new fact as if she had yielded something to be "earthlier happy." But no; . . . She does not feel any fall. There is no compunction on either of their brows. She told me her story . . . with such womanly, referring ways, referring to the youth . . . that I cannot mistrust them. And yet, dear sister, happiness is so vulgar. (*L*, vol. 7, 404)

Emerson here sounds like a rejected suitor, defeated by his rival, clothing his disappointment in platonic rhetoric. But what is surprising in the phrase "I will elect him also" is not so much the "also"—that is, the rivalry—but rather his wanting to be "elected" by her at all. Emerson self-consciously, if somewhat self-ironically, pits himself as the Puritan against the "earthliness" of the youth, as if the youthful Ward had not himself aspired to Emerson's loftiness. In other words, Emerson chooses to interpret the marriage of Barker and Ward as the introduction of an unbridgeable difference between himself and the world. But the whole point of his fantasy of Anna Barker's reflection, as he relates it to Sturgis, is that Barker's renunciation of the ideal friendship with Emerson in favor of the romantic relationship with Ward is Emerson's loss. In light of this condemnation, the possibility of solitary self-reliance that it opens up is clearly not a consoling prospect. Yet it remains the only prospect of "the Puritan at Concord."

Because of the delay between August (the moment he finds out about the engagement of Barker and Ward) and April of the following year (the date of the journal entry on the social tests), one may doubt whether the journal entry on the social tests actually refers to Ward and Barker.[12] Indeed, it is possible, if less likely, that it refers to Sturgis, who was sixteen years younger than Emerson and became close to him just as the friendship with Barker and Ward lost momentum. Like his friendships with Barker and Ward, Emerson's relationship with Sturgis seems to have remained platonic, yet it was erotically charged. (Robert D. Richardson has pointed out that Emerson and Sturgis modeled their friendship after Goethe and Bettina von Arnim's as it was portrayed in *Goethe's Correspondence with a Child*.)[13] But despite the erotic overtones, the dynamic between Emerson and Sturgis seems more to have resembled that between Emerson and Fuller than that between Emerson and the engaged couple. That is, Emerson usually kept Sturgis at bay, rather than feeling rejected by her or excluded from youth. Emerson sometimes did this rather cruelly, as in a letter from March 15, 1841, in which he wrote, "It is always a pleasure to see you. . . . But who is fit for friendship? Not one" (*L*, vol. 7, 447). Even with Sturgis, however, Emerson would from time to time reflect critically on his own stance of enforcing the distance necessary for self-reliance. For instance, during the previous August, about the time Emerson found out about Ward's and Barker's engagement, Fuller reproached him on Sturgis's behalf for displaying "inhospitality of soul" (*JMN*, vol. 7, 509).

At first, in his journal reflections on Fuller's accusation, Emerson seems to take comfort in the ugly necessities of a self-reliant existence in a higher sphere: "Unless that which I do to build up my self, endears me to them, our covenant would be injurious" (*JMN*, vol. 7, 510). This is a resolution that foreseeably leads him to conclude that his friends do not fulfill his requirements: "But this survey of my experience taught me anew that no friend I have surprises, none exalts me" (*JMN*, vol. 7, 510). Yet in a letter to Sturgis, written, like the journal entry, shortly after Fuller's reprimand, he pleads:

> But that which set me on this writing was the talk with Margaret F last Friday who taxed me both on your parts with a certain inhospitality of soul. . . . I confess to the fact of cold & imperfect intercourse but not to the impeachment of will. and not to the deficiency of my affection. I count & weigh, I love also. I cannot tell you how warm & glad the naming of your names makes my solitude. You give me more joy than I could trust your tongue to tell you. (*L*, vol. 2, 325)

The dynamic here is different from that of his reaction to the engagement of Ward and Barker. There, Emerson feels rejected and withdraws into the idealization of friendships to compensate. Here he is criticized for being unapproachable, and his reaction consists of a mixture of seeking the same compensation in idealization, and making an effort to see and break through this defense mechanism.

Both of his reactions—to the felt rejection inherent in the engagement of Ward and Barker, and to the criticism from Fuller and Sturgis—show Emerson reconsidering the idealization of friendship: it is no longer unequivocally desirable as a sign of reaching the higher, spiritual spheres of being. Emerson also comes to see the idealization of friendship as a problematic psychological reflex triggered by the unsatisfactory result of the social test of approbation. This reflex has ramifications not only for him but also for those he taxes with superficiality, as Fuller's censure seems to reveal to him.

With this biographical background in mind, the social tests of the journal entry from April 13, 1841, draw a different picture of approbation from that in the passage from "Circles" quoted earlier. In that essay, approbation becomes a problem insofar as it limits us. It is the praise of our friend that becomes our anguish: "yet, if I have a friend, I am tormented by my imperfections." By contrast, in the journal entry, the appraisal of friends is loved and applauded because it "call[s] out our latent powers." There is no trace of an ambiguity of praise to be found here. It is rather condemnation, the pointing out of our deficiencies, that paralyzes us. In "Circles," on the other hand, this condemnation is precisely what Emerson hopes for in order to "rise . . . to new heights."

Stagnation versus Cavellian Perfectionism

Only now does the scope of the thought event in the journal passage become clearer. Emerson's acceptance of the authority of "social tests" calls into question those interpretations of Emerson's texts that concentrate on the process of upward reciprocity. Consider Stanley Cavell's compelling interpretation of what he calls "Emersonian moral perfectionism," which has been extremely and justifiably influential in recent Emerson studies, and which could be said to derive from the logic of our passage in "Circles." Simply put, Emerson's thinking, according to Cavell, is above all concerned with finding the next self. This next self is never the achievement of perfection, yet perfectionism is the term that best describes an ethic that, because it is not substantiated, keeps the individual striving for the unattainable. This ethic involves acknowledging our relationship to the other, to the friend, who can help us attain the next self to the degree that the friend represents our unattained self. In other words, Cavell is interested in the moment of transition from one self to the next.[14] This transition requires turning away from society and also turning away from the attained self, back to society. This explains the prominence of "shame" in Emerson's thought: our shame about our present self indicates that we are on the verge of achieving the next self. Shame and joy are part of the same circular movement. The same goes for the ambivalence we feel for the friend. When our friend unsettles the self that we have come to embrace, we perceive the friend as an enemy. When we realize, in the next moment, that the friend is the representative who mobilizes our latent powers, we love the friend. The following quotation summarizes Cavell's argument:

Shame manifests the cost as well as the opportunity in each of us as the representative of each. It is why shame, in Emerson's discourse—his contradiction of joy—is the natural or inevitable enemy of the attainable self, the treasure of perfectionism for democracy.

. . . Emerson's turn is to make my partiality itself the sign and incentive of siding with the next or further self, which means siding against my attained perfection (or conformity), sidings which require the recognition of an other— the acknowledgment of a relationship—in which this sign is manifest.[15]

There is no doubt that Cavell's model captures an important facet of Emerson's thinking, specifically concerning the dimension of recognition and acknowledgment. What is difficult to explain from a Cavellian standpoint, however, is the instance of shame and self-loathing in the journal passage: "[T]hose [tests] which detect our deficiencies we hate & malign. The poet who is paralysed in the company of the young & beautiful, where he would so gladly shine, revenges himself by satire and taxing that with emptiness & display." According to Cavell's model, our hatred of our deficiencies may be painful, but it is necessary to help us reveal our latent powers. Here, however, Emerson describes a kind of shame so paralyzing that the only available reaction is spiteful satire rather than a turn to the next self. This is an important point to remember, even if Emerson attempts to reaffirm—unsuccessfully, as I will show—the perfectionist turn in the remainder of the journal entry, as follows:

But when we have been tried & found wanting in any one, the wise heart will cherish that mortification until the flower grows out of the noisome pit. It will learn that not by seeking to do as others do that thing for which it was shown that we had no faculty, but by pious waiting from month to month from year to year & ever new effort after greater selftruth, will the new way at last appear by which we are to do the correspondent act in our circle. (*JMN*, vol. 7, 427)

This is Emerson spinning in circles at maximum speed. What was just dismissed as revenge and satire—the upholding of higher, more spiritual standards in the face of rejection—is now offered as an answer to this very dismissal. And yet, the circle has become elliptical. Recall the self-reflexivity of the journal entry's first paragraph: "The poet who is paralysed in the company of the young & beautiful, where he would so gladly shine, revenges himself by satire and taxing that with emptiness & display." Emerson here fully disclosed the self-deception of satire and condescension. This very insight now accuses the standard resolution offered in the final paragraph, "the wise heart will cherish that mortification . . . [and] the new way [will] at last appear," of being no more than that part of self-loathing which is directed at the public, the "maligning," which may in fact keep us from finding our next attainable self. It is an accusation that sticks, that cannot be blotted out by a simple reassertion of the superiority of solitude.

We see more clearly now the difference between a Cavellian reading and one that takes to heart the metarecognition of the journal passage: Cavell describes an essentially optimistic process—it is both an ethics and a description of how Emerson analyzes social and spiritual life—in which there is little room for the tragic. To be sure, Cavell has a very keen eye for the frustrations that inhabit Emerson's thought, but they are made to promote democratic understanding, education, and the unfolding of the self. By contrast, the journal passage shows that Emerson also has a darker side, one that does not neatly dissolve into a movement spiraling upward.

The Double Standard in the Sermons

A central facet of this darker strain occurs in Emerson's notion of the distance between friends. Distance plays several roles for him. At times, Emerson addresses distance as a necessary corollary of mutual twoness in which reciprocity involves drawing a line between the involved parties. In these instances, Emerson actually encourages distance. But in his darker moments, he regards distance as a barrier to mutuality.[16] Here distance becomes a sign of Emersonian misrecognition as stagnation. I will briefly trace this strain through early pronouncements of his friendship theory in two sermons and two journal passages. In these texts Emerson discusses the question of distance in friendship in conjunction with the relationship between the actual and the ideal. The essential point here is that Emerson increasingly intertwines the ideal and the actual. As a result of this intertwining, the perfectionist solution of turning failure into an advantage for the attainment of future selves becomes less and less feasible. I call this crippling way of connecting the ideal and the actual Emerson's "double standard."

In Sermon 62, from January 1830, Emerson still sounds like a solid Unitarian who discusses friendship in the context of the true believer's relationship to Jesus. For the most part, this sermon displays an Emerson who still fits the perfectionist paradigm sketched out by Cavell. Emerson interprets Jesus as a representative: loving him will set us on a path toward our own growth. He preaches two Unitarian staples, divine benevolence and the importance of self-culture. The former makes it possible, and the latter necessitates, that we love Jesus, rather than fear him. Thus, if the believer has a "feeling of friendship to Christ," it will make him "more and more like him, and so continually more capable of estimating him." As a result, the virtuous mind "should perceive the power of indefinite expansion to which God had appointed it by making it in his image" (CS, vol. 2, 120). However, toward the end a skeptical note creeps into the sermon and disturbs the perfectionist mood. Emerson admonishes his listeners to entertain the same friendly relationships with one another, which would revolutionize social life: rather than living in a society based on competition and greed, they would "cease to envy and oppose each other," instead "aiding in each other's mutual advancement" (CS, vol. 2, 123). He makes it clear that such a heavenly state is not at all yet present and continues: "Meantime it is in the power of every Christian to promote this great social cause by his own devotion to it." Importantly, the sermon leaves open the question of whether this kind of society based on friendship would ever materialize. Thus this cheerful and optimistic sermon ends on a slightly skeptical note.

This skepticism becomes more pronounced two years later in Sermon 140, in which friendship is again the topic. Here Emerson shifts the focus from friendship with Jesus to the interpersonal level, observing (along the lines of the argument of mutual growth) that "[A] true friend is the ideal object which every human mind seeks and with an earnestness proportioned to its improvement" (CS, vol. 4, 50). But now the word *ideal* has become loaded, implying that the materialization of the ideal might be impossible. He confronts his listeners with two quotations from Michel de Montaigne's essay "Of Friendship," the second one being the famous apostrophe "O my friends, there is no friend."[17] This is the occasion for Emerson to declare his friends mere acquaintances: "And I cannot but think that every one of us must have remarked in his own experience the strange solitude in which every soul lives, in this world, let our acquaintances be as many and as intimate as they may" (CS, vol. 4, 51).

It is at this point that friendship is conceived of as the tension between the ideal and the actual. Emerson places himself in the philosophical position most closely associated with Montaigne, whose recitation of "O my friends, there is no friend" confronts the problem of the discontinuity between ideal and actual friendships. Emerson's divergence from Montaigne lies in his claim that while we may experience real intimacy, this intimacy still does not alter our predicament of living in "strange solitude." It is as if he were saying, "O my friend, there is no friend," eradicating Montaigne's plural, thus leveling out the ideal and actual, and yet maintaining the contradiction. This can be partially explained as a dilemma that Emerson creates himself: he wants friendship to be the realization of the ideal, as well as the path toward the realization. Thus, one reason for the strange loneliness is the individual's and the friend's lack of self-reliance—a friend may be intimate, but as long as he lacks self-reliance, he will not show me the way to my own self-reliance. When Emerson writes, "It is not what is in us, that alone determines what we shall say to our companion, but also what is in him and his capacity to understand us" (CS, vol. 4, 51), it is as if he were saying: our friends, in this world, are sadly wanting in this very capacity.

This is an earlier version of the now familiar point from "Circles" about the insufficiency of our friends, except that Emerson here refrains from recommending disposal of them. Instead, he laments the pain of having to live with distant friends: "Among his friends, man feels unknown" (CS, vol. 4, 51).[18] The dilemma ends in a double standard: intimacy is not a sign of true friendship, yet our experience of solitude *is* a sign of friendship's imperfection.

This double standard confounds the difference between the two worlds. The real and the ideal do not become the same, but they become crossed. In the ideal world solitude is the sign of fulfillment: there we can live with others as we would in solitude, and we can live in solitude as we would with others. There is no doubt that this is also the highest degree of intimacy. In the world of the actual, by contrast, solitude is a sign of unfulfillment, yet there, too, we live in intimacy. If we did not, we could simply curse the paucity of this world and oppose the majesty of otherworldliness to it. But since we do know intimacy, the distinction between the worlds becomes unstable and we have to ask ourselves the question of "Experience": "Where do we find ourselves?" Just as Emerson mourns the shallowness of experience in that essay, he here bemoans the solitude of intimacy. In other words, not only is the actual bleak; the ideal itself is losing its allure.

Climax of the Double Standard: Masochistic Emerson

Over the following years, up to the time of his composition of the essay "Friendship," the intertwining of ideal and actual relationships concerns Emerson intensely, specifically when he thinks about friendship. This becomes apparent from two journal passages written in the winter of 1839–40, during the time in which Emerson lives through his intense feelings for Barker, Ward, and Sturgis and works on his first book of essays (of which "Friendship" became the centerpiece) as well as on his lecture series "The Present Age," presented between December 4, 1839, and February 12, 1840, at the Masonic Temple in Boston. All of these experiences play into the two entries. And all of them are directly tied to his struggle as a freelance lecturer having to capture an audience. Here is the first entry, entitled both "Eloquence" and "Lyceum."

Here is all the true orator will ask, for here is a convertible audience, & here are no stiff conventions that prescribe a method, a style, a limited quotation of books & an exact respect to certain books, persons or opinions. No, here everything is admissible, philosophy, ethics, divinity, criticism, poetry, humor, fun, mimicry, anecdotes, jokes, ventriloquism, all the breadth & versatility of the most liberal conversation; highest, lowest, personal, local topics, all are permitted, & all may be combined in one speech;—it is a panharmonicon,— every note on the longest gamut, from the explosion of cannon, to the tinkle of a guitar. Let us try if Folly, Custom, Convention & Phlegm cannot hear our sharp artillery. Here is a pulpit that makes other pulpits tame & ineffectual with their cold, mechanical preparation for a delivery the most decorous,— fine things, pretty things, wise things, but no arrows, no axes, no nectar, no growling, no transpiercing, no loving, no enchantment. Here he may lay himself out utterly, large, enormous, prodigal, on the subject of the hour. Here he may dare to hope for ecstasy & eloquence. (*JMN*, vol. 7, 265)

Emerson is celebrating here the widest possible scope for eloquence, and his breathless enumeration of the plentitude of the permissible, vis-à-vis "Folly, Custom, Convention & Phlegm," conjures the ecstasy of eloquence that is his subject. As I have already noted, Emerson frequently linked the topics of friendship and oration as instances in which individuals enter a communicative relationship of the highest sort, in which both parties mutually profit from each other. Eloquence, in Emerson's vision, could achieve what friendship was designed to do: it could enrich both sides through entry to a transgressive relationship, in which all the boundaries of conformist societies were left behind. This passage is eye-opening insofar as it sketches the bodily and performative aspects of the exalted, spiritual, and ideal relationship, to which belong in Emerson's mind both friendship and public oratory:[19] there are "no stiff conventions . . . everything is admissible." And not only that: all registers of human expression are combined in one speech. In this way, words become "sharp artillery": fully materialized, they possess the power to destroy the confines of convention.[20] To achieve this, the speech must be "on the subject of the hour," by which Emerson means both that each lecture needs to be organized around one coherent topic (a lecture typically lasted fifty minutes)[21] and that it addresses issues relevant to his listeners in the present moment. This is to ensure that the audience can actually be affected by the flurry of performativity.

Emerson is clearly not discussing the institution of the lyceum abstractly here. Rather, he is laying out how he would like to see himself: as an eloquent orator who transgresses the confines of decorous presentation. In other words, he is naming his goals for the upcoming lecture series at the Masonic

Temple.[22] On February 19, 1840, one week after having finished the lecture course, he takes stock of the series, in economic and spiritual terms. It is only now that we fully understand the degree to which he was addressing himself when he spoke of the "pulpit that makes other pulpits tame & ineffectual with their cold, mechanical preparation for a delivery the most decorous."

> These lectures give me little pleasure. I have not done what I hoped when I said, I will try it once more. I have not once transcended the coldest self-possession. I said I will agitate others, being agitated myself. I dared to hope for extasy [sic] & eloquence. A new theatre, a new art, I said, is mine. Let us see if philosophy, if ethics, if chiromancy, if the discovery of the divine in the house & the barn, in all works & all plays, cannot make the cheek blush, the lip quiver, & the tear start. I will not waste myself. On the strength of Things I will be borne, and try if Folly, Custom, Convention, & Phlegm cannot be made to hear our sharp artillery. Alas! alas! I have not the recollection of one strong moment. A cold mechanical preparation for a delivery as decorous,—fine things, pretty things, wise things,—but no arrows, no axes, no nectar, no growling, no transpiercing, no loving, no enchantment. (*JMN*, vol. 7, 338–39)

Emerson's writing technique commonly embraced quotation and copying: he quoted widely from his reading notes, only sometimes naming the source, and often mixing quotation and paraphrase. In his essays and lectures he frequently recycled passages written in letters and in his journals (that was of course the major function of the journal in the first place). And he developed a whole theory about the mutual dependence of genius and quotation.[23] But what is peculiar about the above passage is that it presents a form of self-quotation that can be called masochistic.

Emerson has fallen short of his ideal performance, and in his own estimation he has reached no one: "I have not transcended the coldest self-possession." The entire passage takes *ad absurdum* the old strategy of cherishing rejection (or miscommunication) while resigning oneself to solitude. By quoting himself, he demonstrates that he can create the ecstasy of eloquence once again by writing in his journal, alone, finding friendship in his own text (self-quotation also becomes a self-doubling). This recreation forces the experience of the ideal onto him in the face of his failure to live the ideal. In his failure, he painfully realizes the ideal, thus disallowing the comforting sigh that, alas, reality and the ideal are disparate. The actual and the ideal become intertwined in the masochism with which he encounters his failure. Emerson's lesson is not that we can turn failure into success. Rather, we can only succeed in failure. What is left is pure disgust. His failure is not only negative (centered on what he has not achieved) but positive: it binds him to that which he hates—the cold, mechanical, and decorous.[24]

By calling Emerson's self-quotation masochistic I want to draw attention to how this moment differs from the shame described by Cavell. If in Cavell's model, shame is a moment that marks the movement from one self to the next, with the next self becoming accessible through an act of transformative recognition of and by the other, Emersonian masochism is an attempt to succeed at self-transformation despite the breakdown of the relationship of recognition. But whereas before Emerson habitually declared such breakdowns valuable for receiving an "eternal approbation," and thus for achieving the higher self without the social other, in this case the only option for achieving self-transformation lies in potential self-destruction.

Slightly modified, what I am describing, then, corresponds to Sigmund Freud's late concept of masochism, developed in his 1924 essay "The Economic Problem in Masochism." There Freud describes masochism as deriving from the death drive. The death drive is eager to disintegrate the organism, "and bring each elemental primary organism into a state of inorganic stability."[25] But insofar as primal masochism is erotogenic, the death drive is libidinally bound up with the organism. Thus, "[masochism's] dangerousness lies in its origin in the death-drive, which correlates to that part of the latter that escaped deflection onto the outer world. But since, on the other hand, it has the value of an erotic component, even a person's self-destruction cannot occur without a libidinal gratification" (Freud, "Das ökonomische Problem," 383, my translation). Similarly to Freud's model, Emerson's self-quotation constitutes a force aimed at self-transformation through the infliction of pain that couples a tendency to self-destruction with libidinal gratification.

Is all of this related to friendship only because both eloquence and friendship have to do with interpersonal, and ideally, uplifting, contact? First of all, during that winter of 1839–40, his lecture course and the subject of friendship (as well as his actual friendships) occupy him so much—and for such similar reasons, namely, a general anxiety over the possibility of establishing the contact he envisages—that both issues are regularly treated contiguously in the journal. But moreover, Emerson also makes explicit the link between his failure as an orator and as a friend in the final paragraphs of the journal entry:

And why?

I seem to lack constitutional vigor to attempt each topic as I ought. I ought to seek to lay myself out utterly,—large, enormous, prodigal, upon the subject of the week. But a hateful experience has taught me that I can only expend, say, twenty one hours on each lecture, if I would also be ready & able for the next. Of course, I spend myself prudently; I economize; I cheapen; whereof nothing grand ever grew. Could I spend sixty hours on each, or, what is better, had I such energy that I could rally the lights & mights of sixty hours into twenty, I should hate myself less, I should help my friend.

———

I ought to be equal to every relation. It makes no difference how many friends I have & what content I can find in conversing with each if there be one to whom I have not been equal. If I have shrunk unequal from one contest instantly the joy I find in all the rest becomes mean & cowardly. (*JMN*, vol. 7, 339)

The portion below the break found its way into the essay "Friendship," but the really interesting moment occurs just before: "I should hate myself less, I should help my friend." Clearly, he here again spells out that his self-hatred does not result from failing to live up to some random goal, but rather from failing to enter into a mutual relationship with his audience. This sort of isolation—the Emersonian misrecognition understood as stagnation—issues in self-loathing, not in self-reliance. But why this abrupt jump to friendship? Is "lay[ing] myself out utterly . . . upon the subject of the week" the same as "help[ing] my friend"? Is he equating his audience members with his friends? Are they in an analogous position to each other—both situated in relation to a man who hates himself and who is thus, in Emerson's terms, of no use to them? All of these interpretations draw support from the paragraph below the break, in which the difference between friends and audience is a trivial difference in number, a triviality that reaches into friendship itself: "It makes no difference how many friends I have." Considering the masochistic battle he has just been fighting with himself, the contest he speaks of can thus be read as a contest with himself, and the one to whom he is not equal is the unattained self of the ecstatic speaker. (As we will see, one would hardly arrive at this interpretation if one only knew the sentence from the essay "Friendship.") Again, there is no possibility of turning the unattained self into a force that propels us to the next step on the ladder of perfectionism.

I have turned to these two journal entries in order to show how Emerson comes to think of the chiasmus of ideal and actual relations. Let me pause here for a moment in order to clarify how the threads of this chapter come together: I have argued so far that Emerson's self-reliance can best be understood in the context of what we today call recognition—a term that, for Emerson, would encompass both self-possession and growth through interpersonal relationships (which means transcending self-possession). In order to grow, the self relies on friends as much as on itself. But because Emerson often depicts friendship as mutual growth into the impersonal, both friendship and the recognition we want from our friend tend to seem idealistic, that is, impossible to translate into reality. Thus, self-reliance is at once sought inside friendship and often portrayed as a compensation for the experience of the shortcomings of actual friendship.

One strand of readings of Emerson, exemplified by Stanley Cavell, attempts to show that it would be a mistake to construe this difficulty of translating the ideal into the actual as a rigid disjunction between the two, because the ideal is no more than that which keeps us searching for our next self within the actual. From this perfectionist perspective, there can be no final failure, breakdown, or misrecognition: any such negative experience is put into the service of finding the next self—or, more modestly speaking, it can and should be put into that service. I have claimed that the problem with such a view is that it neglects those moments in Emerson's writings in which he insists on the finality of failure and on the absoluteness of solitude. In these moments, Emerson sees no possibility of individual growth, and this is what most fully captures Emersonian misrecognition. Instead of paving the way for the next self, these experiences disclose a side of Emerson seldom addressed, namely a masochistic lingering on failure.

Yet my reading, like Cavell's, is also unsatisfied with closing the case by affirming an essential difference between the ideal and the actual. Emerson puts too much emphasis on both actual experience and the ideal—and their elusive relationship to each other—to warrant such a reading. The problem I have been concerned with here is how to explain the relationship in his thought between the ideal and the actual (in friendship and in recognition) without explaining away mishaps as perfectionism and thus claiming any difference between the ideal and the actual as a resource for enhancing the actual.

My point in tracing the development of Emerson's theory of friendship has been that he *does* support a perfectionist position—Cavell is not per se mistaken—yet he tends to contradict it by bemoaning solitude and distance in a manner that moves beyond the shame that Cavell integrates into his model. Both strands tie together the ideal and the actual in their own way. Perfectionism makes use of the ideal as a measure of the actual. The necessary shortcomings of the actual produce the shame that becomes the motor for stepping up to the next self. By contrast, the masochistic Emerson cannot turn shame into a source of power. Here, too, the actual is measured by, and must fall short of, the ideal. But at the same time, the actual is also recognized as different from the ideal, and is thus also measured by its own standard. This is the double standard that plagues the pessimistic side of

Emerson: he lets the ideal judge the actual and censure it, yet he then permits the actual itself to become the judge in affirming the censure: "Yes, this is my *actual* limitation."

What is baffling here is the persistence of the ideal, which will not let Emerson come to rest and which keeps him in limbo between perfectionism and resignation. This may sound almost like a Freudian description of battles with the ego ideal, except that in this case the ego ideal is less a specific ego than a capacity to engage in productive social relations, which will then produce an enlarged self. In extreme instances, this battle with the ideal turns into self-hatred, as in the two-part journal entry on his vision of eloquent ecstasy. Here, masochism is the only way the self can make good on the nonrelation with the audience, by entering into a mutual relationship with itself in "agitation and being agitated." Thus, at this point, Emerson registers the psychic toll of the culture of recognition. In this context, self-reliance becomes a morbid endeavor in which social recognition is replaced with pain.

Weak Time

I have focused on these two journal passages not only because they present a climax of suffering due to the double standard. There is also a hint in the last section of the second journal entry of a different and less painful possibility of crossing the ideal and the actual, and thus of coming to terms with the thirst for approbation. This can be detected in Emerson's economy of time, which, as the entry makes clear, is based immediately on the economy of the lecture circuit. I argue that Emerson tries to devise a method of dealing with the vagaries of recognition by emphasizing time as basic to what he calls the "law of friendship." As I will show in this section, time becomes coupled with an ethics of patience. Emerson introduces a concern for time relatively late in the development of his thought on friendship—roughly at the moment when his skepticism about the perfectionist solution to misrecognition arises. His ethics of patience is to provide a way to live friendship— to secure recognition—beyond the ups and downs that either climax in the masochistic reaction to stagnation, or, in the perfectionist mood, lead to a swift succession of friends.

At the end of the second journal entry, Emerson does not treat time as related to patience in friendship or public speaking. However, time is responsible for the speaker's failure to connect with the audience, and the friend's failure to help his friend, because Emerson lacked time for the preparation of the text:

But a hateful experience has taught me that I can only expend, say, twenty one
hours on each lecture. . . . Could I spend sixty hours on each, or, what is better, had I such energy that I could rally the lights & mights of sixty hours into
twenty, I should hate myself less, I should help my friend.

It seems at first as if he were simply saying: had I had more time, my lectures
would have turned out better and I would hate myself less. But this common-
sense logic is complicated by his wish to "rally the lights & mights of sixty
hours into twenty." He describes time as the realm of personified "lights
& mights," who can be rallied by human beings. With the right energy the
"lights & mights" can be lured from their abode of sixty hours and crammed
into twenty hours. Emerson directs our attention to what time hosts, that is,
he distinguishes between time and the "lights & mights," which would usually be thought of as the inherent attributes of a given stretch of time. Thus,
if one had indefinite amounts of energy, one could reach a state in which
time becomes entirely malleable: the "lights & mights" of all time could be
assembled into the now.

In *Above Time: Emerson's and Thoreau's Temporal Revolutions*, from
2001, James Guthrie has argued that Emerson came to believe "that the moment was all, or rather, that the individual's *response* to the moment was all.
Moreover . . . the significance of the individual, for whom the moment was
a temporal analogue, began to grow."[26] The journal passage partially confirms Guthrie: Emerson came to view time less as a linear flow than as a
resource of material that can be molded into forms of varying density. Of
course, the point of the journal entry is precisely that Emerson has failed to
do so, or, in other words, that the linearity of time remains a force that easily
exceeds the individual's energies. Molding moments out of the flow of time
becomes the individual's struggle. What Guthrie does not mention is the
function of this exercise: to reach the audience, to "help my friend," in short,
to create a relationship of recognition.

The Time of Friendship

Not coincidentally, it is during this period that the issue of time assumes a
central position in Emerson's theory of friendship. In the sermons that discussed friendship, as well as in the undated lecture manuscript on friendship from the mid-1830s, time was not a notable concern to him. A few
years later, Emerson discussed friendship in several lectures that became
cornerstones, along with his journal entries from the winter of 1839–40,
of the essay "Friendship." It is striking that both in the winter lecture series

of 1837–38 (entitled "The Philosophy of History") and in the series of the following winter ("Human Culture"), Emerson spent a considerable amount of time in one lecture discussing friendship.[27] Yet, neither lecture touches upon time.

However, in a different lecture from the "Human Culture" series (given in the winter of 1838–39), entitled "Being and Seeming," time does make a significant appearance: "In a true and ingenious mind the appeal is always being made to the future. The boy we know is allowed to be ignorant and helpless because of the tacit appeal to what he shall be and do" (*EL*, vol. 2, 303). Emerson's fascination with boys and youth runs through his entire work,[28] precisely for the reason that for him young men individualized and embodied the hope for an age that would heal modern civilizational alienation. This future-directed outlook approaches time via the virtues of hope and patience: "This patience and trust—patience with obscurity, nay sometimes with a painful sense of imbecility; and this trust that if man will stand by the truth, it will stand by him infinitely—this patience and trust shall not lose their reward" (*EL*, vol. 2, 304). Patience as future-mindedness couples the present and the future by mentally keeping them apart, by thinking in the present about a different future. Yet, at a closer look, Emerson's phrasing questions the chronological chain from present ordeal to future reward. If "patience and trust *shall not lose* their reward," this could mean that the law of future reward, which has saved many, will work for Emerson and his audience, too. Or, read more literally, it could mean that the reward of patience is already being received in the moment of being patient. The same goes for trusting truth: retain this trust, he says, and truth will not leave you. He does not say: retain this trust, and you will find truth.[29]

This repeal of future-mindedness is more clearly discernible when Emerson comes to integrate time into friendship. Again, he conceptualizes time through the virtue of patience. But rather than keeping the present and the future apart, patience in friendship is the attempt to insert the hope for an ideal future into the present. How this is supposed to work is first hinted at in the lecture "Private Life" from the 1839–40 lecture series, which would so cruelly disappoint him. "Private Life" most directly precedes the essay "Friendship" in Emerson's developing thought on friendship. He writes, "Respect so far the holy laws of this fellowship as not to prejudice its perfect flower by your impatience for its opening. We must be our own, before we can be another's." Two paragraphs later he continues: "Our impatience betrays us into rash and foolish alliances which no god attends. . . . By persisting in your path, by holding your peace, though you forfeit the little you gain the great" (*EL*, vol. 3, 254–55).

The Laws of Friendship and "Immanent" Patience

At first, this may sound very similar to Emerson's call to wait out condemnation and thus reap the benefit of eternal approbation. He still makes the promise that if we only persist in our path we will eventually gain the great. However, when applied to friendship, persistence comes to mean obeying the "laws of this fellowship," which he comes to call "the laws of friendship" in "Friendship" (CW, vol. 2, 117). Future-directedness is thus replaced by a perspective that withstands the temptation to "prejudice [the] perfect flower" of friendship. While the common concept of patience implies passing the time of the slow blossoming by anticipating the perfect flower, Emerson's "immanent patience" depends on an appreciation of the closed flower.

To make friendships long lasting is of course a plea that, in itself, is far from original—Plato and Aristotle, for instance, both considered constancy the sign of the purest love. But for Emerson, there is something more specific at stake, which connects back to his wish to "rally the lights & mights." Another section from "Private Life" is revealing here (although we cannot be entirely sure whether this part of the manuscript was originally part of the lecture; compare EL, vol. 3, 248). Here he develops a thought that is related to a topic of his later essay "Nominalist and Realist," which I discussed in chapter 2 under the rubric of "representation of concealment":

> Before it [the soul], Time—which usually we think the strongest of powers,—
> is weak. We think in idle hours that the ancients have perished, are dead and
> inoperative. Then we awake and see that through the force of soul nothing
> alive dies. In the present moment all the past is ever represented. (EL, vol. 3,
> 250)

Clearly, the immediate focal point of this passage is not patience: Emerson is laying out his most consoling version of his theories of history and immortality. Death is redefined as an epistemic problem, and history must be achieved by the soul in the present. What is pertinent to my discussion, however, is the idea of "weak time." Seeing the past and the dead in the present requires the insight that time is falsely considered "the strongest of powers." More precisely, while it is a strong power, it can be weakened if the individual is receptive to the soul.[30]

But while being receptive to the soul implies passivity, Emerson does think of the weakening of time in much more active terms as well. This was already noticeable in the phrase "rally the lights & mights." Here, weakening time took on a heroic dimension insufficiently captured by the passive-sounding reception of the soul. In June 1840, during the last stages of preparing his first collection of essays (among which "Friendship" is placed at the center), Emerson explicitly links heroism and time in his journal. Again, there is, at first glance, the old argument that we have to appreciate failure because the worthy life is ahead, in the future. And again, at second glance he displays an almost pragmatic reorientation in the now:

> Heroism means difficulty, postponement of praise, postponement of ease, introduction of the world into the private apartment, introduction of eternity into the hours measured by the sittingroom clock. (*JMN*, vol. 7, 499)

It might be futile to attempt to unpack this assemblage of interlocking images. But what is clear is that Emerson asks us to postpone praise and ease— in other words: approbation and the gratification we gain from it. While *postponement* could lead one to think that we should await praise, he is not really returning to future-directedness at all. His emphasis on our everyday surroundings—the private apartment, the sittingroom clock—suggests that heroism knows no triumph except in difficulty and postponement. More precisely, his call to introduce eternity into the time of the familiar implies that he is speaking of *indefinite* postponement: the emphasis is on an eternal here and now, and that which is postponed fades into a receding future.

Emerson's active, heroic introduction of the eternal into the familiar not only brings the eternal within the reach of the present. It also entails a sense of defamiliarization and disorientation: the private apartment suddenly must contain the world, and the sittingroom clock does not measure the familiar, linear, standardized flow of time, but rather amorphous eternity. In other words, I argue that the indefinite postponement arising out of "immanent patience" is Emerson's deepest reflection on what it would mean to weaken time, to "rally the lights & mights." As he writes in "Friendship," obeying the laws of friendship means resisting the temptation "to suck a sudden sweetness" (*CW*, vol. 2, 117). By this move, Emerson attempts to make friendship—understood always as a relationship of recognition—sustainable over time.

This has immediate effects on the relationship of friends. It levels out the peaks of attraction and repulsion, and thus keeps the friends at a greater distance from each other in order to ensure a more stable relationship. This helps to avoid the total breakdown of the relationship, which, for Emerson, constitutes misrecognition and stagnation. Emerson's sober friendship theory is thus in alignment with the general development of his thought in the early and mid-1840s. What he describes in "Experience" as the "midworld"—that sphere in which the individual learns, in Maurice S. Lee's phrase, "to accept a stubborn self-reliance more lonely than inspired"[31]—is also the world of friends who have learned that hoping for too much ease, too much recognition, and too much inspiration leads to the cul-de-sac of self-hatred.

"Friendship" and Textual Recognition

We now turn to Emerson the writer. If weak time is the basis of a model of recognition that explains the dynamics of both friendship and eloquence, does weak time find its way into his act of eloquence entitled "Friendship?" As an essay, it must be pointed out, "Friendship" differs from the lectures discussed so far, but it does so only in degree: Emerson's creative process of turning a lecture into an essay seems to have been continuous with the ceaseless revisions to his lectures in between deliveries of them.[32] Where there are notable differences between lecture and essay, he has usually radicalized the disjunctions, leaps, and vaguely suggestive connections. This, in fact, makes "Friendship" all the more useful for interrogating how Emerson transforms his ideas of friendship and recognition into an occasion for textual engagement.

Textual Friendship and Textual Recognition

Borrowing from both deconstruction and Levinasian ethics, Kuisma Korhonen has recently developed a useful concept of "textual friendship" in his 2006 study *Textual Friendship: The Essay as Impossible Encounter*. Textual friendship puts emphasis not on the question of how friendship is treated thematically or hermeneutically in a text, but rather on how the text itself stages a relationship of friendship between itself (not the implied author) and the implied reader. As Korhonen writes, "textual friendship is 'friendship prior to friendship,' or, to put it in the formalistic language of Roman Jacobson, perhaps it refers to those 'conative' and 'phatic' functions of language where the Other is addressed before anything referential or poetic has been said" (Korhonen, *Textual Friendship*, 68).[33] Textual friendship conceives of friendship as residing in between thematic and hermeneutic renderings of friendship in the text. It may be described as the relationship between the reader and the trace of the author in the text: "A text may be a textual machine, but still it carries a reference to its creation in it. Someone has, in some way, made it. But who?" (Korhonen, *Textual Friendship*, 69). Thus, every text, whether it is openly concerned with friendship or not, is an encounter of some sort: "[In] every text, I, in some way, do encounter something that I, at least sometimes, can think of as the voice of some other human being" (Korhonen, *Textual Friendship*, 69). This someone is not as concrete as "the author" or "the implied author": this someone is located on a level prior to such concrete figures.

Keeping in mind that in Emerson's thought, friendship stands in the service of recognition, it makes sense to look at the essay "Friendship" by altering the concept of "textual friendship" to "textual recognition." Korhonen's model of textual friendship aims to defamiliarize the notion of friendship by locating textual friendship as a "trace" that becomes visible "by pointing out the places where the textual economy of thematizations and hermeneutic circles are trying to cover up some rupture" (Korhonen, *Textual Friendship*, 69). The textual recognition in Emerson's "Friendship" likewise acts where the textual, the hermeneutic, and the thematic intersect (though this intersection is hardly covered up), and its work, too, may be described as defamiliarization: what recognition is, what it involves, is not settled in advance, but put into practice by the interaction of the three levels. However, shifting from textual friendship to textual recognition effects one remarkable difference on the level of the textual. In the case of textual recognition, the textual becomes much more palpable than in textual friendship (where the textual is no more than a trace), namely, in the various modes of address. In other words, textual recognition—the interaction between the hermeneutic, thematic, and textual—lets us see how Emerson's various ways of calling on himself, the reader, and others in general become forces in the dynamic of recognition. What I call textual recognition, then, is not a general model for reading; rather, it calls attention to the specific ways Emerson's "Friendship" puts into relationship his assertive statements on friendship, the hermeneutic challenges built into the text (marked by Emerson's characteristically elusive and contradictory exposition), and its various forms of address. The interplay of these levels in the final instance concerns the reception aesthetics of the text: reading "Friendship" becomes the reader's experience of a particular type of recognition.

The Hermeneutic Dimension

The second of the two journal passages I discussed above provides a welcome entry into this dynamic. Recall that the portion below the break in that entry found its way into the essay "Friendship." To approach how this passage becomes involved in textual recognition, I will first reconstruct this portion's place in the essay, with an eye on the hermeneutic dimension. Here is the version of the passage as it appears in the essay:

> I ought to be equal to every relation. It makes no difference how many friends
> I have, and what content I find in conversation with each, if there be one to

whom I be not equal. If I have shrunk unequal from one contest, the joy I find in all the rest becomes mean and cowardly. I should hate myself, if then I made my other friends my asylum. (*CW*, vol. 2, 118)

Following this passage, Emerson quotes four lines from Shakespeare's Sonnet 25, in which Shakespeare considers the fickleness of personal reputation, exemplified, in the lines quoted by Emerson, by a warrior who loses a prince's favor after a single defeat.[34] The sonnet's combative scene connects with the contest between friends brought up by Emerson.

While Emerson thus appears to insist on the necessity of never sliding into a position of inferiority in this passage, it may be surprising that its larger context in the essay undermines this vehemence, as the broader discussion is concerned with something not immediately related, namely the question of time and patience, which, as I have said, not only occupies a central place in "Friendship" but also remains a fresh facet of his thought on friendship at this time.[35] Emerson embarks on the theme of time and patience in the preceding paragraph, bringing back several motifs with which we are already familiar: the law of friendship and the danger of "sucking" benefit from our friends, which here is derived from an Edenic image:

Our friendships hurry to short and poor conclusions, because we have made them a texture of wine and dreams, instead of the tough fibre of the human heart. The laws of friendship are austere and eternal, of one web with the laws of nature and of morals. But we have aimed at a swift and petty benefit, to suck a sudden sweetness. We snatch the slowest fruit in the whole garden of God, which many summers and many winters must ripen. (*CW*, vol. 2, 117)[36]

Halfway through this paragraph, the result of impatient passion is described as "subtle antagonisms, which, as soon as we meet, begin to play, and translate all poetry into stale prose. Almost all people descend to meet" (*CW*, vol. 2, 117). Although it is not quite clear what passion has to do with subtle antagonisms, and what the link is between these antagonisms and the widespread tendency to descend to meet, the apparently harmful effects of descending do provide a transition to the discussion of the necessity of equality. But even this connection remains vague, perhaps even contradictory: would descending to meet not be a viable route toward equality? Probably "descending to meet" designates something like the lowest common denominator (he also says, in this context, "All association must be a compromise") and would contradict a more idealized understanding of equality, which must be measured relationally as well as in absolute terms. However that may be, the paragraph does not linger long enough on this point to make the transition effective. By the time one gets to the journal passage, the point of transition has been nearly forgotten, because in the remaining sentences of the paragraph, Emerson goes on to complain more generally about the "perpetual disappointment" of "actual society" and the sudden apathies by which one is struck "in the heyday of friendship and thought." Instead of bridging the necessity to "be equal to every relation," Emerson concludes the paragraph with the fatalistic outlook that friendships end in solitude because of an epistemological failure: "Our faculties do not play us true, and both parties are relieved by solitude" (CW, vol. 2, 118). But how exactly do our faculties explain the sudden strokes of apathy in the heyday of friendship? And what does that have to do with needing to be equal to every relation? Clearly, as usual, Emerson's technique here is not persuasive argumentation, but rather something like the calculated leap of surprise.

This impression is reinforced by what follows the journal passage. After the (unattributed) Shakespeare quotation, Emerson abruptly jumps back into his discussion of impatience: "Our impatience is thus sharply rebuked" (CW, vol. 2, 118). We might not have been aware of it, but we now realize that we should have known all along that the necessity of being equal and the eternal loss of honor in the case of a single failure have something directly to do with our impatience. But what exactly? Not only does Emerson leave open what he might mean; he does not even make clear whether it is worth trying to find out whether these threads really belong together. Maybe they do, but then, arriving at a solid answer might turn out to be of little interest. But if they do not form a coherent position, why should one keep reading?

Emerson practices a risky kind of writing here, even by his own standards: after just these few paragraphs, it becomes clear that the reader cannot expect anything even close to coherence. Close reading will reveal ever more facets to and connections between his sentences, and between impatience, honor, equality, and epistemology. Forcing these threads together into a waterproof system of thought seems next to impossible. At the same time, in order to allow the reader to follow some of the possible connections, these passages must not be left entirely incoherent. In fact, not only does the essay provide possibilities for drawing connections; it encourages these connections by rhetorical claims of sense-making. The Emersonian speaking voice (which is, of course, not quite the same as "Emerson," although I sometimes find it appropriate to give in to the text's luring us to associate the voice with Emerson) never seems to question whether the succession of statements and paragraphs makes perfect sense. When the authorial voice begins a paragraph with a logical transition such as "Thus," or, even more frequently, "Yet," he sounds as if he expects every one of his readers to have followed his logic up to this point. These declarations of coherence are typically Emersonian in that they manage to affirm and deny themselves simultaneously.

The Thematic Dimension

But besides the hermeneutic challenge of making sense of the essay, there are two further dimensions—the thematic and the textual—that contribute to the mechanism of textual recognition in "Friendship." On the level of the thematic, the essay wavers between celebrating friendship and declaring it impossible. This is a continuous process so that even when friendship has been declared impossible, the speaker's voice will find ways to rekindle his—and, significantly, our—hope that friendship will be possible after all, perhaps on some other level than originally anticipated. On the thematic level, then, the essay moves in circles, the shape favored so often by Emerson.[37]

I will sketch out the first circle, which Emerson draws within the first seven paragraphs. He begins on a confident note, exclaiming "How many we see in the street . . . we warmly rejoice to be with" (*CW*, vol. 2, 113), and then provides two examples of auspicious friendship: the empowering effects of letter writing and the visit of the stranger with whom we converse in a most inspired tone. Halfway through this second example, once the guest has become more familiar, Emerson casts a cloud over friendship. Suddenly, the mutual inspiration has ceased: "But as soon the stranger begins to intrude his partialities, his definitions, his defects, into the conversation, it is all over" (*CW*, vol. 2, 114). Strangely, however, in the next paragraph Emerson continues to celebrate friendship as if nothing had happened. He asks, "What is so pleasant as these jets of affection which make a young world for me again?" (*CW*, vol. 2, 114). In the following (fifth) paragraph, he initially retains the exhilarated tone by expressing gratitude for his friends. Only toward the end does he ask, "Will these too separate themselves from me again, or some of them?" (*CW*, vol. 2, 115), as if he were belatedly acknowledging the infelicitous ending of the stranger's visit. Yet he refuses to linger on the question: "I know not, but I fear it not" (*CW*, vol. 2, 115). However, in the following paragraph, he suddenly leaps into a pessimistic mood again, which turns into a classic case of the anxiety of influence: while new friends sometimes give him the greatest fancies, they lead him neither to new thoughts nor to action. Instead, he realizes that he falsely adulates them: "We overestimate the conscience of our friend. His goodness seems better than our goodness, his nature finer, his temptation less" (*CW*, vol. 2, 115). And yet in the following (seventh) paragraph—the longest and most convoluted up to this point—it turns out that some sort of friendship is possible after all, although it requires that we love our friends' essence rather than their appearance. This, in effect, means that we need to accept the alternation between solitude and friendship, and the succession of actual friends as representatives of essential love: "Thus every man passes his life in the search after friendship" (*CW*, vol. 2, 117). In other words, the first seven paragraphs form an upward spiral: friendship seems intoxicating at first, yet it wears off and begins to limit us. However, this limitation can be overcome if we learn to search for real love, namely in the realm beyond the phenomenal.

But while this might seem like a proper, textbook précis of Emerson's idealist thought on friendship, we need to remember that this first movement has covered no more than a fraction of the essay and that the affirmations and negations continue to spin the reader many more times. In addition, the circular movement sketched out here is not at all obvious because Emerson frequently creates swirls within the larger circle, as in the second half of the example of the stranger. This is where the hermeneutic and the thematic intersect: in an ingenious trick, the theme of friendship becomes tied to the reader's attempts to understand the essay. The reader's hermeneutic circles become conflated with the essay's thematic circling around the possibility and impossibility of friendship. Both levels confront the precariousness of relationships. First, there is the thematic relationship of friendship: because of Emerson's logical leaps, in combination with his rhetoric of logical coherence, the thematic rendering of the relationship of friendship remains problematic. There either is no clearly discernible verdict on the (im)possibility of friendship, or if there is one, it is unclear how to weigh it. Intertwined with this problematic is the interpretive relationship between reader and text: the text's problematizing of friendship becomes the reader's problem of understanding the text.

The Textual Dimension

The intertwining of the thematic and the hermeneutic is deepened by the input of the textual, which concerns a more direct relationship between the writer's voice and the implied reader. This level of textual recognition is activated chiefly through the essay's different modes of address. Emerson switches back and forth between the addressees "one," "we," "I," "you," and "thou." Of special interest are "you," or "thou," and "we." "We" is sometimes inclusive, making universal statements, often about our current shortcomings, as when he writes, in the sentence immediately preceding the portion from the journal: "Our faculties do not play us true, and both parties are relieved by solitude." But "we" can also connote complicity—in these cases, the Emersonian voice will be defiant against the falsity of society, but it will pull the reader onto its side in a logic of "us against them." Shortly after the passage discussed above, he writes: "But to most of us society shows not its face and its eye, but its side and its back. To stand in true relations with men in a false age, is worth a fit of insanity, is it not?" (*CW*, vol. 2, 120). Never mind that the biographical source of the "fit of insanity" is the mentally unstable poet Jones Very. What is crucial for the current context is that Emerson achieves the effect of forming a bond between his voice and the reader against society through the rhetorical question, which only gains weight from the sentence in which it appears. If true relations with men are so rare in society, then asking the reader a rhetorical question that assumes consent can only mean: you are one of the few people with whom I can have a true relationship in this false age.

The uses of "you" are equally differentiated. Sometimes Emerson seems to be addressing a specific friend (though usually this specificity remains abstract, so that the reader does not immediately begin to read the essay as a roman à clef, even if at other times friends such as Jones Very are discernible). In these cases, it is as if the reader were not addressed; often, the result of Emerson's calling on a friend who is not the reader is the kind of complicity we saw above—the reader becomes a witness of sorts. In other cases, the "you" seems to be the reader, and the relationship between the reader and the Emersonian voice is at stake. Sometimes these two cases appear in the same sentence, with a sudden switch in mid-sentence, as here: "Friendship requires that rare mean betwixt likeness and unlikeness, that piques each with the presence of power and consent in the other party. Let me be alone to the end of the world, rather than that my friend should overstep by a word or a look his real sympathy" (*CW*, vol. 2, 122). The addressee seems to change after the comma in the second sentence. In the first part, the addressee of the imperative "Let me" could well be the reader; after the comma, the designation "my friend" puts distance between the reader and the addressee.

The paragraph narrows from a general statement about the requirements of friendship to the case at hand, a direction that ultimately aims "Let me be alone to the end of the world" at the reader. To read the reader as the addressee, the sentence must be placed in its immediate context: Emerson has just made the point that friendship is a relationship that is determined by affection, which is something beyond the individual's control. He then turns this claim into a requirement for prospective friends: "Among those who enjoy his thought, he will regain his tongue" (*CW*, vol. 2, 122). But by framing affection as enjoyment, it is not so clear whether affection is really beyond the individual's control. Might enjoyment not require a conscious effort? The "natural selection" of affection thus turns into a social test.

Although Emerson writes this preceding paragraph in the third person, his specification of friendship as based on affection, which is itself measured by the enjoyment of thought, suggests a close proximity to the relationship of reading. It is as if Emerson asked his readers: "Do you enjoy my thought? Are you my friend?" Thus, in this context, the reader of the phrase "Let me be alone to the end of the world" is rebuked. Only after the comma is the reader ruled out as addressee—otherwise the voice could not tell the reader about "my friend." In this moment, not being the addressee equals relief: "For the time being, we do not have to take the test of affection," or, even better, "We may have passed it already."

At other times, Emerson uses the imperative "let" as if he were address-ing a "you" (singular or plural), but strangely, that "you" is himself, as if he were talking to himself: "Let him to me be a spirit" (CW, vol. 2, 123). In fact, the imperative "let" frequently changes from "me" to "you" to "us." When the three addressees are looked at in isolation from each other, it be-comes uncertain if there is a difference between them. But when reading these sentences in their actual context, the difference can be immense. "Let us," for instance, is a comforting call that tells us we are not alone, that we are at least joined by the Emersonian voice, although this may contradict the manifest meaning of the sentence, as in this one, close to the end of the essay: "Let us feel, if we will, the absolute insulation of man" (CW, vol. 2, 125). This insulation cannot be so bad if it lets us form a bond of resolve.

It is remarkable that in the essay's very last paragraph, after Emerson has insisted adamantly on the necessity of "lofty seeking, . . . spiritual astron-omy, or search for stars" (Nietzsche will later tighten this into his "star friendship"),[38] any apostrophe or pronoun is avoided. The Emersonian voice comes to replace the subject with the "object of love":

> True love transcends the unworthy subject, and dwells and broods on the eternal, and when the poor, interposed mask crumbles, it is not sad, but feels rid of so much earth, and feels its dependency the surer. Yet these things may hardly be said without a sort of treachery of the relation. The essence of friendship is entireness, a total magnanimity and trust. It must not surmise or provide for infirmity. It treats its object as a god, that it may deify both. (CW, vol. 2, 127)

One might be tempted to read this ending as a particularly cruel one: we, the readers, have finally been disposed of. We are cast aside as a mere mask of the essence, and when we feel to the speaker like "so much earth," we must wonder if he is not admitting that he has murdered us. This is rigidly fol-lowed through on the textual level: friendship is now treated as so entirely pure that we have ceased to be addressed. And while Emerson's pure love has reached new heights, "we" are no longer part of that relationship: the essay has found its and our end.

On the other hand, there may be good reasons why the end does not feel nearly as pitiless as this reading would suggest. The total absence of address may be read as the exact opposite, as a reassurance and valorization of the relationship between the Emersonian voice and the reader. Maybe it is only here that we know for sure how artfully, carefully, and consciously Emerson crafts the correlation between the address of his reader and the theme of friendship. If we, the readers, are suddenly no longer addressed at the very moment Emerson pushes toward the "total magnanimity and trust" of friendship at the essay's very end—and if the craftedness shines through because all of this is happening at the text's end—the relatedness of the thematic and the textual, of friendship and ourselves, is finally affirmed. We do trust that Emerson means, recognizes, and approves of *us* when he reaches for the stars and rhetorically rids himself of all earthliness.[39]

But to read him in this way, and to begin to trust him as he asks us to, we need to have had the patience to endure the circles of friendship for fourteen very long pages. And what do we end up with? Certainly not some satisfying reward (unless, of course, having finished the essay alone provides gratification). One would be hard pressed to say at once what friendship is, if friendship is possible after all or if it is a mere ideal construct against which all reality must pale, or to say what other rock-hard philosophical insight one might have gained from the essay. This is typical after reading Emerson: much is left in suspense. Is it even possible, after finishing the essay, to remember what it said? I would argue that this lingering uneasiness is as much a part of the essay's textual recognition as is the feeling of having journeyed through an ebb and flow of confidence and bewilderment. While the essay actually consists to a large extent of passages taken from his journals, lectures, and letters, Emerson has managed to construct a wavering dynamic of recognition through the interplay of the hermeneutic, thematic, and textual that is ultimately experienced by the reader through the reader's own actualization of Emerson's construct.

This raises the question of how, for Emerson, textual recognition is related to interpersonal and social recognition. I see two possible answers. Either he considers reading his essays and listening to his lectures to be an educational act in which one experiences in the field of literature how to master the scarcity of recognition and then translates that literary experience into the world of the interpersonal, or he models his concept of patient friendship after the reading and listening experience. Both possibilities draw on a commonplace of Emerson's time equating books with friends, and both face the problem of evading the difference between social and textual recognition.

As Emerson suggests himself when he recognizes the limitations of his old strategy of transforming misrecognition into a benefit: while a book can be put aside, our social relationships cannot.

From this perspective, Emerson's "Friendship" dishes up poor theory. From another perspective, it makes absolute sense that, while Emerson models his theory of recognition on reading and listening, his theory thereby exceeds its models. Emerson's essay, like his lectures, cannot go as far as the theory of recognition developed therein. As in his theory, the reward of the reading and listening experience remains tentative; yet, the requirements of the lecture form, which are still operative in the essay, are not fulfilled by mere parsimony and demands for heroic, immanent patience. Rather than leveling out peaks of delight and despair, the public lecture—and the textual recognition that evolves from it—centers on an alternating series of contradictory, imaginary experiences of recognition and misrecognition.

Emerson's ethics and practice diverge at this point. But they also begin to cross-pollinate. Taking into account what the performance and experience of immanent patience amount to, his ethics begins to look slightly different. The point is still that, in order to avoid the cul-de-sac of masochism, the wish for immediate gratification available from a reciprocal self-transformation must be recognized to be futile. But its earlier replacement—immanent patience—now appears as the embrace of the entire movement of recognition: a sequence of experiences made up of moments of both recognition and misrecognition. This is the final implication of Emerson's announcement to "blot a line to acknowledge the value of those social tests to which we all are brought in turn to be approved or damned."

III

EMERSON AND THE NATION

[5]

NEW AMERICANIST TURNS:
EMPIRE, TRANSNATIONALISM, AND UTOPIANISM

Empire Criticism

WHEN REVISING THE American Studies paradigm of the Cold War era, New Americanists turned their attention to two related fields of inquiry that, in their perception, were foreclosed by the "field imaginary" of the founders of American Studies. One was the complex of race, class, and gender, which brought questions of identity and recognition to the table (as discussed in chapter 3). The other field concerned the United States' role in the world. Exploring the imperial character of the United States became a hallmark of New Americanist scholarship, and it resulted in the influential 1993 anthology *Cultures of United States Imperialism*, edited by Amy Kaplan and Donald Pease, which inaugurated Pease's *New Americanists* series at Duke University Press.[1]

As the title *Cultures of United States Imperialism* indicates, the critical point of the volume lay not only in replacing the ideology of American exceptionalism with an account of U.S. imperialism but also in extending the critique of empire from foreign policy and economics to culture itself. As Amy Kaplan wrote in her widely noted introductory chapter "Left Alone with America," the anthology's goal was to explore "empire as way of life."[2] This connected the question of America's role in the world, and its cultural expressions, with the issues of race, class, and gender (and ultimately with the question of identity) within the borders of the nation:

> Not only about foreign diplomacy or international relations, imperialism is also about consolidating domestic cultures and negotiating intranational relations. To foreground cultures is not only to understand how they abet the subjugation of others or foster their resistance, but also to ask how international relations reciprocally shape a dominant culture at home, and how imperial relations are enacted and contested within the nation. (Kaplan, "'Left Alone with America,'" 14)

Imperialism was seen to work both at home and abroad, so that the exclusion of minorities and women addressed by multiculturalism and gender studies had to be read as a manifestation of imperialism as much as a culturally constitutive force that propelled U.S. imperialism. Anticipating the transnational turn, Kaplan argued that the connection between imperialism on the one hand, and race, class, and gender on the other, forced scholars to question the form of the nation itself. Multicultural studies that left the national form intact as the container of diverse cultures missed the point that injustice at home could not be explained and resisted without looking at imperial injustice abroad. If the nation acted imperially at home and abroad, then the very distinction between inside and outside became fragile. As Donald Pease put it in an interview:

> You cannot produce a sense of internal counter-hegemony without opposing the US global hegemon. Internal hegemony and global hegemony are interlinked projects, and the critique has to be a double critical consciousness, so that the elsewheres onto which the US imperium projected the dimensions of its own history that it didn't want to acknowledge are also linked to the excluded internal alterities.[3]

In her later essay "Manifest Domesticity," included in her 2002 study *The Anarchy of Empire*, Kaplan exemplified the combined attention to imperialism, class, race, and gender by arguing that, in the aftermath of the annexation of Texas, there was an intimate link between "the language of political union and marital union," based on the common fear of racial intermixture.[4] At a time when imperial expansion destabilized national borders, the language of imperialism was applied to the home, and, likewise, "the discourse of domesticity was deployed to negotiate the borders of an expanding empire and divided nation" (Kaplan, *Anarchy of Empire*, 28). Kaplan's investigation of the intersections between the domestic and the imperial certainly offers valuable insights into how the external and internal, the national and the foreign, constitute each other, although the allegedly *literal* identity of the domestic and the imperial discourses at times begs the question of whether such literalness was really necessary for the ideological work described.

In any case, Kaplan's studies are based on a rather commonsensical point. If the United States engaged in expansion and imperialism (and there is no doubt that it did; indeed, it now seems almost incredible that for a long time U.S. historians insisted that the United States has not, at least at times, acted imperially), then this must have some correlations in culture. In addition, the notion that the discourses around foreign policy and domestic issues permeate each other is in itself not much more than a commonplace. In the ever-lengthening process of U.S. presidential campaigns, for instance, it is anything but a special insight for journalists and strategists to highlight the connections between a political candidate's stance and rhetoric regarding "the war on terror" and his or her self-portrayal regarding same-sex marriage.[5]

The force of the paradigm of empire criticism has less to do, then, with the emphasis on the intersections between the domestic and the foreign. Rather, its provocative power depends on two related notions. The first is that what connects the domestic and the foreign is of a particularly imperialist quality. The second idea is that what is at issue is not the degree to which political candidates or any other individuals fuse the foreign and the domestic (whether "domestic" is understood in the sense of the nation or the home), but the fact that these connections come to carry out their force in culture as a way of life. If "imperial relations are enacted and contested within the nation," as Kaplan writes, then one may be consoled that there is at least a possibility of contestation. And yet, whether one highlights enactment or contestation, culture is imperialist in its totality: even contestation cannot topple the imperialist character of culture.[6]

If these two notions—that American politics, economics, and culture are imperialist, and that this imperialism is total in all realms—stand at the center of New Americanist and related forms of empire criticism, then surely one would expect a theoretical engagement with the fundamental questions on which these notions rely. These fundamental questions concern first and foremost relations (1) between the individual or individual cultural work and culture at large, and (2) between culture and imperialism. It is noteworthy, however, that one generally looks in vain for such theoretical engagement.

I want to turn briefly to the now most famous and celebrated example of empire criticism, Edward Said's *Culture and Imperialism*, which is related to Pease and Kaplan's *Cultures of United States Imperialism* not only in its publication year of 1993 but also in its premise that imperialism must be understood as a cultural project. (Contrary to Pease and Kaplan, however, Said is reluctant to describe the United States of the nineteenth century as a full-fledged empire on the same scale as those of the British and the French.) Said writes, "we must look carefully and integrally at the culture that nurtured the sentiment, rationale, and above all the imagination of empire."[7] Yet while he here explains the role of culture with the metaphor of nurturing, he elsewhere flatly resists explaining theoretically how imperialism, culture, and literature interconnect: "Still, I have deliberately abstained from advancing a completely worked out theory of the connection between literature and culture on the one hand, and imperialism on the other" (Said, *Culture and Imperialism*, 14).

Said justifies this decision by pointing to the historical changes in the relationship between the terms: "Neither culture nor imperialism is inert, and so the connections between them as historical experiences are dynamic and complex" (Said, *Culture and Imperialism*, 14). I concede this point—it surely makes sense that individuals living inside an empire tend to take an imperial world order increasingly for granted the more firmly established that imperial order becomes over time—but Said nevertheless evades the question of how to theorize the correlation between a single cultural artifact such as a novel and imperialism. Instead, he focuses on authorial cognition and will, as well as the limits imposed on them by culture.

Because of this dual perspective, Joseph Conrad is an author of particular interest to Said: as a Polish expatriate in England, Conrad did not quite fit in with the British imperial order. He was, writes Said, "[n]ever the wholly incorporated and fully acculturated Englishman," (Said, *Culture and Imperialism*, 25) and thus self-consciously struggled with imperialism. Yet his own imagination was nevertheless bounded by British imperial culture, which is why he could not begin to think about empire from the perspective of the colonial other: "[In *Heart of Darkness*,] there is no use [for Kurtz or Marlow] looking for other, non-imperialist alternatives; the system has made them unthinkable" (Said, *Culture and Imperialism*, 24).

Said's recourse to a systemic explanation is a remarkable move if one considers how Said describes his position in the opening pages of his book. In the introduction he insists that "even at their worst, [Western imperialism and Third World nationalism] are neither monolithic nor deterministic. Besides, culture is not monolithic either" (Said, *Culture and Imperialism*, xxiv). He also assures the reader, "I do not believe that authors are mechanically determined by ideology, class, or economic history, but authors are, I also believe, very much in the histories of their societies, shaping and shaped by that history and their social experience in different measure" (Said, *Culture and Imperialism*, xxiv).

This is Said, the self-proclaimed humanist, who aims to locate high cultural products in history without succumbing to determinism. Yet, because he never spells out what this might actually mean—and to explain this, he would have to tackle the problem from a theoretical perspective—he comes to subscribe to a theory of systemic force after all. This system, he implies, subjects the individual author, and—unless one resides in a position at the system's margins, like Conrad—*determines* his or her intention and perspective. Thus, Said repeatedly points out that "the full roster of significant Victorian writers" (Said, *Culture and Imperialism*, 105) was in full support of British imperial domination, and "an active consciousness of imperialism, of an aggressive, self-aware imperial mission" became "inescapable" (Said, *Culture and Imperialism*, 106).

Arguing that an imperial culture permeates and fully structures individual works and authors' minds is probably the easiest way of breaking with the tradition that separated high culture from politics and history. However, this seems to me to be no less of a reduction than the view it aims to overcome. I will argue in this chapter that this mirror structure is not wholly accidental and that it is not just an intellectual shortcoming but points to a utopian belief in a world free of domination, which is not so different from the idealism that posited aesthetic works as separate from history and politics in the first place.

I have paid attention to Said's work here not only because it has been especially influential but also because the theoretical challenges with which he would have had to grapple beset much of the empire criticism within American Studies, a fact seen in some prominent studies of authors of the American Renaissance, particularly Emerson. Reading studies concerned with a single author or a limited group, one again encounters the question of what to do with the insight that culture cannot be regarded as an autonomous realm. Most immediately, such studies face the problem of metonymy. Typically, the authors under consideration are treated as exemplars of a "dominant imperial ideology." In a rigorous argument, this would require already knowing what that ideology consists of. However, in many cases (I will discuss two below) the reasoning approaches the tautological: the interpretation of a certain author or limited group must produce the very ideology that the authors are said to represent. As a result, differences in literary interpretation also yield widely divergent, yet supposedly dominant ideologies.

A related problem emerges as well: while Said based his arguments mainly on overt affirmations of imperialism, many critics set themselves the goal of showing how imperialism operates in culture on a covert level. In such cases, the question becomes quite simply, How does one determine whether a particular philosophy, aesthetic form, or narrative structure that is not overtly concerned with imperialism is nevertheless imperialist? One might argue that certain cultural materials lend themselves to appropriation for imperialist purposes, but then again, such appropriations can never shed their contingency and hardly demonstrate that cultural forms are imperialist per se.[8] To establish the covertly imperialist character of culture, the critic has to insist on the metonymic position of the cultural objects under consideration so that specific traits claimed to be covertly imperialist are elevated from their randomness and shown to be directly related to actually existing imperialism. For instance, a certain philosophy that is not explicitly concerned with imperialism can be claimed to be imperialist if that philosophy is read as an expression of an ideology that permeates American culture as a whole. Because the starting assumption is that imperialism is a way of life, any cultural manifestation that metonymically stands for American culture as a whole must be imperialist.[9] I now turn to Myra Jehlen's work as my paradigmatic example of this approach.

Myra Jehlen and the Incarnation Incarnate

Myra Jehlen's chapter on Emerson in her *American Incarnation*, published in 1986 during the formative phase of what would soon be called New Americanist criticism, has been one of the most influential readings of Emerson's relationship to expansionism, and, as I will argue here, it exemplifies the metonymic problem of literary empire criticism.[10] In Jehlen's work, however, metonymy concerns not only the irony that Emerson becomes once again America's "representative man," but also the fact that a theoretical, close reading of a single text (the hypercanonical *Nature*), complemented by a few pages on the essay "The Method of Nature," comes to stand for the entire Emerson. Jehlen is not interested in locating Emerson in his historical context in order to see how his philosophy comports with his political opinions and actions. Neither does she pay attention to the actual history of U.S. expansion, whether the internal conflicts over annexations and acts of imperial aggression, or the international context that would open up a view of the United States not only as the subject of imperial agency but also as the object of imperial rivalry.

In an important way, Jehlen's metonymic approach compels her to make use of a pre–New Americanist framework that can be called, obviously against her intentions, exceptionalist, and that ultimately partakes of the same logic that she criticizes. Her analysis of American expansionism does not lead her to locate American culture within a wider imperialist network in which essentialist notions of America become fractured. Rather her point is that the dominant American ideology can be differentiated from that of Europeans. Ideology critique thus replaces the myth of exceptionalism yet in turn becomes exceptionalized itself. While both Americans and Europeans shared a belief in liberal individualism, Jehlen argues, Americans conceptualized liberal individualism as incarnated in space, whereas Europeans backed up their version of the ideology of individualism with history. Jehlen's result is that Americans conceived of process spatially instead of temporally, so that "process did not mean transformation but expansion."[11]

To substantiate her point, Jehlen takes great pains to argue that Emerson's thought is organized by the valorization of incarnation over disembodiment.

Reading a passage from the 1841 essay "The Method of Nature," in which Emerson describes man as "the mediator betwixt two else unmarriageable facts" who "unites the hitherto separated strands into a perfect cord" (*CW*, vol. 1, 128–29), she concludes:

> [I]n Emerson's world, there is only one positive presence, that of man at one with nature and the world. There is no alternative, but only a more or less complete realization of the one. The "other"—Satan, evil, or just another way—is thus cast as the absence of this "one," not a substantial negative but a negation. In his formulation, the fact that America was not only a historical entity but a physical place was crucial: the assertion that there was the "Me" and the "not-Me," natural and unnatural, America and not-America, was literally carved in stone.
>
> America and the American thus incarnated the good (the affirmative and confirming), while the evil, the rebellious, was definitively *dis*embodied. (Jehlen, *American Incarnation*, 80)

The trajectory of her argument, then, is to show that Emerson was predominantly concerned with calling for the incarnation of the ideal in the realm of the actual. In other words, while he toyed with notions of duality (between reason and the understanding, the ideal and the actual, and so forth), Jehlen's point is that Emerson's dualism is merely "rhetorical," drowning out real antagonism in transcendence. In my reading, this misses the crucial edge of Emerson: while he called for the realization of the ideal, such realization could be no more than glimpsed; it remained a motivating impossibility, which in turn necessitated the continuing renewal of the call for realization.[12]

For my present purpose, however, the question is not predominantly whether Jehlen gets Emerson right or wrong, but what leads her to interpret Emerson as the representative "incarnationalist." She arrives at her conclusion through a series of interpretive decisions that have by now become familiar. She stresses Emerson's fatalistic strain, arguing that, as the divine ideal is to be found inside man, the incarnation of the ideal will transpire "not through the process of historical action, but by the agency of his [man's] self-consciousness. The happy future that Emersonian idealists envision will emerge of itself from itself. It requires neither good deeds nor a revolution" (Jehlen, *American Incarnation*, 85). Thus, in her interpretation, Emerson's idealism puts so much trust in fate that his thought leads directly to political quietism. Furthermore, Jehlen's Emerson despises true creation, so that instead of celebrating a poet-creator, "he suggests that man's truest and best creations are, as it were, dictations from nature." Neither of these arguments are surprising: they pick up on Carolyn Porter's claim that Emerson introduced Spirit as an authority figure to whom the individual had to submit, and they anticipate similar arguments articulated by John Carlos Rowe and Christopher Newfield regarding the political quietism induced by Emersonian idealism.

Finally, and most centrally, Jehlen insists that it is Emerson's Transcendentalist idealism that rationalizes the ideology of expansionism. Writing about the "Transparent Eyeball" scene from *Nature*, she concludes that for Emerson the mental operation of insight amounts to material incarnation and possession:

> In this account of the poet and the landscape, there is no conflict and not even an indirection between seeing, all the way to the landscape's infinite horizon, and having, all the way around the whole countryside. Not that the poet actually owns the countryside. But he could, the better and the more completely for his better sight. His particular practical living is thus infused with the energy that is potential in universal transcendence. And best of all, there is no contradiction between the lives (the truths, the goals) that these two realms require of him. (Jehlen, *American Incarnation*, 100)

Emerson writes in the passage under consideration, "There is a property in the horizon which no man has but he whose eye can integrate all the parts, that is, the poet" (*CW*, vol. 1, 9). If poetic sight really means ownership, Jehlen argues, the idealist vision Emerson aspires to must amount to a claim on the land. As she remarks, "This is orthodox idealism—with one addition. This idealist moves away from the material land to the landscape only to return to the land with enhanced power; he has 'a property in the horizon'" (Jehlen, *American Incarnation*, 99). In other words, whereas orthodox idealism would have distinguished between the idea of landscape and the material land—with the implication that only the material land can become property—Jehlen's Emerson holds out the possibility of owning idea and matter, landscape and land, at the same time. Hence, Emerson's idealism amounts to an ideology of imperial conquest: "The deeds Emerson envisions are real deeds, of expansion and conquest, of industrial production and growth: they are deeds of social and national reproduction, building roads to the horizon" (Jehlen, *American Incarnation*, 84). She closes her chapter with a quotation from the chapter of *Nature* called "Beauty," which virtually all of Emerson's empire-critical readers cite:

> When the bark of Columbus nears the shore of America;—before it, the beach lined with savages, fleeing out of all their huts of cane; the sea behind; and the purple mountains of the Indian Archipelago around, can we separate the man

from the living picture? Does the New World clothe his form with her palm-groves and savannahs as fit drapery? (*CW*, vol. 1, 15)

To Jehlen, "[t]he answers are obvious" (Jehlen, *American Incarnation*, 122), because Emerson here seems to confirm what she takes to be his central message: that the man and the living picture ought to be one, and that therefore, what idealism teaches man is to make use of the land that is already his. And the fact that Emerson celebrates Columbus and rejoices in "savages, fleeing" is ample proof that the union between man and land is to be understood in terms of violent imperialism.

I agree that Emerson revels in imperialist daydreaming in this passage. But reading it as a specific claim to the land of the American Continent takes it out of context. Emerson describes not so much an exceptionalist American errand, but rather the general structure of materializing greatness through individual, heroic acts. Columbus is only one (and the only "American") example, who is preceded by the following:

> When a noble act is done,—perchance in a scene of great natural beauty; when Leonidas and his three hundred martyrs consume one day in dying, and the sun and moon come each and look at them once in the steep defile of Thermopylae; when Arnold Winkelried, in the high Alps, under the shadow of the avalanche, gathers in his side a sheaf of Austrian spears to break the line for his comrades; are not these heroes entitled to add the beauty of the scene to the beauty of the deed? (*CW*, vol. 1, 115)

The point here is not, as Jehlen claims, that Emerson espouses an ideology according to which America is exceptional as the one land predestined to become identical with its heroic explorers and settlers. Rather, any heroic, noble act reveals the inseparability of man from the living picture. The picture, however, comes alive only in and through the heroic act. *Pace* Jehlen,[13] Emerson does not describe the necessary self-actualization, in the manner of an entelechy, of a particularly American fate that already exists fully as potentiality.[14] Emerson's notion of potentiality is much more skeptical: he is not suggesting a fait accompli but instead limits the accomplishment to momentary acts, which, due to their necessity of vanishing, are also possessed by failure.

But beyond the fact that Emerson may turn out to be a poor candidate for exemplifying an ideology of incarnation, Jehlen's empire criticism struggles with two larger problems that I already mentioned earlier. First, how does she arrive at the "dominant ideology" of incarnation in the first place? When she claims that her objects of study—*Nature*, along with Hawthorne's *The Marble Faun* and Melville's *Pierre*—are "texts in which the American incarnation is itself incarnate" (Jehlen, *American Incarnation*, 19), her lack of evidence (beyond her three examples and several historical studies that she cites in her first chapter) that American expansionism at large was propelled by an ideology of incarnation makes her study resemble its own thesis. It is as if her texts incarnate an idea that she has access to through an almost Emersonian insight: she fleshes out what was somehow always there yet had to await critical revelation. This surprising turnaround, however, is less an individual shortcoming of Jehlen's study and more an inherent danger in the assumption that the culture of imperialism finds its embodiment in particular texts. I am not claiming that American imperialism is absent from *Nature*, only that there is no reason why this text or any other should exemplify and incarnate imperialism as a way of life. Properly understood, imperialism as a (whole) way of life does not follow a metonymic formula because the imperialist way of life is not reducible to its many component parts but only emerges from their interaction. At the same time, these components are not reducible to imperialism.

The second overarching problem regarding Jehlen's analysis concerns the question of which insights her study claims to offer. Even if one agreed with her findings, what would remain uncertain is how the "dominant ideology of incarnation" interacted with the U.S. history of expansionism. Of course, an ideology of expansion and conquest is unlikely to mirror the history of expansion; on the contrary, it inevitably produces contradictions that then must be negated or negotiated. But Jehlen does not examine how the ideology reacts to, absorbs, or denies the contradictions that arise between it and the reality of conquest and expansion, which means encountering resistance and imperial rivalry instead of the unfolding of an entelechy. Rather, she reconstructs an ideology that remains abstract and strangely ahistorical.

What insights, then, does the analysis of an abstract and quasi-exceptionalist ideology of incarnation have to offer, if that ideology is not placed within the history of expansion? In my reading, the abstraction of Jehlen's diagnosis serves an unexpected function: it lets her produce a negative *idea* of America, and in the idea's shadow emerges a utopian implication, a familiar, positive inversion. In this light, we witness the rising of an ideal America that is not imperialist or violent and that does not expel and kill indigenous peoples, and so forth. For this inversion to emerge, the concept of American imperialism must be both total and abstract. My critique here is not so much the (surely important) point that, against her best intentions, Jehlen ends up reaffirming an exceptionalist myth of America.[15] What I want to emphasize here is rather the close interdependence of critique and implied ideal. The critique of an idea that remains abstract leads to the production of an implied utopia, rather than to an illumination of the culture of imperialism.

Jenine Abboushi Dallal: Incarnation as Abstraction

In light of my discussion of Jehlen, it is remarkable that, fifteen years after the publication of Jehlen's study, the comparatist Jenine Abboushi Dallal came to a similar result by an opposite route (for her, too, Emerson functions as the exemplar of American imperial ideology). According to her 2001 article "American Imperialism UnManifest: Emerson's 'Inquest' and Cultural Regeneration," the dominant ideology of American expansionism did not promote incarnation but instead celebrated its opposite: abstraction. Dallal observes how little Emerson and the broader expansionist discourse addressed the act of expansion: "When the territorial dominion of the United States increased by nearly 70 percent in the 1840s, the discourse of U.S. expansion was perhaps the most disembodied in its history."[16] Her analysis of the character of U.S. imperialist ideology explicitly reverses Jehlen's definition: "U.S. expansionist ideology . . . translates conquest into 'inquest,' Ralph Waldo Emerson's term for self-inquiry. . . . In this context, *inquest* is an inward search for what is already there—a tautological process of 'self-recovery'" (Dallal, "American Imperialism UnManifest," 48). Thus, rather than valorizing the manifest over the abstract (as Jehlen claimed), in Dallal's analysis imperial discourse depends so much on abstraction that actual expansion never seems to take place.

According to Dallal, this even holds for the locus classicus of the discourse of Manifest Destiny, John O'Sullivan's essay in the *Democratic Review*, where the term first appears in print.[17] As Dallal writes, "What will 'manifest' [according to O'Sullivan] is not land but 'principles,' a process decidedly rhetorical, unanchored in either material space or historical time" (Dallal, "American Imperialism UnManifest," 54). Emerson in particular finds American greatness in abstraction: "Most often, Emerson invests beauty in the incorporeal, regarding it as the source not only of poetry but also of culture" (Dallal, "American Imperialism UnManifest," 59).

Where Jehlen left the reader wondering how imperial praxis and ideology went together, Dallal maintains that the ideology of inquest was the counterpart of actual U.S. expansion. Because the United States was a settler society, she argues, expansion and conquest occurred unofficially: "Settlers typically seize Indian land piecemeal through local battle, thus creating a fait accompli with which rival imperial powers, and in some cases (such as Texas), the U.S. government must contend. Because territorial expansion enters official discourse through documents and legal issues concerning annexations or purchase, it can be represented as a bloodless purchase" (Dallal, "American Imperialism UnManifest," 50). Thus, for Dallal, the ex post facto character of national expansion—carried out by settlers, then "legalized" by the government—is mirrored in a discourse that presents expansion as tau-tology: expansion concerns the conquest of land that is (always) already American, transforming conquest into inquest.

Dallal's connection of a broad public discourse of abstraction—she quotes from a relatively wide spectrum of politicians and writers, including James Polk, Daniel Webster, John C. Calhoun, O'Sullivan, and, perhaps surpris-ingly, Thoreau—with American imperial praxis makes her argument quite persuasive. Yet the link is not as self-evident as she suggests. Tying Emerson (and Thoreau, for that matter) to ex post facto expansionism relies on a specific interpretation of Emerson's idealism that is very close to Jehlen's. For Dallal to make her claim, she must show that Emerson's preference for the abstract diverts attention from the fact that the ideal must be fully in-carnated in the actual. In effect, she interprets his idealism almost as Jehlen did: while Jehlen argued that the antagonism between the universal and the particular, or the abstract and the incarnate, was merely a rhetorical an-tagonism that issued in the solution of all contradiction, Dallal similarly claims that, although Emerson preferred the rhetoric of the abstract over the embodied, this rhetoric masked the fact that the abstract fully incorpo-rated the concrete. In the end, "conquest as inquest" relies on material con-quest, although it conceptualizes it as spiritual inquest. In other words, the difference between Jehlen and Dallal is that for Jehlen Emerson valorizes this incarnation of the ideal explicitly, whereas Dallal maintains that Emer-son conceals the aim of incarnation (read: expansion) behind a rhetoric of abstraction.

In both reconstructions of Emerson's idealism, the individual becomes the mere facilitator of design. Individual fulfillment awaits the individual who becomes the agent through whom an idea, or spirit, "is married" to physical nature. Idea and material expression are predetermined for each other, and all the individual does—but nevertheless *has to do*—is to play the truly heroic matchmaker. While Jehlen claims that the "married couple" of spirit and nature will take nature's name, Dallal bets on the spirit. But the critical point for both is that Emerson is an imperialist thinker because he defines the individual as the one whose errand it is to officiate and enact the fateful marriage. This marriage is fateful because it allows only for same-ness: it is a single spirit that must be materialized, and all materializations, though appearing to be different from each other, must be imbued with, and must lead back to, the same spirit.

This concern with sameness is also central to the readings of several other critics who read Emerson as an imperialist. In his essay "Global and Babel," Jonathan Arac, for instance, repeats Jehlen's argument that where Emerson seems to praise antagonism, he really endorses sameness. Trying to show that Emerson favors global homogeneity over diversity, he quotes a paragraph from Emerson's "Plato" (from *Representative Men*), in which Emerson contrasts the principles of "oneness and otherness" and associates them with Asia and Europe. Emerson writes: "Our strength is transitional, alternating; or, shall I say, a thread of two strands. The sea-shore, sea seen from shore, shore seen from sea . . . the experience of poetic creativeness, which is not found in staying at home, nor yet in traveling, but in transitions from one to the other . . . " (*CW*, vol. 4, 31–32).[18] Arac concludes, "The chiasmus here does not punctuate an antithesis but rather holds up a mirror—more of the same, from sea to shining sea. Emerson fixes on a transition that I take as that between America globalizing and the globe Americanizing" (Arac, "Global and Babel," 103). (Arac's use of the verb *to punctuate* is a reference back to Said, whose ideal of the contrapuntal, formulated in *Culture and Imperialism*, has left a deep impact on critics such as Arac, Paul Bové, and Homi Bhabha.)[19]

Similarly, Eric Cheyfitz reads Emerson as an ethnocentrist, whose penchant for sameness blinds him to cultural difference: "The limits of Emerson's progressive thought are in his inability to sustain the imagination of value of other cultures *on their own terms* and to imagine this cultural difference as a crucial critique of Western power" (emphasis in original).[20] Cheyfitz is correct that Emerson's thought is ethnocentric insofar as he does not value other cultures on their own terms. His strategy of accommodating otherness lies in abstraction. If New Englanders, or the U.S. white middle class, can be described as striving for the achievement of a life in obedience with the spirit, this description can be extended to other cultures, even to the point of claiming their superiority: in his "An Address . . . on . . . the Emancipation of the Negroes in the British West Indies," from 1844, for instance, Emerson argues that "the black race" is becoming "indispensable for the civility of the world" because of blacks' "more moral genius" (*AW*, 31).

While the abstraction of a moral principle heightened Emerson's tolerance, it was ethnocentric qua its universalism: it allowed for only one moral law, although that law remained impossible to fix. A further limitation concerned his imagination of what it meant to be subjected to empire. There is little indication that he grappled with what it might mean to be a colonial subject. Although he was self-consciously critical of the British Empire in its habit, as he wrote in *English Traits*, of "trampl[ing] on nationalities to reproduce London and Londoners in Europe and Asia" (*CW*, vol. 5, 143), his reflections on being trampled on by empire nevertheless tend to sound like being receptive to the Spirit in the act of inspiration. In his journal, he compared being a subject of an ancient Indian empire to *reading* the Bhagavad Gita:[21] "I owed,—my friend & I,—owed a magnificent day to Bhagavat

Geeta.—It was the first of books; it was as if an empire spake to us, nothing small or unworthy but large, serene, consistent, the voice of an old intelligence which in another age & climate had pondered and thus disposed of the same questions which exercise us. Let us not now go back & apply a minute criticism to it, but cherish the venerable oracle" (*JMN*, vol. 10, 360).[22]

Keeping in mind the interplay of receptivity and expression (which I discussed at length in chapter 2) as constitutive phases of inspiration also suggests that obedience to the Spirit did not necessarily imply that the individual had to be understood as an agent who fulfilled a divine master plan by facilitating the materialization of Reason. The lack of a truly "punctuating" difference, which Jehlen, Arac, and Cheyfitz bemoan, is an attack on Emerson's idealist assumption of universal Reason. This attack may be legitimate, but it does not establish the imperialist character of Emerson's thought: if universal Reason remains an undefined realm whose function is to challenge the actual, and if for this very reason the actual and the ideal cannot be fixed congruently on top of each other, then Emersonian idealism is less systemically repressive and less manifest than Jehlen, Dallal, Arac, and Cheyfitz argue.

What these critics suggest is a specific conception of imperialism that works on the basis of an ideology of sameness and incarnation (even if incarnation is masked as abstraction). The problem, I suggest, is not just that they try to bend Emerson until he fits this description. More fundamentally, the crux is that imperial power does not necessarily need such totalizations. If one wants to read Emerson in order to understand the connection between culture and imperialism, it is more productive to look at his internal contradictions. His imperialism does not lie in his alleged overcoming of all contradictions. Rather, he is imperialist in his contradictions. By this I do not mean that his contradictions are the site from which an imperialist ideology emerges, but that his imperialism is no more than contradictory. This is not an attempt to rescue his reputation. It is rather an argument that imperialism does not have to totalize culture in order to draw on it.

Too often, critics of empire have rendered absolute the claim that culture is imperial, thereby constructing a view of culture that is monolithic. At the core of this idea I see the assumption that an imperial order based on power inequities between colonizer and colonized must find its mimetic representation in culture, so that artifacts from the cultural mainstream are organized by and express sameness that is imperialist, while products from the margins punctuate and are anti-imperialist or resistant. As soon as one considers that one and the same author, and even an individual work, can function both imperialistically and anti-imperialistically, however, these easy distinctions between sameness and punctuation become inadequate.

Emerson is a particularly good example of this. As I will argue in my next chapter, his positions are at times imperialist, but at other times fundamentally anti-imperialist. His idealism, because of its fractures, is so flexible that it can lay the groundwork for both positions. His structure of thought is thus neither inherently imperialist nor anti-imperialist.

What is needed, then, is a different way of conceptualizing the relationship between culture and imperialism. Reducing culture to a homogenized way of life not only underestimates the complexity of culture but also overestimates the dependence of imperialism on its pervasive presence in culture. This is not at all to say that the old liberal consensus of divorcing culture from politics should be revived, nor is it to suggest that analyses of imperialism should be left to students of foreign policy. I am arguing that the analysis of imperialism and culture should start from the premise that imperialism, beyond the work of government, administration, and the military, is a practice that activates cultural repertoires, making them usable for imperialist purposes. This kind of analysis would require a critical reconstruction of potentially endless chains of appropriations—chains that extend through history and across contexts. It could be demonstrated that Emerson, for instance, was used by arbiters of imperialism by means of selection, reduction, and recontextualization. Emerson himself could also be inserted into the chain of appropriating agents by revealing the means and sources that allowed him to construct imperialist appeals. The culture of imperialism would no longer be thought of as a way of life, but as a conglomerate of situational activations—extending synchronically and diachronically—of cultural material for imperialist purposes.

The Transnational Turn

In the last decade, "the transnational turn" has directed American Studies toward a new master paradigm. Since then, many of the annual conventions of the American Studies Association have taken as their topic the transnational, and the most influential Presidential Addresses from this period have concerned themselves with the attempt to finally move beyond American exceptionalism by adopting a transnational perspective.[23]

While for empire critics, Donald Pease's label "New Americanists" worked well as a sign of radicalism, the transnational turn has made the promise captured in the term "New Americanists" come true in a literal sense— being a "New Americanist" now merely means being an Americanist of the present moment. As Michael Kramer has written in a review essay in 2001, "Many of their [the New Americanists'] assertions are our assumptions;

what seemed radical and threatening then (at least to Crews) is ordinary now."[24]

But transnational American Studies did not merely pull New American-ist empire criticism into the mainstream; neither was this mainstreaming accompanied by a simple dilution of its radicalism. Rather, the transnational turn has brought one element to the fore that empire criticism had contained only by implication: it has made room for the articulation of a visionary pro-gram to counter imperialist nationalism, and it has conceptualized this uto-pianism as a theoretical radicalization of the approach of empire criticism.

Shelley Fisher Fishkin and the Transnational Imaginary

A look at Shelley Fisher Fishkin's 2004 Presidential Address underlines this point. In her view, transnational American Studies surpasses empire criticism as well as race, class, and gender studies because only now have the limits of the national perspective been transcended:

> The field has been dramatically transformed over the last four decades as scholars recovered the voices of women and minorities and replaced earlier exceptionalist visions of unsullied innocence with a clear-eyed look at the lust for empire that America shared with other western powers. But the national paradigm of the United States as a clearly bordered geographical and political space remained intact.[25]

Fishkin goes on to mention that Amy Kaplan expressed "a sense of irony and dismay" (Fishkin, "Crossroads of Cultures," 21) in her 2003 Presiden-tial Address at the fact that while she had tried, in the early 1990s, to get readers to acknowledge that the United States has been an empire, right-wing politicians and pundits have in the meantime begun to openly embrace American empire, thus creating an eerie alliance between left-wing aca-demic criticism and right-wing political ideology. Yet despite her reference to Kaplan, Fishkin neglects to mention that Kaplan had already insisted in her introduction to *Cultures of United States Imperialism* that empire criti-cism required interrogating the form and borders of the nation. The as-sumption that only the transnational turn questioned "the United States as a clearly bordered geographical and political space" is a misrepresentation of what empire criticism set out to achieve.

And yet, in a crucial way, Fishkin's insistence that the perspective of transnational studies differs from that of empire criticism is correct. Empire criticism, almost by definition, focuses on the United States as the imperial actor. This perspective has recently provoked criticism from various angles. Paul Giles, for instance, has remarked that "there is an important sense in which we should read the United States itself as one of the objects of global-ization, rather than as merely its malign agent."[26] But while Giles's answer to the overemphasis on the imperial subject has been to look at the United States as a global object, "so that all the insecurities associated with trans-nationalism are lived out experientially within the nation's own borders" (Giles, "Deterritorialization," 57), this is not the route that the majority of transnational Americanists have taken to complement the focus of empire criticism. Rather, the most popular approach has adopted the focus of ear-lier race, class, and gender studies on resistant and oppositional subjectivi-ties to show how, in Fishkin's words, "borderlands, crossroads, and contact zones . . . disrupt celebratory nationalist narratives" (Fishkin, "Crossroads of Cultures," 19). Transnational American Studies is thus claimed to tran-scend the notion of the United States as a clearly bordered space by examin-ing the agency of identities that reach across national borders. Importantly, as American Studies has long identified with progressive activism, scholarly work on resistant, transnational formations has enabled the scholars involved to construct models of identification.

In fact, I would venture to claim that transnational American Studies could only achieve its prominence by adding a broad grounding of imagi-nary identification to the negativity of empire criticism. Whereas empire criticism interrogated national borders in light of an imperial way of life, the world of oppositional, anti-imperialist formations examined by transnational American Studies is often portrayed as achieving a surprising degree of free-dom. And as transnational scholars seem to directly promote that freedom by elucidating it, they have tended to adopt a self-understanding as, and an imaginary identity of, emancipators.

Fishkin's address is a good example of this mirroring between scholars and their object of study. She quotes David Palumbo-Liu and Paul Lauter on the openness of the transnational world. While Palumbo-Liu argues that the circulation of ideas, peoples, capital, and cultures throughout the world requires that we view America "as a place always in process" (quoted in Fishkin, "Crossroads of Cultures," 21), the passage Fishkin picks out from Lauter even goes as far as claiming that America must be regarded as part of "a world system, in which the exchange of commodities, the flow of capital, and the iterations of cultures know no borders" (quoted in Fishkin, "Crossroads of Cultures," 21). It is striking how easily the interrogation of geographical and political borders slides into affirmations of "no borders" for commodities, capital, *and culture*. Circulation as "ceaseless process," "iterations that know no borders"—it is, indeed, difficult not to think here of Emerson's descriptions of the incessant circular flows of universal energies in such essays as "Circles": "every action admits of being outdone. Our life is an apprenticeship to the truth, that around every circle another can be drawn; that there is no end in nature, but every end is a beginning" (*CW*, vol. 2, 179).[27]

The mirroring becomes fully discernible in Fishkin's descriptions of the history of American Studies:

> [O]ne of the reasons many of us were attracted to American studies in the first place was its capaciousness, its eschewal of methodological or ideological dogma, and its openness to fresh syntheses and connections. I honor that openness in my talk tonight, as I probe some of the syntheses and connections being made in the field today and where they might take us. (Fishkin, "Crossroads of Cultures," 19)

To be sure, the self-congratulatory tone is in part to be explained (and excused) by the occasion and genre of the Presidential Address. Nevertheless it is striking how closely her descriptions of American Studies resemble those of first-generation American Studies scholars[28] who were later so vigorously attacked by New Americanists such as Donald Pease for perpetuating an exceptionalist ideology that thrived on the idea that America and American Studies were concerned with humanist matters that transcended methods and theories. The point I want to make here, however, is not that transnational American Studies has revived tenets widely shared in the early decades of the field; rather, I want to show how the articulation of the utopian self-understanding of American Studies was particularly facilitated by the transnational turn.

Fishkin's celebration of the alleged openness of American Studies is grounded on two facets of transnationalism. The first should plainly be called "internationalism," as it refers to the fact that, at the ASA convention over which she presided, the participants came from many different countries, with training in different disciplines, interests in different fields, skills in different methodologies, and so forth. The second, more properly transnational, facet addresses the transnational outlook of their work:

> Today American studies scholars increasingly recognize that that understanding [of the multiple meanings of America] requires looking beyond the nation's borders and understanding how the nation is seen from vantage points beyond its borders. At a time when American foreign policy is marked by nationalism, arrogance, and Manichean oversimplification, the field of American studies is an increasingly important site of knowledge marked by a very different set of assumptions—a place where borders both within and outside the nation are interrogated and studied, rather than reified and reinforced. (Fishkin, "Crossroads of Cultures," 20)

Fishkin's statement serves the obvious purpose of charging the work of American Studies with an oppositional political force (the mirroring force that makes American Studies indistinguishable from its objects of study), but in order to arrive at this goal she must stretch the logic of her point. While it makes sense that understanding the multiple meanings of America requires taking different vantage points beyond U.S. borders, this interest in other perspectives very much relies on the *difference* of perspectives, and thus on borders, as well as on the distinction between inside and outside. How this project is related to the issue of the interrogation of borders versus their reification and reinforcement is not at all self-evident. In fact, recognizing America's multiple meanings may directly contradict the interrogation of borders. Her logic implies that nationalist arrogance is defined by taking no interest in other perspectives and also by naturalizing the national form (nationalism), so that the counterargument must develop an interest in other views and question the form of the nation. But as she demonstrates in her own quotations, the project of questioning borders leads directly to the affirmation that "the iterations of culture" know "no borders."

Thus, "interrogating and studying" borders of nation-states involves overcoming borders of culture. This threatens to undermine the very premise of her argument, which relied on the difference in views, meanings, and so forth. Taking into account outside perspectives thus becomes subordinated to the political goal of countering nationalism because the way she imagines to counter nationalism consists of taking down the borders and boundaries that are themselves the product of nationalism. In other words, if the violence of nationalism is seen to lie in its reification of borders, crossing borders becomes the most important counternationalist act. "Other perspectives" can only be pursued within the project of demonstrating the nationalist artificiality of reified otherness and thus are relegated to a secondary level.

Transnationalism, then, is a project that puts extremely high hopes on the transcendence—and ultimately the abolishment—of borders, because what is promised to lie in the very act of transcending the borders is a vision of limitless freedom. The thrust of the logic of transnationalism is "inherently expansive"[29] because the promise of freedom relies on the continuous movement of transcendence. One may claim at this point that the development from empire criticism to transnationalism has come full circle, as the transnational turn subscribes to the same process of limitless growth that empire critics decried as the connection between transcendentalism and imperialism. But my point is not to criticize transnationalism for its tacitly imperial aspirations, but to explain why the transnational successors of empire criticism (and it is certainly possible to inhabit both positions at once)[30] could so rapidly turn against the convictions of their predecessors. The reason lies in the fact that both paradigms subscribe to a concept of freedom that is essentially utopian and that envisions a life without external or internal pressures and limitations.

Culture, Organicism, Freedom

In a series of illuminating essays and books, Pheng Cheah has traced this particular concept of freedom back to its philosophical articulation in eighteenth-century German idealism and developments in the natural sciences. As he demonstrates, it is the metaphor of the organism that has provided the link between the notion of culture, or *Bildung*, and an idea of freedom that is understood as the freedom from the limitations of the given.[31] In this sense, I argue, both empire critics and transnational American Studies scholars habitually invoke a concept of emancipation that is based on the image of the organism.

At first, this seems a counterintuitive claim, because the organism is commonly understood to describe a state of extreme communality in which the individual cannot be distinguished from the group. In this understanding, organicism describes the opposite of such states as social anomie, extreme individualism, or, indeed, cosmopolitanism and transnationalism. After all, if transnationalism is defined by the transcendence of those forces that keep a limited group tightly knit together by means of ideology and force (the nation here appears as organicism gone bad), then transnationalism, understood as the formation of mobile alliances beyond circumscribed boundaries, seems to be much too dynamic and ephemeral to be aptly described by the organic metaphor.

Yet while the organism is most easily recognizable as the complete union of the individual and the group, the organizing idea (Cheah speaks of "ontology") underlying the image is not limited to this particular shape. For what the union of the individual and the group describes is a state that is from one perspective absolutely compatible with the self-description of transnationalism: the attractiveness of the union of the individual and the group derives from the dissolution of the boundary between inside and outside, and precisely this dissolution resurfaces in the transnational vision. This dissolution is underwritten by the idea that the individual is freed from outside forces and pressures that impose their limits on freedom. Significantly, in the genealogy of the organism it is not some "unencumbered" individual that poses as its counterterm, but the mechanism, which is a mere relay of external forces. Organism and mechanism oppose each other because the organism is, in Cheah's words, "capable of auto-construction, auto-maintenance, auto-regulation, auto-repair, and auto-genesis," while the machine remains dependent on a "creator outside of it," is merely "the sum of its parts," and "is more vulnerable to changes in surrounding conditions."[32]

As Cheah demonstrates, in the philosophical elaborations by German idealists, the metaphor of the organism finds its domain in culture, and it there comes to stand for the closest approximation of actualizing the freedom ascribed to Reason (classically defined as the realm of absolute freedom from determining forces) via the transcendence of finitude through purposive rationality: "The philosopheme of culture articulates the formative power over nature that co-belongs with humanity, not only as an animal capable of contemplation, but as a purposive being with the ability to shape its natural self and external conditions in the image of rationally prescribed forms" (Cheah, *Spectral Nationality*, 39). What the organismic metaphor suggests is that culture allows the individual to become capable of emancipating himself or herself from the natural forces that act on, and limit, the bodily self. Through and in culture, humans shape nature rather than being shaped by it.

While the organismic metaphor quickly became the underlying idea of Romantic nationalism, it can be extended to that which appears to us without a clearly bounded, bodily shape: "[T]he putative antithesis between cosmopolitan universalism and nationalist particularism misleadingly obscures the fact that both philosophical nationalism and cosmopolitanism articulate universal institutional models for the actualization of freedom and are underwritten by the same organismic ontology" (Cheah, *Spectral Nationality*, 2). In his article titled "Given Culture," Cheah fleshes out this "organismic ontology," demonstrating that Kant's universal cosmopolitanism, Hegel's and Fichte's nationalism, and even Homi Bhabha's rearticulations of cosmopolitanism based on hybridity all presuppose an idea of culture that promises the actualization of freedom as the overcoming of limitation.[33]

Cheah pursues a double purpose with this genealogy. His argument aims to reconsider postcolonial nationalism in the global South. Rather than following the critical trend of rejecting such nationalisms in favor of some version of hybrid cosmopolitanism, Cheah's analysis insists that nationalism per se is neither good nor bad—in other words, that postcolonial nationalism is in no way inferior to the postcolonial hybridity generally favored by scholars of postcolonialism. Taking his argument further, however, he also claims that postcolonial nationalisms, while borrowing support from the organicist legacy, develop a different understanding of freedom, which does not aspire to the transcendence of limiting forces but rather valorizes a "responsibility to the given" (Cheah, "Given Culture," 292). What he sees emerging in the nationalisms of the global South is what he calls (borrowing from Derrida) "spectral nationality," that is, the confrontation with and acceptance of the aporia that resides in the reinvestment in the postcolonial nation-state. This aporia describes the fact that the postcolonial nation-state is both medicine and poison: in Cheah's reading, the nation-state is the only effective weapon of defense against the processes of "neocolonial globalization," yet the same postcolonial nation-state is also susceptible to becoming "recompradorized," that is, to inviting "neocolonial" investment in a way that exacerbates the ramifications of globalization.

From the confrontation with this double bind, Cheah attempts to extrapolate a radically different philosophical concept of freedom: "The theoretical significance of postcolonial nationalism . . . is that as given culture in neocolonial globalization, it is a historical case of the gift of life in finitude. . . . A spectral life—life perpetually haunted by the spectrality from within that constitutes it" (Cheah, "Given Culture," 323). Spectrality is another description of the aporia mentioned above: while the metaphor of the organism promises freedom from limitations, the organism is itself enabled by limiting forces from the outside that can "contaminate" the organism. In Cheah's words (which, in a way, reverse Adorno and Horkheimer's argument in *Dialectic of Enlightenment*), "the becoming-objective of culture as the realm of human purposiveness and freedom depends on forces that are radically other and beyond human control" (Cheah, "Given Culture," 308).[34] If culture itself is "merely given" (Cheah, "Given Culture," 308), this not only means that organic freedom in the ideal sense is impossible. It also means that utopian and repressive forms of organicism (for instance, nationalism) cannot be categorically differentiated: they are internally linked by the dependence on the given, by the principal vulnerability to malign forces. The possibility of reversal from a benign to a malign organism is therefore inscribed into the very condition of the project of organic freedom.

In his book *Spectral Nationality*, Cheah emphasizes that spectrality—understood as the "questioning of the modern philosopheme of freedom"—is:

> emphatically not a form of postmodern pessimism or nihilism. For the point is not that ideas cannot be incarnated, that one should therefore dismiss efforts toward transcendence as useless and futile. It is rather that what makes incarnation possible—a ghostliness linked to the gift of time—also makes it impossible. This ghostliness both enables and impedes the living nation's self-perpetuation because it is the condition of (im)possibility of the epigenesis of life itself. (Cheah, *Spectral Nationality*, 247)

The "(im)possibility of incarnation" again describes the aporia of given culture: Postcolonial nationalism cannot but invest the nation with an idea of freedom based on the belief that the national body will be the incarnation of freedom. Yet the incarnation in the nation-state can never really become freedom's incarnation, since it is also the portal through which the "in-organic" and "mechanical" forces of globalization enter.

While Cheah's genealogy of organicism as "freedom from" is highly con-vincing, I want to extend the range of articulations of the "responsibility to the given." The responsibility to the given, and the acceptance of the aporia that freedom is immanent to the given (to that which subjugates us), could similarly be elucidated from a reading of pragmatism's various versions of the figure of "reconstruction." For instance, in chapter 2 I discussed Peirce's description of experimentalism as the sequence of belief, surprise, and re-construction. Reconstruction here is literally a response to the unexpected given, perceived by Peirce as a step toward the universal truth. For Peirce, the reconstruction that consummates the experimental act is the closest he gets to a notion of freedom. What the dependence of Peirce's "realist mo-nism" on reconstruction suggests, and what interests me more than pragma-tism here, is that certain kinds of idealism (and there is clearly an idealist residue in Peirce's thinking) can also be understood to facilitate an under-standing of freedom as responsibility to the given.

Crucial for idealism to do so is the realization that the ideal cannot be seamlessly actualized or incarnated, and that there is nevertheless no alter-native to promoting the incarnation of the ideal. Idealist thinkers who self-consciously limit organisms to the side of the actual, despite measuring them by the ideal, work toward the dual strategy of remaining loyal to the aim of actualizing freedom, while also distinguishing the actual from the ideal. This kind of idealism, too, follows "the (im)possibility of incarnation." I will argue in the next chapter that Emerson's idealism tends to produce a similar sense of aporia: he calls for the incarnation of a nationalist organism, yet as a next step he tends to disown the putative products of incarnation.

For now, however, the point I want to maintain from my excursus into Cheah's examination of the organismic metaphor is that transnationalism is a project steeped deeply in the organicist legacy. It has come to define na-tionalism (in a reversal of the nineteenth-century understanding of the na-tion) as a confining mechanism that has erected naturalized borders, which create the conditions for imperial domination. As a remedy, transnational-ism suggests a concept of freedom rooted in ever-emergent transcendence, in which borders are crossed, new coalitions are forged, and culture knows no boundaries (and hence no outside). What remains to be demonstrated now is that the way Emerson has been read by transnational Americanists fits this description. As I will show, it has recently become possible to claim Emerson either as a force of imperialist and nationalist ideology, or as a force of transnational transcendence. In both cases, however, the aspirations to organic freedom on the side of the critic remain firmly in place.

John Carlos Rowe: Comparatism versus Imperialism

Pheng Cheah's seminal intervention has not gone wholly unnoticed in the debate over the transnationalization of American Studies. In his contribution to a 2003 special issue of PMLA on "America: The Idea, the Literature," John Carlos Rowe makes an attempt to accommodate Cheah's claim that postcolonial nationalisms may be "an indispensable means of resisting one-way globalization,"[35] but he does so only with the caveat that Cheah is mistaken in his warning not to make "easy distinctions between good and bad nationalisms" (Rowe, "Literary Culture and Transnationality," 88):

> transition or modulation [between oppressive, hierarchical nationalism and a good, demotic nationalism] is not as ambiguous or indeterminate as Cheah implies . . . ; it can be understood by careful historical interpretation and understanding. (Rowe, "Literary Culture and Transnationality," 88)

As Rowe's insistence on the possibility of distinguishing between good and bad nationalism rests on historical analysis, he does not sufficiently engage with Cheah's argument that good and bad nationalism (as well as cosmopolitanism) work with the figure of the organism, that organic freedom depends on being "haunted" by the forces of the given, and that therefore benign and malign organisms can slide into each other. Rowe's response to Cheah, however, does have the advantage of illuminating the persistence of an organicist utopia in transnational American Studies.

Rowe structures his article around the attempt to "distinguish between a genuinely comparatist understanding of political, cultural, and historical otherness or foreignness and the cultural imperialism that finds itself replicated everywhere either as instances of its civilized superiority or in the sympathetic identification whereby the national subject substitutes its own image to silence and suppress other peoples" (Rowe, "Literary Culture and Transnationality," 88). This Manichean structure is driven by the assumption "that critical studies of colonialism and nationalism have as their aim the political as well as intellectual transformation of inherently exclusive and repressive systems" (Rowe, "Literary Culture and Transnationality," 79). "Transformation" sounds like an engagement with the given rather than transcendence, but since systems that are *inherently* exclusive and repressive cannot be transformed but only replaced, Rowe's progressivist agenda is precisely one of transcendence, if not of nationalism per se, then of those nationalisms whose "inherently exclusive and repressive" character can be established through historical analysis. Tellingly, the transnational criticism Rowe envisions takes part "in the ultimate project of defining new kinds of social organization that will dispense with the hierarchies, exclusions, and fears of the past" (Rowe, "Literary Culture and Transnationality," 88).

Rowe refrains from simply aligning progressive and reactionary with transnationalism and nationalism respectively. According to him, there are forms through which transnationalism is underwritten by reactionary values or becomes plainly imperialist. On the other hand, there are also reconfigurations of nationalism that "in certain qualified ways" contribute to the ultimate project (Rowe, "Literary Culture and Transnationality," 87). Yet whenever nationalism crosses over to this side of the divide, "we have national discourse that enunciates the concerns of transnationality and postcolonial study" (Rowe, "Literary Culture and Transnationality," 82). The program for literary criticism that accompanies this utopian project sets out to distinguish between texts that conform to this progressive project and those that do not, but it never becomes clear in Rowe's writings what the criteria are for establishing on which side an author or a text stands. Even an author's claims of commitment to activism (as discussed in chapter 1) can be revealed as "inefficacious," if that commitment, as in Emerson's case, is perceived to be too idealistic.

In his contribution to the special issue of PMLA, Rowe reads Emerson as an imperialist on grounds that resemble Jehlen's, though here, too, the argument is essentially historical: "It is difficult to find examples of transnationality in the writings of the transcendentalists that do not serve imperialist aims and purposes. . . . The transcendentalists were particularly good in developing analogies between the physical frontier and the psychic and metaphysical boundaries to be overcome by the contemplative, educated man" (Rowe, "Literary Culture and Transnationality," 81). As in his chapter on Emerson in *At Emerson's Tomb*, discussed in chapter 1, Rowe uses Emerson's antislavery writings (the texts on which his apologists most rely) to demonstrate Emerson's imperialist complicity. Rowe claims that even in Emerson's "An Address . . . on . . . the Emancipation of the Negroes in the British West Indies," from 1844, "Emerson invokes the British abolitionist Thomas Clarkson's argument to Prime Minister William Pitt that an end to the British slave trade would have the advantage of opening Africa to British commercial and political colonization, likely to be of far greater profit to Britain than the slave trade" (Rowe, "Literary Culture and Transnationality," 81).

Rowe is only partially correct. Emerson is, as usual, less than clear on the matter. At first, he indeed refers to the argument that the civilization of Africa would provide new markets.[36] Yet in the passage to which Rowe points, Emerson does not elucidate Clarkson's and Pitt's interest in the material prospects of colonialism but instead sees them as joining forces *against* the materialist dehumanization caused by slavery. Emerson here endorses the imperial civilizing mission by pitting culture against economics: what the West, or humanity, can gain from colonialism is not material but cultural riches.[37] Moreover, early on in the address, Emerson makes an economic antislavery argument, but he explicitly does so for strategic reasons. It is the only way to persuade the most selfish and stubborn slaveholders of the advantages of abolition:

> If the Virginian piques himself on the picturesque luxury of his vassalage . . . , I shall not refuse to show him, that when their free-papers are made out, it will still be their interest to remain on his estate, and that the oldest planters of Jamaica are convinced, that it is cheaper to pay wages, than to own a slave. (AW, 8)

Emerson leaves no doubt that he cannot help looking down on the "Virginian's" perspective of economic self-interest. He ridicules the slaveholders' selfishness with an image of grotesque disproportion: "If there be any man who thinks the ruin of a race of men a small matter, compared with the last decoration and completions of his own comfort,—who would not so much as part with his ice-cream, to save them from rapine and manacles, I think, I must not hesitate to satisfy that man, that also his cream and vanilla are cheaper, by placing the negro nation on a fair footing, than by robbing them" (AW, 8). Material self-interest, ridiculed as indulgence in "cream and vanilla," is thus ruled out as an argument for slavery on both economic and moral grounds; in fact, the moral grounds make the economic perspective itself untenable. Thus, when Emerson argues that slavery is not defensible economically, he also insists that economic arguments are categorically inappropriate to the question of slavery ("the ruin of a race of men"). In other words, Emerson's position in the 1844 Address consists of at least three different and incommensurable speech acts, ranging from the invocation of the material gains to be had from abolition to the irrelevance of material gains for the question of abolition.

As I will discuss in the next chapter, such ambivalences are typical of Emerson's stance on imperialism. He tended to affirm *and* reject it, convinced that there were good (spiritual) and bad (material) forms of imperialism. The fact that Emerson, following the conventions of nineteenth-century imperialist reasoning, tended not to distinguish between the terms *imperialism* and *cosmopolitanism*, begins to suggest the complicated intertwining of imperialism with the aims of emancipation pursued on universalist grounds. This is an intertwining with which cosmopolitical theory is still struggling today,[38] and it is directly linked to Cheah's aporia that is at the core of the concept of freedom as haunted. For Rowe, however, insisting on such ambiguities is a sign of a lack of political commitment. This impatience with ambiguity is an expression of his activist aspirations, which depend on being able to tell which texts enable emancipation and which ones enforce limitations.[39]

Tales of Imprisonment

The critic's game of writing books and articles that divide a list of authors into progressive and reactionary, comparatist and hegemonic, or simply transnationalist and nationalist, is popular among many of transnationalism's proponents, and it can be viewed as a result of the felt need to adjust and potentially reduce literary analysis to a utopian politics. Jonathan Arac and Eric Cheyfitz, whose critiques of Emerson I quoted earlier, pursue similar projects. For both, Emerson acts as the inversion of what transnationalism must do. In Arac's view, the most critical steps toward transnational incarnation (or toward what one could call an ever-emergent organism of the diverse) are taken by the late critic Edward Said, who prefers "sublime disruption" over the faux antagonism of an Emerson (Arac, "Global and Babel," 110). Cheyfitz, on the other hand, contrasts Emerson's ethnocentrism with Pequot Methodist minister William Apess, who in the 1830s was "defending Indian rights, rewriting New England history from a Native perspective, and calling, like Emerson, institutional Christianity in question, though for its racism not the aridity of its traditional forms" (Cheyfitz, "Common Emerson," 261).

Not all transnationalist critics have read Emerson as the apex of imperialism. If the appeal of transnational American Studies lies in its capacity to amend the negativity of empire criticism with new figures of identification, it was to be expected that critics would find ways to salvage as transnational visionaries the very writers who previously played the role of the imperialist villain. Wai Chee Dimock's recent work is the best example of such a rescue attempt. In her recent study *Through Other Continents: American Literature across Deep Time*, she describes an Emerson who, by way of his interest in Hinduism, Islam, Buddhism, and so forth, "bursts out of the confines of the nation-state, becoming a thread in the fabric of world religions" (Dimock, *Through Other Continents*, 32). In her reading, Emerson's disenchantment with the Church is based on his view of Jesus as a mere local and national figure. According to Dimock, Emerson holds up figures whom he deems truly universal against Christianity's deification of Jesus. Among these are Goethe, whose work, however, lacks a certain warmth, and the more widely accessible vernacular poet Hafiz.

Dimock's point is that the "low" poetry of Hafiz afforded Emerson with a "different scale with which to measure beauty" (Dimock, *Through Other*

Continents, 44). "Different" here means different from the standardized measures of the nation-state. In Dimock's hands, the very term *deep time* (originally used in geography to describe stretches of time beyond our imagination) becomes an expression of transnationalist transcendence: "As an associative form, the nation-state is a late arrival in human history; it had a definitive beginning, and, just as conceivably, it might also have a finite end. Rather than naturalizing its clock and its border, I try to loosen up both" (Dimock, *Through Other Continents*, 4).

While Rowe, Cheyfitz, Arac, and others require engagement in anti-imperialist politics for an author to qualify as genuinely transnational, for Dimock it is sufficient that an author identifies with literatures across world history. In fact, against the initial impetus of empire criticism that aimed to analyze "cultures of imperialism," literature itself once again becomes the domain of transcendence: "Literature is the home of nonstandard space and time. Against the official borders of the nation and against the fixed intervals of the clock, what flourishes here is irregular duration and extension, some extending for thousands of years of thousands of miles, each occasioned by a different tie and varying with that tie, and each loosening up the chronology and geography of the nation" (Dimock, *Through Other Continents*, 4).

In one sense I agree with Dimock: literature cannot be reduced to nationalist ideologies. But converting this reservation into an emancipatory potential of literature not only seems rash but also runs the risk of replicating the logic underlying the opposite argument that the realm of literature is fully co-opted by imperialist and other ideologies. Although Dimock seems to have changed her politics quite dramatically since her earlier work (she was included in the 1990 special issue of *boundary 2*, in which Pease appropriated the term *New Americanists* from Crews), there are two corresponding continuities. Now as before, she subscribes to the New Americanist (and now transnationalist) agenda of locating sites and methods of resistance, with resistance leading to the emergence of new orders that transcend the old limitations of the given. Second, what makes such utopian resistance necessary in the first place is the assumption of a force that tends to subordinate the subject in its entirety. Dimock thus shares the belief of all the empire and transnational critics discussed in this chapter that the nation is a confining force field, or mechanism, not taking into account that in the nineteenth century the nation was generally defined as the exact opposite of the mechanism, that is, as an emancipating organism.

This is, in fact, what aligns New Americanist and post–New Americanist readings of the nation with the issues of representation and identity that I discussed in Parts I and II: just as the New Americanists understand representation to interpellate the subject by symbolic means, and just as identity is analyzed as a violent imposition on the individual, so the nation keeps the individual imprisoned within its spatial (and, according to Dimock, temporal) borders. In other words, theories that imagine freedom as a state of being without any outside pressure typically picture being subjugated to virtually any force (whether it is language, identity, or the nation) as a kind of incarceration in which the subject is tied up in chains and left almost completely impotent. I say almost, because some subjects must still find ways to break out and resist.

The liveliest debate in empire and transnational criticism has concerned two related issues: much scholarship has focused either on arguing over which authors are reactionary and which emancipatory, or on devising ever-new ways of resistance. But if these debates come to such widely different results as, for example, those of Rowe and Dimock, one must ask whether this has to do with the problem that, while nationalism and imperialism are generally understood to work in imprisoning ways, the very concept of power as an imprisoning force (whether via the nation, language, or identity) has remained largely unquestioned. In other words, I suggest it is time to turn attention away from the artistry of resistance to a retheorization of power. As attractive as it may be to develop models of emancipation and utopia, the exuberant focus on this side of the equation has led to a lack of scrutiny of what precisely resistance contends with. Power, whether that of a nation (empire), representation, or identity, may work far less unilaterally than the various theories of resistance lead us to believe, as I have suggested in the earlier chapters regarding both representation and identity.

If one is willing to dispense with the common assumptions about imperialist culture as a totalized category, studying Emerson in the context of a culture of imperialism turns out to be a promising field of inquiry. It lets us see that, while U.S. politics in the mid-nineteenth century was becoming increasingly imperialist, this imperialism drew on culture without requiring that culture be reduced to imperialism or being able so to reduce it. For the most part, empire critics have been willing to concede this under the assumption that fissures in the imperialist outlook evolve from the margins. But as I will argue in the following chapter, Emerson's thought, as well as his politics, wavered between imperialism and anti-imperialism. They did so because of his own brand of organicism, which underlies both those moments in his career when he reiterated imperialist positions and those moments when he formulated sharp critiques of imperialism and actively fought for the abolition of slavery. It would be too simple, then, to conclude that Emerson was an imperialist because he was an organicist thinker. Rather, his organicism could easily develop in an imperialist direction, but it also enabled his most progressive moods.

From the early nineteenth century on, the belief that America's achievement or destiny is to realize freedom has legitimized imperial expansion. What makes Emerson interesting even today is that he remained reluctant to square the ideal of freedom with a belief in the possibility of its realization. In earlier chapters, I have called this his "fractured idealism." This reluctance has directly to do with his engagement in the institution of the public lecture, which produced the generic expectation of a clash between (at least) two different voices, one of them taking up matters of the actual world, and another proceeding to idealist generalization. As a result of this engagement, Emerson's writings can be reconstructed as an early grappling with the aporia Pheng Cheah calls "the (im)possibility of incarnation." From this aporetic viewpoint, Emerson's conception of freedom is situational and momentary, rather than utopian. It is this risky immanence of his thought that the premises of empire criticism and transnationalism have all but occluded. I will attempt to uncover this outlook in my final chapter.

[6]

EMERSON'S ORGANICIST NATIONALISM

Nationalism as Idealist Organicism

EMERSON'S RECORD ON the issues of nationalism, imperialism, and racism is mixed: his statements are often contradictory, his opinions seem to swerve from one extreme to the other, and often he does not even inform the reader whether a given viewpoint is his own or just one worthy of reporting. Without doubt, this equivocality (his famous inconsistency) has been essential for keeping readers and scholars interested in him. As discussed in the previous chapter, Emerson's thought on the nation and on empire lends itself to scholarly projects showing either how deeply complicit a hypercanonical figure such as Emerson was in the expansionist and imperialist aspects of United States history and culture, or, on the other side of the spectrum, how cunningly he opened up possibilities of identification and solidarity beyond the temporal and spatial confines of the nation.

In this chapter, I will demonstrate that both of these reading practices neglect the function of Emerson's disquisitions on the nation for his career as a public lecturer. From this perspective, Emerson neither simply promoted nationalist and imperialist views nor heroically resisted them. Instead, he produced a series of truly incompatible positions that served him well on the lecture circuit. The topic of the nation—whether focusing on the Anglo-Saxon, American, or British nation—was central to his public engagement from his early lecture series in the mid-1830s through his performances during and after the Civil War. Emerson tried to capture his audiences' interest by expanding on the differences, the similarities, and, at times, the identity between the British and the Americans, particularly after returning from his European trips in 1833 and 1848. In 1835 he gave a lecture series on English literature; between his return from Europe in 1848 and the publication of *English Traits* in 1856, he delivered lectures such as "England," "London," "France, or Urbanity," and "The Anglo-American." A few years earlier, in 1843, he had traveled along the eastern seaboard reading a series of lectures on New England. This corpus of texts provides the material for this chapter.

The question of the nation was particularly well suited for the lyceum stage. Several historians have argued that the institution of the lyceum, especially after it had developed from a local institution of mutual education into a national lecture system, played an important role in forming an "imagined community" in the United States.[1] Audiences knew they were listening to the very lectures that had already been heard in other parts of the country and that had been written about in local newspapers and in those, like the *New York Tribune*, that were circulating more widely. Moreover, if these lectures addressed the question of the nation, the identity work provided by such performances intensified.

The question of the nation suggested itself for another reason as well. Because the lyceum, even when it began increasingly to pay attention to the demands of entertainment, never fully let go of its educational aspirations, lecturers were expected to address particular topics without dividing the audience by taking partisan positions (compare Ray, *Lyceum and Public Culture*, 29). Here the topic of the nation was ideally suitable: American national characteristics concerned everyone in the audience and reaffirmed a unifying identity over against a different nation, most often the British (though, as I will show, this differential logic was unstable, considering the heavy emphasis that Emerson put on the myth of the Anglo-Saxon). Still, it was impossible to refrain from partisanship when discussing American achievements and shortcomings. At this point, a related convention of the public lecture was helpful. While the particular was essential for grounding lectures, it was to make way for generalization in order to convey the suggestion of deeper insight (compare Scott, "Popular Lecture," 797).

These two voices—one of engagement with the particular and one of metaphysical reflection—also structured Emerson's public performances. As I will show in this chapter, regarding the nation Emerson most often based his assessment of the particular on a philosophical premise that I call idealist organicism. The leading idea, derived most obviously from Victor Cousin, was that every nation corresponded to one "idea"; the imperative for each member of the nation was to find ways to embody that idea. This idealist organicism became a useful engine for Emerson's lectures, because it allowed for ever new differentiations between the ideal and the actual, as well as for the combination of a concern for the nation with a striving for the sphere of universal Reason.

Emerson's assessment of the British Empire is one example. Starting from the premise of idealist organicism, Emerson could declare the British Empire either an instance of the incarnation of the ideal or precisely the opposite: a regrettable failure to actualize what the ideal would truly mean. It was, in fact, not foreseeable in which direction Emerson would be led by his premise at any given point. And at critical moments, he fractured his idealism by coming to suggest that the ideal could never be incarnated, although the goal of incarnation could not be given up. This aporetic fracturing became particularly necessary when Emerson tried to hold on to his premise while distancing himself from its political implications. Thus, when the Hungarian revolutionary Lajos Kossuth, toward the end of his tour through the United States in 1851–52, came to visit Concord, Emerson introduced him to the audience by *politicizing* abstraction, in order to affirm the principles of Kossuth's politics while rejecting the use to which Kossuth and his supporters in the United States had put them.

It is not that Emerson's idealist organicism gives coherence to his inconsistencies after all. Rather, his holding onto a vague and unelaborated organicist idealism serves as the starting point for arriving at contradictory positions and assessments that can no longer be integrated into one stable subject. Emerson, the public speaker, became a subject in flux, a subject affected by the situational diversity of speaking before a modern public. I am not arguing, then, that Emerson consciously chose to be inconsistent in order to be flexible enough to speak about everything to—and potentially for—everyone. I am rather claiming that the inconsistencies at which he arrived, to a large degree due to his unsystematic idealist organicism, *worked particularly well* in the marketplace of the modern lecture system. His idealism provided a basic, recognizable framework—a habitual return to pitting the ideal against the actual, or Reason against the Understanding—on top of which he pleased and displeased, reassured and confused, bored and surprised his audiences by taking up and generalizing the particular, at times coming close to undermining the basic idealist structure altogether. As I explained in my introduction, it will be necessary to resort to the language of authorial intention when delineating Emerson's idealist études concerning the nation. But the subject standing behind this authorial intention is neither metaphysically grounded nor an effect of cultural power (Emerson is never just spoken by discourse), but nonidentical and protean.

Emerson and Anglo-Saxonism

Emerson's organic nationalism finds its first sustained expression in his 1835 lecture series on English literature. As I will show in this section, this early formulation of organic and idealist nationalism pays little attention to the national identity of the United States and instead has recourse to mythic Anglo-Saxonism. Fully conflating the categories of nation and race,

Emerson comes to deflect attention from an American cultural nationalism seeking cultural emancipation from the British. Instead, he celebrates the characteristics of the English language and endorses British imperialism. Importantly, he also aligns nationalism with universalism, thereby giving priority to the individual over the group. Becoming the truest embodiment of the nation comes to stand for particularizing the universal.

It is noteworthy that it is in this lecture series on *English* literature that Emerson works out some of the key tenets of his idealism that appeared in *Nature* one year later. In particular, we find fragments of the chapters "Language" and "Beauty" (these also appear in partial form in an even earlier lecture series on science). Emerson returned from his first trip to Europe in 1833, and while it is an open question to what degree his lecture series was directly prompted by the impressions of his trip (there are no autobiographical reminiscences of the trip in the lectures), there are certain structural resemblances between this series and 1856's *English Traits*, which resulted from his second trip to Europe in 1848. In both cases, he approached England by combining observations regarding material and spiritual aspects of life, or more precisely, considerations of national traits, race, trade, and history, with an examination of literature. The difference lies in proportion, with the earlier lecture series focusing on literature (as the title suggests) and the later book concentrating on race, history, and institutions.[2]

He introduced the 1835 series with a lecture focusing on the role of language and literature in man's relationship to nature and the spirit, including paragraphs that would appear verbatim in the "Language" chapter of *Nature*. He then spent two lectures ("Permanent Traits of the English National Genius" and "Age of Fable") covering English racial traits and the history of the English race, which can also be described as Emerson's version of the process of civilization, from the medieval period of war to the modern, peace-loving age of science, a process exemplified by the history of genre, moving from fable and romance to poetry and prose of a plain style.[3] From here on, he turned to his major authors: Chaucer, Shakespeare, and Bacon (he accorded two full lectures to Shakespeare, although they tended toward recitation rather than criticism). The final three lectures discussed various groups of authors—one lecture covered some not quite major writers (Ben Jonson, Herrick, Herbert, Wotton), another some "ethical writers" (Milton, Addison, Samuel Johnson). "Ethical" for Emerson denoted a quality genuine to truth-loving Anglo-Saxons, but ever since Locke, ethics had become overly concerned with the Understanding, and thus the authors discussed were, for the most part, only minor in Emerson's estimation. Finally, "Modern Aspects of Letters" rounded out the series with some near-contemporary writers (Byron, Sir Walter Scott, Coleridge, Dugald Stewart, James Mackintosh, all minor, with the exception of Coleridge) and ended with several paragraphs known from the "Beauty" chapter in *Nature*. In fact, the final two paragraphs of the series are almost identical with Emerson's description of Columbus's arrival in the New World that I discussed in the previous chapter.

The editors of the *Early Lectures* preface the series with an independent lecture titled "On the Best Mode of Inspiring a Correct Taste in English Literature," given at the American Institute of Instruction three months before the series began. It indeed fits in with the series in that it elaborates on American cultural impoverishment, a lament that Emerson repeats in the final lecture. In expressing his anxiety over America's cultural inferiority (as he would again and again in his most famous early essays), he echoed a long-standing debate, which, some fifteen years earlier, had been famously carried out on the pages of the *Edinburgh Review* and the *North American Review*. But while the Emerson of *Nature* has often been understood to cope with some kind of anxiety of influence by demanding to forget history and the (English) fathers alike, here he calls for "effective literary associations" (*EL*, vol. 1, 216) and "a revolution in our state of society[, the first step of which] would be to impress men's minds with a deep persuasion of the fact that the purest pleasure of life were at hand unknown to them" (*EL*, vol. 1, 212), all the while insisting on the importance of English traditions for his quest for an American identity.

In fact, in "On the Best Mode of Inspiring a Correct Taste in English Literature," which stands out in Emerson's early work for its concreteness regarding social institutions, he proposes the establishment of an equivalent to eighteenth-century British coffeehouse culture, "places where the scholar might come to utter himself to other scholars without passing the piquet and guard posts of etiquette" (*EL*, vol. 1, 216).[4] Likewise, in order to find cultural resources for the fulfillment of America's promise it was not at all necessary or even wise to turn away from English literature: "The Instructor should consider that by being born to the inheritance of the English speech he receives from Nature the key to the noblest treasures of the world in the native and translated literature of Great Britain and America" (*EL*, vol. 1, 212). It would have been surprising, in fact, had Emerson used the English literature lectures to suggest that America should from now on concentrate on its own independent culture in order to promote a national identity. On the contrary, Emerson argues throughout that American national identity consists of shared racial traits and a shared racial history with England—subsumed under the category of the Anglo-Saxon. Emerson's nationalism is so focused on the idea of Anglo-Saxonism that its object of boosterism rarely coincides with the American nation-state.

Emerson's reliance on Anglo-Saxonism in these lectures is highly derivative. While Anglo-Saxonism was popular both during Emerson's time and
even more so during the Revolutionary period,[5] Emerson draws support not
from American articulations of the Anglo-Saxon myth but from a British
source: for the two lectures dedicated to Anglo-Saxon history, Emerson relies almost completely on Sharon Turner's *History of the Anglo-Saxons*, published between 1799 and 1805. It was Turner's thesis that throughout history the Anglo-Saxons displayed the traits of a freedom-loving, democratic
people. Turner himself was anything but original. His views went back to
sixteenth-century reformers;[6] they were then pushed in a political direction
by English Parliamentarians, who declared the Anglo-Saxon to be the original democrat. Furthermore, scholarship during both the Tudor period and
the Restoration delved into the pre-Conquest period in England to trace the
lineage of the Anglo-Saxons before 1066. As Reginald Horsman writes, from
the work of these scholars arose a "well-defined myth of Anglo-Saxon history," according to which:

> Anglo-Saxons were viewed as a freedom-loving people, enjoying representa-
> tive institutions and a flourishing democracy. This early freedom was crushed
> by the Norman Conquest, and only gradually through Magna Carta and the
> subsequent struggles were the English people able to regain their long lost
> freedoms.[7]

Anglo-Saxonism also connected with the myth of the "Gothic" (the two
came to be seen as synonyms). The Goths were known to have undermined
the Roman Empire after they crossed the Danube in AD 376, and thus they
came to stand for the morally pure and courageous "original democrats of
the world" (Kliger, "Usable Anglo-Saxon Past," 476). As Samuel Kliger
notes, German humanist reformers later claimed the Goths as their precursors so that "the Goths of antiquity became associated with a tradition of
political liberty and religious enlightenment" (Kliger, "Usable Anglo-Saxon
Past," 476).

Pride in the allegedly Anglo-Saxon characteristics of love of liberty, truth,
moral purity, bravery, and persistence was reaffirmed by singling out those
who were seen to differ from the Anglo-Saxons. These were above all the
Normans, along with anything "Latin" or "Roman." A strong anti-French
feeling thus accompanied the myth of the Anglo-Saxon past,[8] and it no doubt
accounts for much of Emerson's own resentments against the French, which
he voiced throughout his writings on England and New England. (Only
later, during the Civil War, when he turned against the English with a ven-
geance, would he come to reconsider the French, especially regarding their

revolutionary record, which suddenly looked pretty good to him, particularly when compared to the miserable failure of the Chartists.)

Despite this long history of Anglo-Saxon and Gothic myths, it is also true that the conception of this myth in racial terms was more recent. Prior to Sharon Turner's three-volume study, its racial version was chiefly disseminated by Thomas Percy in the preface to his translation of Paul-Henri Mallet's 1770 work *Northern Antiquities*, and by John Pinkerton's *Dissertation on the Origin of the Scythians or Goths*, from 1787. Both insisted on the difference between the Goths and the Celts, and Pinkerton especially established the view of the Celts as both weaklings and savages, a view picked up by Emerson numerous times. For instance, in his 1848 lecture titled "England," he evokes the racial categories "Norman-Saxon" and "Celtic" in a remark on England's social inequality and the failure of the Chartists.[9]

While Percy and Pinkerton racialized Anglo-Saxonism, Sharon Turner took this racialism in a direction that was particularly useful for Emerson. As Horsman remarks, the myth underwent a shift toward Romanticism that became noticeable in the writings of Turner, Walter Scott, and others: "Although the basic arguments were still along traditional lines [with roots in the 'free Anglo-Saxon' arguments of the seventeenth century], a new Romanticism was present; an emphasis on personal, individual traits rather than on abstract institutional excellence" (Horsman, "Origins of Racial Anglo-Saxonism," 393). Turner appealed to Emerson especially because, in his view, general racial traits became effective in the individual. Turner became compatible with Emerson's interest in formulating a philosophy of the individual that posited the fulfillment of the individual in the materialization of a deindividualized idea. Turner did not elaborate on these metaphysical spheres (as we will see, Victor Cousin and Coleridge became much more important for Emerson in this area). Indeed, in late 1835 Emerson dismissed Turner in his journal as predictable and lacking access to ideas: "It will not do for Sharon Turner or any man not of Ideas to make a System. Thus Mr. Turner has got into his head the notion that the Mosaic history is a good natural history of the world, reconcilable with geology &c. Very well. You see at once the length & breadth of what you may expect, & lose all appetite to read" (*JMN*, vol. 5, 106).

But despite disparaging notes such as this one, Emerson's lectures on the history of the Anglo-Saxon derive their historical information almost entirely from Turner, to the point that some passages read like paraphrases and summaries of Turner. Emerson begins by celebrating the island of Great Britain as the high point of civilization, as the apex of the development of moral man: "Nowhere is greater sincerity and benevolence. Nowhere greater ability of display" (*EL*, vol. 1, 235). He extends his praise unabashedly to the British Empire: "It is in the world a sort of ganglion or nervous centre. It radiates like a sun its light and heat" (*EL*, vol. 1, 236). While he cynically acknowledges colonial discontent—"where she is not loved, men buy her goods" (*EL*, vol. 1, 236)—he clearly describes England as a benevolent empire whose print public sphere takes up the cause of the oppressed in all of Europe: "Its stormy and warlike press is the advocate of every unproved opinion and injured party in Europe as in the Islands" (*EL*, vol. 1, 236). At this point he begins his paraphrase of Turner, delineating the English ancestors, first the Asiatic Cimmerians, with their savage Druidic religion, and then, about 1100 years later, Germanic or Saxon tribes from the Elbe, Jutland, and the three islands of North Strandt, Busen, and Heligoland. These savages "enjoyed a disorderly freedom" and "held the female sex in great respect" (*EL*, vol. 1, 237). Finally, the "Danes and Northmen," "very little distinguish[ed] unless by even more beastly ferocity from the Anglo-Saxons" (*EL*, vol. 1, 241, brackets by editors).

Turner had emphasized the savagery of the English ancestors, and Emerson gladly embraced the notion. It comported well with the cyclical philosophy of history that he developed around this time, according to which the original savage strength of a race determined its power and durability in its civilized state.[10] The enormous savage strength of the English thus became a sign of the longevity of the British Empire. And although, as his writings on England emphasized continuously, England was now in a state of decline, the same foundation of savage strength also gave that part of the English race that had been transplanted to American soil its strength, before the decline of the English fully set in.

Literature and the Embodiment of the National Idea

Emerson's purpose of following Turner's delineation of Anglo-Saxon history was to show the identity of the English race over time. But speaking of the race only interested Emerson in connection with individual minds that embodied the nation or race, and the means of embodiment were language and literature. For this reason, Emerson reiterated the belief that the English language had largely resisted the influence of the Normans, with the exception of the language of the courts, which, as an elite and administrative language, clearly did not express the genius of the people in the first place. The alleged continuity of the English language—the resistance to Latin influence—thus became a sign of racial permanence.

At this point a paradox emerged: if literature was supposed to demonstrate the unchanged character of a race while the race itself underwent demonstrable historical changes, a literature that remained essentially unchanged risked losing its power to be one with its people. This organic unity with the people was a precondition for any vital literature: "[B]ooks only have life as long as they express the thoughts of living men," Emerson writes in "Age of Fable" (*EL*, vol. 1, 262). One possible solution to the paradox of historical change despite racial permanence was to argue that what became visible in a literary history of changing genres *was* the history of a people. Yet, this concept of historical change in both literature and the people risked the credibility of the claim of permanent national traits. The solution Emerson opted for was to define organicism itself, or the inner connection of literature and the people, as the permanent racial trait, which then became exclusively Anglo-Saxon. In literary terms, this organicism exclusive to the Anglo-Saxon was defined as the "plain style." As Emerson explains in "Age of Fable":

> The whole imagery of the Allegro of Milton is of the same kind [of homeliness, love of plain truth, and a strong tendency to describe things as they are, without rhetorical decoration]. And this is exclusively English poetry. It is neither French nor Italian nor Spanish nor Oriental. It is the poetry of a nation in which is much knowledge and much business so that their speculation and their fancy is filled with images from real nature and useful art. (*EL*, vol. 1, 265)

"Images from real nature and useful art" are, on the one hand, no more than a particular aesthetic style that corresponds to a practical, business-minded culture. But if books are claimed "to express the thoughts of living men," the commonness of the style exceeds its role as the expression of a particular culture; it becomes a facilitator of the expression of "living men" by and of itself. In other words, Emerson argues that the plain style becomes the condition for literature to "express" a people, and in the case of the English it at the same time *is* the expression of a people. Thus, via the notion of popular and organic literature as the expression of the defining national trait, Emerson reaffirmed the myth of the naturally democratic race. But of course, if this essentially Romantic organicism became both the content and the mechanism of English nationalism, English distinctiveness was not at all secured, given that organic nationalism spread everywhere in the nineteenth century. This opened up a loophole in nationalist logic, which, as we will see, Emerson seized on by extending to individuals from potentially all groups the individual's ability to particularize a national idea.

The idea of a popular literature of a plain style that organically expressed the thought of the people of course required another decisive step of argumentation, namely the distinction between books that were alive and those that had "withered into pedantry" (*EL*, vol. 1, 262). This problem shifted the emphasis to the individual reader and writer, both of whom had to have access to the genius of the nation in order to write a "healthy" book. And it is this aspect of nationalist organicism that Emerson was most interested in throughout his career. In *Nature* and the early essays, Emerson isolated this concern over the individual's continued shortcomings in the effort to fully achieve the ideal union, so that it often seemed that his idealism indeed called for a divorce from the social body of the nation. It is after all striking how little Emerson discussed America in his "The American Scholar," and even *Nature*'s "sepulchers of the fathers," though adapted from Daniel Webster's 1825 oration on the Bunker Hill Monument and thus alluding to the history of the American Revolution, are not necessarily to be read as a manifestation of cultural nationalism.[11]

What the lectures on English literature reveal, then, is that Emerson devised a version of the idealism of *Nature* that had nationalist underpinnings (and by nationalist I here mean not necessarily chauvinist, but simply based on the category of the nation). This is not to say that *Nature* itself should be read in narrowly nationalistic terms. Rather, major strands of *Nature* are derived from Emerson's organicist nationalism, although *Nature* is also an example of how, in Emerson's idealist organicism, nationalist implications could be muted.

The link between organicist nationalism and the emphasis on the individual's achievements (or lack thereof) becomes visible in the introductory lecture of the 1835 series. Here we find images familiar from the idealist period of *Nature* (where nature is a readable book rather than a ceaseless torrent): "All reflection goes to teach us the strictly emblematic character of the material world. Especially is it the office of the poet to perceive and use these analogies. . . . [H]e makes the outward creation subordinate and merely a convenient alphabet to express thoughts and emotions" (*EL*, vol. 1, 224). Although thoughts and emotions, as well as their material emblems, appear to be completely universalized here, they turn out to be based on the nation. Thus, a few pages later, Emerson claims—again, on seemingly universalist grounds—that great literature cannot be neatly categorized by epoch or genre. Yet suddenly he grounds universals in the nation: "There is no insulated genius or book, but rather is it to be contemplated with genius and awe, as the striving for long periods, this way and that, of the *great national mind*, now under the openings and progressive force of *one Idea*, which, before it is spent, is opposed by or blended with another" (*EL*, vol. 1, 231, my emphasis).

The relationship of man to Spirit becomes the relationship of a representative of the nation to the "one Idea" of the nation, and the genius of the writer who attempts to find material analogies to the national idea in the medium of the national language can only be determined by his reception among the nation's readers—if not during his lifetime, then in posterity. Only if the writer's compatriots (at least future compatriots) truly find their own thoughts expressed in his writings can the writer be called "great" and thus a representative of the national idea. Likewise, such a writer will "deepen and fix in the character of his countrymen those habits and sentiments which inspired his . . . song" (*EL*, vol. 1, 275).

Emerson's thought up to this point is of course not at all exceptional. He repeats many of the central thoughts expressed by Victor Cousin in his *Introduction to the Philosophy of History*, which Emerson read in the early 1830s, and by which he was greatly impressed. In the opening pages of his tenth lecture on great and representative men, Cousin develops the notion of the nation's proper idea: "It must appear evident to you that a people can be considered as truly such only on condition of expressing an idea, which, infusing itself into all the elements which compose the interior life of that people . . . give[s] to that people a common character, a distinct physiognomy in history."[12] He also proposed another thought that Emerson repeated in the above quotation, namely that this idea would spend itself, at which point the nation would no longer have a future of its own: "The spirit of a people is not a dead substance. . . . It is a force from which a people borrows its own; which moves and sustains it while it endures, and which, when it retires after its development is completed and exhausted, leaves it a prey to the first conqueror" (Cousin, *Philosophy of History*, 294–95).

Where Emerson did differ was in his endorsement of self-reliance, which he emphasized even in the lectures on English literature: "[The great men who now make up the body of English literature] made themselves obedient to the spirit that was in them and preferred its whisper to the applause of their contemporaries" (*EL*, vol. 1, 231–32). Emerson here anticipates his theory of the minority of great minds that remains in tension with the concept of literature as the organic expression of the national idea. Distinguishing between spirit and popular recognition drives a wedge into the image of organic unity: while for Cousin the great man's embodiment of the national idea aligns him with the masses of the nation, in Emerson's eyes the same achievement sets him apart, at least for the time being.

Although Emerson's idealism is grounded in the nation, this generally does not diminish his emphasis on the universal. According to his idealist organicism, the national and the universal are not contradictions but rather depend on each other. Chaucer, one of the "great national poets" of the series, is at the same time a "man of the world" and even a "Universal Man," through whose veins flows "the milk of human kindness" (*EL*, vol. 1, 272). The truly national man, by this logic, must be truly universal, because the idea of a particular nation must itself be universal—after all, Emerson's idealism by definition places true ideas in its separated domain. Grasping and expressing this national idea, which is itself housed in the realm of the universal, can thus only be accomplished by a hero of universal stature.

The Critique of Materialism and the Two Cosmopolitanisms

In the 1835 lectures on English literature, Emerson described the English nation and its literature for the most part in an overwhelmingly celebratory tone. He could not help closing the series with the same feeling of cultural inferiority that had already marked his lecture at the American Institute of Instruction in Boston, given a few months prior to the series: "A degree of humiliation must be felt by the American scholar," he wrote in the final lecture, "Modern Aspects of Letters,"

> when he reviews the constellation of great geniuses from Chaucer down who in England have enlarged the limits of wisdom and then returns to this country where Humanity has been unbound and has enjoyed the culture of Science in the freedom of the Wild and reckons how little has been here added to the stock of truth in mankind. (*EL*, vol. 1, 381)

But Emerson's critique of American culture—its shortcomings in furthering truth, despite the advances of science and the events of the Revolution ("Humanity unbound")—found a similar target in contemporary English culture, although this criticism did not dominate the tone of any of these early lectures. Nevertheless, the English, too, had apparently lost their ability to produce literature in the same league as Chaucer, Shakespeare, and Bacon. "In general," he complained,

> we cannot but feel that with the exceeding multitude of English books reason and virtue do not gain in proportion. It must be felt that a torpidity has crept over the greater faculties which the Masters were wont to touch which is ill supplied by incessant appeals to the passion, to the love of literary gossip, and to superficial tastes. (*EL*, vol. 1, 381)

"Too little addition to the stock of truth," "torpidity crept over the greater faculties"—such were the terms in which Emerson voiced his early forays into cultural critique. Only several years later did he fill this critique of English and American cultural poverty with concrete, though typically equivocal, analyses of modern trends toward excessive materialism, first in the 1843 lecture series on New England, later in his 1856 book *English Traits*, and in lectures such as "England," "London," "France, or Urbanity," and

"The Anglo-American," which he gave between his return from Europe in 1848 and the publication of *English Traits*.

Although his criticism of England and New England generally focused on similar targets, the symptoms had different causes in each case. Briefly put, Emerson saw England as culturally already on a downward slope—its idea had spent itself—and the lack of contemporary cultural productions on a par with works from the Elizabethan period was, while deplorable, in line with the nation's position in the cycle of history. England was slowly but inevitably coming down with "a great deal of hereditary disease," as he put it in the 1843 lecture "The Genius and National Character of the Anglo-Saxon Race" (*LL*, vol. 1, 17–18). In America, on the other hand, the situation was both more hopeful and more grave: here the great future still lay ahead: "innocent, rusty complexions . . . abound here" (*LL*, vol. 1, 17–18). Yet if Americans still produced little of moral and spiritual virtue, this could only imply—and here Emerson's critique partakes of the logic of the jeremiad—that Americans were not living up to their promise. The bright side was that America obviously had not yet reached its peak, and thus did not have to face its decline in the near future. As Emerson said in "The Anglo-American": "[W]e ought to be thankful that our hero or poet does not hasten to be born in America, but still allows us others to live a little, and warm ourselves at the fire of the sun; for when he comes, we others must pack our petty trunks and be gone" (*LL*, vol. 1, 294).[13]

I have already mentioned that Emerson's cyclical theory of history was a corollary to his (derivative) national idealism.[14] In turn, this gave the critique of materialism a nationalist hue that only sometimes surfaced in his texts: materialism was deplorable not only because spiritual life was preferable for its own sake; a life in which matter and spirit were wed in proper proportion was also the condition for embodying the national idea and thus for forming an organic whole with the nation. Materialism as the lack of spirit was, in other words, also deplorable as a shortcoming in the embodiment of the national idea. (It is a bit of a chicken-and-egg question whether the ultimate goal was the fulfillment of the nation or a spiritual life; the point is that both could only be had together.)

This idealist and antimaterialist conception of national embodiment at times clearly distanced Emerson from robust, jingoistic nationalism: national domination played itself out in the realm of the material, especially when the nation's strength was measured by its imperial reach. Not even Emerson could miss the fundamentally exploitative nature of military and economic imperialism, as several remarks in *English Traits* attest.[15] Thus, in its overemphasis on the material, actually existing nationalism continually lagged behind the goals set by idealist nationalism. Again, the problem with a culture's excelling merely in material endeavors was that it hindered the fruition of a full-fledged American nationalism. It would be a mistake, however, to read the spiritual elevation and complementation of an overly materialist nationalism as a call to withdraw from engagement in the world. On the contrary, the ideal nationalism Emerson had in mind sounded decidedly active and even expansive: "We have innocence in our manners and habits, but not a vigorous virtue which dares all and performs all" (*LL*, vol. 1, 18).

And yet it is necessary to keep in mind that "daring all and performing all" was not a simple endorsement of the reckless pursuit of national self-interest in the Western hemisphere or the world. The national idea, after all, could only be grasped from the perspective of the universal, which ruled out the pursuit of self-interest. More precisely, while idealist nationalism found its fulfillment in the combination of the nation's outward strength and its artistic (chiefly literary) production, the literary side mattered not for the sake of the literary achievement as an end in itself but as the spiritual expression of the national idea. This also meant that great national literature had to reach the internally connected goals of furthering the nation and opening up to readers the *universal* realm that housed the national idea. Hence the Transcendentalist norm that literature be morally virtuous. I am belaboring this point here because it implies that, despite the tendency of nationalism toward chauvinism and aggression, Emerson deployed the very same nationalism to promote the universal ideals of the Enlightenment, while remaining vague as to how aggressively it was to proceed in furthering the nation on the side of matter.

Emerson's social conscience awakened not despite his nationalism but because of it. It is not surprising, from this perspective, that with the abolition of slavery his nationalism underwent a transformation: once abolition was within reach, Emerson tended to view the tension between actual and ideal nationalism as resolved, and thenceforth he promoted a triumphant nationalism in which his skeptic reflexes for a while seemed to disappear almost entirely.

Two Faces of Cosmopolitanism

Emerson's foundational idea of idealist organicism also led him to articulate a theory of cosmopolitanism which, perhaps surprisingly in today's understanding of cosmopolitanism, was not conceptualized as a transcendence of the national, but rather as its consummation. But in addition, Emerson also formulated a competing version of cosmopolitanism that, in fact, *was* conceptualized as a liberating critique of the nation. In this section, therefore, I aim to show how his underlying idealism generated a productive ambiguity.

Through the clash of his two concepts of cosmopolitanism, his idealism threatened to become undone. Whether planned or unplanned, by contradicting himself Emerson mobilized his thought, bestowing praise on his audience that was declared illegitimate by his own premises.

In his book *Representative Men*, from 1850, he made his readers familiar with the strategy of cheering for his great men until the very last pages of each essay, at which point he suddenly objected to their shortcomings. This rhetorical strategy had already been the blueprint for his lectures on New England (written in 1843, about two years before the lectures that would result in *Representative Men*), and he would repeat it in *English Traits*. In the latter, the first half of the essays is generally more favorable to the English than the second half. (The turning point is the chapter titled "Wealth.") In the book's first half,[16] the chapters "Land," "Race," and "Character" end on a largely positive note; the chapters "Abilities," "Manners," "Truth," and "Cockayne" either end ambivalently or emphasize critical points. The second half of the book is more unified in its effect of theatrically shoving the English off the pedestal onto which Emerson himself had heaved them.

Even in the New England lectures this rhetorical formula had already become formulaic. The second lecture, "The Trade of New England," praises American commercial triumphs for page after page, celebrating farmers, merchants, and sailors, until the paean finally is deflated with a sudden objection: "But when we have said all this for the genius of the people of New England, it yet remains to ask whether they have played a great and high part in the history of man: whether they have done anything for the greatest and highest" (*LL*, vol. 1, 36). Emerson follows this objection with an elaboration of the Coleridgean distinction, which by 1843 was rather conventional, between Reason and the Understanding, the duality of which forms the very structure of shifting from praise to blame.

But if the act of sudden deflation here becomes somewhat mechanical, the real drama resides, as usual, in the lecture's ambiguities. The celebration of the particular and partial—in this case, "the genius of the people of New England"—leaves its traces even after it has been denigrated as merely partial. In this lecture, the remaining tension between the triumph in the realm of the Understanding, and the shortcoming in that of Reason, is most pointed regarding the question of cosmopolitanism. Emerson begins by describing cosmopolitanism as a symptom of the advancement of international trade: "The citizens of every nation own property in the territory of every other nation" (*LL*, vol. 1, 32). A quick look at the opposing categories—national citizenship based on inalienable national territory versus ubiquitous land ownership—indicates that trade-based cosmopolitanism has disrupting consequences, legally, and potentially morally. What is surprising is that Emerson speaks of "marriage" in the context of these property relations:[17] "[The cities that line the Atlantic coast are scarcely] two centuries old, yet related by commerce to all the world. The sea is the ring by which they are married, and these cities are the altars and temples of the marriage rite" (*LL*, vol. 1, 31).[18] Despite the image of marriage, this trade-based cosmopolitanism dissolves all national bonds (themselves often described as resembling a family): "The old bonds of language, country, and king give way to the new connexions of trade. It destroys patriotism and substitutes cosmopolitanism" (*LL*, vol. 1, 32). This cosmopolitanism, it seems, creates a social vacuum, since the "old bonds" are replaced by trade, which is precisely not a bond in the old sense.[19]

But the image is more ambiguous than this. If cosmopolitanism seems to do away with all that holds together the organic nation, and thus endangers the most profound kind of freedom, it is also presented as kin to the self-propelled unfolding of cosmic freedom. Here one hears an Emersonian voice that pits universal freedom *against* patriotism and nationalism. Thus, by celebrating cosmopolitanism (to be dismissed later on in the lecture as lacking in Reason), Emerson for a little while treats nationalism and universalism as incompatible rather than as interdependent.[20] Significantly, this cosmopolitanism disposes not only of "language and country," but also "of kings," which, on the ideological spectrum of 1843, redeems it at once, and, paradoxically, turns cosmopolitans into the true representatives of Anglo-Saxon ur-democracy. But not only does cosmopolitanism put an end to monarchy, "it makes peace and keeps peace" (*LL*, vol. 1, 32). In itself, this idea is not original. It reaches back to Adam Smith, who argued in his *Wealth of Nations*, from 1776, that global free trade would diminish the importance of nations and advance peace, because war would be in no one's interest. But in the current, ambivalent context, the argument that cosmopolitanism ensures peace gives further evidence that Emerson is actually subscribing to trade-based cosmopolitanism, despite the fact that he later disparages the materialism of trade.

In fact, if we keep in mind Emerson's suggestions that cosmopolitanism paves the way for freedom and weakens the importance of nations, his espousal at the end of the lecture of Reason over the Understanding, and thus his implicit preference for national organicism over cosmopolitan materialism, seem no less than a self-inflicted regression. Thus, "The Trade of New England" is largely self-contradictory: Its overall idealism rejects cosmopolitanism (defined through trade relations) as limited to the Understanding. Yet Emerson's praise of cosmopolitanism—and thus of his audience's genius—subverts this very idealist framework.

But Emerson abandons his praise of cosmopolitanism by having recourse to irony—a rhetorical strategy Emerson commonly uses to subordinate the particular to the universal when the particular has come to look eerily glorious.[21] Thus, he attempts to obliterate the prestige of the worldwide spread of trade that he himself has just reiterated: "The New Bedford sailors tell us that the very savage in the Northwest coast of America, has learned to hold up his sea-shell in his hand, and cry 'a Dollar!' to the passing mariners. Even the ducks of Labrador that laid their eggs for ages on the rocks, must send their green eggs now to Long Wharf" (*LL*, vol. 1, 32). Although I read this hyperbole as an effort to reinstall an organic, truly idealistic nationalism over the merely sensuous union enabled by trade, by showing how ridiculous the spread of trade has become, Emerson—seemingly unwittingly— also criticizes national and economic expansionism by delimiting the realm of acceptable (that is, nonridiculous) expansion. Note that he does not say "American Northwest coast" or "America's Northwest coast": the clumsier "Northwest coast of America" signals, at the height of the debate over the Oregon Territory,[22] that continent and nation may not naturally coincide. Not to mention that he manages to point his listeners' attention to the victims of the extension of trade. Of course, imagining Native Americans as victims of an unfortunate leap in the civilization process from savage to idiotic materialist, which is not really a leap at all, hardly qualifies as serious criticism of capitalism, unless perhaps one capitalizes on its flip side: that traders are as savage as "the very savage." Clearly, even the political subtext is spinning out of control, wavering between anti-expansionism and expansionist racism.

While Emerson risked toppling his distinction between the Understanding and Reason by celebrating a cosmopolitanism of trade, only to dismiss it ironically, his attempt to reinstate the reign of Reason over the Understanding was complicated by the fact that he had elsewhere repeatedly articulated a version of cosmopolitanism that belonged in the sphere of Reason. *This* cosmopolitanism did not rest on an opposition to patriotic nationalism, but rather defined the highest level of individual nationalist achievement as coterminous with cosmopolitanism. Such an idealist cosmopolitanism was already implied in his 1835 lectures on English literature when he insisted that the greatest national heroes—Chaucer, Shakespeare, and Bacon—had to be men of the world. And as full national embodiment represented the apex of populism, these national cosmopolitans were also of a decidedly democratic spirit, being themselves "representative men." Though thoroughly idealistic, Emerson did not envision this "cosmopolitanism of the spirit" as an armchair cosmopolitanism in which everything, with the exception of books, remained firmly in its place. Rather, in his eyes, it put people in touch with each other, promoted peace, and made citizens from all over the world familiar with each other at a level that mere commerce could never reach. Such were the lofty ambitions of organic cosmopolitanism, as Emerson makes clear at the climax of his 1837 lecture titled "Society":

> Books and Arts and Sciences, those famous cosmopolites and pacificators, weave the ties of acquaintance, hospitality, and love. The American, the European, finds to his surprise that the Patagonian, the Otaheitan, the Caraib is neither centaur nor satyr, has neither tails nor horns, is neither hoofed nor webfooted; but that his tattooed bosom beats with the same heart, and his dark eye flashes with the selfsame soul as his own. (*EL*, vol. 2, 112)

Of course it is not quite clear whether books, arts, and sciences remain reserved for Americans and Europeans, who, awakened to universalist virtue, realize that the selfsame soul is distributed among all races, even those commonly deemed savage and diabolical; or whether "Patagonians, Otaheitans and Caraibs" themselves become mutual partners of acquaintance, hospitality, and love, thus also becoming involved in the advancement of books, arts, and sciences. Or, from a different perspective, the question is whether Emerson assumes here a universal civilizing process that ultimately assimilates everyone to the Western concept of virtue, or whether his thought can combine "selfsameness of soul" with cultural difference. But in any case, the passage is remarkable considering the widespread views of racial hierarchy of the time, promoted both by increasingly prominent "scientific" racial theories and the racial stereotypes disseminated by Romantic literature.[23]

In sum, Emerson entertained two incompatible notions of cosmopolitanism, one of them located on the side of Reason, the other on the side of the Understanding. While this bespeaks an Emersonian lack of systematicness, it created a productive confusion that let him praise and dismiss his audience's daily endeavors at the same time.

"Racial Science" and the Nation

By the mid-1840s, the new racial theories had gained such discursive cachet (especially with Emerson, who had been interested in incorporating the findings of science into his philosophical thought from his very first lecture series forward) that the confidence with which he had pronounced universal all-inclusiveness in 1837 was challenged. In his study *Race and Manifest Destiny*, Reginald Horsman notes that racial theories caught on first in the South, where slaveholders hoped for—and, with the work of Josiah Nott, acquired—proslavery arguments from science, and in the West, where expansionists found justification for disposing of Native populations.[24] New England periodicals such as the *North American Review* and the *American Whig Review* generally remained reluctant to accept the theories of racial "science" throughout, in part because racial theories—especially of the polygenist kind—questioned Mosaic history, but possibly also because, as Horsman claims in a somewhat exceptionalist tone, "[t]he moral and religious core that persisted in the New England mind made it more difficult for ideas which totally ignored other peoples to gain acceptance" (Horsman, *Race and Manifest Destiny*, 176).

Nevertheless, even these writers made concessions to racial thinking step-by-step. When the *American Whig Review* commented extensively on the debate over human unity in December 1850, the reviewer tried hard to find fault with the leading racial thinkers but had to admit that racialist discourse (in particular Johann Friedrich Blumenbach's division of five different races) had become a commonplace—although such popularity hardly had authority in the reviewer's mind, especially since Blumenbach himself spoke of "variety" rather than "race": "Who has not heard of the Caucasian, Ethiopian, Mongolian, Malayan, and American races? Races, we remark, is not the designation adopted by the author himself, but *variety*,—a distinction which, however, he does not very precisely define."[25]

In great detail, Philip Nicoloff and Laura Dassow Walls have traced which of these theories had a particularly strong influence on Emerson and wherein lay his misconceptions. (He reacted to Darwin's *The Origin of Species* with a shrug that suggests his limited understanding of Darwin's thought: "Darwin's 'Origin of Species' was published in 1859, but Stallo, in 1849, writes 'Animals are but foetal forms of men,' &c" [*JMN*, vol. 16, 298].) Generally speaking, his interest was roused whenever a theorist took a developmental, meliorist angle, which seemed to satisfy Emerson's need for proof of a benevolent and ascending tendency of the universe.[26] He especially praised Robert Chambers's 1844 bestseller *Vestiges of the Natural History of Creation*, which supported the theory that the embryological development of each human being mirrored the stages of evolution, which is essentially the idea he believed Darwin was explaining. According to this theory, evolution unfolds by design, and each being's development is "arrested" at a certain point on the general evolutionary track, depending on the circumstances. Thus, in Chambers's words, "from the humblest lichen to the highest mammifer," all organisms were companions on the same path and simply stopped at different points on it.[27] That path, Chambers insists, was laid out in advance by God: "[A]ll the various organic forms of our world are bound up in one ... system, the whole creation of which must have depended upon one law or decree of the Almighty, though it did not all come forth at one time" (Chambers, *Vestiges of Natural History*, 197).

While scholars have begun to investigate Emerson's concern with race theories and other scientific currents of his day, what has gained less attention is the question of whether these theories posed a challenge to his nationalism and (idealist) cosmopolitanism. Many racial theories still followed the practice of mixing race and nation, partly for the reason that scientists required the input of Romantic writers to provide the alleged character traits of each race, since quantitative projects, like the measurement of skulls, hardly offered the desired information about cultural and behavioral hierarchies. In his chapter on the "Early History of Mankind," Chambers, for instance, begins with the sentence, "The human race is known to consist of numerous nations, displaying considerable differences of external form and colour, and speaking in general different languages" (Chambers, *Vestiges of Natural History*, 277). Yet he goes on to contend that, "Numerous as the varieties are, they have all been classifiable under the five leading ones" (Chambers, *Vestiges of Natural History*, 277), at which point he reiterates Blumenbach's conventionalized racial taxonomy. For nationalist purposes, grouping nations within larger races did not necessarily solve the problem— Emerson had struggled all along with the paradox of pushing for an American national identity and severance from Britain on the basis of a ("prescientific") racial Anglo-Saxonism.

While Nicoloff argues that Emerson rejected racial categories when they were applied to the individual, yet affirmed them for nationalist purposes, because "the racial designations conveyed correctly enough the truth that each nation possessed a persistent and definable character when viewed in its totality,"[28] this was precisely not what racial designations provided, especially if one applied Blumenbach's popular five-race taxonomy. Of course, racial taxonomies hierarchized races, conveniently placing white Europeans on top. But even if one belonged to that category—Blumenbach called it Caucasian—it was designed much too broadly to use in the establishment of a specific nation's racial traits.

By questioning the fixity of race, Emerson seems to have tried to reintegrate race and nation—a strategy that led him into a conceptual mess. In *English Traits*, from 1856, he spent the entire chapter called "Race" wrangling with the various racial theories with which he had familiarized himself, among them those of Robert Knox, Chambers, Alexander von Humboldt, Charles Pickering, and Blumenbach. What makes the chapter disconcerting is that Emerson reverses his usual rhetorical pattern of praise followed by dismissal. Thus the first third of the essay wavers between affirmation and rejection, with rejection gaining the upper hand, while the final two thirds accept race as a category, if only "for convenience, and not as exact and final" (CW, vol. 5, 29). Walls has interpreted Emerson as giving relevance to race here because it has gained an undeniable existence on the level of discourse: "[R]ace may be a nominal not a real category—but usage makes it real enough, and so he will proceed with his fine-grained analysis of the English racial character" (Walls, *Emerson's Life in Science*, 177).

Beyond accepting racial categories for their merely nominal existence, Emerson also ascribes a real foundation to race. But although he considers race real, he thinks of it as fluid, both epistemologically and ontologically. On the epistemological level, Emerson objects to the scientists' attempts to quantify and qualify particular races; specifically, the 1840s fad of phrenology earns his disdain. When race appears fixed, he claims, this is merely a problem of perspective, of our inability to see across the immense time spans of natural history (here he is influenced by the conception of time advanced by geology): "The fixity or inconvertibleness of races as we see them, is a weak argument for the eternity of these frail boundaries, since all our historical period is a point to the duration in which nature has wrought" (CW, vol. 5, 27). On the ontological level, he claims that scientists cannot perceive race as fixed because *it is not* fixed: "Yet each variety shades down imperceptibly into the next, and you cannot draw the line where a race begins or ends" (CW, vol. 5, 24). His assertions of racial fluidity take him as far as rejecting the very racial histories of the Anglo-Saxons that he himself appropriated earlier: "Who can call by right name what races are in Britain? Who can trace them historically? Who can discriminate them anatomically, or metaphysically?" (CW, vol. 5, 28).

However, while these questions address the impossibility of perceiving (naming, tracing, discriminating) the racial makeup of the nation, he maintains that there are "races in Britain." Emerson, in other words, accepts race, despite the impossibility of qualifying and quantifying it, and he never fully distinguishes it from the nation. Racial traits remain national traits. Thus, his infamously racist affirmation, "Race in the negro is of appalling importance," is followed directly by the national traits of French Canadians: "The French in Canada, cut off from all intercourse with the parent people, have held their national traits" (CW, vol. 5, 26).

Race as Fate: The Challenge to Organicism

The challenge race posed for Emerson's nationalism, however, went deeper than the spatial incongruity between the borders of race and nation, and it is this challenge that led him to similar gyrations in his espousal of cosmopolitanism. The categories of race and nation suggested two different, seemingly irreconcilable, organizing principles, which I will call organicist and antagonistic. According to organicism, which was developed in his early nationalism, it was presumed that one could "achieve" one's country if one managed to embody the national idea, which was given in advance. Race, on the other hand, operated according to the logic of antagonism, which designated race as a materially determining force. While in idealist organicism, "one idea" determined each nation, the antagonism of race exercised a determining force from the direction of matter. Instead of something to be achieved, race was something to be contended with. In "Race," Emerson therefore characterized civilization as one among several forces that "resisted" race (CW, vol. 5, 26). Race could not be achieved, then, because doing so would have required, perversely, making ideas conform to matter, while idealism proper consisted of making matter transparent by entering the realm of ideas, and thus, subduing matter. (Emerson's rejection of the Democratic Party's politics of expansion may be understood from precisely this vantage point: in his view, the Party falsely attempted to achieve the Anglo-Saxon race, thus ending up in a veritable apotheosis of matter that mistook destiny to be overly manifest.)

If the distinction between nation and race lay in their respective imperatives of achieving versus resisting, and if a nation's constitutive racial traits required a response different from the larger national organism, what would become of nationalism? How, in other words, could achievement and resistance be negotiated?

In a way, Emerson seems never to have tried to solve the problem. It was rather an instance that was productive enough to concern him through the 1850s, issuing in Notebook EO, a lecture (now lost), and an essay. To all three he gave the title "Fate."[29] He enters into the problem by aligning race with several other antagonistic forces explored by the new (or newly vitalized) sciences of statistics (especially as taught by Adolphe Quételet), astronomy, and geology. "Whatever limits us, we call Fate," he writes (CW, vol. 6, 11). Emerson's first step toward making achievement encounter resistance is to broaden fate's spectrum: "If we are brute and barbarous, the fate takes a brute and dreadful shape. As we refine, our checks become finer. If we rise to spiritual culture, the antagonism takes a spiritual form. . . . The limitations refine as the soul purifies, but the ring of necessity is always perched on top" (CW, vol. 6, 11).

In a characteristically perceptive reading, Barbara Packer has noted two different ways in which the essay suggests that fate be handled: "One way is to restate the philosophical idealism that had always attracted him." (Packer, "History and Form," 442). As Emerson writes later in the same essay, "Thought dissolves the material universe, by carrying the mind up into the sphere where all is plastic" (CW, vol. 6, 15). Packer does not point out, however, that because Emerson has just laid out that our rise to idealist thought is answered by fate's rise to the same level, not much is gained if all matter is dissolved. The second approach to fate that Packer identifies in the essay does not imagine "the conflict between power and limitation . . . as a contest between opposing forces but as erotic evasion and pursuit. . . . Every time limitation takes a new disguise, power pursues it; every time power rises to new heights, limitation precedes it" (Packer, "History and Form," 442). Packer bases this reading on Emerson's reference to the Hindu tale of Vishnu and Maya, which is indeed the story of erotic pursuit. As Emerson writes, "In the Hindoo fables, Vishnu follows Maya through all her ascending changes . . . ; whatever form she took, he took the male form of that kind, until she became at least a goddess, and he a man and a god" (CW, vol. 6, 11). In my reading, however, the story merely illustrates how limitation follows power (with conventional, misogynist gender implications). The point of my argument, then, is not that the forces of erotic pursuit do not oppose each other; they clearly do, precisely in pursuing and evading each other. The point is rather that the ceaseless antagonism has entered the domain of the spirit. In this way, the distinction between organicism, or the achievement of the nation, and antagonism, or the resistance to race, begins to falter.

In fact, the essay repeats the old lament about America's lack of spiritual achievement ("Our America has a bad name for superficialness," [CW, vol. 6, 2]), but instead of calling, as is usual, for the embodiment of the national idea, Emerson now redefines achievement as resistance: "Great men, great nations, have not been boasters and buffoons, but perceivers of the terror of life, and have manned themselves to face it" (CW, vol. 6, 2). Facing the terror is the new strategy for becoming a nation worthy of the name. At this point it seems that Emerson has resolved the conflict between his old conception of the nation and the claims of science by elevating limitation to spiritual heights. Thus, resistance displaces achievement, the logic of race defeats the logic of nation, antagonism supersedes idealist organicism.

Except that Emerson will not let matters rest there. Terror cannot remain terror for Emerson. Thus, throughout the remainder of the essay, he works toward a reversal of his provisional result by subordinating necessity to an overarching organicism. By the end of the essay, he has turned terror into beauty, and he has found a law that controls even necessity and its antagonistic relationship to freedom: "Let us build altars to the Beautiful Necessity, which secures that all is made of one piece; that plaintiff and defendant, friend and enemy, animal and planet, food and eater, are of one kind" (*CW*, vol. 6, 26). The Beautiful Necessity reigns above necessity and terror, transforming antagonism into unity. Worshipping this highest law and highest idea has nothing to do with resistance, but everything to do with achievement. In the end, the danger of race to the national organism is contained, and while resistance—facing the terror—is not erased, it has become subordinated to idealist organicism.

The term *Beautiful Necessity* is closely associated with this late essay, but it is revealing that Emerson had already employed it in his early lectures. More precisely, he had used it in the 1835 series on England. In the introductory lecture of that series he had written:

> [T]he good of the whole is evolved, the discordant volitions of men are rounded in by a great and beautiful necessity so as to fetch about results accordant with the whole of nature, peaceful as the deep heaven which envelopes him, and cheerful as the green fields on which the sun finds him. Over men the purposes of Providence are thrown like enormous nets enclosing masses without restraining individuals. (*EL*, vol. 1, 225)

That Emerson might well have written this passage twenty-five years later, at the end of "Fate," not only shows how hard he tried to integrate new information into an old system but also hints at his determination not to let go of his idealist (and nationalist) organicism. This was not so much because he needed it for his nationalism; after all, antagonism would have accomplished that task quite well, as his provisional solution in "Fate" demonstrates. Rather, his idealist organicism remained the only theoretical path available to him for overcoming external restraints—as counterintuitive as this may sound in the context of "Fate." But his not letting go also suggests that he may have held on to his idealist organicism because it was generative of a multiplicity of positions that were at odds with each other and that often risked displacing organicism altogether.

This is exemplified by the fact that organicism often had nationalist and racist underpinnings, yet it also allowed him to radically oppose the racial hierarchies of his time and to proclaim "Toussaint, and the Haytian heroes, or . . . the leaders of their race in Barbadoes [sic] and Jamaica" "the anti-slave," in his 1844 "An Address . . . on . . . the Emancipation of the Negroes in the British West Indies": "here is the anti-slave: here is man: and if you have man, black or white is an insignificance" (*AW*, 31). Antislavery activism was nothing compared to the heroic self-emancipation that alone could put an end to slavery. And self-emancipation was only possible under the condition of the embodiment of an idea: "When at last in a race, a new principle appears, and idea;—*that* conserves it; ideas only save races" (*AW*, 31). Of course, this reasoning remains troubling: it is marred by a characteristically Emersonian longing for passivity that will celebrate the results of the active work of others as Providence, and, in its gloomiest manifestation, will shrug off the plight of others as the logical consequence of the lack of a strong idea: "[A] compassion for that which is not and cannot be useful or lovely, is degrading and futile" (AW, 31). In his journal, the passage on the anti-slave—the climax of his address—is followed by a long complaint about the pressures to be actively involved in the abolitionist movement:

> Does he not do more to abolish Slavery who works all day steadily in his garden, than he who goes to the Abolition meeting & makes a speech? The anti-slavery agency like so many of our employments is a suicidal business. . . . Do not, then, I pray you, talk of the work & the fight, as if it were anything more than a pleasant oxygenation of your lungs. (JMN, vol. 9, 126–27)

Surely, these sentences remain grating to any reader of Emerson. Nevertheless, they also carry a half-hidden self-critique that should not be missed: the passage decries the thinly veiled air of superiority and condescension displayed by white abolitionists. And if he is talking to himself here, as I believe he partly is, then the admonishment that the fight "is no more than a pleasant oxygenation of your lungs" also bespeaks his suspicion regarding his own narcissism: not least of all, the pleasure is on the side of the speaking body.

Cosmopolitanism as Imperialism

While Toussaint L'Ouverture fulfilled the requirements of being a "cosmopolite of the spirit," one edge of this cosmopolitanism is its compatibility with a certain form of imperialism, which was pointed out by Emerson himself. Both cosmopolitanism and imperialism are often understood to fracture the national imaginary.[30] For Emerson, however, they ideally were corollaries to a fully developed sense of national embodiment.

To see the link between cosmopolitanism and empire, it is necessary to observe that, while potentially everyone may become a cosmopolite (just as everyone may become self-reliant), in reality cosmopolitans are by definition a minority, a sort of unofficial club of achievers of their nation. As Emerson writes in English Traits, "there is at all times a minority of profound minds in the nation, capable of appreciating every soaring of intellect and every hint of tendency" (CW, vol. 5, 145). Cosmopolitans, by staying aloof of the vices that result from an excess of the Understanding, are capable of communicating with each other across national boundaries without being limited by national stereotypes—again, because each fully embodies his respective national idea, although this may set him apart from his contemporary compatriots. This Emerson has to concede in "The Fortune of the Republic," written in 1863, at a critical moment during the Civil War, when England is perceived to be supporting the South, war drags on, and in the North voices for a compromise become increasingly audible.[31] For the most part, the essay is an anti-British tirade in which Emerson leans toward American jingoism. And yet there is this acknowledgment:

> In speaking of England, I lay out the question of the truly cultivated. They exist in England, as in France, in Italy, in Germany, in America. The inspirations of God, like birds, never stop at frontiers or languages, but come to every nation. This class like Christians, or poets, or chemists, exist for each other, across all possible nationalities, strangers to their own people,—brothers to you. (*AW*, 151)

While this cosmopolitan elite of the "truly cultivated" would seem to be at odds with the forces of imperialism, Emerson's organicist idealism here ultimately will lead him to an outright endorsement of the British Empire that again threatens to topple the idealist dichotomy of Reason and the Understanding. In *English Traits*, he spends one chapter on the *Times*, Britain's leading—and conservative—newspaper, which he read regularly during his second trip to England in 1847–48. In the end, however, what mars this publication for Emerson is its failure to heed the minority principle. Writing in an "imperial tone," the paper's predicament is a reflection of the British Empire more generally: "The 'Times' shares all the limitations of the governing classes, and wishes never to be in a minority. If only it dared to cleave to the right, to show the right to be the only expedient, and feed its heart from the central batteries of humanity, it might not have so many men of rank among its contributors, but genius would be its cordial and invincible ally" (*CW*, vol. 5, 153).

What Emerson desires is an idealist version of the *Times*, in which the tone is "high," instead of "official, and even officinal" (*CW*, vol. 5, 153). Such a morally elevated and universalist tone, Emerson implies, would pose an alternative to the imperial language "of a powerful and independent nation," which is the language in which the actual *Times* is written. At this point, Emerson's thought seems to operate according to the familiar distinction between a truly universalist cosmopolitanism (the ideal *Times*) and imperialism (the actual paper). For while British imperialism casts a web of trade relations around the entire globe, in comparison with an ideal cosmopolitanism it is, in Emerson's estimation, highly parochial: "As they [the British] trample on nationalities to reproduce London and Londoners in Europe and Asia, so they fear the hostility of ideas, poetry and religion,— ghosts which they cannot lay;—and, having attempted to domesticate and dress the Blessed Soul itself in English broadcloth and gaiters, they are tormented with the fear that herein lurks a force that will sweep their system away" (*CW*, vol. 5, 143).[32]

The imagery of being haunted by glimpses of ideas, by intuitions of humanity, suggests the benevolent tendency of the universe, the invincibility of Reason, which undermines all efforts of spiritual domestication (one could say: repression).[33] At first sight this tidy division of terms—cosmopolitanism versus imperialism, the power of ideas versus the domestication of the Soul— would really amount to no more than the latest installment in the Coleridgean saga of the struggle between Reason and the Understanding. However, Emerson rounds out the chapter on "The 'Times'" by imagining the ideal cosmopolitan newspaper in a way that renders these dichotomies unstable yet again:

> [The ideal *Times*] would be the natural leader of British reform; its proud function, that of being the voice of Europe, the defender of the exile and patriot against despots, would be more effectually discharged; it would have the authority which is claimed for that dream of good men not yet come to pass, an International Congress; and the least of its victories would be to give to England a new millennium of beneficent power. (*CW*, vol. 5, 153)

The combination of a Kantian League of Nations with a millennium of British power or empire is of course hard to swallow, however "beneficent" this power may be. The problem here is that in specifying the ideal in terms of the actual—the voice of reform, the defender of the exile, and so forth— the ideal comes close to being indistinguishable from the actual. We end up with what we already have: British power. Emerson here is taking *ad absurdum* his goal of "shooting the gulf" (as he put it in "Circles") between the actual and the ideal by idealizing actual power. This, too, was within the scope of his idealist organicism.

Kossuth and the Politics of Abstraction

More often than not, Emerson insisted on the difference between the ideal and the actual, the universal and the particular, but he also created dramatic effects of ambiguity by injecting the particular into the universal and extracting the particular from the universal. With regard to the ideology of Manifest Destiny, of America's mission to subdue the continent and to control the Western Hemisphere, this led to an uncomfortable ambiguity: national expansion seemed to be implied in his idealist organicism, yet actual expansion tended to appall him. And when expansion had made yet another

step forward, he tried to "fatalize" his nausea by arguing that, while imperialist policies looked paltry and savage to him, when seen with hindsight
they would surely turn out to confirm the benevolent course of the universe.
Thus, in an oft-quoted passage from his journal, he contends that: "It is very
certain that the strong British race, which have now overrun so much of this
continent, must also overrun that tract, & Mexico and Oregon also, & it
will in the course of ages, be of small import, by what particular occasions
and methods it was done. It is a secular question" (*JMN*, vol. 9, 73). However, what gets quoted much less often is the rest of the passage. For it turns
out that he deems resistance indispensable nonetheless: "It is quite necessary
& true to our New England character that we should consider the question
in its local & temporary bearings, & resist the annexation with tooth &
nail. It is a measure which goes not by right nor by wisdom but by feeling"
(*JMN*, vol. 9, 73–74).[34]

After the failure of resistance, Emerson still tried to find something consoling in the course of events that was more immediate than the prospect
that eventually one would see that it was all for the best. In the essay titled
"Power," he speculated on a dialectics of power, according to which annexation fed a burgeoning counterforce. First, power itself seems to belong
naturally to the Democratic Party's policies of expansion and displacement:
"Men expect for good Whigs put into office by the respectability of the country, much less skill to deal with Mexico, Spain, Britain, or with our own
malcontent members, than from some strong transgressor like Jefferson or
Jackson, who first conquers his own government and then uses the same
genius to conquer the foreigner" (*CW*, vol. 6, 33–34). But while this "Power
of Lynch law" (*CW*, vol. 6, 34) seems to prey easily on weakly Whig respectability, it bears "its own antidote: . . . all kinds of power usually emerge
at the same time; good emerges and bad; . . . the ecstasies of devotion with
the exacerbations of debauchery" (*CW*, vol. 6, 34). Emerson here evokes a
familiar thought—polarity, or compensation—but in the face of an annexation policy he wishes to resist, this takes on an unusually immediate political
meaning. While in the journal passage he sounded like a fatalist who was
willing to accept Manifest Destiny, even if he felt the urge to put his shoulder to the wheel, the divine law of compensation in "Power" elevates spiritual resistance to as much of a destiny as Manifest Destiny itself. Nevertheless, this does not solve his dilemma: if the law of compensation elevates
resistance to destiny, it still affirms the destiny of expansion as well.

The dilemma that caused Emerson to waver on the question of imperialism and expansionism resulted from the very idealist organicism the varied
ramifications of which I have traced throughout this chapter. The concept of
design behind the ideology of Manifest Destiny accorded with his idea of the

successful achievement of a nation, which included both outward strength and inward virtue. In fact, however, outward strength and inward virtue tended to be at odds with each other. Violently overrunning others did not conform to the idea that the masses would be persuaded by genius and character. If force was necessary, spirit was lacking. And if spirit was lacking, expansion was paltry and savage. In other words, the very thought that allowed him to embrace national embodiment let him express his uneasiness about actual national expansion.

The Case of Kossuth

How this dilemma determined Emerson's political and rhetorical decisions can be observed in his involvement in the excitement over Lajos Kossuth. The leader of the failed Hungarian Revolution put the United States into a condition of virtual hysteria when he came to the country in December 1851, after having been extracted from his internment in Turkey. In the following eight months, Kossuth traveled throughout the country, rallying private financial support for the cause of Hungarian independence, as well as popular, legislative, and executive support for an intervention of the U.S. in Europe. (He succeeded only in his first goal.) Before his arrival, the American press had turned him into an almost mythical hero. He had aided this reception with the timely publication of a small book of lectures in English. (He had supposedly learned the language while imprisoned in Turkey, with only the help of Shakespeare and the Bible.) Upon his arrival in New York, about a quarter of a million people lined the streets on his way from Castle Garden to Central Park. As the *New York Times* reported, it was "such a scene as the world seldom beholds."[35] Larry Reynolds has described the so-called Kossuth Fever that spread throughout the United States in the following months. Along with the famous Kossuth hat (decorated with an ostrich plume), "Kossuth marches, Kossuth dances, Kossuth oysters, Kossuth restaurants, Kossuth buttons, flags, and photographs became the signs of the times."[36]

According to the judgment of his contemporaries, Kossuth was an exceptionally charismatic, but also argumentative, stubborn, and at times erratic character (compare Spencer, *Louis Kossuth and Young America*, 1–4, 164–73). Throughout his stay in the United States he did not meet only with praise. By deciding to travel to the South, he alienated northern abolitionists—and also was received coolly in the South. He was met with enthusiasm in the West, where expansionist ideology loomed large and many refugees from the 1848 revolutions had settled. Meanwhile, a few New Englanders besides the abolitionists became skeptical of Kossuth's brand of nationalism. Francis

Bowen, the scholarly editor of the *North American Review*, who had recently been appointed to a professorship at Harvard, wrote an extended critique of Kossuth, pointing out that the Magyars were suppressing other ethnic groups in Hungary such as the Slavic population. Yet Bowen's view was unpopular and decidedly disadvantageous: Harvard even revoked his appointment.[37]

Toward the end of his trip, Kossuth traveled to New England, where he was greeted with overwhelming enthusiasm. His itinerary led him to Concord, where Emerson introduced him. Although Emerson's introductory address is included in the Centenary edition of Emerson's works, few critics seem to have looked at it closely. To my knowledge, Larry Reynolds is the only scholar who more than mentions it in passing, in his *European Revolutions and the American Literary Renaissance*. In Reynolds's assessment, Emerson's welcome to Kossuth was lukewarm: "He tried to praise Kossuth without flattery" (Reynolds, *European Revolutions*, 161). According to Reynolds, "All in all the address was appropriately complimentary, vacuous, and vague" (Reynolds, *European Revolutions*, 161). I agree with Reynolds, but while he uses this reading to support his view of Emerson's response to the European revolutions of 1848 as largely reactionary, in my understanding, Emerson's reluctance did not have much to do with conservatism. It rather bespeaks his struggle with the plight of incarnation, or, put differently, the organic materialization of the Spirit to which his idealism tended.

In order to demonstrate this, it is necessary to reconstruct the meaning that Kossuth had taken on in the United States for both international and domestic politics. Kossuth's arrival in the United States coincided with Emerson's increasing disgust with national politics. The Compromise of 1850 had radicalized his stance against slavery because of the Fugitive Slave Law that was part of the Compromise. The new Fugitive Slave Law had been proposed by Henry Clay, the Whig senator from Kentucky, who up to this point had not been an advocate of slavery. As Barbara Packer explains, Clay "hoped to regain his role as a party leader" through the Compromise, after having lost the presidential nomination of 1848 to Zachary Taylor.[38]

Clay's case is informative for understanding Kossuth's significance. A veteran politician (he had been a "war hawk" back in 1812), he was skidding through the ideological spectrum with the Compromise bill: at almost exactly the same time that he was proposing the Fugitive Slave Law, he also became a figure of ridicule among expansionist Democrats. The reason was none other than Kossuth. When the Hungarian uprising was suppressed by Austria with the help of the Czar, parts of the Democratic Party, who came together under the label "Young America," promoted Federal intervention against Austria and Russia. It was Clay who spoke out in the Senate against the Young American motion advanced by Lewis Cass (who was not exactly a Young American himself; indeed, he belonged to the old Democratic cadre that chief Young America ideologue George Sanders worked hard to oust as "Old Fogies").[39] Clay's position against Federal intervention was itself surprising, as the Democrats did not fail to point out, because some thirty years earlier he had supported recognition of the democratic movements in Latin America and then in Greece (Spencer, *Louis Kossuth and Young America*, 30–35). Nevertheless, within the political context of 1850, reluctance to stretch American influence into Europe and the proposal of a slavery-friendly Compromise bill at the same time, must have seemed like discordant acts. After all, national expansion (in the Western Hemisphere) was dreaded by anti-slavery forces because it implied the extension of slavery. It is likely that Clay's behavior suggested to abolitionists that resistance to slavery was evaporating even among nonexpansionist Whigs. But the hostile reaction Clay elicited from Young America might also be read by northern abolitionists as a confirmation that zealous support for an intervention in Europe, whether by means of diplomatic shunning (as Cass had suggested) or through military action, was closely linked to the proslavery stance of Democrats.

Emerson's outrage over the Fugitive Slave Law found its target not in the Kentuckian Clay, but in the support for Clay's bill from Massachusetts Senator Daniel Webster, who for many decades had been a model of eloquence and a personal hero of Emerson's. Webster's desertion of the northern anti-slavery cause brought Emerson to despair: from now on, anything Webster touched was tainted: "He has undone all that he has spent his years in doing; he has discredited himself" (*JMN*, vol. 11, 348). And as it was Webster who managed to get Kossuth out of prison in Turkey and into the United States, Emerson rejected any claim on Webster's part of authentic democratic convictions:

> [Webster] has gone over in an hour to the party of force, & stands now on the precise ground of the Metternicks [sic], the Castlereaghs, and the Polignacs. . . . He to talk of liberty, & to rate an Austrian? He would dragoon the Hungarians, for all his fine words. I advise Kossuth . . . not to trust Webster. He would in Austria truckle to the Czar, as he does in America to the Carolinas; and hunt the Hungarians from the Sultan as he does the fugitives of Virginia from Massachusetts. (*JMN*, vol. 11, 348)

It would be inaccurate to simply claim that Emerson did not believe in Kossuth's cause of democratic freedom. His insistent analogizing of Webster's support for slaveholders with his secret support for the opponents of the Hungarians was rather meant to drive home the point that American enthusiasm for Kossuth and an intervention in Europe was sheer hypocrisy. What seemed like engagement for the organic, democratic cause was nothing but an espousal of the "party of force," which ruled by the same principle by which all cruel expansionism ruled, whether it was British imperialism or the American annexation of Oregon and Texas. What needs to be kept in mind, then, is that for Emerson, the case of Kossuth, and the reaction it demanded, could not be disentangled from what to Emerson looked like a bleak domestic political situation in which proslavery forces were on the rise. This was what it came down to when the particular (the messiness of domestic political interests) and the universal (the cause of Hungary's national independence on the basis of idealist organicism) slid into each other.

One gets an even clearer idea of the concrete discursive field Emerson had to enter after accepting the task of introducing Kossuth to a nearly hysterical New England crowd by reading the speeches of Kossuth's hosts that accompanied him on his trip through New England (collected in *Kossuth in New England*, which was published immediately after the tour, as if to cash in on the hype while it lasted).[40] At Faneuil Hall in Boston, Democratic Governor James Boutwell used his introduction of Kossuth to call for a military intervention against Russia and Austria based on geopolitical and economic considerations that he gladly shared: "Russia and the United States are as unlike as any two nations which ever existed. If Russia obtains control of Europe by the power of arms, war will be inevitable. . . . Centralization, absolutism, destroy commerce. The policy of Russia diminishes production and limits markets."[41] A few days later, at a "Legislative Banquet" for Kossuth, Boutwell was even more explicit, as related by the editors of *Kossuth in New England*: "War is a great evil, but it is not the greatest of evils. Prostrated humanity is a greater evil than war" (*Kossuth in New England*, 101). Kossuth encouraged this interventionist awakening by altering a phrase from John Quincy Adams into his slogan: "be a power upon earth." Even the Conscience Whig and Free Soiler Anson Burlingame, who later joined first the Know-Nothings and then the newly formed Republican Party, joined the interventionist chorus in his address in Worcester by reviving the debate over George Washington's 1796 Farewell Address,[42] in which Washington had advised an isolationist, neutral foreign policy: "Let us not wrong our fathers by believing they intended to chain this nation to infancy forever" (*Kossuth in New England*, 63).

Many of the other speakers invoked Faneuil Hall, and New England more generally, as "the cradle of liberty" and usurped the Kossuth case to boost American nationalism by remembering—and with the help of Kossuth, almost reliving—the American Revolution.[43] Kossuth knew how much he depended on this nationalism of memory, and he fed it incessantly. But he also possessed the chutzpah to one-up the Americans' narcissistic and exceptionalist appropriation of himself. At Faneuil Hall he insisted:

> You should change 'American Liberty' into 'Liberty';—then liberty would be forever sure in America and that which found a cradle in Faneuil Hall never would find a coffin through all coming days. I like not the word cradle connected with liberty,—it has a scent of mortality. (Kossuth in New England, 88)

Although Kossuth and his hosts argued from a universalist perspective throughout—Kossuth claimed that liberty had to be understood as a principle rather than as an American privilege—he tried to justify his silence on slavery by declaring it an "interior" question:

> I claim the right for my people to regulate its own domestic concerns. I claim this as a law of nations, common to all humanity; . . . now, that being my position and my cause, it would be the most absurd inconsistency, if I would offend that principle which I claim and which I advocate. (Kossuth in New England, 93)

Emerson and Kossuth had a comparable philosophical starting point, but they ended up with different results. Both Kossuth and Emerson based their notion of freedom on the idea of nationalist organicism so common in the nineteenth century. But while Emerson's idealism let him conceptualize organisms that remained to be achieved by the individual, which might then lead to the embodiment of previously unpenetrated ideas and thus to nations that were still to be articulated, Kossuth construed organic freedom on the assumption of a fixed set of existing nations. In effect, he, too, had to have some notion of national emergence to make his own case; and by the same token, Emerson's concept of emergence, like Kossuth's, depended on previously given (if as yet unpenetrated) ideas. In the end, the main difference was that Emerson hesitated to limit idealist organicism to actually existing organisms, while Kossuth argued the other way around and granted the universal right to freedom only to those who were already recognizable as a nation (or as a nationalist movement that claimed to have a national past). As a result, Kossuth could securely distinguish between domestic and international issues, while for Emerson, inside an organic nation a new organic nation might spring up. The domestic was thus potentially international. But of course, Kossuth most likely had decided to tour the South on purely pragmatic grounds, hoping for support from any quarter. Had he not underestimated the forces of U.S. sectionalism, and decided that siding with the abolitionist North might be in his self-interest, he might have argued that supporting slavery would have been "the most absurd inconsistency."

In the case of Kossuth, with all its domestic political ramifications, Emerson hesitated to align the realm of national ideas with particular nationalist manifestations. This accorded with the dominant application of his idealism: while his project consisted of bringing the ideal to coincide with the actual, this was only one side of his endeavor. His skepticism affirmed Reason by distinguishing it from the Understanding, and by pointing out that what was generally taken to be an incarnation of the Spirit (for instance, the popular worship of heroes) was in fact a merely partial phenomenon. It was this program that he put to concrete political use in his address to Kossuth. Thus, he praised Kossuth predominantly on individual grounds, as a master of organic achievement, as if it were Kossuth's person that mattered, rather than the political movement in Hungary:

> We have seen, with great pleasure, that there is nothing accidental in your attitude. We have seen that you are organically in that cause you plead. The man of Freedom, you are also the man of Fate. You do not elect, but you are also elected by God and your genius to the task. (W, vol. 11, 399)

One recognizes here Emerson's belief in the Beautiful Necessity, in the co-dependence of freedom and fate, and one may read this statement, as Reynolds does, as a nicely composed stock phrase. But this particular passage contains a thinly veiled critique, not of the principles of Kossuth's engagement, but of the way both Kossuth and his American supporters instrumentalized it in a politics of self-interest. Thus for Emerson, "the cause you plead" is decidedly no more than a cause. It does not deserve further amplification as the alleged incarnation of the Spirit. "Hungary" only enters the address once, in the very last sentence. And even here, Emerson resists the particularization of the cause by pushing it into a distant future: "And, as the shores of Europe and America approach every month, and their politics will one day mingle, when the crisis arrives, it will find us all instructed beforehand in the rights and wrongs of Hungary, and parties to her freedom" (W, vol. 11, 401).

For Kossuth, the crisis had arrived long ago, and the politics of Europe and the United States were already fully mingled. He demanded action now. This he preached in lecture after lecture, in village after village. (His remarks were usually fully transcribed in the newspapers.) With this in mind, Emerson's vagueness cannot be sufficiently explained by the abstractions inherent in philosophical idealism, or by mere conservatism. The temporal imprecision about politics that "will one day mingle" is a friendly but definite denial of the specific demands that were the reason for Kossuth's trip. It was difficult to overlook the rebuke contained in these final words of the welcoming address. Nathaniel Hawthorne, present in the audience, clearly understood it. Himself no big fan of Kossuth (compare Reynolds, *European Revolutions*, 198), he added a short postscript to a letter to Emerson soon after the occasion: "P.S. We think that you said the only word that has yet been worthily spoken to Kossuth" (*L*, vol. 4, 292).

Emerson's reluctance to partake in the wave of Kossuth jubilees did not just concern the temporal vagueness about future political involvement in Europe. He evidently was concerned that Kossuth risked letting his organic unity with his cause be disrupted by his populism; he even implied that Kossuth's campaign for financial support, along with his knack for adulation from the masses, might throw Kossuth in with those striving for material gain:

> We are afraid that you are growing popular, Sir; you may be called to the dangers of prosperity. But, hitherto, you have had in all centuries and in all parties only the men of heart. I do not know but you will have the million yet. Then, may your strength be equal to your day. But remember, Sir, that everything great and excellent in the world is in minorities. (*W*, vol. 11, 399)

If Kossuth needed a reminder about the necessity of being in a minority, this could only mean that he was already losing his moral stature and was descending to the same level Emerson ascribed to the *Times* of London in *English Traits*. In his notebook EO, filled from the early to mid-1850s, he included Kossuth—side by side with Webster!—as an example of the natural trend of the decline of great men into measly materialists (thus reiterating his cyclical theory of history, transposed to the level of the individual): "But strong natures, New Hampshire giants, Napoleons, Burkes, Websters, Kossuths, are inevitable patriots, until their life ebbs, & their disease, gout, palsey, or money, warp their politics" (*TN*, vol. 1, 71).[44]

Kossuth understood Emerson's criticism quite well, and he took on the challenge at the outset of his lecture with a deft retort:

> One thing I may assume, and one thing own,—should the Almighty give me prosperity, yet in my life it would not carry me away, not to be frank, not only in adversity, but in duty, which is a good guard as well against ambition in prosperity as in adversity. One thing I may own,—that it is, indeed, true, everything good has yet been in the minority; still mankind went on, and is going on, to that destiny the Almighty designed, when all good will not be confined to the minority, but will prevail among all mankind. (*Kossuth in New England*, 224)

Kossuth thus picked up the belief in meliorism preached by Emerson himself and used it as an argument against Emerson's reluctance about immediate action. Again and again, he addressed Emerson directly during his lecture. If he pressed his American audiences elsewhere on the promises of their Revolutionary past, here he reinforced this strategy by treating Emerson as the representative American, taking him to the task over his own implications:

> Sir, I implore you [Mr. Emerson] give me the aid of your philosophical analysis, to impress the conviction upon the public mind of your nation that the Revolution, to which Concord was the preface, is full of a higher destiny—of a destiny broad as the world, broad as humanity itself. (*Kossuth in New England*, 227, brackets added by editors)

The main reason for Emerson's disagreement may not at all have been a democratic movement of Kossuth's kind (even if he came to doubt that Kossuth was truly of "strong nature"). After all, he did agree to introduce Kossuth, which disgusted Thoreau.[45] The problem was rather that supporting Kossuth meant subscribing to an ideology according to which present-day America—and especially Concord and New England—embodied the ideal to which, eventually, the world would have to conform. Shortly after the fall of Webster, this view had become untenable for Emerson.

Thus Emerson's biggest problem was not Kossuth, but America's reception of him. In his lecture "The Anglo-American," first presented about five months after Kossuth's departure, in December 1852, he interprets the enthusiastic reception of Kossuth in New York as a typical sign of America's hasty and superficial excitement, which is not backed up by true conviction: "If Kossuth had received on his landing in England, such a welcome as he found in the city of New York, it might have been relied on, whereas the very actors in the New York scene knew it meant nothing" (*LL*, vol. 1, 284). This also relates back to Emerson's belief in the importance of appealing to a minority only. Throughout his address, he emphasized the mixed reactions Kossuth had received during his travels throughout the United States. But rather than apologizing for those Americans who had greeted Kossuth coldly (presumably in the South), Emerson seems to have appreciated the resistance to Kossuth as a sign that he was "drawing to your part only the good" (*W*, vol. 11, 399). Clearly, Emerson's belief in the power of minorities (that is, in the gap between those truly embodying the national spirit and the masses of a nation) fit in well with the deepening rifts of American sectionalism.

Emerson was also particularly careful to avoid joining those nationalist voices that saw in Kossuth's appraisal of American liberty a confirmation of America's—and especially New England's—exceptionalist status of having materialized freedom. While others uniformly reiterated the slogan of the "cradle of liberty," Emerson distinguished between the achievements of the Founding Fathers and contemporary America. A few weeks after Kossuth's visit to Concord, he wrote to Robert Carter, who was preparing *Kossuth in New England* for publication, with several corrections from the newspaper transcripts Carter used as his source. The first correction reads: "[E]rase the words '[Concord is one of the monuments of freedom;]'" (*L*, vol. 8, 318). It was not that the remaining paragraph in Emerson's address denigrated Revolutionary history: "[I]t is the privilege of this town to keep a hallowed mound which has a place in the story of the country; . . . you could not take all the steps in the pilgrimage of American liberty, until you had seen with your eyes the ruins of the bridge where a handful of brave farmers opened our Revolution. Therefore, we sat and waited for you" (*W*, vol. 11, 397). But without the sentence about Concord being the *monument* of freedom, what remained of the Revolution were the ruins of a bridge; and rather than being naturally infused with liberty, the "hallowed mound" was no more than a part of America's "story"—one is almost inclined to read: myth.

Instead of reiterating the logic with which Kossuth's case was usually linked to New England—as the introductory speaker in Lexington earlier the same day expressed it: "[A] brighter day has dawned upon our country. . . . So may it be with your beloved country!" (*Kossuth in New England* 218)— Emerson created a parallel between the United States and Hungary along the opposite axis: "We know the austere condition of liberty—that it must be reconquered over and over again; yea, day by day; that it is a state of war; that it is always slipping from those who boast it to those who fight for it" (*W*, vol. 11, 397). Emerson may have had in mind the very real fights over a fugitive slave known as Shadrach Minkins, who, in March 1851, had escaped a Boston courtroom with the help of African American rescuers and had finally made his way to Canada. Webster himself was ordered to prosecute Minkins's helpers. Emerson may have also thought of the case of Thomas Sims, another fugitive slave, who, one month after Minkins, was shipped back to Georgia, guarded by three hundred men (compare Packer, "Historical Introduction," *CW*, vol. 6, xli–xlii).

In any case, the radicalization of Emerson's antislavery stance directly impinged on his divided reaction to the case of Kossuth. Thus, Emerson attempted to maintain a fine balance between supporting Kossuth's revolutionary cause, and distancing himself from the way this cause was used for a politics that increasingly appalled Emerson. Emerson's balancing act hinged on a "politics of abstraction"—the strategy of not letting a universal principle be reduced to narrow particularity. Rather than explicitly distinguishing between a principle and its manifestations (as Kossuth did), this required answering the impositions of the particular by remaining pointedly general and vague. In politicizing abstraction, Emerson turned on its head the lecture hall convention of muting a politicized bias by means of abstraction. In effect, it was his organic, idealist nationalism that gave him the tools to do so, although it also implicated him in nationalism.

How fragile this balance was, and how easily being implicated in nationalism on the level of theory could turn into open promotion of a particular nation's special standing becomes apparent in Emerson's late writings, during and after the Civil War. Here I only want to come back once more to the aforementioned lecture "Fortune of the Republic," which Emerson used like a campaign speech for the war effort and Lincoln's renomination. In order to avert a crisis over the North's future, Emerson diverged from his earlier "politics of abstraction" and employed American exceptionalist discourse to motivate his listeners to continued support of the war: "We are these days settling for ourselves and our descendants questions, which, as they shall be determined in one way or another, will make peace or prosperity, or the calamity of the next ages" (AW, 139). Exceptionalism in his case meant above all rending ties to the British, whom Emerson had up to this point usually presented as the Americans' Anglo-Saxon relatives. Now, America's definitional dependence on the British was turned inside out, with England becoming a negative foil:

> We are coming—thanks to the war,—to a nationality. Put down your foot, and say to England, we know your merits. In pastime we have paid them the homage of ignoring your faults. . . . We who saw you in a halo of honor which our affection made, now . . . we must compare the future of this country with that, in a time when every prosperity of ours knocks away the stones from your foundation. (AW, 145)

Having supposedly freed itself from the influence of the British, and having emancipated the slaves, America, in Emerson's view, came closer than ever before—and closer than any other nation—to embodying the ideal: "At every moment some one country more than any other represents the sentiment and the future of mankind. At present time, no one will doubt that America occupies this place in the opinions of nations" (AW, 139). In this moment (as in others), Emerson stifles the engine of his thinking, that is, the insistence on the difference between the ideal and the actual, and the impossibility of achieving the ideal. Even if only for the purposes of political propaganda, Emerson here celebrates the incarnation of an ideal.

Emerson has been critiqued from different angles, on account of either the expansionist or the quietist tendencies of his thought, or a combination of both. These two aspects of critique directly impinge on the image I have just sketched. One critique, voiced for instance by Myra Jehlen, argues that Emerson's idealism strives toward, and finds fulfillment in, incarnation. While this incarnation aggressively amasses wealth, land, and power for

Emerson's class and race, it exploits, expels, and kills others. Another critique, articulated in exemplary fashion by John Carlos Rowe in *At Emerson's Tomb*, claims that Emerson's idealism keeps him from pursuing transformations in the realm of the actual; Rowe thus claims that Emerson does not muster sufficient vigor to push the ideal toward the actual. In both types of critique, the question remains, what type of emancipation and freedom do Emerson's critics envision? I have argued that, all too frequently, they insist on the realization of a freedom uncontaminated by the current order of things, and thus untrammeled by the kinds of aporia that result from a responsibility to the given. While this amounts to a utopian idealism that is problematic on philosophical grounds, it also lets the New Americanists, and revisionist critics more generally, overlook that Emerson may be read as having been concerned with a fragile, implicated, and necessarily aporetic concept of freedom and change, a concept that was strengthened by the need to find a voice that promised success in the lecture hall.

EPILOGUE

IN ORDER TO ATTRACT and relate to an audience, Emerson had to partially affirm his listeners' worldviews. But despite Emerson's working within an ideological framework, the listening experiences Emerson enabled his audiences to have are not reducible to this ideology. What I have described throughout the foregoing chapters as fractured idealism allowed him to imbue his lectures with a dramatic potential that could be translated into listening (and, once published, reading) experiences of inspirational excess. It is not that the requirements of the public lecture hall forced him to distort his philosophy. Rather, his professional engagement bolstered the eclectic character of his thinking, a characteristic that can be traced back to his days as a student. As I have argued, Emerson's thought is marked by a tension between aiming for limitlessness and questioning the feasibility of this aim in the face of limitation, whether he considers language and representation, friendship and identity, or the nation and empire.

Thus, his idealist nationalism lets him promote the embodiment of what he calls, following Cousin and others, a "national Idea." Yet when he comes across a putative achievement of embodiment, he turns into a skeptic, raising doubt not only about whether the individual in question really embodies the idea but also about whether such embodiment is possible at all.

Similarly, when Emerson ruminates on the conditions and potential of friendship, he affirms the generative and enriching effect of meeting friends. In conversing with friends, the individual receives a kind of spiritual enlargement that allows both friends to achieve their higher selves. Yet the beneficent effects of friendship quickly wear off and tend to leave the individual isolated and spiritually depleted. It is not enough to say that true friendship now appears as an ideal moment only to be experienced on rare occasions. The possibility of such an elevating friendship is called into question altogether (though it is not denied). Instead, Emerson tries to formulate alternative modes of interpersonal contact in which sustainability replaces rapid growth.

Finally, language promises the Emersonian figure of the Poet a means of giving expression to the highest truth, which will allow all others to witness the Poet's experience. Yet language, in Emerson's writings, turns out to be insufficient for representing or expressing an experience of insight, because this insight consists of that which eludes language. In fact, because the insight cannot be represented, neither can it be remembered. Between reception and expression there emerges a fissure that is ultimately unbridgeable, and what remains of reception is decidedly less than an idea: it is the faintest idea. But if Emerson's idealism is marked by fractures and fissures, his philosophical thinking does not therefore indulge in failure.

On the contrary, whether concerned with representation, identity, or the nation, Emerson imagines moments of failure to generate a dynamic of excessive overcoming. Representation is the best example of this dynamic. For Emerson, the shortcomings of expression lay the groundwork for signifying acts that, because they can never capture what was obtained in reception, must engage in an ever-shifting semiosis. The best language use is creative precisely because of its failure to grasp what was received in a moment of spiritual abandonment. Furthermore, by transforming failure into creativity, expression itself enables new moments of receptive abandonment. Key to this argument is the idea that expression and reception constitute types of signification that are incommensurable but that are nevertheless capable of energizing each other. The dynamic of aiming for limitlessness and encountering limitation is thus productive of an excess that incessantly refuels this very dynamic.

In order to turn Emerson's gyratory performances of fractured idealism into an experience of inspiration, his listeners had to contribute their share. When Emerson motivated them to move from the world of the Understanding to that of Reason, and when he juxtaposed particulars with generalizations, they had to provide the mental connections called for by these juxtapositions. They were, in fact, morally compelled to do so. It was not that the mental work of the audience was able to make Emerson's sentences add up to coherent and rational insights. Nor was it supposed to. Rather, Emerson's juxtapositions were designed to stimulate his listener's minds, allowing them to perceive his vague promises of deep meaning as a web of unlimited connections. Entering this imaginary sphere in which everything seemed connected could lead to an imaginary experience of pure potentiality. Emerson switched back and forth from scolding to lauding his audiences. But for the moment of the inspirational effect, as fleeting as it may have been, he enabled a degree of self-confirmation that was worth all the rebuffs. For the imaginary experience of pure potentiality, looked at from a slightly different perspective, provided an experience of the unlimited potential of the self.

In a world in which the demand for social recognition became ever more urgent, and its allocation increasingly insecure, the occasion for self-recognition that Emerson offered to his audiences helps explain the extraordinary appeal his often obscure writings had with a mass public. In this light, we read anew Emerson's oft-quoted statement from 1840: "In all my lectures, I have taught one doctrine, namely, the infinitude of the private man" (*JMN*, vol. 7, 342). If teaching meant provoking—as he had explained in the Divinity School Address—then Emerson seems to have been well aware of what lay at the root of his appeal: He did not merely prioritize the individual. More crucially, he allowed his listeners to experience their own infinitude.

Today, it may be difficult to imagine that Emerson ever achieved a popular following. But the principle of his appeal propels the popular to this day. We still crave Emerson's challenge.

NOTES

Introduction

1. See Philip Gura, *American Transcendentalism: A History* (New York: Hill and Wang, 2007).

2. William H. Gilman et al., eds., *The Journals and Miscellaneous Notebooks of Ralph Waldo Emerson*, vol. 7 (Cambridge, MA: Belknap Press of Harvard University Press, 1960–1982), 342; hereafter cited in text as *JMN*.

3. See, for instance, Len Gougeon, *Virtue's Hero* (Athens: University of Georgia Press, 1990); the essay collection, Gregory Garvey, ed., *The Emerson Dilemma: Essays on Emerson and Social Reform* (Athens: University of Georgia Press, 2001); and Phyllis Cole's various essays on Emerson and the women's movement, for instance, "The New Movement's Tide: Emerson and Women's Rights," in *Emerson Bicentennial Essays*, ed. Ronald A. Bosco and Joel Myerson (Boston: Massachusetts Historical Society; Charlottesville: Distributed by the University of Virginia Press, 2006), 117–52.

4. In his recent, illuminating study *Emerson's Ghosts: Literature, Politics, and the Making of Americanists* (New York: Oxford University Press, 2007), Randall Fuller has traced the influence Emerson has had on critics of American literature from the late nineteenth century to the present. He argues that Emerson has "haunted" Americanists, particularly because of his ideal figure of the "American Scholar," who performs cultural criticism through literary means. For Fuller, Emerson becomes the proper subject of a monograph because Fuller deliberately puts Emerson in the position Emerson once claimed for himself, namely that of the "central man." My angle is a different one: Emerson is important for my project not because of the indebtedness of revisionists to Emersonianism, but because of the capacity of his own writings to make visible the problems of the premises underlying revisionist criticism.

5. As a reflection of this self-positioning, Americanists in recent years have generally tried to de-emphasize the link between the discipline's and the nation's names by changing the spelling of "American Studies" to "American studies." Throughout this study, I retain the older spelling.

6. Winfried Fluck, "The Humanities in the Age of Expressive Individualism and Cultural Radicalism," in *Futures of American Studies*, ed. Donald E. Pease and Robyn Wiegman (Durham, NC: Duke University Press, 2002), 216; hereafter cited in text as "Humanities."

7. See Richard F. Teichgraeber III, *Sublime Thoughts/Penny Wisdom: Situating Emerson and Thoreau in the American Market* (Baltimore: Johns Hopkins University Press, 1995). For related views of Emerson, see Eduardo Cadava, *Emerson and the Climates of History* (Stanford, CA: Stanford University Press, 1997); Lawrence Buell, *Emerson* (Cambridge, MA: Harvard University Press, 2003); Anita Haya Patterson, *From Emerson to King* (New York: Oxford University Press, 1997); and John Michael's essay "Democracy, Aesthetics, Individualism: Emerson as Public Intellectual," *Nineteenth-Century Prose* 30, nos. 1–2 (Spring/Fall 2003): 195–226.

8. My understanding of modernity as it concerns the growing responsibility put on the shoulders of the individual is informed by Ulrich Beck's theory of individualization. Beck's analysis is tied to "reflexive modernity" rather than what he considers a first modernity; "reflexive modernity" sets in, in his view, in the second half of the twentieth century. It should be noted that this periodization is based to a large degree on the fate of the European welfare state. The story in the United States is obviously a different one. Many of the traits of "reflexive modernity" are visible in the emerging market culture of the nineteenth-century United States. In his foreword to Ulrich Beck and Elisabeth Beck-Gernsheim's *Individualization: Institutionalized Individualism and Its Social and Political Consequences* (London: Sage, 2002), ix, Scott Lash writes "The non-linear individual [of second modernity] . . . puts together networks, constructs alliances, makes deals. He must live, is forced to live in an atmosphere of risk in which knowledge and life-changes are precarious." In this sense, Emerson's career is marked by non-linearity as well.

9. Stuart Hall, "The Work of Representation," in *Representation: Cultural Representations and Signifying Practices*, ed. Stuart Hall (London: Sage in association with the Open University, 1997), 15; hereafter cited in text as "Work of Representation."

10. The term comes from Richard Poirier's *A World Elsewhere: The Place of Style in American Literature* (New York: Oxford University Press, 1966), which is often seen as belonging to Myth and Symbol criticism. Poirier takes the phrase from Shakespeare's *Tragedy of Coriolanus*.

11. See Wai Chee Dimock, *Through Other Continents: American Literature across Deep Time* (Princeton, NJ: Princeton University Press, 2006), hereafter cited in text as *Through Other Continents*.

12. See in particular Pheng Cheah's article "Given Culture: Rethinking Cosmopolitical Freedom in Transnationalism," in *Cosmopolitics: Thinking and Feeling beyond the Nation*, ed. Pheng Cheah and Bruce Robbins (Minneapolis: University of Minnesota Press, 1998), 290–328; hereafter cited in text as "Given Culture."

13. The term is James P. Warren's, see his *Culture of Eloquence: Oratory and Reform in Antebellum America* (University Park: Pennsylvania State University Press, 1999).

14. R. Jackson Wilson, "Emerson as Lecturer: Man Thinking, Man Saying," in *The Cambridge Companion to Ralph Waldo Emerson*, ed. Joel Porte and Saundra Morris (New York: Cambridge University Press, 1999), 77; hereafter cited in text as "Emerson as Lecturer."

15. Compare Wilson, "Emerson as Lecturer," in Porte and Morris, eds., *Cambridge Companion*, 78.

16. Donald M. Scott, "The Popular Lecture and the Creation of a Public in Mid-Nineteenth-Century America," *Journal of American History* 66, no. 4 (March 1980): 795; hereafter cited in text as "Popular Lecture."

17. Walter Benn Michaels, "The Shape of the Signifier," *Critical Inquiry* 27, no. 2 (Winter 2001): 277.

1. The New Americanists and Representation

1. Several of the critiques from the early 1970s have reached classic status, among them Bruce Kuklick, "Myth and Symbol in American Studies," *American Quarterly* 24, no. 4 (Autumn 1972): 435–50; Robert Sklar, "American Studies and the Realities of America," *American Quarterly* 22, no. 2, part 2 (Summer 1970): 597–605; and R. Gordon Kelly, "Literature and the Historian," *American Quarterly* 26, no. 2 (Summer 1974): 141–59. For a European perspective that critically scrutinizes the implied aesthetic theory of the Myth and Symbol school, see Winfried Fluck, "Das ästhetische Vorverständnis der 'American Studies,'" *Jahrbuch für Amerikastudien* 18 (1973): 110–29; English version: "Aesthetic Premises in American Studies," in Winfried Fluck, *Romance with America? Essays on Culture, Literature, and American Studies*, ed. Laura Bieger and Johannes Voelz (Heidelberg: Winter, 2009), 15–38.

2. Thomas S. Kuhn, *The Structure of Scientific Revolutions* (Chicago: University of Chicago Press, 1962), x; hereafter cited in text as *Structure*.

3. It is of course true that such a view was not available to the Myth and Symbol practitioners themselves. The whole point of Henry Nash Smith's and Leo Marx's articles on the lack of method in American Studies was to justify their sense that whatever American Studies might be, it did not add up to anything like a method or paradigm. Indeed, Smith even felt obliged to put "American Studies" in quotation marks, so marginal and inchoate did his enterprise appear to himself. See Henry Nash Smith, "Can 'American Studies' Develop a Method?" *American Quarterly* 9, no. 2, part 2 (Summer 1957): 197–208; and Leo Marx, "American Studies: A Defense of an Unscientific Method," *New Literary History* 1, no. 1 (Autumn 1969): 75–90.

4. In Lawrence Buell's apt description, American Studies since 1970 has become "a combination of home base, contact zone, and debating ground for an increasingly complex, politicized, and centrifugal array of revisionisms—gender and sexuality studies, race and ethnicity studies, and (trans)national theory in particular" (commentary on Henry Nash Smith, "Can 'American Studies' Develop a Method?" in *Locating American Studies: The Evolution of a Discipline*, ed. Lucy Maddox [Baltimore: Johns Hopkins University Press, 1999], 14).

5. Gene Wise, "'Paradigm Dramas' in American Studies: A Cultural and Institutional History of the Movement," *American Quarterly* 31, no. 3 (1979): 295; hereafter cited in text as "'Paradigm Dramas.'"

6. Wise characterized the Myth and Symbol school in the following terms: "Reduced to essentials, these assumptions [of the intellectual history synthesis] are as follows: a) There is an 'American Mind.' . . . b) What distinguishes the American Mind is its location in the 'New' World. Because of this, Americans are characteristically hopeful, innocent, individualistic, pragmatic, idealistic. . . . c) The American Mind . . . comes to most coherent expression in the country's leading thinkers. . . . d) The American Mind is an enduring form in our intellectual history. . . . e) . . . America is revealed most profoundly in its 'high' culture" (Wise, "'Paradigm Dramas,'" 306–7). While Wise's summary is correct in

stressing the belief in an American mind, it is also a caricature in that it overlooks the critical impetus with which Myth and Symbol scholars legitimated their work and the value of American culture. As Winfried Fluck writes, "On the surface, the [Myth and Symbol school's] argument goes, American culture seems to perpetuate certain foundational myths such as the belief in progress or the regenerative potential of the frontier. But on a covert level, the major works of American literature are characterized by a unique potential for radical resistance, of saying 'No! in Thunder'" [Winfried Fluck, "Theories of American Culture (and the Transnational Turn in American Studies)," *REAL—Yearbook of Research in English and American Literature* 23 (2007): 63].

7. Wise did refer to Kuhn in explaining his use of *paradigm*. However, he highlighted a dimension usually not considered central to Kuhn's theory, namely the function of a paradigm as an act: "In *The Structure*, Kuhn handles paradigms not only as patterns of belief but also as the characteristic acts which function to dramatize those beliefs. . . . For Kuhn, then, a paradigm is not just the content of a thought pattern, but, more fundamentally, *an actual instance of that pattern of thinking in action*" (Wise, "'Paradigm Dramas,'" 297, emphasis in original). Wise is right, but for Kuhn it is nevertheless the organizational function of the paradigm that matters, a dimension Wise underplays. In fact, his emphasis on the paradigm as an instance of action displays the impact of Kenneth Burke's idea of "symbolic action" on his thought.

8. Wise, "'Paradigm Dramas,'" 295.

9. One should take seriously here Leo Marx's insistence that, in its formative years, the American Studies movement was highly critical of nationalism and therefore, in self-consciously Jeffersonian and Lincolnian fashion, associated "the idea of America" with universalist, Enlightenment ideals: "In our 1930s lexicon, nationalism was a reactionary habit of mind, a seedbed of xenophobia and fascism. Our Left was internationalist" (Leo Marx, "On Recovering the 'Ur' Theory of American Studies," *American Literary History* 17, no. 1 [Spring 2005]: 127; hereafter cited in text as "On Recovering the 'Ur' Theory." Of further importance is Heinz Ickstadt's reminder that the Myth and Symbol Americanists did assume a position toward the myths analyzed that was often very critical of their hegemonic power (Heinz Ickstadt, "American Studies in an Age of Globalization," *American Quarterly* 54, no. 4 [December 2002]: 547).

10. Donald E. Pease and Robyn Wiegman, "Futures," in *The Futures of American Studies*, ed. Donald E. Pease and Robyn Wiegman (Durham, NC: Duke University Press, 2002), 11; hereafter cited in text as "Futures."

11. Pease and Wiegman write, "The contributors to this volume [*The Futures of American Studies*] do not assume that the field of American studies is reducible to the dimensions of a single overarching paradigm, nor do they think that the genealogy of the field can be described as a struggle to predominate among conflicting paradigms" (Pease and Wiegman, "Futures," 4).

12. This "negative reciprocity" was already described by Robert Sklar in one of the early critiques of the Myth and Symbol school, "American Studies and the Realities of America": "While the American Studies revolution has considerably aged, another revolution has taken place in the colleges and universities to which American Studies has been only tenuously connected—the development of programs studying American social problems, programs in minority cultures and history, in urban studies, in environment and ecology. To students and staff attracted to these new programs American Studies appears

not as irrelevant but rather as different: you in American Studies study the arts and ideas, we over here will study society" (Sklar, "American Studies and the Realities of America," 602–3).

13. As a caveat, one needs to keep in mind how quickly "theory" turned into a niche of its own in the American academy. Thus, English departments frequently hired a designated theorist, which in effect contributed to the containment of theory. See Gerald Graff, *Professing Literature: An Institutional History* (Chicago: University of Chicago Press, 1987), chapter 15. Nevertheless, theory provided disciplinary "glue" that worked even for those who did not venture deeply into theory.

14. Foucault's *Madness and Civilization*, for instance, appeared as early as 1961, but as he claimed in an interview in 1977, "without the political opening [that followed '68] I would perhaps not have had the courage to take up the thread of these problems and to pursue my inquiry in the direction of punishment, prison, and disciplines" (Quoted in Luc Ferry and Alain Renaut, *French Philosophy of the Sixties*, trans. Mary Cattani [Amherst: University of Massachusetts Press], xix).

15. Several scholars, including William Paulson and Lawrence Buell, have recently pointed out the significance of the fact that the reception of theory in the United States and the development of new academic disciplines were from the start linked to identity questions. Although environmentalism was part of the activist agenda, its lack of identitarian representatives led to the belated arrival of ecological theory in academia. See William Paulson, *Literary Culture in a World Transformed* (Ithaca, NY: Cornell University Press, 2001, 56), and Lawrence Buell, *The Future of Environmental Criticism: Environmental Crisis and Literary Imagination* (Malden, MA: Blackwell, 2005).

16. Refraining from calling it a new paradigm, Pease has recently described the term *New Americanists* as a "supplement," that is, as a term that implied the unending openness of "new" American Studies, but also its interdependence with older Americanist approaches. In "9/11: When Was 'American Studies after the New Americanists'?" Pease writes, "The individual and collective aims of the scholars Crews gathered under the New Americanists' banner were more perplexing than the ones he attributed to them. The New Americanists were involved in a relationship of supplementarity to traditional American studies. In adding what the field had been lacking, the New Americanists did not effect a definitive overthrow of the ruling orthodoxy of American studies. The establishment americanist [sic] and the New Americanist each brought out something that was lacking, or excessive, or unthought by the other" (Donald Pease, "9/11: When was 'American Studies after the New Americanists'?" *boundary 2* 33, no. 3 [Fall 2006]: 85–86; hereafter cited in text as "9/11").

17. This became most obvious in Pease's dismissal of Sacvan Bercovitch's influential essays on ideology, which Bercovitch published in conjunction with the impending publication of *The Cambridge History of American Literature*, of which he was the general editor. Bercovitch's well-known point is that the American ideology has been able to absorb all forms of dissent into a consensus. While Myth and Symbol scholars had claimed that America's classic authors subverted mainstream culture, Bercovitch claimed that "these classics turned the ideological norms they represented—independence, liberty, enterprise, opportunity, individualism, democracy, 'America' itself—against the American way," thereby reaffirming the culture, rather than undermining it (Sacvan Bercovitch, "The Problem of Ideology in American Literary History," *Critical Inquiry* 12, no. 4

[Summer 1986]: 643–44). For Crews, Bercovitch's focus on ideology made him a New Americanist. But Pease maintained that Bercovitch's espousal of a concept of ideology as a true prison left no possibility of politically efficacious resistance.

18. Philip Fisher, "Introduction: The New American Studies," in *The New American Studies: Essays from "Representations,"* ed. Philip Fisher (Berkeley: University of California Press, 1991), xii; hereafter cited in text as "New American Studies."

19. In fact, creating the New Americanists was a poor defense against the erosion of the social and political gains of the '60s, because, as an academic category, it could do no more than solidify a social-democratic academic consensus. This was certainly not enough to confront the rise of neoconservatism and the consolidation of a Republican majority in both houses of Congress. In this respect, the insistence on the close links between American Studies and social movements, which Pease emphasized in his second programmatic article, "National Identities, Postmodern Artifacts, and Postnational Narratives," was dangerously self-deceptive in its political ambitions. In retrospect, however, the impact of the New Americanists, limited though it may have been, can also be interpreted as a political achievement: in light of the aggressive, yet so far largely futile, attempts of neoconservatives to get a foothold in the academic system (most crucially in the humanities), the fact that the New Americanists contributed to defending this bastion of humanist inquiry should not be neglected.

20. There is a parallel between the New Americanists and Cultural Studies in this regard. As Bill Readings has argued, Cultural Studies practitioners' self-description "is characterized above all by resistance to all attempts to limit its field of reference—such as distinctions between high and popular culture, between factual texts . . . and fictional ones" (Bill Readings, *The University in Ruins* [Cambridge, MA: Harvard University Press, 1996], 98). Commenting on a typical Cultural Studies introduction by Anthony Easthope (*Literary into Cultural Studies* [London: Routledge, 1991]), Readings describes the Cultural Studies version of Pease's New Americanist nonparadigm: "In effect, Easthope is offering to recenter the University around a decentered absence that will then be invoked as if it were a center" (Readings, *University in Ruins*, 99).

21. Crews discusses the following works: Walter Benn Michaels and Donald E. Pease, eds., *The American Renaissance Reconsidered: Selected Papers from the English Institute, 1982–83* (Baltimore: Johns Hopkins University Press, 1985); Russell J. Reising, *The Unusable Past: Theory and the Study of American Literature* (New York: Methuen, 1986); Sacvan Bercovitch and Myra Jehlen, eds., *Ideology and Classic American Literature* (Cambridge: Cambridge University Press, 1986); Donald E. Pease, *Visionary Compacts: American Renaissance Writings in Cultural Context* (Madison: University of Wisconsin Press, 1987); Jane Tompkins, *Sensational Designs: The Cultural Work of American Fiction, 1790–1860* (New York: Oxford University Press, 1986); David S. Reynolds, *Beneath the American Renaissance: The Subversive Imagination in the Age of Emerson and Melville* (New York: Alfred A. Knopf, 1988); and Philip Fisher, *Hard Facts: Setting and Form in the American Novel* (New York: Oxford University Press, 1985).

22. Frederick C. Crews, "Whose American Renaissance?" *The New York Review of Books* 35, no. 16 (October 27, 1988): 68; hereafter cited in text as "Whose American Renaissance?"

23. See, for instance, Edmund Wilson, *The Cold War and the Income Tax: A Protest* (New York: Farrar, Straus, 1963).

24. Compare Louis Menand's description of Wilson: "Edmund Wilson disliked being called a critic. He thought of himself as a journalist, and nearly all his work was done for commercial magazines. . . . Most of his books were put together from pieces that had been written to meet journalistic occasions" (Louis Menand, "Missionary: Edmund Wilson and American Culture," *The New Yorker* 81, no. 23 [August 8 and 15, 2005]: 82).

25. Donald E. Pease, "New Americanists: Revisionist Interventions into the Canon," *boundary* 2 17, no. 1 (Spring 1990): 4; hereafter cited in text as "New Americanists."

26. For Jameson, what needs to be recovered from the "political unconscious" in literary texts is the continuing narrative famously outlined by Marx in *The Communist Manifesto*: "The history of all hitherto existing society is the history of class struggles." Thus Jameson writes: "It is in detecting the traces of that uninterrupted narrative, in restoring to the surface of the text the repressed and buried reality of this fundamental history, that the doctrine of a political unconscious finds its function and necessity" (Fredric Jameson, *The Political Unconscious: Narrative as a Socially Symbolic Act* [Ithaca, NY: Cornell University Press, 1981], 20). While many New Americanists "restore" to the surface traces that are legitimated in their status as traces by the sheer appearance in the critic's text (in other words, by the critic's textual performance), Jameson devised a more rigorous method: a literary text had to be placed in three overlapping horizons in order to "mark a widening out of the sense of the social ground of a text through the notions, first, of political history, in the narrow sense of punctual event and a chroniclelike sequence of happenings in time; then of society, in the now already less diachronic and time-bound sense of a constitutive tension and struggle between social classes; and, ultimately, of history now conceived in its vastest sense of the sequence of modes of production and the succession and destiny of the various human social formations, from prehistoric life to whatever far future history has in store for us" (Jameson, *Political Unconscious*, 75).

27. Compare Louis Althusser, "Ideology and Ideological State Apparatuses," in *Lenin and Philosophy and Other Essays*, trans. Ben Brewster (New York: Monthly Review Press, 1971), especially 170–77. For Donald Pease's most extensive discussion of Althusser, see Donald E. Pease, "Negative Interpellations: From Oklahoma City to the Trilling-Matthiessen Transmission," *boundary* 2 23, no.1 (Spring 1996): 1–33.

28. Louis Althusser, *Lenin and Philosophy and Other Essays*, trans. Ben Brewster (New York: Monthly Review Press, 1971), 170; hereafter cited in text as *Lenin and Philosophy*.

29. For Gramsci's reading of Dante, see Antonio Gramsci, *Selections from Cultural Writings* (London: Lawrence and Wishart, 1985), 252–78; for his thoughts on linguistics, see Gramsci, *Selections from Cultural Writings*, 279–329.

30. Bringing both dimensions of her analysis together, Holub concludes, "From his scattered notes on linguistic matters to his notes on philosophical and political issues there is little doubt that Gramsci prefers a theoretical communicative model where the subject is not caught in inexorably determinate linguistic structures. What Gramsci tends to prefer is a theoretical communicative model where the subject is in a position to interact with an object and with other subjects, and it is in the very interaction with the object and other subjects that the subject can create his or her own object of knowledge according to the circumstances or the goals the subject intends to achieve. Dante's reader in part fulfils the requirements of this model. The reader, as we recall, creatively assembles the sensory data, whether visible or invisible, unexpressed or expressed, in the act of creating

his/her own object in this act of interpretation" (Renate Holub, *Antonio Gramsci: Beyond Marxism and Postmodernism* [London: Routledge, 1992], 135).

31. Gramsci discussed James and pragmatism in general (both American and Italian) several times in his notebooks, usually somewhat ambiguously. On the one hand, he typically dismissed the pragmatists as utilitarian and conservative. On the other hand, he sensed potential in their work. He thus writes, for instance, "It seems to me safe to say that the conception of language held by Vailati and other pragmatists is not acceptable. But it also seems that they felt real needs and 'described' them with an exactness that was not far off the mark, even if they did not succeed in posing the problems fully or in providing a solution" (Antonio Gramsci, *Selections from the Prison Notebooks* [London: Lawrence and Wishart, 1971], 664; hereafter cited in text as *Prison Notebooks*). The presence of the pragmatists in Gramsci's mind is not surprising, considering that he studied linguistics in Turin at a time when Italian pragmatists like Giovanni Vailati were highly influential there. (Vailati himself based his work closely on Peirce's; compare Robert E. Innis, "Pragmatism and the Analysis of Meaning in the Philosophy of Giovanni Vailati," *Differentia: Review of Italian Thought*, nos. 3–4 (Spring/Autumn 1989): 177–98). Martin Jay has ventured to argue that although "Gramsci never fully identified with their position, he seems to have built his own theory of language partly on pragmatic foundations" (Martin Jay, *Marxism and Totality: The Adventures of a Concept from Lukács to Habermas* [Berkeley: University of California Press, 1984], 160). For the influence of American pragmatists in Italy, see also Gerald Myers, "The Influence of William James's Pragmatism in Italy," in *The Sweetest Impression of Life: The James Family and Italy*, ed. James W. Tuttleton and Agostino Lombardo (New York: New York University Press, 1990), 162–81; and Claudio Gorlier, "Listening to the Master: William James and the 'Making of the New' in Italian Culture," in *The Sweetest Impression* (see previous citation), 182–96.

32. Pease admits as much in "Negative Interpellations: From Oklahoma City to the Trilling-Matthiessen Transmission." Here he speaks of "the highly polemical introduction I linked to a volume for this journal entitled 'New Americanists: Revisionist Interventions into the Canon'" (Pease, "Negative Interpellations," 10).

33. This reassessment is strategically motivated in two ways: First, in "9/11: When was 'American Studies after the New Americanists'?" Pease toys with the idea that he is writing from a point in time after the New Americanists, and thus can usefully incorporate Crews's agreement with the New Americanists as a form of legacy building. Second, Crews has been replaced by Alan Wolfe and Leo Marx as the New Americanists' main antagonists. He can thus be integrated without threatening a collapse of the New Americanists' position of difference.

34. Crews also repeated this point in his Introduction to Frederick C. Crews, *The Critics Bear It Away: American Fiction and the Academy* (New York: Random House, 1992), which was published in somewhat different form as a separate article in the *New York Review of Books* under the title "The New Americanists" (*The New York Review of Books* 39, no. 15 [September 24, 1992]: 32–34). In this article, which is not mentioned by Pease, Crews positioned himself in opposition to the "cultural nostalgics as William Bennett, Allan Bloom, Lynne Cheney, and Roger Kimball" on the right and to the "Left Eclecticists" on the other side, with a clear leaning toward the left. Crews writes: "In my view there can be no such thing as a sacrosanct text, an innately civilizing idea, or an

altogether disinterested literary critic. . . . In contrast, I see political belief of one kind or another as part of the motive force behind most intellectual and cultural interests. The problem with Left Eclecticism, in my opinion, is not that it allows 'subversives' access to the academy but that it makes for a closed shop in which scholarly questions tend to be answered aprioristically and in which only a small band of opinion is considered tolerable. . . . The left, unlike the right, has made some indisputably fertile contributions to the recent evolution of literary study. It is radicals who brought about today's general realization that criticism must become more self-aware about the ideological coordinates of the positions it takes" (Crews, "The New Americanists," 32).

35. In Crews's description, "Delbanco referred demeaningly to 'prosecutorial' books and articles that 'have the quality of a belated inquest convened not to determine if a crime took place—the crime is called culture—but to determine the degree of Melville's complicity in it'" (Frederick C. Crews, "Melville the Great," *New York Review of Books* 52, no. 19 [December 1, 2005]: 8). Crews cites Andrew Delbanco, "Melville in the '80s," *American Literary History* 4, no. 4 (Winter 1992): 711, 715.

36. "In specifying racialized exclusions and gendered hierarchies as structural realities that were at once insistently present to the field's disciplinary perspectives yet persistently absent from americanist practices, New Americanists were obliged to think about racial and gendered distinctions in terms of what Joan Scott has called the contradictory logic of the supplement. . . . When New Americanists restored the content to the events that the Liberal Imagination had disallowed signification, this surplus knowledge opened up the paradoxical gap separating the liberal from the democratic ambitions of the liberal democracy in which they practiced their scholarship" (Pease, "9/11," 89).

37. Donald E. Pease, "National Identities, Postmodern Artifacts, and Postnational Narratives," *boundary 2* 19, no. 1 (Spring 1992): 9.

38. Georg Lukács, "Reification and the Consciousness of the Proletariat," in *History and Class Consciousness: Studies in Marxist Dialectics*, trans. Rodney Livingstone (Cambridge, MA: MIT Press, 1971), 89; hereafter cited in text as "Reification."

39. "In the theory of 'reflection' we find the theoretical embodiment of the duality of thought and existence, consciousness and reality, that is so intractable to the reified consciousness. And from that point of view it is immaterial whether things are to be regarded as reflections of concepts or whether concepts are reflections of things. In both cases the duality is firmly established" (Lukács, "Reification," 200).

40. This tendency is visible even in Raymond Williams's otherwise useful chapter "From Reflection to Mediation" in *Marxism and Literature*. Although the general direction of his argument—to point out the productive work that mediation does in connecting *processes* of base and superstructure—is well taken, he ends the chapter by noting, "But when the process of mediation is seen as positive and substantial . . . it is really only a hindrance to describe it as a 'mediation' at all. For the metaphor takes us back to the 'intermediary,' which, at its best, this constitutive and constituting sense rejects" (Raymond Williams, *Marxism and Literature* (Oxford: Oxford University Press, 1977), 100; hereafter cited in text as *Marxism and Literature*.

41. Martin Jay explains, "As Lukács himself came to understand after reading Marx's *1844 Manuscripts* a decade later, he had erroneously conflated the processes of objectification and reification in an essentially idealist way. By equating praxis with the objectification of subjectivity, instead of seeing it as an interaction of a subject with a pre-given

object, Lukács had missed the importance of the dialectic of labor in constituting the social world" (Jay, *Marxism and Totality*, 114).

42. A summary article of her book appeared under the title "Reification in American Literature," in *Ideology and Classic American Literature* (ed. Sacvan Bercovitch and Myra Jehlen, 1986), one of the essay collections reviewed by Crews.

43. Carolyn Porter, *Seeing and Being: The Plight of the Participant Observer in Emerson, James, Adams, and Faulkner* (Middletown, CT: Wesleyan University Press, 1981), 97; hereafter cited in text as *Seeing and Being*.

44. Sharon Cameron explains that the relationship between self and Spirit should not be understood as a struggle between different entities. She writes, "although the essays perform the task of ravishment—that process by which the person is annihilated by the impersonal—no sacrifice is customarily really exacted because rarely is it the case that a discrete or particularized self initially occupies the subject position" (Sharon Cameron, "The Way of Life by Abandonment: Emerson's Impersonal," *Critical Inquiry* 25 [Autumn 1998]: 17).

45. Carolyn Porter, "Reification and American Literature," in *Ideology and Classic American Literature*, ed. Sacvan Bercovitch and Myra Jehlen (Cambridge: Cambridge University Press, 1986), 215.

46. Axel Honneth has recently attempted to salvage the concept of reification by distinguishing between an official version in Lukács's text that issues in the Fichtean identity theory, and an "unofficial view," organized around such intersubjective notions as "participation," "organic unity," and "cooperation," which Honneth attempts to couple with a normative theory of recognition (compare Axel Honneth, *Verdinglichung: Eine Anerkennungstheoretische Studie* [Frankfurt/Main: Suhrkamp, 2006], especially 26–27).

47. John Carlos Rowe, "Deconstructing America: Recent Approaches to Nineteenth-Century Literature and Culture," *ESQ* 31, no. 1 (Spring 1985): 60.

48. Other articles from this time include John Carlos Rowe, "'To Live outside the Law, You Must Be Honest': The Authority of the Margin in Contemporary Theory," *Cultural Critique*, no. 2 (Winter 1985): 35–68; and John Carlos Rowe, "Surplus Economies: Deconstruction, Ideology, and the Humanities," in *The Aims of Representation: Subject/Text/History*, ed. Murray Krieger (Stanford, CA: Stanford University Press, 1987), 131–58.

49. As Priscilla Wald writes in her review of *At Emerson's Tomb*, Rowe's criticism of the Emersonian tradition thereby becomes imbued with self-criticism regarding Rowe's own earliest work: "But Emersonianism [for Rowe] is not Emerson; rather, it is a tradition—almost a belief system—culled from Emerson's (often contradictory) writings. In *At Emerson's Tomb*, it encompasses any critical or theoretical tradition that confuses formal and aesthetic innovation with social engagement or political dissent. That includes—perhaps most pointedly—the poststructuralist tradition that represents Rowe's own brand of 'aesthetic dissent'" (Priscilla Wald, "Fabulous Shadows: Rethinking the Emersonian Tradition" [review of *At Emerson's Tomb*], *American Quarterly* 50, no. 4 [December 1998]: 837).

50. John Carlos Rowe, *At Emerson's Tomb: The Politics of Classic American Literature* (New York: Columbia University Press, 1997), 23; hereafter cited in text as *At Emerson's Tomb*.

51. See, for example, Judith Butler, *The Psychic Life of Power: Theories in Subjection* (Stanford, CA: Stanford University Press), 1997.

52. Newfield's influence is discernible in such New Americanist readings of Emerson as Dana D. Nelson's article "Representative/Democracy: The Political Work of Counter-symbolic Representation," in *Materializing Democracy: Toward a Revitalized Cultural Politics*, ed. Russ Castronovo and Dana D. Nelson (Durham, NC: Duke University Press, 2002), 218–47; and Jay Grossman's study *Reconstituting the American Renaissance: Emerson, Whitman, and the Politics of Representation* (Durham, NC: Duke University Press, 2003; hereafter cited in text as *Reconstituting the American Renaissance*). Both Nelson and Grossman emphasize the link between linguistic and political representation and re-locate Emerson in the constitutional debate between Federalists and Anti-Federalists. In Nelson's view, Emerson's figures of the "Central Man," the "Great Man," and the "Rep-resentative Man" resonate with the Federalist position. She thereby equates Emerson's theory of representativeness with the representation of a people by a president. In her view, Emersonian representativeness relies on a fixed hierarchical relationship between the rep-resentative and the represented. As this model links the multitude with the great man, it becomes the burden of the individual constituent to learn to conform to the representa-tive. Therefore, both transcendentalism and constitutionalism depend, she argues, "on the (false) ideal that peoples' particular *desires* for political participation and community can be satisfied through their identification with a singular, symbolic representative" (Nel-son, "Representative Democracy," 219). Similarly, Grossman proposes that to "see the shifts toward democratic, and away from merely republican, systems of self-representation as a development largely unforeseen by the Founders places us in a position to acknowl-edge and to investigate the *residues* rather than (only) the disjunctions between Revolu-tionary and Renaissance texts, and so to reconstruct a genealogy for the discursive or generic discriminations that constitute American Romanticism in general and the writings of Emerson and Whitman in particular" (Grossman, *Reconstituting the American Renais-sance*, 15). While Grossman cites Newfield to point to "the highly compromised nature of agency across Emerson's classic essays" (Grossman, *Reconstituting the American Re-naissance*, 23)—which is largely a misunderstanding, because Newfield is interested not in the limited *nature* but the *notion* of agency in Emerson's essays—he embraces Al-thusser's interpellation theory to demonstrate that Emerson and Whitman are "'represen-tative' subjects, particularly with regard to the cultural institutions and practices of social class" (Grossman, *Reconstituting the American Renaissance*, 121). Thus, Grossman ar-gues that "Emerson retained a foundational belief in his own elevated status as truth-giver to the masses. . . . To precisely that extent, he remained both his father's son, as well as a true Federalist heir" (Grossman, *Reconstituting the American Renaissance*, 137).

53. Christopher Newfield, *The Emerson Effect: Individualism and Submission in Amer-ica* (Chicago: University of Chicago Press, 1996), 5; hereafter cited in text as *Emerson Effect*.

54. In the *Cratylus*, Plato's dialogue on representation and the power of naming, Cra-tylus takes the position that proper names must be correct, that is, have a referent in na-ture: "SOCRATES: So all names have been correctly given? CRATYLUS: Yes, as many of them as are names at all" (Plato, *Cratylus*, 429b, in *Plato: Complete Works*, ed. John M. Cooper [Indianapolis: Hackett, 1997]).

55. Compare Christopher Newfield's article "Democratic Passions: Reconstructing Individual Agency," in *Materializing Democracy: Toward a Revitalized Cultural Politics*, ed. Russ Castronovo and Dana D. Nelson (Durham, NC: Duke University Press, 2002),

314–44, in which he criticizes the Left for having neglected individual agency, which, in his view, has led to something of a colonization of individual agency by neoliberals, who misconstrue it as best taken care of in the "free market." Unburdened agency, in Newfield's opinion, can only take place in nonmarket settings. As an example, he favorably opposes a model of contact to that of networking. The materialization of "contact" can be paradigmatically studied in the terrain of sexuality: "Unlike a self-regulating market, sexual exchange works through ranges restricted only by the practitioners. Desire is variable within one person, is changeable, is nonlinear, is not exactly predictable" (Newfield, *Materializing Democracy*, 333).

56. I would maintain that Friedrich Schlegel is a problematic candidate for Newfield's vision of linguistic agency. Newfield quotes Schlegel from the *Athenaeum* fragment 116: "Poetry 'alone is infinite, as it alone is free, and its first law is that the poet's arbitrariness is subject to no law'" (Newfield, *Emerson Effect*, 43). As Tzvetan Todorov notes, Schlegel, in this sentence, is "formulating a maxim that is contradicted, as he knows full well, by other fragments of the *Athenaeum*" (Tzvetan Todorov, *Theories of the Symbol*, trans. Catherine Porter [Oxford: Basil Blackwell, 1982], 198). But even within this fragment, and even this very sentence, Schlegel's point requires qualification. It is significant that in his phrasing both Romantic poetry itself and the poet's arbitrariness are free and subject to no law. This suggests that Schlegel here is proposing a radical form of Romantic reason (or creativity), which is defined by its organic structure and thus by the absence of determining, outside forces. While Romantic poetry is not governed by external rules, it is driven by a law that is self-organized. But this self-organization should not be anchored in the random will of an individual. It is rather subject to its own law (its own nature) of organic becoming. As Schlegel writes two sentences earlier, "Romantic poetry is still in a state of becoming; that is even its specific nature, not to be able to do anything but become, eternally, and never to be accomplished" (quoted in Todorov, *Theories of the Symbol*, 195). Schlegel is here much closer to Emerson than Newfield admits; after all, in Emerson the "moral law," which Newfield misleadingly externalizes, is itself fundamentally a law of *becoming*.

57. It is for this reason that I have not discussed here Sacvan Bercovitch's article "Emerson, Individualism, and Liberal Dissent," included in his *The Rites of Assent: Transformations in the Symbolic Construction of America* (New York: Routledge, 1993), 307–52. Bercovitch generally is treated as an antipode by the New Americanists. While Pease dismisses Bercovitch's pessimism regarding the possibility of change outside of containment, Rowe is repelled by Bercovitch's work because it misses the potential of real change in texts like Frederick Douglass's (here, his point mirrors Pease's) and because it is too optimistic regarding the possibility of change *inside* containment—here Bercovitch is, in other words, too liberal: "What Bercovitch fails to do . . . is provide an effective hermeneutic for distinguishing literary 'subversions' that contribute to progressive change from nominally 'liberal' or 'progressive' sentiments that merely help ideology adapt to new circumstances" (Rowe, *At Emerson's Tomb*, 9).

58. Donald E. Pease, *Visionary Compacts: American Renaissance Writings in Cultural Context* (Madison: University of Wisconsin Press, 1987), 204; hereafter cited in text as *Visionary Compacts*.

59. Donald E. Pease, "'Experience,' Antislavery, and the Crisis of Emersonianism," *boundary* 2 34, no. 2 (Summer 2007): 92; hereafter cited in text as "'Experience.'"

60. This particular version of the space-in-between has been central to Pease's recent work more generally, as can be seen in his articles on C. L. R. James—see for instance "C. L. R. James, *Moby-Dick*, and the Emergence of Transnational American Studies," in *The Futures of American Studies*, ed. Donald E. Pease and Robyn Wiegman (Durham, NC: Duke University Press, 2002), 135–63; and "The Extraterritoriality of the Literature of Our Planet," *ESQ* 50, nos. 1–3 (2004): 177–222. Here, too, he emphasizes the position in between exclusion and the not yet formulated. This aligns C. L. R. James, held captive in the no-man's-land of Ellis Island, with those stories of the Pequod's crew that Melville had felt forced to leave out of his narrative: "Melville's scene of writing thereby became the locus for a change in James's position from the 'you' who was subject to the law's power to the 'I/We' capable of doing narrative justice to Melville's crew. James wrote from a position in between the Jamesian 'I' the Cold War state had disinterpellated and the 'I' Melville had promised to the mariners in the passage James cited. When James resumed his interpretive project on Ellis Island, he substituted the untenable position in which the culture had placed him for this as-yet-unoccupied narrative position within Melville's text" (Pease, "Extraterritoriality," 210).

2. Representing Potentiality

1. Stanley Cavell has repeatedly examined Emerson's resistance to severing style from substance, particularly in his essay "The Philosopher in American Life." Having established that "Self-Reliance" is a reflection on "(philosophical) writing," Cavell remarks: "Our philosophical habits will prompt us to interpret the surface of writing as its manner, its style, its rhetoric, an ornament of what is said rather than its substance, but Emerson's implied claim is that this is as much a philosophical prejudice as the other conformities his essay decries, that, so to speak, words are no more ornaments of thought than tears are ornaments of sadness and joy" (Stanley Cavell, *Emerson's Transcendental Etudes*, ed. David Justin Hodge [Stanford, CA: Stanford University Press, 2003], 55). Drawing on Cavell, Thomas Augst has recently taken important steps in connecting Emerson's vernacular philosophy to its historical condition of possibility: "[Emerson and Thoreau] use an ordinary language for a philosophy concerned not with arguments, not with the Continental tradition committed to accumulating a canon of objectively certain knowledge, but with a *style* of philosophy, an 'intimacy with experience' and an 'economy of living'" (Thomas Augst, *The Clerk's Tale: Young Men and Moral Life in Nineteenth-Century America* [Chicago: University of Chicago Press, 2003], 122; hereafter cited in text as *Clerk's Tale*). As elaborated below, I part with Augst, however, in his insistence that this style of philosophy was so intimate with everyday experience that it came down to providing audiences with moral and managerial guidance in a disorienting market culture. In my reading, Emerson's philosophical style offered his listeners an experience sui generis, one that is irreducible to everyday life, though made possible by it.

2. Mary Kupiec Cayton, "The Making of an American Prophet: Emerson, His Audiences, and the Rise of the Culture Industry in Nineteenth-Century America," *American Historical Review* 92, no. 3 (June 1987): 610; hereafter cited in text as "American Prophet."

3. See also the analysis in her 1989 biography *Emerson's Emergence*: "By elaborating seemingly universal laws of human nature that in reality had their base in the specific

conditions of a particular social and economic order, he provided the new hegemonic culture with a language of morality that defined the nature of legitimate moral questions, and at the same time precluded certain other questions from being asked or even clearly articulated" (Mary Kupiec Cayton, *Emerson's Emergence: Self and Society in the Transformation of New England, 1800–1845* [Chapel Hill: University of North Carolina Press, 1989], 159).

4. Augst, *Clerk's Tale*, 3.

5. On the level of intellectual history, this interpretation is corroborated by Neal Dolan's recent study *Emerson's Liberalism* (Madison: University of Wisconsin Press, 2009). Dolan disagrees with what he calls Emerson's social-democratic critics (like Bercovitch and Michael Gilmore) who detect a critique of materialism in the early Emerson and then describe his gradual co-optation by the ideology of the market. According to Dolan, Emerson never possessed that "radical" side; his wariness of potential spiritual impoverishment caused by the market in no way challenged his commitment to it: "Like his friends Carlyle and Thoreau, Emerson was profoundly attuned to the dangers of the potential commodification of consciousness in a commercial culture governed by what Carlyle himself had dubbed 'the cash nexus.' . . . But Emerson also understood that free markets and private property were essential to the still fledgling emancipation of Western society from the thousand-year stranglehold of a tiny aristocratic elite. . . . Emerson looked to the spiritually elevating power of what he called 'culture' as a counterpoise to the spiritual diminishments of the capitalist marketplace" (Dolan, *Emerson's Liberalism*, 117–18). Even in his early, "radical" writings, Dolan maintains, Emerson "engaged in class politics . . . , but only of a conservative-liberal American Whig variety entirely in keeping with his own elite upper-middle-class status" (Dolan, *Emerson's Liberalism*, 116). Dolan's wording suggests that he himself subscribes to a belief in the emancipatory powers of free markets. Ironically, this makes him draw a picture of an Emerson who is so conservative that it is only matched by the characterizations of Emerson's Marxist critics. He even radicalizes Mary Kupiec Cayton, who, writing from a leftist (thought not outspokenly Marxist) perspective, still considered Emerson's ideological complicity unintentional. Thus she writes in *Emerson's Emergence*: "Emerson's perspective sought to escape the moral dangers of economic individualism. In implying that the locus of moral decision making and the focus of moral questions ought legitimately to be limited to the individual, however, he provided unawares a moral rationale for reproducing the order to which he objected" (Cayton, *Emerson's Emergence*, 159). Dolan's re-revisionist angle certainly has its merits. But in explaining away Emerson's contradictions, he also misses their functionality.

6. John Albee, *Remembrances of Emerson* (New York: Robert Grier Cooke, 1901), 5–6.

7. For a typical example from the early 1840s, see this description from the New York *Weekly Herald*: "Mr. Emerson's lecture was attended by a not very numerous, but highly respectable audience. There were a great many gentlemen, with fine phrenological developments, and tastefully arranged heads of hair present. There were also a fair portion of handsome ladies present, with classical features, and sparkling eyes" (*The Weekly Herald*, March 5, 1842). These descriptions, replete with racial, gender, and class markers, did not simply delimit who belonged to a respectable public. From what we know today, Emerson's audiences were relatively diverse. In Lawrence Buell's words, the lyceum "cli-

entele was mixed, ranging from teens to elders of both sexes, professionals to tradesmen. Not that the audiences were social microcosms, exactly. Immigrants and factory workers were underrepresented; white Protestants of British descent predominated. . . . But to a comparatively sheltered, well-bred Bostonian like Emerson, . . . this was real diversity" (Buell, *Emerson*, 23–24). This suggests that assertions of the audience's respectability became necessary precisely because of this relative diversity. In a democratic institution like the lyceum and the lecture system, the conformity to codes of manners could no longer be taken for granted. By the same token, assertions of the audience's respectability could serve the function of a community's congratulatory self-affirmation. As Cayton notes, after Emerson became accepted as a "great American," this logic of self-affirmation began to be extended to the very act of having invited him to speak: "After the Civil War, when Emerson had become a household word as a literary figure and popular lecturer, newspaper accounts increasingly congratulated audiences on their wisdom in appreciating such a great man" (Cayton, "American Prophet," 617).

8. For details, see the "Historical and Textual Introduction" to the *Later Lectures*, especially *LL*, vol. 1, xxviii–xxx.

9. Boston *Evening Transcript*, February 9, 1844.

10. Quoted in Nancy Craig Simmons, "Emerson and his Audiences: The New England Lectures, 1843–44," in *Emerson Bicentennial Essays* (see note 3 to Introduction), 68.

11. Emerson presented the lecture course on New England during this trip. The surviving lecture manuscripts are collected in *LL*, vol. 1. See Simmons, "Emerson and his Audiences," for a detailed analysis of the lecture tour's circumstances.

12. *Spirit of the Times*, January 15, 1843, quoted in Simmons, "Emerson and his Audiences," 68.

13. Boston *Evening Transcript*, February 8, 1849.

14. Quoted from reprint in *New-York Daily Tribune*, February 6, 1849. Emphasis added by *New-York Daily Tribune*.

15. Considering Emerson's own overblown expectations regarding his upcoming lecture course in the winter of 1839–40, the reporter turns out not to be all that far off the mark: "Let us try if Folly, Custom, Convention & Phlegm cannot hear our sharp artillery. Here is a pulpit that makes other pulpits tame & ineffectual with their cold, mechanical preparation for a delivery the most decorous,—fine things, pretty things, wise things, but no arrows, no axes, no nectar, no growling, no transpiercing, no loving, no enchantment. Here he may lay himself out utterly, large, enormous, prodigal, on the subject of the hour. Here he may dare to hope for ecstasy & eloquence" (*JMN*, vol. 7, 265).

16. One finds the same image, for instance, in Henry Ward Beecher's *Eyes and Ears* (Boston: Ticknor and Fields, 1863), in his chapter on the lecture system: "It does not take a community long to perceive that some lectures instruct them wearisomely, that some instruct and inspire, that some inspire but do not instruct, that some, like fire-works, are magnificent while going off and nothing afterwards, and others, like a pomological show, are fine in the exhibition, and very juicy and refreshing afterwards" (Beecher, *Eyes and Ears*, 103–4). Beecher's text makes the interesting point that lectures were evaluated by communities according to the amount of "after-discussion" inspired throughout the following week. Beecher uses this as an argument against the claim that public lecture audiences favored the sensational over the substantial—perhaps a self-serving point, considering that Beecher, as one of the most popular lecturers in the United States, relied on

a good deal of theatricality himself (Compare Carl Bode, *The American Lyceum: Town Meeting of the Mind* [New York: Oxford University Press, 1956], 213–14; hereafter cited in text as *American Lyceum*). Though more people might come to hear P. T. Barnum than some learned professor, what mattered was "what opinion was formed of Mr. Barnum's lecture; whether people *afterwards* were as much pleased, as before they were curious" (Beecher, *Eyes and Ears*, 105). The importance of after-discussion also provides a further context for the newspapers' secondary discourse.

17. James Russell Lowell, "Emerson the Lecturer," in *My Study Windows* (Boston: Houghton, Mifflin, 1871), 384; hereafter cited in text as "Emerson the Lecturer."

18. See also John Albee: "I think I can still faintly detect the air of the lecture room; the upturned faces, expecting the sentence which should cut clean, sound to the depths, soar to the heights, and which never disappointed that expectation" (John Albee, *Remembrances of Emerson* [New York: Robert Grier Cooke, 1901], 99).

19. We know, of course, that this reporter was not alone in ending up as the butt of a joke after trying to translate Emerson's motivational calls to action. Albee states that "It is safe to say that nearly all the young men who took Emerson for a master, themselves either wrote or soon began to write poetry" (Albee, *Remembrances of Emerson*, 52). This led, however, to "a sorrowful fact—the dilemma in which I and my companions who wished to follow the Emersonian ideas found ourselves when it was necessary to choose some definite careers in life" (Albee, *Remembrances of Emerson*, 72). While Albee notes that ultimately his followers were capable of adapting Emerson's doctrines to bourgeois life—"There are idealists in the stock exchange and on lonely New England farms whose pedigree can be traced back to Concord" (Albee, *Remembrances of Emerson*, 71)—this adaptation, *pace* Augst, was nevertheless to be wrested from a dilemma.

20. This provides an alternative interpretation to Cayton's take on some newspapers' refusal to summarize Emerson's lectures. In the explanations offered for the refusal, she finds suggestions of misunderstanding. In her particular example, a newspaper reporter from the Alton *Weekly Telegraph* in Illinois indeed seems to have become befuddled about Emerson's point—he claims Emerson called for the suppression of all spontaneous emotions in order to make men into "cultivated automatons." But his misunderstanding notwithstanding, he also points to the distinction between the individual sentence—each "perfect in itself"—and the overall effect, which was so "closely condensed" that a synopsis "would be almost impossible." This distinction bespeaks the difficulty of conveying the listening experience by means of quotation. It also undermines Cayton's point that the newspapers reduced Emerson to a flat materialist whose lectures did not contain a spiritual dimension. Reporters rather made the point that this spiritual dimension could not be summarized (compare Cayton, "American Prophet," 614).

21. For the most important studies, see David Mead, *Yankee Eloquence in the Middle West* (East Lansing: Michigan State College Press, 1951); Carl Bode, *The American Lyceum: Town Meeting of the Mind*; Donald Scott, "The Popular Lecture and the Creation of a Public in Mid-Nineteenth-Century America"; Donald Scott, "The Profession that Vanished: Public Lecturing in Mid-Nineteenth-Century America," in *Professions and Professional Ideologies in America*, ed. Gerald L. Geison (Chapel Hill: University of North Carolina Press, 1983), 12–28; and Angela G. Ray, *The Lyceum and Public Culture in the Nineteenth-Century United States* (East Lansing: Michigan State University Press, 2005), hereafter cited in text as *Lyceum and Public Culture*. For an overview of the final phase

of the lyceum movement and its successor in the form of Chautauqua, see James McBath, "The Platform and Public Thought," in *The Rhetoric of Protest and Reform 1878-1898*, ed. Paul H. Boase (Athens: Ohio University Press, 1980), 320–41. Among the contemporaneous accounts, Thomas Wentworth Higginson's essay "The American Lecture-System," *Macmillan's Magazine* 18 (May 1868): 48–56 remains essential.

22. Bode, *American Lyceum*, 30. Bode points out that one of the reasons for the lyceum's rapid success was its harmlessness: neither in its early phase nor after its transformation into the lecture system did it pose "any economic threat to the rich" (Bode, *American Lyceum*, 30). Ray takes the point farther, suggesting that the lyceum's pedagogy furthered capital: "The implicit and sometimes explicit focus on the improvement of the products of work—particularly in farming and manufacturing—established a capitalist underpinning as a primary motive for education (Ray, *Lyceum and Public Culture*, 15–16).

23. Compare Ray, *Lyceum and Public Culture*, 28.

24. See George Rogers Taylor, *The Transportation Revolution, 1815–1860* (New York: Rinehart, 1951). For a recent interpretation, which highlights the communication revolution in describing the transformations of the nineteenth century, see Daniel Walker Howe's *What Hath God Wrought: The Transformation of America, 1815–1848* (New York: Oxford University Press, 2007).

25. Peter S. Field provides us with numbers for the previous decade: "His reputation well established by the end of the decade [that is, the 1830s], Emerson delivered more than fifty public addresses annually throughout the 1840s, with gross receipts for 1846 alone, for example, totaling between $825 and $900. Approximately two fifths of the lecture income came from subscriptions to multiple-lecture series in Boston and around New England in the winter months. The remainder resulted from invitations from lyceums, mercantile associations, and similar organizations, which paid anywhere from $10 to $25 for a lecture" (Peter S. Field, "'The Transformation of Genius into Practical Power': Emerson and the Public Lecture," *Journal of the Early Republic* 21, no. 3 [Autumn 2001]: 474–75).

26. In 1859–1860 the *Tribune* listed 202 lecturers with professional titles and hometowns. Most came from Boston and New York, but one also finds Cincinnati and Iowa City (compare Ray, *Lyceum and Public Culture*, 197–202).

27. According to Scott, "For some people, lecturing became a major part of their careers, even though they remained in some other office or profession. Figures like [Henry Ward] Beecher, Theodore Parker, [Dr. Oliver Wendell] Holmes, Louis Agassiz, Benjamin Silliman, George William Curtis, Edward Starr King, and Josiah Holland continued to hold positions as ministers, professors, and editors. Nonetheless, for ten years or more most of them devoted almost four months of each year to lecturing" (Scott, "Popular Lecture," 799).

28. Edward T. Channing, *Lectures Read to the Seniors at Harvard College* (Boston: Ticknor and Fields, 1856), 23. The quotation also appears in "Introduction: Transformations of Public Discourse in Nineteenth-Century America," in *Oratorical Culture in Nineteenth-Century America*, ed. Gregory Clark and S. Michael Halloran (Carbondale: Southern Illinois University Press, 1993), 17. For the transformation of eloquence in the nineteenth-century United States, see also Kenneth Cmiel, *Democratic Eloquence: The Fight Over Popular Speech in Nineteenth-Century America* (New York: William Morrow,

1990); and Lawrence Buell, *New England Literary Culture* (New York: Cambridge University Press, 1986), chapter 6.

29. Lionel Trilling, *Sincerity and Authenticity* (Cambridge, MA: Harvard University Press, 1971), 9; hereafter cited in text as *Sincerity and Authenticity*.

30. On the connection between sincerity, the confidence man, and the city, see Karen Halttunen, *Confidence Men and Painted Women* (New Haven, CT: Yale University Press, 1982).

31. Clark and Halloran, "Introduction," 17.

32. Poignant examples of this can be found in his most activist phase. In the "Seventh of March Speech on the Fugitive Slave Law," given in New York City in 1854, he begins by repeating his habitual lament about the self-diminishing effects of having to engage in public affairs. He then makes clear that his responsibility is entirely to himself: "I am not responsible to the audience for what I shall say; I am responsible to myself for now and forever for what I say to this audience" (*LL*, vol. 1, 334).

33. In 1853, Emerson notes in his journal the envious admiration he received from Oliver Wendell Holmes when Holmes tried to persuade Emerson not to visit his own lecture: "I am forced to study effects. You and others may be able to combine popular effect with the exhibition of truths. I cannot. I am compelled to study effects" (*JMN*, vol. 13, 270).

34. In "Emerson As Lecturer," R. Jackson Wilson offers a slightly different (but compatible) explanation of Emerson's shock-and-appeasement strategy. "[Emerson's] writing . . . took much of its energy from the tensions he generated in the prose between the startling and the conventional, between the rough and (as he would have said) 'manly' edge it could take on, and the smoother and sweeter stretches of calm with which he knew how to smooth his writing" (Wilson, "Emerson as Lecturer," 90). According to Wilson, alternating between these two modes allowed Emerson to offer two kinds of wisdom, so that he became of interest to both the Victorian middle class and those readers, like Nietzsche, who were radically averse to this class (compare Wilson, "Emerson as Lecturer," 94–95).

35. Locke writes: "*Spirit*, in its primary signification, is Breath; *Angel*, a Messenger: And I doubt not, but if we could trace them to their sources, we should find, in all Languages, the names, which stand for Things that fall not under our Senses, to have had their first rise from sensible *Ideas*" (*E*, book 3, chap. 1, para. 5, 403). References to Locke's *Essay* refer to the Nidditch edition.

36. When complex ideas are of "mixed mode," that is, when they combine simple ideas of things that do not occur together in nature, the annexation of a word is not just a supplement to an idea. Rather the annexed word becomes functional for the idea in that it holds it together (compare Michael Losonsky, "Language, Meaning, and Mind in Locke's *Essay*," in *The Cambridge Companion to Locke's "Essay Concerning Human Understanding,"* ed. Lex Newman [Cambridge: Cambridge University Press, 2007], 299). Certain ideas, for Locke, therefore do not exist independently of words.

37. There are also cases in which words not only signify the idea, but in addition refer to the thing. This is the case for names of substances (see Losonsky, "Language, Meaning, and Mind"). Nevertheless, this "double reference" still leaves in tact the tripartite structure of idea-word-object. Each of these relationships—the representation of objects by ideas, and the signification of ideas by words—has long been the subject of debate among

Locke scholars. For a discussion of the contradictory interpretations of Locke's sense of "representation," see Thomas M. Lennon, "Locke on Ideas and Representation," in *The Cambridge Companion to Locke's "Essay Concerning Human Understanding,"* ed. Lex Newman (Cambridge: Cambridge University Press, 2007), 231–57. Roughly speaking, the claim that ideas represent an object can either mean that ideas *stand for* an object (as a lawyer represents a client), or that they *present* an object (as a lawyer presents a case to the court). Lennon takes the position that, generally, Locke's concept of representation is to be understood in the latter sense. A similar ambiguity concerns Locke's claim that words signify ideas. This can either mean that words *refer to* ideas or that ideas constitute the *sense* of words. Although Locke has been frequently attacked for the claim that words *refer* to ideas (famously by Leibniz), Losonsky argues persuasively that "Locke himself simply does not distinguish between sense and reference" (Losonsky, "Language, Meaning, and Mind," 310).

38. On the "Adamic doctrine," see Hans Aarsleff's *From Locke to Saussure: Essays on the Study of Language and Intellectual History* (Minneapolis: University of Minnesota Press, 1982). On its presence in Emerson's thought, see Warren, *Culture of Eloquence,* chapter 2.

39. In his "Preliminary Essay" to Coleridge's *Aids to Reflection,* Marsh criticizes Locke and Scottish philosophy more generally: "According to the system of these authors, as nearly and distinctly as my limits will permit me to state it, the same *law of cause and effect* is the *law of the universe.* It extends to the *moral* and *spiritual*—if in courtesy these terms may still be used—no less than to the properly *natural* powers and agencies of our being. The acts of the *free-will* are pre-determined by a cause *out of the will,* according to the same law of *cause and effect,* which controls the changes in the physical world. We have no notion of *power* but uniformity of antecedent and consequent. The notion of a power in the will to *act freely,* is therefore nothing more than an inherent capacity of *being acted upon,* agreeably to its *nature,* and according to a *fixed law,* by the motives which are present in the *understanding*" (James Marsh, "Preliminary Essay," in Samuel Taylor Coleridge, *Aids to Reflection,* 1st American ed. [Burlington, VT, 1829], xxx, emphases in original). For Sampson Reed's critique, see his *Observations of the Growth of the Mind* [1826] (Boston: Otis Clapp, 1838).

40. In "The Poet," he attacks the mystic, for he "nails a symbol to one sense, which was a true sense for a moment, but soon becomes old and false" (*CW,* vol. 3, 20). Although in "The Poet" Emerson praises Swedenborg for providing a counterexample to the mystic, in "Swedenborg, or The Mystic" he attacks Swedenborg for the very same reason: "He fastens each natural object to a theologic notion . . . and poorly tethers every symbol to a several ecclesiastic sense. The slippery Proteus is not so easily caught" (*CW,* vol. 4, 68). For a recent affirmation of the centrality of Swedenborg for Emerson, see Joan Richardson, *Natural History of Pragmatism* (New York: Cambridge University Press, 2007), chapter 3.

41. I am arguing, then, against the generally accepted notion in the literature on Emerson that *Nature* and "The Poet" stand for radically different theories of symbolism. Compare the statement, for instance, of Barbara Packer, who describes the difference as follows: "At the time of *Nature* Emerson is thinking, or hoping, that the book of nature is written in a single tongue. But his growing dissatisfaction with the Swedenborgian theory of 'correspondences'—the most fully worked out system of translation—had, by

the early 1840s, made him painfully aware that, as Wimsatt remarks, 'formulary or ste-reotyped symbolism as a creative technique is a contradiction.' . . . Hence by the early 1840s Emerson is forced to develop a different conception both of nature and of symbol-ism, a conception he refers to as 'the metamorphosis'" (Barbara Packer, *Emerson's Fall* [New York: Continuum, 1982], 190).

42. Emanuel Swedenborg, *Concerning Heaven, and its Wonders, and Concerning Hell; From Things Heard and Seen* [1758] (Boston: Boston New Church Printing Society, 1837), 65; hereafter cited in text as *Concerning Heaven*.

43. In "Poetry and Imagination," he emphasizes succession as metonymy: "All think-ing is analogizing, and it is the use of life to learn metonymy. The endless passing of one element into new forms, the incessant metamorphosis, explains the rank which the imag-ination holds in our catalogue of mental powers" (W, vol. 8, 15).

44. "The poet has a new thought: he has a whole new experience to unfold; he will tell us how it was with him, and all men will be the richer in his fortune" (CW, vol. 3, 7).

45. Packer, *Emerson's Fall*, 181.

46. Packer notes several different similarities between the two essays and concludes: "[T]he repetition of phrases and metaphors . . . is far too systematic to have been acci-dental" (Packer *Emerson's Fall*, 197). Consequently, she argues that "there is the same relationship between 'The Poet' and 'Experience' as between the mystical idealism of the Mahabharata and the skeptical idealism of Hume; they are the manic and depressive sides of the same coin" (Packer, *Emerson's Fall*, 198). My argument is a slightly different one in that I see a larger retroactive influence of "Experience" on the "Poet" than a somehow more optimistic anticipation of "Experience" in "The Poet." Rather than seeing both as two sides of one coin, they become parts of a series; this is by necessity an alignment on the terms of "Experience." On Emerson's use of irony, see Julie Ellison's *Emerson's Ro-mantic Style* (Princeton, NJ: Princeton University Press, 1984; hereafter cited in text as *Emerson's Romantic Style*). Ellison interprets irony in Nietzschean terms as a hegemonic principle that invests power with a reflex of self-deprecation in order to insure the effi-cacy of power: "This habit of abandoning authority once he has it saves his will to power from brutality. Before the superman can oppress anyone, he resigns and joins the revolu-tion that would have resisted him" (Ellison, *Emerson's Romantic Style*, 130–31). But the focus on power does not explain the function irony has for the process of significa-tion. I see Emersonian irony as a function of signification that undercuts moments of self-congratulatory success and thus keeps signification going.

47. Compare Susanne Rohr's precise explanation: "Perception as a process mediated by signs is principally to be understood as an act of interpretation. And if interpretation marks the beginning of any perception, then one begins to explain the meanings of one's own interpretations by formulating perceptual judgments (the extreme cases of abduc-tion). In understanding these in subsequent representations, the cognizing subject, as it were, traces its own trace, or, chases its own creativity. This is why we could claim earlier that interpretant and meaning are constitutive elements of each sign, but that they be-come present only in subsequent representations and thus interpretations" (Susanne Rohr, *Über die Schönheit des Findens: Die Binnenstruktur Menschlichen Verstehens nach Charles S. Peirce: Abduktionslogik und Kreativität* [Stuttgart: M&P, Verlag für Wissen-schaft und Forschung, 1993], 127, my translation).

48. Peirce connects the impossibility of introspection into pure consciousness with a few lines from Emerson's poem "The Sphinx," although he seems compelled to disparage Emerson at the same time: "Possibly this curious truth was what Emerson was trying to grasp—but if so, pretty unsuccessfully" (*CP*, vol. 1, para. 301).

49. At other moments, Peirce emphasizes the similarity in structure between artistic and scientific activity. Both proceed in a sequence of steps from radical passivity—the opening of the self to Firstness—to intersubjective exchange: "It begins passively enough with drinking in the impression of some nook in one of the three Universes. But impression soon passes into attentive observation, observation into musing, musing into a lively give and take of communion between self and self" (*CP*, vol. 6, para. 459). I thank Susanne Rohr for pointing out this passage to me.

50. In his insightful early article "Charles Sanders Peirce: Pragmatic Transcendentalist," Frederic Carpenter argues that Peirce's thought grew as much out of Emerson and Thoreau as out of the German idealists. He establishes a substantial connection between Emerson and Peirce in regard to intuition. However, in contrast to my argument, rather than aligning intuition with Firstness, he links it with Thirdness: "[Peirce] valued instinctive insights as the source of all intellection, and translated the Emersonian 'intuitions' into the 'hypotheses' of modern science. Just as thought realizes itself in action, so unconscious intuition realizes itself in conscious thought" (Frederic I. Carpenter, "Charles Sanders Peirce: Pragmatic Transcendentalist," *New England Quarterly* 14, no. 1 [March 1941]: 41). Carpenter's interpretation seems quite plausible, indeed. His argument lets us establish a parallel temporality in Emerson's and Peirce's thought: just as Emerson bemoans the fact that we can never put our intuition into words because it is too far off in our memory, Peirce can be read as saying that we cannot express our creative insight of abduction in the interpretant. The difference is crucial, though: For Peirce, the hypothetical insight is only barred from the current interpretant, but, in the course of devising more and more signs, we will come to the truth of our abduction. For Emerson, on the other hand, what we receive in the moment of intuition can never finally be expressed. And this is more clearly captured by the relationship between Firstness, Secondness, and Thirdness than by the chain of Thirds, although ultimately, the two claims do not exclude each other.

51. Ulla Haselstein, "Seen from a Distance: Moments of Negativity in the American Sublime: Tocqueville, Bryant, Emerson," *Amerikastudien/American Studies* 43 (1998): 420–21.

52. This tension in Emerson's writings can be extended to his equivocal treatment of passivity and activity. Here Lawrence Buell is helpful in his discussion of Myra Jehlen's and Christopher Newfield's analyses of Emerson as "opposite pathologies as imperial will and corporate conformity." Buell points out how these two "pathologies" habitually work together in Emerson's works: "[Not only his later writings, but] even 'Self-Reliance' makes both moves. On the one hand, the exploits of Columbus and Napoleon clearly excite the writer; on the other, he urges readers to confide themselves 'childlike' to the spirit of the age and 'accept the place the divine Providence has found for you'" (Buell, *Emerson*, 70).

53. See Richard Poirier, *Poetry and Pragmatism* (Cambridge, MA: Harvard University Press, 1992), and Jonathan Levin, *The Poetics of Transition: Emerson, Pragmatism, and American Literary Modernism* (Durham, NC: Duke University Press, 1999).

54. Laura Dassow Walls, *Emerson's Life in Science: The Culture of Truth* (Ithaca, NY: Cornell University Press, 2003), 158–59; hereafter cited in text as *Emerson's Life in Science*.

55. Emerson ends "Experience" with a sobered up version of a clarion call: "Never mind the ridicule, never mind the defeat: up again, old heart!—it seems to say,—there is victory yet for all justice; and the true romance which the world exists to realize, will be the transformation of genius into practical power" (*CW*, vol. 3, 49).

56. See Joseph M. Thomas's article "Poverty and Power: Revisiting Emerson's Poetics," in *Emerson Bicentennial Essays* (see note 3 to Introduction), 213–46, for a genealogy of Emerson's thought on eloquence. See also Warren, *Culture of Eloquence*, chapter 2.

57. The literature on Emerson's use of metaphor and allegory is extensive. For my context, Barbara Packer's observation of Emerson's *metaphorical* use of philosophical terms such as "idealism" and "experience" in the essay "Experience" is of particular interest: "he employs the technical vocabulary of epistemology to talk about things like grief, guilt, ruthlessness, and isolation" (Packer, *Emerson's Fall*, 161). Packer goes on to note that Emerson ironically exploits the various meanings these technical terms take on in various philosophical systems. Picking up on Cavell's phrase "epistemology of moods," she concludes that "one of the chief ways of arriving at an epistemology of moods is by studying the shadings these words take on as the paragraphs pass by" (Packer, *Emerson's Fall*, 162). If Packer's metaphorical analysis studies a movement of meaning in the re-appearance of philosophical terms, my metonymic perspective works complementarily: it describes a movement of terms enabled by their richness of meaning. The reader is en-abled to jump from one term to the next to make new, spontaneous connections of his or her own. For some classic studies that investigate Emerson's use of metaphor and al-legory, see Jonathan Bishop, *Emerson on the Soul* (Cambridge, MA: Harvard University Press, 1964); Kenneth Dauber, "On Not Being Able to Read Emerson, or 'Representative Men,'" *boundary 2* 21, no. 2 (Summer 1994): 220–42; Julie Ellison, "Aggressive Alle-gory," *Raritan* 3, no. 3 (Winter 1984): 100–115; and Olaf Hansen, *Aesthetic Individual-ism and Practical Intellect* (Princeton, NJ: Princeton University Press, 1990).

3. The New Americanists and the Violence of Identity

1. Clearly, this claim requires a qualification. John Carlos Rowe, for instance, in his book *The New American Studies*, has emphasized that "New historicism, feminism, criti-cal race theory, and postcolonial and cultural studies have radically transformed the study of American literature both by broadening its scope to include the several Americas and by treating literary functions other than the purely aesthetic" (John Carlos Rowe, *The New American Studies* [Minneapolis: University of Minnesota Press, 2002], xxv). Still, there is little reference to the common theoretical assumptions that underlie the ruling arguments of these various fields and subfields.

2. A similar requirement shaped the adaptation of Foucault's philosophy by American literary scholars who worked under the label of new historicism in the 1980s, as Winfried Fluck has shown in "Die 'Amerikanisierung' der Geschichte im *New Historicism*," in *New Historicism: Literaturgeschichte als Poetik der Kultur*, ed. Moritz Bassler (Frankfurt/Main: Fischer, 1995), 229–50; English version: "The Activist and the Actor: The Re-

Authorization of Historical Criticism in New Historicism," in Winfried Fluck, *Romance with America? Essays on Culture, Literature, and American Studies*, ed. Laura Bieger and Johannes Voelz (Heidelberg: Winter, 2009), 39–48. They, too, had to ensure the relevance of their discipline and thus found ways to argue for the special relevance of the literary text in their new historicist reconstructions of discourse.

3. For the necessity of revisionist movements in order to keep the field of American literary studies alive, see Michael Boyden's study *Predicting the Past: The Paradoxes of American Literary History* (Leuven: Leuven University Press, 2009), which describes the field from the perspective of Luhmann's systems theory.

4. The term was used in passing by the liberal philosopher John Rawls in *A Theory of Justice* (Cambridge, MA: Harvard University Press, 1971), 516. It was the communitarian philosopher Michael Sandel who made the term popular in his critique of Rawls (see his article "The Procedural Republic and the Unencumbered Self," *Political Theory* 12, no. 1 [Spring 1984]: 81–96). Since then, "the unencumbered self" has become a straw man of sorts employed in critiques of the "thinness" of liberalism.

5. Habermas has entered the debate, for instance, in a commentary on Charles Taylor's "The Politics of Recognition," which is found in *Multiculturalism: Examining the Politics of Recognition*. In his argument, based on his theory of discursive public space and deliberative democracy, the communitarian charge that liberal neutrality excludes questions of cultural specificity overlooks that in liberal societies, the individual must understand himself or herself not only as bound by the law but also as the author of laws: "Once we take the internal connection between democracy and the constitutional state seriously, it becomes clear that the system of rights is blind neither to unequal social conditions nor to cultural differences" (Jürgen Habermas, "Struggles for Recognition in the Democratic Constitutional State," in *Multiculturalism: Examining the Politics of Recognition*, ed. Charles Taylor and Amy Gutman [Princeton, NJ: Princeton University Press, 1994], 113). Thus, Habermas insists on the validity of (democratically committed) individual liberty by challenging the distinction between liberal neutrality (the individualist perspective) and group rights. In his article "Three Normative Models of Democracy," he posits his discourse-theoretical or proceduralist approach as an alternative to both liberal and communitarian theories: "According to this proceduralist view, practical reason withdraws from universal human rights, or from the concrete ethical substance of a specific community, into the rules of discourse and forms of argumentation. In the final analysis, the normative content arises from the very structure of communicative actions" (Jürgen Habermas, "Three Normative Models of Democracy," in *Democracy and Difference: Contesting the Boundaries of the Political*, ed. Seyla Benhabib (Princeton, NJ: Princeton University Press, 1996, 26).

6. Kwame Anthony Appiah, *The Ethics of Identity* (Princeton, NJ: Princeton University Press, 2005), 79; hereafter cited in text as *Ethics of Identity*.

7. Charles Taylor, "The Politics of Recognition," in *Multiculturalism: Examining the Politics of Recognition* (see note 5 above), 25.

8. One position that does not neatly fit into my framework is Nancy Fraser's, who has tried to insert a politics of recognition (understood by her as a politics of difference) into a politics of equal justice. The norm behind her argument is "participatory parity." This equality-based norm puts her on the liberal side, for it takes no interest in the individual's cultural, racial, and sexual identifications per se. However, these aspects do come into

play when it is the lack of social esteem for an individual's identification that stands in the way of the possibility of participating. In "Recognition without Ethics," she writes, "recognition is a remedy for social injustice, not the satisfaction of a generic human need. Thus, the form(s) of recognition justice requires in any given case depend(s) on the form(s) of *mis*recognition to be redressed. . . . In every case the remedy should be tailored to the harm" (Nancy Fraser, "Recognition without Ethics," in *Recognition and Difference: Politics, Identity, Multiculture*, ed. Scott Lash and Mike Featherstone [London: Sage, 2002], 30). In other words, if the case at hand demands it, she suggests temporarily taking a liberal communitarian position. Her approach thus has to find a solution for the same problem faced by liberal communitarianism: what is to be done when one remedy (for instance, affirming and institutionalizing a specific identity) creates harm for another person (who now also belongs to that group identity and feels so imprisoned by it that he or she feels barred from participation)?

9. I borrow the term "hard pluralists" from K. Anthony Appiah. See his description in Appiah, *Ethics of Identity*, 73–77.

10. As is usual with grids such as this one, one can find sentences in each example that question the entire grid. For instance, Bhikhu Parekh, who may be as much of a hard pluralist as one can find, writes sentences like these: "A culture has no authority other than that derived from the allegiance of its members, and it dies if they no longer subscribe to its system of beliefs and practices" (Bhikhu Parekh, *Rethinking Multiculturalism: Cultural Diversity and Political Theory*, 2nd ed. [New York: Palgrave Macmillan, 2006], 169). But thankfully, he also writes: "Since [John Stuart] Mill's theory of diversity was embedded in an individualist vision of life, he cherished individual but not cultural diversity, that is diversity of views and lifestyles within a shared individualist culture but not diversity of cultures including the nonindividualist" (Parekh, *Rethinking Multiculturalism*, 44). One may well wonder whether it makes sense to maintain that nonindividualist cultures only derive authority from the allegiance of their members. This begs the question whether allegiance can be understood outside of an individualist framework. Even cultures that emphasize group values over individualism may be more individualist, and even more liberal, than Parekh suggests.

11. For a concise discussion, see Diane Macdonell, *Theories of Discourse: An Introduction* (Oxford: Basil Blackwell, 1986).

12. The most concentrated engagement of the New Americanists with the idea of radical democracy is found in the essay collection *Materializing Democracy* (see note 51 to chapter 1). The contributors include Donald Pease, Christopher Newfield, Wai Chee Dimock, Lauran Berlant, Wendy Brown, and the editors. The early key disseminators of the term *radical democracy* were the political philosophers Ernesto Laclau and Chantal Mouffe; see their cowritten and widely influential book *Hegemony and Socialist Strategy: Towards a Radical Democratic Politics*, 2nd ed. (London: Verso, [1985], 2001). For William E. Connolly and his discussion of the necessity to radicalize toleration as contestation, see *The Ethos of Pluralization* (Minneapolis: University of Minnesota Press, 1995). For Wendy Brown's argument for resisting attachment to self-affirmed yet nevertheless harmful identities, see *States of Injury: Power and Freedom in Late Modernity* (Princeton, NJ: Princeton University Press, 1995). A good measure of the appeal of radical democracy among deconstructive pluralists in the 1990s is provided by the essay collection *The Identity in Question*, edited by John Rajchman (New York: Routledge, 1995), which col-

lects papers and discussions from a conference held in New York in 1991. Among the speakers were Mouffe, Laclau, Brown, Judith Butler, Homi Bhabha and Cornel West. Almost uniformly, the speakers brought up the concept of radical democracy as a solution to the danger of identitarian imprisonment.

13. Many proponents of deconstructive pluralism aim to undermine the practice of prioritizing the individual over the group by arguing that the individual is not a unitary subject but a conglomerate of subject positions. Hence their validation of the communitarians' and hard pluralists' rhetoric regarding group identity and the common good. However, the deconstructive component of their theory foregrounds individualized recognition claims. Thus, any emphasis on the formations of community and the common good must be opened up precisely for the sake of the individual's liberty. In a move reminiscent of Emerson's call for a new community available after the individuals' emancipation, many deconstructive pluralists envision a community of difference that will arise from the deconstruction of current identity binarisms. Homi Bhabha, for instance, writes that "To live in the unhomely world, to find its ambivalences and ambiguities enacted in the house of fiction, or its sundering and splitting performed in the work of art, is also to affirm a profound desire for social solidarity" (Homi Bhabha, *The Location of Culture* [New York: Routledge, 1994], 18). While this may be a legitimate hope, my point is that its individualizing element has been generally disavowed because it is too closely aligned with a specific kind of liberal individualism that these writers want to overcome.

14. Jay Grossman, *Reconstituting the American Renaissance*, 120.

15. Grossman quotes from Evelyn Barish, *Emerson: The Roots of Prophecy* (Princeton, NJ: Princeton University Press, 1989), 14.

16. See Nelson's essay "Representative/Democracy" (see note 51 to chapter 1).

17. On this level, Grossman clearly has a point: looking at Emerson's early journals (especially in the years after his graduation from Harvard College), one finds an abundance of philosophical thoughts and formulations that can be traced back to Scottish common sense philosophy, which was the main point of reference for the Unitarian and Federalist New England elite, and which dominated the curriculum at Harvard. See Robert D. Richardson, Jr., *Emerson: The Mind on Fire* (Berkeley: University of California Press, 1995), especially 29–33; Sheldon W. Liebman, "The Origins of Emerson's Early Poetics: His Reading in the Scottish Common Sense Critics," *American Literature* 45, no.1 (March 1973): 23–33; Dottie Broaddus, "Authoring Elitism: Francis Hutcheson and Hugh Blair in Scotland and America," *Rhetoric Society Quarterly* 24, nos. 3 and 4 (Summer/Fall 1994): 39–52; and—most meticulously—Dolan, *Emerson's Liberalism*.

18. In his study *American Transcendentalism: A History*, Gura argues that "The transcendentalists were split . . . over how best to effect such reformation. One group, which Emerson epitomized, championed introspection and self-reliance. . . . Another group, centered on [George] Ripley and [Orestes] Brownson, stressed the brotherhood of man and outer-directed behavior for the common good" (Gura, *American Transcendentalism*, xiv). Criticism of Emerson's political detachment has also had a long history in the scholarship on Emerson. Among the prominent early voices is George Santayana, who, in a section on Emerson in his book *Interpretations of Poetry and Religion*, criticized Emerson's lack of intellectual rigor as well as his lack of interest in the world's problems: "There is evil, of course, he tells us. Experience is sad. . . . But, ah! the laws of the universe are sacred and beneficent. . . . Perfect? we may ask. But perfect from what point of

view . . . ? . . . To that of a man who renouncing himself and all naturally dear to him, ignoring the injustice, suffering, and impotence in the world, allows his will and his conscience to be hypnotized by the spectacle of a necessary evolution, and lulled into cruelty by the pomp and music of a tragic show?" (George Santayana, *Interpretations of Poetry and Religion* [New York: Scribner's Sons, 1900], 128). In 1931, Bliss Perry, while affirming the continuing importance of Emerson (hence the title of his book, *Emerson Today*), also criticized the social irresponsibility of self-reliance.

19. I cannot discuss the work of Dimock and Patterson at any length here. See the early article, Wai Chee Dimock, "Scarcity, Subjectivity, and Emerson," *boundary 2* 17, no. 1 (Spring 1990): 83–99; and Patterson, *From Emerson to King*. Dimock argues that Emerson's focus on scarcity as it pertains to subjectivity enabled him—and his readers—to overlook material scarcity as it results from economic inequality. Patterson argues from a different direction—she claims Emerson as a critic of Lockean possessive individualism—but for her, too, Emerson's self-reliance leads to political passivity and, in addition, to an affirmation of imperialism.

20. Russ Castronovo, *Necro Citizenship: Death, Eroticism, and the Public Sphere in the Nineteenth-Century United States* (Durham, NC: Duke University Press, 2001), 2.

21. The terms "positive" and "negative liberty" were coined by Isaiah Berlin in his essay "Two Concepts of Liberty," published in his *Four Essays on Liberty* (London: Oxford University Press, 1969).

22. This is precisely the point the proponents of radical democracy would deny. In fact, Castronovo only repeats the views of proponents of radical democracy such as Chantal Mouffe in calling for republicanism and a pluralist politics of difference at the same time. As Mouffe argues in her essay "Democratic Citizenship and the Political Community," it is essential for a radical democratic politics to create an open, political community (a *respublica*), in which concern for the group, on the one hand, overrides individual interest, but, on the other hand, does not in any way interfere with the articulation of particularities: "To belong to the political community what is required is that we accept a specific language of civil intercourse, the *respublica*. Those rules prescribe norms of conduct to be subscribed to in seeking self-chosen satisfactions and in performing self-chosen actions. The identification with those rules of civil intercourse creates a common political identity among persons otherwise engaged in many different enterprises. This modern form of political community is held together not by a substantive idea of the common good but by a common bond, a public concern. It is therefore a community without a definite shape or a definite identity and in continuous re-enactment" (Chantal Mouffe, "Democratic Citizenship and the Political Community," in *Dimensions of Radical Democracy: Pluralism, Citizenship, Community*, ed. Chantal Mouffe [London: Verso 1992], 233). The distinction between a common good and a common bond can hardly solve the contradiction of prioritizing the group and the individual at once. And in order to construct a common bond open to revision, it is hardly necessary to diverge from liberal democracy at all. As usual, Mouffe invokes Michael Sandel's communitarian argument against John Rawls's "unencumbered self" (Mouffe, "Democratic Citizenship," 226), as if the self in liberal democracy lived in a state of complete anomie, only concerned about its individualized rights.

23. Compare Amartya Sen, *Identity and Violence: The Illusion of Destiny* (New York: Norton, 2006), especially 156–57.

24. "It is not enough to politicize identity, as Wendy Brown argues, because a radical democratic project must ask how political identities themselves are 'also potentially reiterative of regulatory, disciplinary society in its configuration of a disciplinary subject.' A focus on death, I suggest, is one way to ensure that the material and discursive constituents of political identities are not overlooked. So often productive of unsublimated materiality and rigid disciplinary subjects, death prevents discussion of politics as either episodic or independent of culture's nitty-gritty everydayness" (Castronovo, *Necro Citizenship*, 5–6; quotation from Brown, *States of Injury*, 65).

25. In order to invoke Habermas for this point, it is not necessary to agree with him all the way when it comes to his conception of interest-free rationality as the ideal of democratic deliberation.

26. I am using *radical democracy* in the somewhat loose sense in which it is often used by politicized literary scholars. Political philosophers, like Ernesto Laclau and Chantal Mouffe, generally proceed more circumspectly than their colleagues in literature departments. Laclau and Mouffe, for instance, acknowledge that their own norms build on those enshrined in the principles of liberal democracy. Furthermore, they remind their readers, if in somewhat vague terms, that the political order of liberal democracy is not to be displaced in its entirety by radical democracy. In the preface to the second edition of *Hegemony and Socialist Strategy*, Laclau and Mouffe write: "Certainly it is important to understand that liberal democracy is not the enemy to be destroyed in order to create, through revolution, a completely new society. . . . In our view, the problem with 'actually existing' liberal democracies is not with their constitutive values crystallized in the principles of liberty and equality for all, but with the system of power which redefines and limits the operation of those values. This is why our project of 'radical and plural society' was conceived as a new stage in the deepening of the 'democratic revolution', as the extension of the democratic struggles for equality and liberty to a wider range of social relations" (Laclau and Mouffe, *Hegemony and Socialist Strategy*, xv). It remains unclear, however, to what extent "the system of power" can be reformed without dismantling liberal democracy in its entirety, if this systemic power is built into the very foundation of conceiving of the individual as a rights-bearing citizen.

27. For a critical, yet anything but one-sided, consideration of the lengthening distance between state and subject as a result of manifold processes of deformalization, see Saskia Sassen, *Territory, Authority, Rights* (Princeton, NJ: Princeton University Press, 2006).

28. Gregg D. Crane, *Race, Citizenship, and Law in American Literature* (New York: Cambridge University Press, 2002). Crane espouses Richard Poirier's transition-oriented interpretation of Emerson, yet he diverges from Poirier in the latter's resistance to linking literature directly to politics. Crane argues that it is precisely Emerson's treatment of language, in which meaning is always open to revision, that brought Emerson in touch with America's democratic revisions, which were fuelled by the concept of a "higher law": "[Emerson] brings to the constitutional crisis of his day an improvisational approach to language skeptical of the fixity or finality of any expression. He approaches the Constitution in a proto-pragmatist fashion as a text continually in the process of being made and remade by aggressive, visionary readers and authors, anticipating William James's association of the mutability of language and the changes in our idiom of justice" (Crane, *Race, Citizenship, and Law*, 104).

29. Robert D. Richardson, "Schleiermacher and the Transcendentalists," in *Transient and Permanent: The Transcendentalist Movement and Its Contexts*, ed. Charles Capper and Conrad E. Wright (Boston: Massachusetts Historical Society, 1999; distributed by Northeastern University Press), 121–47.

30. In *Race, Slavery, and Liberalism in Nineteenth-Century American Literature*, Arthur Riss has argued that liberal American literary criticism operates from an ideological investment in formalistic notions of hermeneutics and the subject, which it presents misleadingly as transhistorical givens. Riss's prime example is Sacvan Bercovitch, who, according to Riss, has coupled an assumption about the openness of signs to interpretation (the example at hand is *The Scarlet Letter*'s "A"), with a liberal, formalistic concept of the person (exemplified in Bercovitch's assumption of racial anti-essentialism). Riss contends that liberal criticism hides its own ideological involvement in this coupling. He thus calls for a historicization of the way these two concepts have been joined, claiming that it is not accidental that for a nineteenth-century reader like Sophia Hawthorne, the meaning of the letter was fixed (it meant: adulteress), because the common notion of the person at that time was based on essentialist racial views. Riss could extend his critique to my coupling of an understanding of the reading process based on an imaginary transfer with a view of the subject as the result of reciprocal recognition, as indeed I am coupling these two notions. But Riss's call for a historicization of the notions of the person and hermeneutics runs the risk of confounding historicization with the futile hope of transcending one's own theoretical premises. Historicization alone has little to say about which theoretical premises one finds most plausible for literary analysis, because the call for historicization itself is obviously based on a certain set of theoretical premises. Thus, even fine-tuned historical sensibilities face the problems that they transhistorically impose premises about the importance of history, a problem that lies in the nature of any premise.

31. Ryan in particular, as a scholar of the younger generation—her book evolved out of a 1999 dissertation—may be cited as an example of the influence the New Americanists have had on the mainstream of American literary scholarship. But here it is important to remember a point from chapter 1: the New Americanists never constituted a coherent paradigm or a closely defined group. The New Americanists put a name to a widely shared consensus about a number of theoretical premises that had been emerging years before the term was coined. Ryan's generation has little use for the term because these premises have come to dominate large sections of the mainstream of American Studies. The new has become the norm.

32. Julie Ellison, "The Gender of Transparency: Masculinity and the Conduct of Life," *American Literary History* 4, no. 4 (Winter 1992): 593; hereafter cited in text as "Gender of Transparency."

33. Susan M. Ryan, *The Grammar of Good Intentions* (Ithaca, NY: Cornell University Press, 2003), 17; hereafter cited in text as *Grammar of Good Intentions*.

34. "In this book I will be regarding American liberalism as continually seeking harmony between such apparent opposites as private freedom and public order, liberty and union. And I will be suggesting that, in Emerson's powerful version, the reconciliation of terms diminishes both" (Newfield, *Emerson Effect*, 2).

35. Stanley Aronowitz made the attempt to redirect attention to Mead in his contribution to a prominent New York conference on identity in 1991, and to the subsequent

essay collection *The Identity in Question* (Stanley Aronowitz, "Reflections on Identity," in *The Identity in Question*, ed. John Rajchman [New York: Routledge, 1995], 112–15). During the discussion, transcribed in the book, his proposal to reintroduce Mead into the debate provoked no further comment.

36. Charles Taylor briefly mentions Mead, along with Bakhtin, in his explanation of the dialogical conception of identity. He falsely attributes the term of the "significant other" to Mead (as does Aronowitz). The term was introduced by psychiatrist Harry Stack Sullivan and never used by Mead. Taylor and Aronowitz seem to confuse the "significant other" with Mead's terms "significant symbol" and "generalized other" (see Hans Joas, "Ein Pragmatist wider Willen?" *Deutsche Zeitschrift für Philosophie* 44, no. 4 [1996]: 666).

37. I am indebted to Harald Wenzel for his suggestion of the metaphor of the map.

38. In this essay, Mead sketches the transition from taking the roles of individual others to taking the role of the generalized other: "Thus the child can think about his conduct as good or bad only as he reacts to his own acts in the remembered words of his parents. Until this process has been developed into the abstract process of thought, self-consciousness remains dramatic, and the self which is a fusion of the remembered actor and this accompanying chorus is somewhat loosely organized and very clearly social. Later the inner stage changes into the forum and workshop of thought. The features and intonations of the dramatis personae fade out and the emphasis falls upon the meaning of the inner speech, the imagery becomes merely the barely necessary cues. But the mechanism remains social, and at any moment the process may become personal" (George Herbert Mead, *Selected Writings*, ed. Andrew J. Reck [Chicago: University of Chicago Press, 1964], 146–47).

39. In his late work, especially in his Carus lectures, posthumously published as *The Philosophy of the Present*, Mead extends the notion of sociality from an account of the intersubjective constitution of the subject to the social constitution of objects. He also eliminates the terminology of the "I" and "Me," which avoids the misunderstanding that the "I" is a metaphysical or Romantic remnant of the authentic, presocial self. Instead, he focuses on the term "emergence" to theorize novelty in the context of the relativity of time. The emergent, like the "I" previously, can only be conceptualized after the fact, in this case once it has been reintegrated into the past: "The emergent when it appears is always found to follow from the past, but before it appears, it does not, by definition, follow from the past" (George Herbert Mead, *The Philosophy of the Present* [1932] [New York: Prometheus Books, 2002], 36). In terms of the social genesis of the self, Mead's turning away from the terms "Me" and "I" lets him conceptualize the difference between the generalized other and the various individuals purely from their adoption of several roles at once, which structures the way they construct the past, present, and future, without having recourse to some function of spontaneous creativity. At this point, he uses the term *communication* to describe the social process: "Communication as I shall use it always implies the conveyance of meaning; and this involves the arousal in one individual of the attitude of the other, and his response to these responses. The result is that the individual may be stimulated to play various parts in the common process in which all are engaged, and can therefore face the various futures which these roles carry with them, in reaching finally the form that his own will take. . . . The final step in the development of communication is reached when the individual that has been aroused to take the

roles of others addresses himself in their roles, and so acquires the mechanism of thinking, that of inward conversation" (Mead, *Philosophy of the Present*, 103).

40. George Herbert Mead, *Mind, Self, and Society* [1934] (Chicago: University of Chicago Press, 1955), 168.

41. For an account in which Axel Honneth couples the three levels of (mis)recognition with Mead, see his article "Recognition or Redistribution? Changing Perspectives on the Moral Order of Society," in *Recognition and Difference: Politics, Identity, Multiculture*, ed. Scott Lash and Mike Featherstone (London: Sage, 2002), 43–56.

42. On this point, see the fourth section of the collection of Winfried Fluck's essays, *Romance with America? Essays on Culture, Literature, and American Studies*, particularly "Playing Indian: Aesthetic Experience, Recognition, Identity" (431–55).

4. Identity and the Parsimonious Recognition of "Friendship"

1. By using the female pronoun, I point to the fact that Emerson's thought on friendship was shaped in part by his own friendships, which included both men and women.

2. Aristotle *Nicomachean Ethics* 1156b. I refer to the pagination of the standard Bekker edition of the Greek text. See also Aristotle, *Nicomachean Ethics*, 2nd ed., trans. Terence Irwin (Indianapolis: Hackett, 1999), 122 (bk. 8, chap. 3).

3. In the chapter entitled "Literature" from *English Traits*, Emerson associates this thought explicitly with Schelling: "the identity-philosophy of Schelling, couched in the statement that 'all difference is quantitative'" (*CW*, vol. 5, 136). Schelling here serves as one of many examples of a class of thinkers throughout time who organized their thought around unity rather than diversity. As the editors of the *Collected Works* point out, Emerson's source is not Schelling himself, however, but John Bernard Stallo, *General Principles of the Philosophy of Nature* (Boston: Crosby and Nichols, 1848); (compare *CW*, vol. 5, 323).

4. Emerson's choice of the term *approbation* to describe the recognition we gain *from others* is a highly significant resemanticization of the way the term had been used by Scottish moral philosophers, whether of the first generation, for example, Francis Hutcheson, or of following generations, for example, Dugald Stewart and Thomas Reid. (Having received his education at Harvard, Emerson was deeply familiar will all three of these thinkers.) In his *Inquiry into the Origins of Our Ideas of Beauty and Virtue*, Hutcheson begins the introduction of the second treatise ("An Inquiry Concerning Moral Good and Evil") with the following words: "The Word Moral Goodness, in this Treatise, denotes our Idea of some Quality apprehended in Actions, which procures Approbation, and Love toward the Actor, from those who receive no Advantage by the Action. Moral Evil, denotes our Idea of a contrary Quality, which excites Aversion, and Dislike toward the Actor, even from Persons unconcern'd in its natural Tendency" (Francis Hutcheson, *Inquiry into the Origins of Our Ideas of Beauty and Virtue* [1725] [London: Darby, Bettesworth et al., 1726], 111). Approbation, or disapprobation (*aversion* and *condemnation* are common synonyms of the negative term in the parlance of both Scottish philosophy and Emerson), for Hutcheson, is almost a reflex: it is noncognitive, prior to any consideration of self-interest, and thus derived from a moral sense. In the years following his graduation from college, Emerson commonly used the term *approbation* in this sense. At

age nineteen, he formulates a version of the moral law that highlights his immersion in common sense philosophy: "This Sentiment [the moral sense] differs from the affections of the heart and from the faculties of the mind. The affections are undiscriminating and capricious. The Moral Sense is not. The powers of the intellect are sometimes wakefull [sic] and sometimes dull, alive with interest to one subject, and dead to the charm of another. There are no ebbs and flows, no change, no contradiction in *this*. Its lively approbation never loses its pleasure; its aversion never loses its sting. Its oracular answers might be sounded through the world, for they are always the same. Motives and characters are amenable to it; and the golden rules which are the foundation of its judgements we feel and acknowledge, but do not understand" (*JMN*, vol. 2, 50). It was only throughout the following decade, roughly contemporaneous with his discovery of Coleridge's differentiation between "the Understanding" and "Reason," that Emerson came to distinguish between an intuitive dimension of recognition of the moral sense, and the social allocation of recognition—now called *approbation*—based on conformist criteria decoupled from the moral sense. Emerson's mature usage of recognition and approbation as two different processes thus lets us understand the transition from Federalist Enlightenment thought to Romanticism as the emerging split between social recognition and self-recognition.

5. For an original reading of the problem of equality in Emerson's thought on friendship, see Kerry Larson, "Emerson's Strange Equality," *Nineteenth-Century Literature* 59, no. 3 (Autumn 2004): 315–39.

6. See Buell, *Emerson*, particularly 297–312.

7. Kuisma Korhonen, *Textual Friendship: The Essay as Impossible Encounter* (New York: Humanity Books, 2006), 58.

8. Tocqueville observes that "They [Americans] have abolished the troublesome privileges of a few of their fellow men only to meet the competition of all. The barrier has changed shape rather than place. Once men are more or less equal [Tocqueville here means the transition from aristocracy to democracy, not an equality of distribution] and pursue the same path, it is very difficult for any of them to move forward quickly in order to cleave his way through the uniform crowd milling around him" (Alexis de Tocqueville, *Democracy in America* and *Two Essays on America*, trans. Gerald E. Bevan [New York: Penguin Classics, 2003], 625). The development described by Tocqueville is not to be confused with a movement toward economic equality. On the contrary, historians have stressed that the market revolution produced new levels of inequality. Thus, Harry L. Watson shows, in his *Liberty and Power: The Politics of Jacksonian America*, that the transformation of subsistence farming in accordance with the mechanisms of the market produced new inequalities: "Not everyone succeeded in the search for a personal 'competence,' and a permanent population of landless laborers now found themselves working as hired help on the farms of others or as unskilled operatives in the early factory system. As the Age of Jackson dawned, in other words, growth was accompanied by serious and increasing social and economic inequality" (Harry L. Watson, *Liberty and Power: The Politics of Jacksonian America* [New York: Hill and Wang, 1990], 19). In the Jacksonian period, the Enlightenment ideal of self-culture increasingly turned into competitiveness and resulted in an emphasis on individual distinction. For instance, in *The Market Revolution: Jacksonian America, 1815–1846*, Charles Sellers points to the surge in literacy in the early decades of the nineteenth century and connects it with the market revolution: "The literacy/schooling takeoff got its initial impetus from parents equipping children for

the chancy competition of market revolution and agrarian crisis" (Charles Sellers, *The Market Revolution: Jacksonian America, 1815–1846* [New York: Oxford University Press, 1991], 366). The individualism of the Jacksonian era can itself be seen as arising out of a shift in social relations. Following Tocqueville, Lawrence Kohl, in *The Politics of Individualism*, maintains that in comparison to members of aristocratic societies, "Americans related more widely but not as intensely" (Lawrence Kohl, *The Politics of Individualism* [New York: Oxford University Press, 1989], 11). Individualism, then, does not lead to a state of social anomie in which society no longer matters to the individual. On the contrary, Jacksonian individualism can be understood as synonymous with a race for recognition set off by the social structure of democracy. As a result of this speedup, recognition undergoes a change: rather than coming from a few select persons, it is now sought in ever-widening circles. This new type of recognition is fleeting and shallow, rather than reaching into the depths of character. For a discussion of Emerson's (and Thoreau's) placement in the market revolution that foregoes new historicist complicity arguments, see Richard F. Teichgraeber III, *Sublime Thoughts/Penny Wisdom: Situating Thoreau and Emerson in the American Market.*

9. In "Behavior," Emerson himself illustrates these two cases of misrecognition: "Fashion is shrewd to detect those who do not belong to her train, and seldom wastes her attentions. Society is very swift in its instincts, and, if you do not belong to it, resists and sneers at you; or quietly drops you. The first weapon enrages the party attacked; the second is still more effective, but is not to be resisted, as the date of the transaction is not easily found. People grow up and grow old under this infliction, and never suspect the truth, ascribing the solitude which acts on them very injuriously, to any cause but the right one" (*CW*, vol. 6, 98–99).

10. Eleanor M. Tilton gives the fullest account of Barker and Ward's relationship in her article "The True Romance of Anna Hazard Barker and Samuel Gray Ward," *Studies in the American Renaissance* 11 (1987): 53–72. Tilton takes issue with Fuller's representation of the relationship and further suggests that Fuller read too much into Ward's kindness to herself.

11. Compare Tilton, "True Romance of Anna Hazard Barker and Samuel Gray Ward," 68.

12. The letters Emerson wrote around the date of the journal entry do not provide secure evidence to whom he might be referring. From late March to June, Emerson exchanged letters neither with Sturgis nor with Ward. One week after the April journal entry, however, Emerson mentions Ward in his journal, in association with the topic "youth": "Beautiful among so many ordinary & mediocre youths as I see, was S[amuel]. G. W[ard]. when I first fairly encountered him and in this way just named" (*JMN*, vol. 7, 432).

13. Compare Robert D. Richardson, Jr., *Emerson: The Mind on Fire*, 327–30.

14. Although he would protest this claim, this interest in transition brings Cavell close to what those critics look for who insist on the similarities between Emerson and the pragmatists (for instance, Richard Poirier, Herwig Friedl, and Jonathan Levin). Cavell has triggered an extensive and somewhat self-indulgent debate among Emersonians through his resistance to treating Emerson as a protopragmatist. Several critics have felt the urge to respond to his article "What's the Use of Calling Emerson a Pragmatist?" among them Vincent Colapietro ("The Question of Voice and the Limits of Pragmatism: Emerson, Dewey, and Cavell") and James Albrecht ("What's the Use of Reading Emerson Pragmati-

cally? The Example of William James"). The most sensitive position on this issue, which emphasizes the similarities between Cavell's interpretations and those of the adherents of the protopragmatist thesis, while also taking seriously Cavell's reason for repudiating pragmatist readings, is Naoko Saito's study *The Gleam of Light: Moral Perfectionism and Education in Dewey and Emerson* (New York: Fordham University Press, 2005).

15. Stanley Cavell, *Conditions Handsome and Unhandsome: The Constitution of Emersonian Perfectionism* (Chicago: University of Chicago Press, 1990), 30–31.

16. George Kateb distinguishes between three different attitudes Emerson displays toward distance: "He sometimes advocates distance, knowing that the passion of friendship is to overcome distance; he sometimes feels troubled that since the growth of individualism in the 1820s, all sentiments have weakened and an extreme distance or detachment, not intrinsic to the human condition, has developed; and he sometimes resigns himself sadly to the inevitable existence of distance, to the 'infinite remoteness' in even the closest relationships, including friendship" (George Kateb, *Emerson and Self-Reliance* [Thousand Oaks, CA: Sage, 1995], 108–9). Kateb then goes on to say that the most radical passages "are those in which he speaks as the advocate of more distance—that is, of distance recognized as such, accepted as inevitable, and deliberately turned into a source of benefit" (Kateb, *Emerson and Self-Reliance*, 109). This is radical only if one is interested in pursuing a reading in a Cavellian vein. For my present purposes—and considering the consensus among Emerson scholars—it is indeed more radical to consider how Emerson deals with his doubts about the possibility of turning distance into a source of benefit.

17. Montaigne attributes the sentence to Aristotle, and so does Emerson. The attribution to Aristotle originally stems from Diogenes Laertius. But the latter's Greek sentence can also be translated as "To whom who has friends, no one is a friend." As Diogenes Laertius refers to the *Eudemian Ethics*, where Aristotle reasons that only a few friends can be true friends, the latter translation is more likely correct. Compare Caleb Crain, *American Sympathy: Men, Friendship, and Literature in the New Nation* (New Haven, CT: Yale University Press, 2001), 296, n. 21; and Jacques Derrida, *The Politics of Friendship* (London: Verso, 1997), 177.

18. Most of the quotations taken from this sermon also appear in a lecture manuscript on friendship that dates from the mid-1830s and was published for the first time in 1985 in *Studies of the American Renaissance*. The manuscript is remarkable in that Emerson here states most directly how the ideal friendship is to negotiate the poles of society and solitude: "That society is therefore best & unobjectionable which does not violate our solitude but permits you to communicate the very same train of thought. And then will one true heaven be entered, when we have learned to be the same manner of persons to others that we are alone; say the same things to them we think alone & pass out of solitude into society—without change or effort" (Karen Kalinevitch, "Emerson on Friendship: An Unpublished Manuscript," *Studies in the American Renaissance* 9 (1985): 58). In other words, the ideal friendship is achieved when recognition or approbation is so secure that it has become a nonissue. A slightly different version of the above quote can also be found in a journal entry from November 29, 1832 (*JMN*, vol.4, 66).

19. In the essay "Friendship," we find a moment that is equally exalting of the transgressive side of the relationship. Here, too, friendship resists the limits dictated by convention and leads to a climactic state described by Emerson with an almost Whitmanian

metaphor of nakedness: "A friend is a person with whom I may be sincere. Before him, I may think aloud. I am arrived at last in the presence of a man so real and equal, that I may drop even these undermost garments of dissimulation, courtesy, and second thought, which men never put off" (*CW*, vol. 2, 119). Emerson presents both friendship and oratory as social arenas of sincerity, occasions for the experience of uplift, defined against the genteel values of autonomy, and, as we will see, particularly against self-possession.

20. Note the similarity to the essay "Montaigne" from *Representative Men*. There, too, words are described using a metaphor from ballistics: "For blacksmiths and teamsters do not trip in their speech; it is a shower of bullets." Moreover, words are not only bullets but also targets: "Cut these words, and they would bleed" (*CW*, vol. 4, 95). Both of these phrases come from a journal entry written in June 1840, only a few months after the dates of the passages under consideration here (*JMN*, vol. 7, 374).

21. In 1837, Emerson noted in his journal self-ironically: "In these Lectures which from week to week I read, each on a topic which is a main interest of man, & may be made an object of exclusive interest I seem to vie with the brag of Puck 'I can put a girdle round about the world in forty minutes.' I take fifty" (*JMN*, vol. 5, 286).

22. We can only assume that this entry was penned before the beginning of the lecture course. Emerson wrote it on a separate sheet, then attached it to the first page of journal E. The first entry in journal E is dated October 11, 1839, seven weeks before the first lecture of the series. If the entry on the sheet was written around that time, his mood soon began to change: on October 18, he reflects more directly on the upcoming series. In brief, this entry shows a certain similarity to the above passage—he writes, "I am to fire with what skill I can the artillery of sympathy and emotion"—but the overall tone is much more skeptical. He wonders whether the entire series is not a mistake, and he self-disparagingly points to the megalomaniac dimensions of this task: "Adam in the garden, I am to new name all the beasts in the field & all the gods in the sky" (*JMN*, vol. 7, 271).

23. See especially the "Shakspeare" chapter of *Representative Men* (*CW*, vol. 4), and the essay "Quotation and Originality," included in *Letters and Social Aims* (*W*, vol. 8).

24. Is it possible that this entry predates the undated sheet? There is no evidence for it. The manuscript of the loose sheet shows several slips of the pen, the entry of February 19 only a single one, which, if anything, is evidence that the loose sheet predates the entry from February (assuming that Emerson would have copied the phrases for the February entry from the loose sheet). But what if the chronological order were, indeed, reversed, and he had written the entry on the loose sheet as a generalized, depersonalized response to his disappointment, perhaps, in order to use it in a lecture (as he would soon after, in "New England: Genius, Manners, and Customs," *LL*, vol. 1, 48)? We would still be looking at a case of masochistic self-quotation, because the textual production of the ecstasy of eloquence on the loose sheet would be informed by Emerson's concrete failure to live out this eloquence. I suspect that creating the flurry of expression on the loose sheet would have felt not only stale and artificial after his disappointing experience, but, indeed, painful.

25. Sigmund Freud, "Das ökonomische Problem des Masochismus" [1924], in *Gesammelte Werke*, vol. 13 (Frankfurt/Main: Fischer, 1999 [London: Imago, 1940]), 369–84; hereafter cited in text as "Das ökonomische Problem."

26. James R. Guthrie, *Above Time: Emerson's and Thoreau's Temporal Revolutions* (Columbia: University of Missouri Press, 2001), 45.

27. These lectures, called "Society" and "The Heart," expand many of the elements already present in the sermons: "What constitutes the charm of society, of conversation, of friendship, of love?" he asks in "Society," and answers with a modification of an idea we have already discussed in relation to *recognition*: "This delight of receiving again from another our own thoughts and feelings . . . " (*EL*, vol. 2, 100). Thus, "The service rendered each human being by his fellows is inestimable in acquainting him with himself" (*EL*, vol. 2, 104). In "The Heart," Emerson stresses another familiar point, namely that the attempt to disentangle oneself from all social ties and to search for eternal approbation in solitude is a misunderstanding of our essential social connectedness: "This solitude of essence is not to be mistaken for a view of our position in nature. . . . We are tenderly alive to love and hatred" (*EL*, vol. 2, 280).

28. Think of the "nonchalance of boys" in "Self-Reliance," the lecture title "The Young American," and, as noted by Robert Richardson, Emerson's penchant for having his photo taken with little children on his arm.

29. Several recent commentators, among them Anita Patterson and Jay Grossman, have criticized Emerson's calls for patience as ways of evading real political engagement. Patterson questions the way Emerson combines patience and prudence with reform: "Just as in 'The American Scholar' Emerson concludes with the suggestion that patience, rightly viewed, constitutes a viable mode of political activism, so here he upholds the ideal of prudence to justify his own commitment to inaction and withdrawal into solitary passivity" (Patterson, *From Emerson to King*, 95). Similarly, Grossman reads the end of "Experience"—"up again, old heart! . . . there is victory yet for all justice; and the true romance which the world exists to realize will be the transformation of genius into practical power"—as a call to patient passivity: "Emerson asks us here at the end of 'Experience' to be satisfied once again with the deferral of 'practical power,' in favor of the 'genius' we can presumably have now" (Grossman, *Reconstituting the American Renaissance*, 204). Such readings tend to take for granted the future-mindedness of Emerson's calls for patience. But as I argue, patience for Emerson is not always linked to passivity. Rather, it becomes a means of extracting and molding the present moment from the stream of time to create a sustainable relationship of recognition.

30. It is here that Emerson's "weak time" rhymes most smoothly with Wai Chee Dimock's concept of "deep time." Dimock proposes this term to conceptualize the situatedness of American literature within world history. Most immediately, this requires redrawing the widest possible relationships of works of literature across time and space. Insofar as this is an extension beyond knowledge based on the nation-state, it also entails transcending standardized, metric time, which, historically, is itself bound up with the nation-state: "Literature is the space of nonstandard space and time. Against the official borders of the nation and against the fixed intervals of the clock, what flourishes here is irregular duration and extension." (Dimock, *Through Other Continents*, 4). Emerson's idea that time is "weak before the soul" captures this sense of infinite historical connectedness, except that it does not assume, as Dimock does, that we can choose from a variety of different existing models of time. Rather, to arrive at a different understanding of time, the "fixed intervals of the clock" must be weakened. This is also where my pointing to "weak time" differs from Dimock's project: weakening time, for Emerson, is a heroic and painful activity, which not only gives us epistemic access to our planetary connectedness, but becomes the only answer to our impossible thirst for approbation. This is not because a

reconstruction of our ties to world history would let us know "who we are," but because tenaciously weakening time opens the way to reconciling the ideal and the actual when our perfectionist models have arrived at a dead end.

31. Maurice S. Lee, *Slavery, Philosophy, and American Literature, 1830–1860* (New York: Cambridge University Press, 2005), 185.

32. The editors of the *Later Lectures* note that "Emerson's lectures grew in length with repeated reading and became increasingly sharpened in thesis and scope with each successive delivery. They were then revised again, in much the same way, for publication" (*LL*, vol. 1, xxviii).

33. Korhonen's theory thus differs substantially from Wayne Booth's notion of literary friendship (developed in his *The Company We Keep*), which is concerned with the relationship between the reader and the implied author. Booth adopts the Aristotelian distinction between pure friendships and those entertained for mere pleasure or utility. He treats stories as "friendship offerings," and it is for the reader to find out whether the implied author offers a true friendship or merely one for pleasure or utility.

34. Emerson's quotation runs as follows: "The valiant warrior famoused for fight, / After a hundred victories, once foiled, / Is from the book of honor razed quite, / And all the rest forgot for which he toiled" (*CW*, vol. 2, 118). The original says "painful" for "valiant."

35. Few commentators have pointed out that Emerson puts considerable emphasis on patience, time, and constancy in this essay, because, I suspect, it is such an inconspicuous, long-established topic in the philosophy of friendship. Some commentators touch on the subject in passing; see for instance George Sebouhian, "A Dialogue with Death: An Examination of Emerson's 'Friendship,'" *Studies in the American Renaissance* 13 (1989): 219–39; Jason A. Scorza, "Liberal Citizenship and Civic Friendship," *Political Theory* 32, no. 1 (February 2004): 85–108; and George Kateb, *Emerson and Self-Reliance*. To my knowledge, none of Emerson's readers has noted the surprising absence of this question in the earlier phases of his writings on friendship.

36. Recall the passage early on in "Circles," where I claimed that his "thirst for approbation" takes on a quasi-cannibalistic dimension, the sign of which is the brutal succession of friends. As a corollary to the necessity for patience, "sucking" returns toward the end of "Friendship," this time in conjunction with the admonition to grant the friend enough space and to refrain from treating her as property: "Leave it to girls and boys to regard a friend as property, and to suck a short and all-confounding pleasure, instead of the noblest benefit" (*CW*, vol. 2, 123).

37. During the heyday of reader-response criticism, several critics analyzed the tasks of the reader in the essay "Circles," generally coming to the conclusion that the reader must herself follow the text's circles in her own circles and transitions. See especially David M. Wyatt, "Spelling Time: The Reader in Emerson's 'Circles,'" *American Literature* 48, no. 2 (May 1976): 140–51. See also James M. Cox, "R. W. Emerson: The Circles of the Eye," in *Emerson: Prophecy, Metamorphosis, and Influence*, ed. David Levin (New York: Columbia University Press, 1975), 57–81.

38. Compare *The Gay Science*, sec. 279: "We were friends and have become estranged. But that was right, and we do not want to obscure it from ourselves as if we had to be ashamed of it. . . . Let us then *believe* in our star friendship even if we must be earth en-

emies" (Friedrich Nietzsche, *The Gay Science: With a Prelude in German Rhymes and an Appendix of Songs* [Cambridge: Cambridge University Press, 2001], 159).

39. In "Emerson's Strange Equality," Kerry Larson argues that, at the end of the essay, "friendship deifies itself, and in so doing it affirms an equality that would appear to be out of this world" (Larson, "Emerson's Strange Equality," 327). He concludes that "'Friendship' is an exceptionally rigorous, even fanatical attempt to apply its logic [of equality] to the realm of personal relations" (Larson, "Emerson's Strange Equality," 327). While I agree with the general direction of Larson's argument, I also consider his account to be incomplete, because the textual recognition of the essay addresses our needs for an actual relationship, which remains in tension with the essay's thematic celebration of starry, impersonal, and equal approbation.

5. New Americanist Turns

1. Pease had originally planned to begin the series with the reprint of the 1990 special issue of *boundary 2* (*New Americanists: Revisionist Interventions into the Canon*) under the slightly altered title *Revisionist Interventions into the Americanist Canon*. He chose *Cultures of United States Imperialism* instead because, as he later explained in the preface of the postponed reprint of the special issue, "[the *boundary 2* volume] threatened to renew preconstituted categories and master narratives of an earlier American studies. To call attention to the need for a global rather than national analytic framework for this emergent field [of New Americanist scholarship] I have placed this text in the New Americanist series after *Cultures of United States Imperialism*" (Donald E. Pease, "Preface," in *Revisionist Interventions into the Americanist Canon*, ed. Donald E. Pease [Durham, NC: Duke University Press, 1994], vii). Compare also Elizabeth M. Dillon, "Fear of Formalism: Kant, Twain, and Cultural Studies in American Literature," *Diacritics* 27, no. 4 (Winter 1997): 51.

2. Amy Kaplan, "'Left Alone with America': The Absence of Empire in the Study of American Culture," in *Cultures of United States Imperialism*, ed. Amy Kaplan and Donald E. Pease (Durham, NC: Duke University Press, 1993), 14; hereafter cited in text as "'Left Alone with America.'"

3. Donald E. Pease, "American Studies: An Interview with Donald Pease. Interview by John Eperjesi." *Minnesota Review*, nos. 65–66 (Spring 2006): unpaged; http://www .theminnesotareview.org/journal/ns6566/iae_ns6566_americanstudies.shtml (accessed July 7, 2007).

4. Amy Kaplan, *The Anarchy of Empire in the Making of U.S. Culture* (Cambridge, MA: Harvard University Press, 2002), 28.

5. To give just one example, on September 9, 2007, the *New York Times Magazine* ran a cover story on Rudolph Giuliani (then a candidate for the Republican nomination for president), who at the time was in the midst of constructing his self-image as a hard-liner on terrorism by attempting to link "the war on terror" to his "achievements" in having made New York "safe" as its mayor (as well as to his reassuring presence in the public immediately following the attacks of September 11, 2001). Matt Bai, the article's author, began by listing reasons why many political prognosticators found it inconceivable that

Giuliani might end up with the Republican nomination. The first reason was this: "As New York's mayor, he was pro-choice, pro–gun control and pro–gay rights" (Matt Bai, "The Crusader," *New York Times Magazine*, September 9, 2007, 48). This appeared to clash with Giuliani's self-portrayal on foreign policy. According to Bai, "Giuliani's answer to all foreign-policy dilemmas was essentially the same: the American president had to be someone the rest of the world feared, someone a little too rash and belligerent for anyone else's comfort" (Bai, "The Crusader," 51). In other words, in the view of these analysts, Giuliani's avowedly imperialist foreign politics could only persuade voters if he displayed the same imperialist belligerence (defined as pro-life, pro-gun, and antigay) in the domestic realm.

6. Kaplan borrows the phrase *empire as a way of life* from the title of a study by William A. Williams. But the phrase also echoes Raymond Williams's description of culture as "a whole way of life." However, for R. Williams, the idea of culture as a whole way of life." However, for R. Williams, the idea of culture as a whole way of life served the purpose of emphasizing the potential of working-class culture for resistance, despite the widespread view that working-class culture had been reduced to mass culture. "[C]ulture is not only a body of intellectual and imaginative work; it is also and essentially a whole way of life. The primary distinction [between working-class and bourgeois culture] is to be sought in the whole way of life, and here, again, we must not confine ourselves to such evidence as housing, dress and modes of leisure. . . . The crucial distinction is between alternative ideas of the nature of social relationship" (R. Williams, *Culture and Society 1780–1950* [New York: Columbia University Press, 1958], 325). In order to recognize in working-class culture more than mere mass culture, R. Williams distinguished between individual cultural items—which indeed were often reduced to the level of mass culture—and a whole way of life in which solidarity remained a key value. In Kaplan's hands, however, the distinction between the way of life and individual cultural manifestations is dismissed: imperialism has come to invade all spheres of life. For R. Williams, working-class solidarity was an effective counterforce to bourgeois individualism. For Kaplan, by contrast, the (whole) way of life becomes an argument for U.S. culture's total co-optation by imperialism.

7. Edward Said, *Culture and Imperialism* (New York: Knopf, 1993), 12; hereafter cited in text as *Culture and Imperialism*.

8. An example that makes this point particularly clear, although it is far removed from the present context, concerns the Nazis' contradictory relationship to jazz: while jazz was generally outlawed as a product of Jewish culture, or alternatively, "Negermusik," or both at once, the Nazis at times also attempted to reclaim "German dance music" derived from jazz for their own ideological purposes. See, for instance, Detlev Peukert's work *Volksgenossen und Gemeinschaftsfremde: Anpassung, Ausmerze und Aufbegehren unter dem Nationalsozialismus* (English edition: *Inside Nazi Germany: Conformity, Opposition, and Racism in Everyday Life*). Peukert speaks of the "fascist ideological mix" that permitted Goebbels to appropriate jazz while continuing to censor it (Detlev Peukert, *Inside Nazi Germany: Conformity, Opposition, and Racism in Everyday Life* [New Haven, CT: Yale University Press, 1987], 38). See also Michael Kater's article "Forbidden Fruit? Jazz in the Third Reich." Kater describes how, before the 1936 Olympics, Goebbels tried to strike a balance between the appearance of cultural tolerance and the enforcement of the purging of jazz from German broadcasting: "Goebbel's staff . . . fashioned a new compromise: to broadcast as much German jazz-like dance music as possible, but simultane-

ously to keep out the genuine article . . . in order to placate Nazi fanatics" (Michael H. Kater, "Forbidden Fruit? Jazz in the Third Reich," *American Historical Review* 94, no. 1 [Spring 1989]: 17). My point is that, while jazz is usually considered to be inherently anti-imperialist and antitotalitarian, even it was not safe from co-optation for imperialist purposes. Per se, jazz is neither totalitarian nor antitotalitarian.

9. My analysis of metonymy is informed by the work of Winfried Fluck, who has persuasively argued that the problem of metonymy for cultural criticism arises from cultural radicalism's assumption that systemic cultural power is constituted by one specific "category of difference." Depending on the critic's view, this basic differential category may be gender, race, imperialism, and so forth. In each case, the assumption is that this difference becomes constitutive of American culture as a whole and thus permeates any specific cultural product, even if that particular text, on the manifest level, criticizes the effects of that category. Once one accepts the assumption that systemic power is built on a constitutive differential category that pervades every cultural manifestation, metonymic interpretations are indeed the only logical consequence: each individual manifestation comes to represent the system as a whole, and the system can only be represented in its manifestations. See Winfried Fluck, "Die Wissenschaft vom systemischen Effekt: Von der Counter-Culture zu den Race, Class, and Gender Studies," in *Der Geist der Unruhe. 1968 im Vergleich. Wissenschaft—Literatur—Medien*, ed. Rainer Rosenberg, Inge Münz-Koenen, and Petra Boden (Berlin: Akademie-Verlag, 2000), 111–24.

10. Jehlen's association with the New Americanists was established through two publications. She coedited (with Sacvan Bercovitch) *Ideology and Classic American Literature*, which was one of the targets of Frederick Crews's review article in which he coined the term New Americanists. And her article "Why Did the Europeans Cross the Ocean? A Seventeenth-Century Riddle" was included in Pease and Kaplan's *Cultures of United States Imperialism*.

11. Myra Jehlen, *American Incarnation: The Individual, the Nation, and the Continent* (Cambridge, MA: Harvard University Press, 1986), 9; hereafter cited in text as *American Incarnation*.

12. See also Richard Grusin's critique of Jehlen: "Her insistence that for Emerson dualism is merely rhetorical, while transcendence is real, seems arbitrary to say the least. One could just as easily argue that transcendence for Emerson is as much a formal, rhetorical condition of action as is duality—that the absolute is not a transcendental signi-fied, a fundamental ground, but rather the formal, rhetorical condition of all action" (Richard Grusin, "Revisionism and the Structure of Emersonian Action," *American Literary History* 1, no. 2 [Summer 1989]: 423). This *is*, in fact, what Grusin argues, and persuasively so.

13. Jehlen sees the logic of entelechy at the core of the American incarnation: "At the heart of the American teleology was an entelechy (a perfect and complete potentiality moving of itself to its realization) that continues to animate the new discovery story" (Jehlen, *American Incarnation*, 25).

14. For an insightful reading of this passage, which sees Emerson's figures as consti-tuting a historical trajectory in line with the Whig interpretation of history, and which is thus more optimistic than my take, see Dolan, *Emerson's Liberalism*, 93–97. In Dolan's view, Emerson provides the reader with an exposé of the gradual and continuing emanci-pation of the individual through the course of history. Dolan anticipates the objection

that sacrificial figures such as Leonidas and Winkelried represent the republican virtue of the prioritization of the common good, rather than liberal, individualist values. In response, he points out that Emerson continues his list by including, besides Columbus, English Whig heroes Harry Vane and Lord Russell. Dolan concludes, "the sequence as a whole can be seen as following a recognizable historical trajectory. It has moved from the classical-republican polis (Leonidas), to the late-medieval emergence of nation-states (Winkelried), to the Renaissance discovery of the New World (Columbus), to the early-modern struggle for rights and constitutional self-government (Harry Vane and Lord Russell), to what Emerson sees as the contemporary freedom, dignity, and potential for moral excellence of the ordinary private individual" (Dolan, *Emerson's Liberalism*, 95).

15. This point was made in a review by Nina Baym, who noted its unacknowledged exceptionalism, by way of which a single idea (or myth) came to stand for America as a whole, suppressing internal difference: "At a juncture in American literary studies when scholars are increasingly aware that the 'whole' of America is not representable by a unitary model, Jehlen's intelligent book is strikingly conservative in its underlying purpose" (Nina Baym [review of Myra Jehlen, *American Incarnation*], *American Literature* 59, no. 2 (Summer 1987): 288).

16. Jenine Abboushi Dallal, "American Imperialism UnManifest: Emerson's 'Inquest' and Cultural Regeneration," *American Literature* 73, no. 1 (Spring 2001): 49; hereafter cited in text as "American Imperialism UnManifest."

17. O'Sullivan writes: "In its magnificent domain of space and time, the nation of many nations is destined to manifest to mankind the excellence of divine principles; to establish on earth the noblest temple. . . . [I]ts floor shall be a hemisphere—its roof the firmament of the star-studded heavens, and its congregation an Union of many Republics, comprising hundreds of happy millions" (John O'Sullivan, "The Great Nation of Futurity," *United States Democratic Review* 6, no. 23 [November 1839]: 427; quoted in Dallal, "American Imperialism UnManifest," 54).

18. Quoted in Jonathan Arac, "Global and Babel: Two Perspectives on Language in American Literature," *ESQ* 50, nos. 1–3 (2004): 102.

19. The musical metaphor of the counterpoint, however, requires some revision; after all, the way composers like J. S. Bach conceptualized the counterpoint was marked by a high degree of quasi-mathematical rigidity that is hardly reconcilable with the anti-imperialist vision of cultural contact-in-difference.

20. Eric Cheyfitz, "A Common Emerson: Ralph Waldo Emerson in an Ethnohistorical Context," *Nineteenth-Century Prose* 30, nos. 1–2 (Spring/Fall 2003): 275; hereafter cited in text as "Common Emerson."

21. This comparison suggested itself because what interested Emerson most in Indian culture was the concept of unity, so that the Bhagavad Gita, as an expression of Indian culture, also seemed to be an expression of the unity of Spirit. On Emerson's reception of Hindu thought, see Russell B. Goodman, "East-West Philosophy in Nineteenth-Century America: Emerson and Hinduism," *Journal of the History of Ideas* 51, no. 4 (October 1990): 625–45.

22. In *U.S. Orientalisms*, Malini Johar Schueller has read Emerson's engagement with East and South Asian thought along the lines proposed in Edward Said's *Orientalism*, with added emphasis on gender. In her reading, Emerson equates the American nation with the male individual and equips the national with an "athletic" drive to empire: "The

new nation was embodied in the strong, virile male whose mission it was to morally regenerate the world" (Malini Johar Schueller, *U.S. Orientalisms: Race, Nation, and Gender in Literature, 1790–1890* [Ann Arbor: University of Michigan Press, 1998], 163). The counterpart of this imperialist construction is his abstraction of India (and Asia in general) as passive, tied to fate, and female: "The East was the complement to the power and energy of the West" (Schueller, *U.S. Orientalisms*, 171). Moreover, Schueller argues that Emerson's emphasis on Asia's link to unity needs to be seen in the political context of the conflicts over slavery that threatened the Union: "Emerson's explanation of the philosophies of the Vishnu Purana as 'The Same, the Same: friend and foe are of one stuff' could well serve as a rallying cry of Unionists" (Schueller, *U.S. Orientalisms*, 171). By reading Emerson's construction of Asia as the feminized object of imperialism, Schueller overlooks Emerson's fascination with India as "ancient empire," in which unity was coupled with an agency spiritually sanctioned. The contextualization within U.S. sectionalism is also more complicated than she suggests. In his antislavery writings, Emerson stepped away from seeking to maintain the Union because this could only be achieved by turning the entire United States into a slave society, as the Compromise of 1850 suggested. Thus, in his Address to the Citizens of Concord on the Fugitive Slave Law, he dismissed the Unionist justification for the Compromise bill: "'A measure of pacification and union.' What is its effect? To make one sole subject for conversation and painful thought throughout the continent, namely, slavery" (*AW*, 64).

23. The recent Presidential Addresses focusing on transnationalism include Janice Radway, "What's In A Name?" which questioned whether American Studies had to free itself from a name that itself seemed to prescribe an exceptionalist agenda. In 2002, Stephen Sumida asked, "Where in the World is American Studies?" which was answered in the following year by Amy Kaplan in "Violent Beginnings and the Question of Empire Today." In 2004, Shelley Fisher Fishkin acknowledged that the transnational had become a "turn," in her "Crossroads of Culture: The Transnational Turn in American Studies." After an excursion into issues of "place" in 2005 (which was well-suited to hosting a range of panels on transnationalism), the ASA convention returned to the topic of transnationalism in 2006, leading Emory Elliott to entitle his Address: "Diversity in the United States and Abroad: What Does It Mean When American Studies Is Transnational?" While the ASA increasingly turned toward transnationalism, further evidence of the growing importance of the transnational appeared in the founding of the International American Studies Association (IASA) in 2000. According to its charter, "The work of IASA supports, complements, and internationalizes ongoing efforts by regional, national, and multinational associations of American Studies" (http://www.iasaweb.org/charter.html; accessed July 20, 2007). The IASA has held four biannual meetings so far: 2003 in Leiden, 2005 in Ottawa, 2007 in Lisbon, and 2009 in Beijing.

24. Michael P. Kramer, "Imagining Authorship in America: 'Whose American Renaissance?' Revisited," *American Literary History* 13, no. 1 (Spring 2001): 108.

25. Shelley Fisher Fishkin, "Crossroads of Cultures: The Transnational Turn in American Studies—Presidential Address to the American Studies Association, November 12, 2004," *American Quarterly* 57, no. 1 (March 2005): 20.

26. Paul Giles, "The Deterritorialization of American Literature," in *Shades of the Planet: American Literature as World Literature*, ed. Wai Chee Dimock and Lawrence Buell (Princeton, NJ: Princeton University Press, 2007), 57.

27. Wai Chee Dimock's "Introduction: Planet and America, Set and Subset" in *Shades of the Planet: American Literature as World Literature*, an essay collection she recently coedited with Lawrence Buell, is a splendid example of the appropriation of Emersonian language for the description of the transnational project. First, she adopts Ross Posnock's use of the language of "Circles" in her summary of his contribution on Philip Roth, Emerson, and Milan Kundera: "American literature is very much a subset of this republic [Pascale Casanova's 'world republic of letters'], 'simply the first circle,' Posnock says, around which a series of larger circles can be drawn" (Wai Chee Dimock, "Introduction: Planet and America, Set and Subset," in *Shades of the Planet: American Literature as World Literature*, ed. Wai Chee Dimock and Lawrence Buell [Princeton, NJ: Princeton University Press, 2007], 10). Then, at the very end of the introduction, she returns to Emersonian imagery, imbuing it with further authority: "What is intimated here is the field [that emerges from linking American Studies, area studies, and comparative literature] as a multilingual and intercontinental domain. Its features are just becoming legible, and we invoke it in that spirit: as a cipher, a cradle, a horizon yet to be realized" (Dimock, "Introduction," 13). See the beginning of "Circles": "The eye is the first circle; the horizon which it forms is the second; and throughout nature this primary figure is repeated without end. It is the highest emblem in the cipher of the world" (*CW*, vol. 2, 179).

28. See for instance Henry Nash Smith's classic article "Can 'American Studies' Develop a Method?" Smith claimed that "The defining characteristic of American Studies is not the size of its problems but the effort to view any subject of investigation from new perspectives, to take into account as many aspects as possible" (Henry Nash Smith, "Can 'American Studies' Develop a Method?" *American Quarterly* 9, no. 2, part 2 [Summer 1957]: 197). Leo Marx's article "American Studies: A Defense of An Unscientific Method" firmly locates the debate over method in the affirmation of the liberal subject. Referring to *Moby-Dick* as his example, he writes, "But the measure of that significance cannot be located in any objective realm, uncompromised by human judgment. It derives from choices by human subjects, hence they are the ultimate basis for the method we call humanistic" (Leo Marx, "American Studies: A Defense of an Unscientific Method," *New Literary History* 1, no. 1 [Autumn 1969]: 89–90).

29. In his essay "Commentary: Hemispheric Partiality," Paul Giles notes the tendency of critics working within hemispheric studies to scold their colleagues for not being quite inclusive enough yet. He correctly identifies this as a structural reflex built into the project of hemispheric studies: "Because of the subject's intrinsically expansive nature, there is always a temptation to accuse any specific example of hemispheric studies of not drawing its hermeneutic circle widely enough, of focusing too narrowly upon the specific angles of incidence most proximate to where the observer stands." Giles instead suggests using the hemispheric approach as "a kind of agent provocateur," instead of "seeking an imaginary plentitude or establishing any new internationalist orthodoxy" (Paul Giles, "Commentary: Hemispheric Partiality," *American Literary History* 18, no. 3 [Fall 2006]: 654).

30. See for instance the titles of two of John Carlos Rowe's books, *Post-Nationalist American Studies*, and *Literary Culture and U.S. Imperialism*.

31. See especially his essay "Given Culture: Rethinking Cosmopolitical Freedom in Transnationalism," in *Cosmopolitics: Thinking and Feeling Beyond the Nation*, a collection Cheah coedited with Bruce Robbins, as well as "Spectral Nationality: The Living On [*sur-vie*] of the Postcolonial Nation in Neocolonial Globalization," *boundary* 2 26, no. 3

(Autumn 1999): 225–52; *Spectral Nationality: Passages of Freedom from Kant to Postcolonial Literatures of Liberation* (New York: Columbia University Press, 2003); and *Inhuman Conditions: On Cosmopolitanism and Human Rights* (Cambridge, MA: Harvard University Press, 2007).

32. Cheah, *Spectral Nationality*, 55; hereafter cited in text as *Spectral Nationality*. Cheah points to the importance of the debates between epigenetic and preformist theorists for the articulation of the concept of the organism as distinguished from the machine. Johann Friedrich Blumenbach's writings became particularly crucial: "Blumenbach's vitalist theory of epigenesis (first formulated in 1781) was pathbreaking because it sharply distinguished the living organism from an artificial machine. He argued that a living body was created by a *Bildungstrieb*, a formative drive which was also responsible for the body's continuing regeneration. . . . [S]ince no preformed germ was detected in seminal fluids prior to fertilization, this organic form did not issue from a divine hand. It was spontaneously generated from within the organism, and could undergo deviations as a result of changes that acted as external stimuli" (Cheah, *Spectral Nationality*, 54–55).

33. For Bhabha, culture is of course no longer the domain of purposive rational endeavor that it was for German idealists. But because nature and culture remain clearly differentiated from each other—culture is the domain of the symbolic system—culture remains responsible for the transcendence of both natural and ideological ("naturalized") limitations, because hybridity theory imagines the instabilities of the sign system to undermine the coherence of subjugating forces. As Cheah writes, "[E]ven as hybridity theorists evacuate the human agent *qua* intentional consciousness, its role is surreptitiously filled by language or culture, a nonnatural sign system or a process *sans* subject that is a relay of human freedom" (Cheah, "Given Culture," 299).

34. Adorno and Horkheimer based their critique on an ambiguity in Enlightenment thinking (particularly in Kant's first *Critique*) that describes Reason both as the domain of utopian, cosmopolitan freedom and as the imposition of order by means of purposive or instrumental rationality: "Everything—even the human individual, not to speak of the animal—is converted into the repeatable, replaceable process, into a mere example for the conceptual model of the system" (Theodor W. Adorno and Max Horkheimer, *Dialectic of Enlightenment* [1947] [London: Verso, 1997], 84). Thus, Reason's utopian potential for organic freedom is usurped by *a priori* systematicness: "Even if the secret utopia in the concept pointed . . . to their common interest, reason—functioning, in compliance with ends, as mere systematic science—serves to level down that same identical interest" (Adorno and Horkheimer, *Dialectic of Enlightenment*, 84). In contradistinction, for Cheah, the problem is not the authoritarian control instituted by Reason, that is, the degradation of Reason to instrumental rationality. Rather, the utopian realization of reason through purposive rationality is itself necessarily subject to outside forces. This goes back to Derrida's idea of ontological impurity, and it is especially Derrida's *Specters of Marx* that Cheah uses to develop his idea of the spectrality of given culture. According to Derrida, "To haunt does not mean to be present, and it is necessary to introduce haunting into the construction of a concept. Of every concept, beginning with the concepts of being and time. That is what we would be calling here a hauntology. Ontology opposes it only in a movement of exorcism" (Jacques Derrida, *Specters of Marx* [New York: Routledge, 1994], 161). Deconstruction in this view is the proper philosophy to address the constitutive impurity that enables life itself: "[Deconstructive thinking inscribes] the possibility of

the reference to the other, and thus, of radical alterity and heterogeneity, of *différance*, of technicity, and of ideality in the very event of presence, in the very presence of the present that it dis-joins *a priori* in order to make it possible" (Derrida, *Specters of Marx*, 75).

35. John Carlos Rowe, "Nineteenth-Century United States Literary Culture and Transnationality," *PMLA* 118, no. 1 (2003): 87; hereafter cited in text as "Literary Culture and Transnationality."

36. See *AW*, 21–23, where Emerson begins the discussion by referring to the rationale of English manufacturers: "In every naked negro of those thousands, they saw a future customer. Meantime, they saw further, the slave-trade, by keeping barbarism in the whole coast of eastern Africa, deprives them of countries and nations of customers" (*AW*, 21).

37. Emerson describes the exchange between Clarkson and Pitt as responsible for the idea of "the civilization of Africa" (*AW*, 29). After criticizing Lord Mansfield for treating slaves as animals, Clarkson and Pitt represent for Emerson "a more enlightened and humane opinion" that finds its correlative in William Wilberforce's speech in the House of Commons, according to which "we have obtained for these poor creatures the recognition of their human nature" (*AW*, 29). In this portion of Emerson's account, the project of the "civilization of Africa" arises not from economic interest but from the realization of the wealth of African culture: "Mr. Clarkson, early in his career, made a collection of African productions and manufactures, as specimens of the arts and culture of the negro; . . . These he showed to Mr. Pitt. . . . 'On sight of these' says Clarkson, 'many sublime thoughts seemed to rush at once into his mind, some of which he expressed'" (*AW*, 29). From today's perspective, the project of civilizing Africa, even and especially if declared to be directed toward fighting a dehumanizing commercialism, must be seen as a key legitimation of imperialism. Nevertheless, Emerson's antislavery address cannot be reduced to an imperialist interest in market expansion, at the very least because Emerson's imperialism relied in part on his Romantic anticommercialism.

38. See, for instance, the essays by Amanda Anderson and Allen W. Wood in Pheng Cheah and Bruce Robbins's collection *Cosmopolitics: Thinking and Feeling Beyond the Nation*.

39. Examples that, according to Rowe, are promising in overcoming nationalist imperialism include Martin Delany, Harriet Beecher Stowe, Frederick Douglass, Harriet Jacobs, John Rollin Ridge (Yellowbird), and, somewhat surprisingly perhaps, Herman Melville (because of his criticism of imperialism in the Pacific in *Typee*, *Omoo*, and *Mardi*). By contrast, he regards the "transnational utopia" suggested by Hawthorne and Susan Warner as "reactionary" because it relies on "Christian values" (Rowe, "Literary Culture and Transnationality," 83).

6. Emerson's Organicist Nationalism

1. See Scott, "Popular Lecture"; and Ray, *Lyceum and Public Culture*.

2. In between these two collections of texts, Emerson composed a lecture series on New England dating from 1843 that anticipated the chapter subdivisions of *English Traits*.

3. The names of the lectures were, for the most part, not supplied by Emerson.

4. Emerson was in the midst of what his critics commonly call "his crisis of vocation" when he wrote and gave this lecture. His looking back to a literary coffeehouse of the

eighteenth century, rather than ahead to the lyceum or lecture hall, may be taken as a reminder that in 1835 lecturing was still a profession yet to come.

5. On August 14, 1776, John Adams wrote to his wife about Jefferson's ideas for the Great Seal of the United States: "Mr. Jefferson proposed the children of Israel in the wilderness, led by a cloud by day and pillar of fire by night; on the other side, Henigst and Horsa, the Saxon chiefs from whom we claim the honor of being descended, and whose political principle and form of government we have assumed" (quoted in Samuel Kliger, "Emerson and the Usable Anglo-Saxon Past," *Journal of the History of Ideas* 16, no. 4 [October 1955]: 486; hereafter cited in text as "Usable Anglo-Saxon Past"). For a concise overview of Jefferson's "doctrine of expatriation," see Joseph J. Ellis, *American Sphinx: The Character of Thomas Jefferson* (New York: Knopf, 1997), chapter 1.

6. Reginald Horsman writes: "The break with Rome and the creation of an English Church stimulated an interest in a primitive Anglo-Saxon church. Reformers wished to demonstrate that England was merely returning to older, purer religious practices dating from before the Norman Conquest" (Reginald Horsman, "Origins of Racial Anglo-Saxonism in Great Britain before 1850" *Journal of the History of Ideas* 37, no. 3 [Summer 1976]: 387).

7. Horsman, "Origins of Racial Anglo-Saxonism," 388.

8. Compare, for instance, Walter Scott's post-Conquest novel *Ivanhoe*, a good portion of which is the story of the clash between French—the language of the court—and the "manly" and "rustic" language of the Saxon. Note, for example, this dialogue between Aymer and Cedric: "'I marvel, worthy Cedric,' said the Abbot, as their discourse proceeded, 'that, great as your predilection is for your own manly language, you do not receive the Norman-French into your favour, so far at least as the mystery of woodcraft and hunting is concerned. Surely no tongue is so rich in the various phrases which the fieldsports demand, or furnishes means to the experienced woodman so well to express his jovial art.' 'Good Father Aymer,' said the Saxon, 'be it known to you, I care not for those over-sea refinements, without which I can well enough take my pleasure in the woods. I can wind my horn, though I call not the blast either a *recheat* or a *mort*; I can cheer my dogs on the prey, and I can flay and quarter the animal when it is brought down, without using the new-fangled jargon of *curée, arbor, nombles*, and all the babble of the fabulous Sir Tristrem'" (Walter Scott, *Ivanhoe* [1817] [New York: Modern Library, 2001], 48).

9. In "England," Emerson writes, "The first effect of the extraordinary determination of the [English] national mind for so many centuries on wealth has been, in developing colossal wealth, to develop hideous pauperism. These fair, ruddy, muscular, well-educated bodies go attended by poor, dwarfed, starved, short-lived skeletons. There are two Englands;—rich, Norman-Saxon, learned, social England,—seated in castles, halls, universities, and middle-class houses of admirable completeness and comfort, and poor, Celtic, peasant, drudging Chartist England, in hovels and workhouses, cowed and hopeless" (*LL*, vol. 1, 205). Typical of Emerson's thought, the analysis of social inequity becomes infused with racial fatalism.

10. Nicoloff summarizes Emerson's cyclical theory of British history in twelve steps, which I paraphrase here: (1) The race which composes the new nation evolves directly out of savage conditions; (2) the race or nation is a racial hybrid superior to its components; (3) geographical forces shape the constitutional temperament of the nation; (4) the golden age of the nation occurs in its youth when idea and national trait become synthesized;

(5) a single representative figure (Bacon) signals influx of the idea; (6) the idea extends to the entire citizenry; (7) decay sets in, and high speculation gives way to materialism; (8) the nation's new state of mind finds expression in philosophical empiricism (Locke); (9) the nation undergoes a prolonged phase of spiritual impoverishment; (10) outward power begins to decline, while high speculation is scorned; (11) formerly splendid institutions become encumbrances; (12) the cycle can only begin anew in a different geographical setting (Philip L. Nicoloff, *Emerson on Race and History* [New York: Columbia University Press, 1961], 48–49).

11. See Buell's remark on "The American Scholar": "[T]he explicitly American parts are striking but brief flourishes: a nod at the start, a resounding finale. Fittingly, it was first published simply as 'An Oration, Delivered before the Phi Beta Kappa Society at Cambridge,' the standard title for such performances. The title we know was added a dozen years later, acknowledging its acquired reputation, when Emerson republished it together with *Nature* and other pieces in 1849" (Buell, *Emerson*, 45). See also Eduardo Cadava's suggestion that "the essay *Nature*—which generally has been read as Emerson's plea to the American writer to shed the burden of history in order to begin to write a literature that would be peculiarly 'American'—inaugurates Emerson's revolutionary politics" (Cadava, *Emerson and the Climates of History*, 97). Cadava's term "revolutionary" is to be understood in a qualified sense as the engagement with the given. He refers to the opening of Marx's *The Eighteenth Brumaire* to make the point that "we must struggle with the past to give the future a chance" (Cadava, *Emerson and the Climates of History*, 101). Cadava's point, then, is that *Nature* is precisely not a culturally nationalist call to do away with indebtedness to the Old World.

12. Victor Cousin, *Introduction to the Philosophy of History* (Boston: Hilliard, Gray, Little, and Wilkins, 1832), 294; hereafter cited in text as *Philosophy of History*.

13. Emerson here also addresses the position he creates for himself in bemoaning America's cultural inferiority. In this self-image he is no more—but certainly no less—than a provisional hero-poet.

14. It needs to be pointed out that this cyclical theory was not Emerson's only approach to history. In "History," the opening piece in his first volume of essays from 1841, he approached the topic from the perspective of the self-reliant individual. From this vantage point, history seemed to lose its binding, cyclical form and could be replaced by an empowering present: "All inquiry into antiquity . . . is the desire to do away with this wild, savage, and preposterous There and Then, and introduce in its place the Here and the Now" (*CW*, vol. 2, 7). These two accounts of history can only be reconciled by interpreting the "here and now" as a particular moment in the cycle of history in which the individual becomes capable of fully synthesizing idea and national trait. Emerson, to my knowledge, never provided this reconciliation. Neal Dolan has recently questioned whether Emerson's thought on history is really based on a cyclical theory: "I suggest that Emerson's earliest conception of history was not one of repeating cycles of decay but rather his own distinctly American and personally reflexive variant of eighteenth-century Scottish liberal and Victorian Whig stories of the history of liberty—a decidedly linear narrative of gradual ascent" (Dolan, *Emerson's Liberalism*, 32). I would maintain that the cyclical and linear narratives are far from incommensurable. For Emerson, each cycle could be seen as a step on the ladder of progress. Importantly, the effect of the decay in one circle was at times to call into question the larger narrative of progress.

15. In "Cockayne," Emerson notes of the British Empire: "The English sway of their colonies has no root of kindness. They govern by their arts and ability; they are more just than kind; and, whenever an abatement of their power is felt, they have not conciliated the affection on which they rely" (CW, vol. 5, 85). In the summary chapter called "Result," Emerson attributes English policies to the interests of the governing classes and furthermore diagnoses English culture as driven by the materialist interests of the privileged: "Truth in private life, untruth in public, marks these home-loving men. Their political conduct is not decided by general views, but by internal intrigues and personal and family interest. . . . They cannot see beyond England, nor in England can they transcend the interest of the governing classes" (CW, vol. 5, 169).

16. The main chapters of *English Traits* are framed by travelogue chapters, which I am not considering here.

17. In *From Emerson to King*, Anita Haya Patterson has demonstrated that Emerson turned against Locke's conception of the person—and of social bonds—as organized in accordance with the idea of property rights. See Patterson, *From Emerson to King*, especially chapters 1 and 2.

18. The image reappears in *English Traits*: "The sea . . . proved to be the ring of marriage with all nations" (CW, vol. 5, 22).

19. One should note here that Emerson's warning against the marriage of nations does not seem to rest on a belief in the inferiority (and infertility) of racial hybrids. Emerson did not generally support this theory, despite its prominence in the racial theories of his time. Sharon Turner's *History of the Anglo-Saxons* had convinced him that the English themselves were the product of mixing. As he writes in the essay "Race" from *English Traits*, "Everything English is a fusion of the most distant and antagonist elements" (CW, vol. 5, 27). In the same essay, he even deduced a rule of thumb from this example (here, perplexingly, affirming maritime cosmopolitan trade relations): "The best nations are those most widely related; and navigation, as effecting a world-wide mixture, is the best advancer of nations" (CW, vol. 5, 27). Nevertheless, the fact that one kind of marriage (that at the core of the Anglo-Saxon race) brought forth a nation, while another kind (that of *all* nations, through commerce) merely destroys older national bonds without producing new ones, clearly does toy with the idea that racial hybrids could produce no offspring. By the same token, however, had these marriages developed into a more profound union than mere trade, they might have provided just what marriage through trade lacked. After all, it is trade that is detrimental to the national spirit, not cosmopolitanism.

20. This voice is also pronounced at a few points in *English Traits*, for instance at the end of "Cockayne," where he gives priority to the individual over all communal forms in matters spiritual: "Coarse local distinctions, as those of nation, province, or town, are useful in the absence of real ones; but we must not insist on these accidental lines. Individual traits are always triumphing over national ones. There is no fence in metaphysics discriminating Greek, or English, or Spanish science. Aesop and Montaigne, Cervantes and Saadi are men of the world; and to wave our own flag at the dinner table or in the University, is to carry the boisterous dullness of a fire-club into a polite circle" (CW, vol. 5, 85). Of course, the whole point of *English Traits* is to show that national distinctions are not merely accidental. It is important, then, to keep in mind the context of this passage: Emerson here is criticizing English patriotic jingoism, which he, somewhat paradoxically, singles out as a national or racial trait of the British.

21. In her article "The Laws of Ice: Emerson's Irony and 'The Comic,'" Julie Ellison derives Emerson's irony from Schlegel's concept of Romantic irony, which challenges the Romantic sublime: "Schlegel imagines, as Emerson would a generation later, a mind in which Reason is not permitted to subdue sense experience or critical reflection, but in which antithetical ways of thinking go on simultaneously or alternately, in energetic competition and correction" (Julie Ellison, "The Laws of Ice: Emerson's Irony and 'The Comic,'" *ESQ* 30, no. 2 (Summer 1984): 74). Thus, in her reading, "overtly ironic passages play a crucial role in the dynamics of [Emerson's] essays, where they represent 'spasms' of protest against the serenity of the moral faculty" (Ellison, "Laws of Ice," 73). By contrast, my point is that Emerson's irony also comes from the opposite direction, not by acting against the sublime, but as "protest" against the glorification of the sensory world.

22. Emerson's lecture, first delivered in January 1843 and repeated several times until January 1844 (compare editors' note: *LL*, vol. 1, 19), coincided with Democratic expansionists' demands for the simultaneous annexation of both Texas and the entire Oregon Territory. The debate dominated the presidential campaign leading up to the 1844 election of James Polk.

23. Racial theory did not reach its greatest prominence until the 1840s and 1850s, but as early as the 1830s, it gained considerable force both in the scientific community and in public discourse. The early popularizers of racial theory in the United States included Charles Caldwell, whose widely read *Thought on the Original Unity of the Human Race* appeared in 1830; J. G. Spurzheim, who traveled the United States in 1832; and George Combe, who came from England at the end of the decade. The 1830s were also the decade in which phrenology was held in considerable scientific esteem (before "practical phrenologists" turned it into a form of fortune-telling in the 1840s). One of the earliest American proponents of phrenology was George Calvert. Caldwell, too, focused on phrenology in much of his work. Other early promoters of racial science were Southerners attempting to justify slavery, among them Thomas Cooper and Thomas Dew. One of the most influential American racial theorists was Samuel George Morton, whose *Crania Americana* appeared in 1839. Morton was not first and foremost a defender of slavery, but he became a core member of the American school of ethnology, an influential group that also included Josiah C. Nott (whose interest in defending slavery was more pronounced than Morton's) and gained support from Louis Agassiz (compare Reginald Horsman, *Race and Manifest Destiny: The Origins of American Racial Anglo-Saxonism* [Cambridge, MA: Harvard University Press, 1981], chapter 7).

24. For instance, as early as 1837, the *Democratic Review*, operating from New York and famous for being the organ of the "Young America" movement, called for a more "realistic" attitude regarding the Indian, and objected to the "sickly sentimentality" with which Natives were treated. Compare Horsman, *Race and Manifest Destiny*, 146.

25. Anonymous review, *American Whig Review*, December 1850, 577.

26. This does not mean that Emerson, by casting a glance at science, was only looking for vague confirmations of his beliefs. As Nicoloff notes, Emerson was interested in the specifics of various subfields of the sciences of his day: "He became to a greater or lesser extent acquainted with the craniometry of Blumenbach, the environmental theories of Robert Owen, the radical constitutional determinism of Robert Knox, the facial geometry of Lavatar, the brain studies of Cabanis, the materialistic neurology of Gall and Spurz-

heim, the statistical studies of Quetelet . . . and, quite likely (through Oliver Wendell Holmes and Agassiz), the osteological work of the American Samuel Morton" (Nicoloff, *Emerson on Race and History*, 108).

27. Robert Chambers, *Vestiges of the Natural History of Creation* (London: John Churchill, 1844), 197.

28. Nicoloff, *Emerson on Race and History*, 157.

29. The essay is included in *The Conduct of Life*, from 1860. The lecture was first presented, as part of the series "The Conduct of Life," on December 22, 1851. The editors of the *Later Lectures* have included a text entitled "Fate" but warn that it may bear little resemblance to the lecture. Barbara Packer has surmised that since "the 'Fate' printed in *LL* contains passages that make reference to events in 1854 and another passage referring to journal articles in 1856, it may be the sketch of a later lecture with the same title, or a collection of notes and variants that had accumulated during the 1850s" (Barbara Packer, "History and Form in Emerson's 'Fate,'" in *Emerson Bicentennial Essays* [see note 3 to Introduction], 448–49, n. 16; hereafter cited in text as "History and Form"). For Notebook EO, see *TN*, vol. 1, 57–92.

30. For a recent example, see Stephanie LeMenager's *Manifest and Other Destinies*. She discovers an "unhappy transnationalism" in the imagination of American space by "anxious profit seekers." Exploring Western deserts, oceans, and rivers as sites of "a loose collection of national and international economies," she concludes that none of these regions "were particularly amenable to nationalist sentiment or even the 'bipolar unities' and uneasy incorporation of dissidence that Sacvan Bercovitch has argued constitute 'the symbol of America'" (Stephanie LeMenager, *Manifest and Other Destinies* [Lincoln: University of Nebraska Press, 2004], 15).

31. Len Gougeon points out that at this point Northern frustration over the war endangered Lincoln's renomination. In this situation, Emerson traveled through Massachusetts, New York, Maine, and Vermont, giving the address fourteen times in a row, more frequently than any other lecture (Len Gougeon, "Emerson and the British: Challenging the Limits of Liberty," *REAL* 22 [2006]: 200).

32. Commentators anxious to prove Emerson's imperialism frequently overlook passages such as this one that show how seriously he tries to distinguish between erecting a world republic of the Spirit and imposing the dominant culture on others. Susan Castillo, for instance, has recently put emphasis on Emerson's idea that America will be England's imperial successor: "He is viewing England as an earlier, inferior version of what imperial America . . . is destined to become" (Susan Castillo, "'The Best of Nations'? Race and Imperial Destinies in Emerson's *English Traits*," *The Yearbook of English Studies* 34 [2004]: 111). While Castillo is surely right, her statement says next to nothing about Emerson's complicated stance toward the imperial. For a less reductionist recent reading of *English Traits*, which, in turn, runs the risk of underestimating Emerson's fascination with empire, see Andrew Taylor: "We are hampered in any attempt we may make to read the book as either proudly nationalistic or fawningly neo-colonial. Although the tendency of *English Traits* may seem to reverse the trajectory of Charles Dickens' narrative of disillusion in his *American Notes* (1842), the prophecy of a rising American civilisation in Emerson's text is nevertheless articulated in the most guarded manner" (Andrew Taylor, "'Mixture is a Secret of the English Island.' Transatlantic Emerson and the Location of the Intellectual," *Atlantic Studies* 1, no. 2 [Summer 2004]: 173). For older, still useful,

readings of *English Traits*, see Phyllis Cole, "Emerson, England, and Fate," in *Emerson: Prophecy, Metamorphosis, and Influence* (see note 37 to chapter 4), 83–106; Julie Ellison, "The Edge of Urbanity: Emerson's *English Traits*," *ESQ* 32, no. 2 (Summer 1986): 96–108; and David M. Robinson, *Emerson and the Conduct of Life: Pragmatism and Ethical Purpose in the Later Work* (New York: Cambridge University Press, 1993), chapter 6.

33. Emerson's idea of haunting is thus the exact opposite of Pheng Cheah's, as discussed in the previous chapter. For Cheah, who picks up on Derrida, the idealist organism is haunted by the forces that enable, influence, and "contaminate" it; for Emerson, the absence of the idealist organism—what one could describe as materialist mechanicality—is haunted by the Spirit's tendency toward the ideal organism.

34. Jenine Abboushi Dallal reads the second part of the entry as a confirmation of her claim that Emerson resisted the expansion of slavery but not expansion itself: "Emerson never in fact considered expansionism in its immediate context. The 'local and temporary issue' to which he refers is the extension of slave territory" (Dallal, "American Imperialism UnManifest," 56). Her point, as discussed in chapter 5, is that Emerson regards expansion as a fait accompli, as national destiny. What I am stressing, by contrast, is that Emerson's fatalism did not entirely preclude the possibility and necessity of action. In this case, he in fact poses a New England counterforce to expansion that is as fate-driven as expansion itself.

35. Donald S. Spencer, *Louis Kossuth and Young America: A Study of Sectionalism and Foreign Policy, 1848–1852* (Columbia: University of Missouri Press, 1977), 5. Compare also 5–9.

36. Larry J. Reynolds, *European Revolutions and the American Literary Renaissance* (New Haven, CT: Yale University Press, 1988), 159.

37. Merle E. Curti, "The Impact of the Revolutions of 1848 on American Thought," *Proceedings of the American Philosophical Society* 93, no. 3 (June 1949): 213.

38. Barbara Packer, "Historical Introduction," in *The Collected Works of Ralph Waldo Emerson*, vol. 6, *The Conduct of Life* (Cambridge, MA: Harvard University Press, 2003), xxxvi.

39. For a still-useful account of this second phase of the Young America movement, see Merle E. Curti, "Young America," *American Historical Review* 32, no. 1 (Autumn 1926): 34–55. For a distinction between the movement's two phases—the first one literary, centered on O'Sullivan and the Duyckinck brothers, the second one political, led by George Sanders—see Edward L. Widmer, *Young America: The Flowering of Democracy in New York City* (New York: Oxford University Press, 1999).

40. Outside New England, both the support for intervention and the hysteria over Kossuth's person were rapidly declining. A week after Kossuth left the country in July 1852, the *New York Herald* wrote: "He entered the city with all the pomp, and ceremony, and enthusiasm, which of old attended the victorious general in a Roman triumph, and has left it secretly and in disguise, without a solitary huzza to bid him God-speed" (*New York Herald*, July 22, 1852, quoted in Spencer, *Louis Kossuth and Young America*, 170).

41. *Kossuth in New England: A Full Account of the Hungarian Governor's Visit to Massachusetts* (Boston: John P. Jewett, 1852), 85.

42. In his Farewell Address, Washington wrote: "In the execution of such a plan, nothing is more essential than that permanent, inveterate antipathies against particular nations, and passionate attachments for others, should be excluded; and that, in place of

them, just and amicable feelings towards all should be cultivated. The nation which indulges towards another a habitual hatred, or a habitual fondness, is in some degree a slave" (George Washington, *Washington's Farewell Address to the People of the United States and Webster's First Bunker Hill Oration* [Boston: Houghton Mifflin, 1909], 38).

43. I take this to be an example of what Ernest Renan, in his 1882 essay "What is a Nation?" called the importance of forgetting and remembering in nationalist imaginings. As Benedict Anderson explains in *Imagined Communities*: "Having to 'have already forgotten' tragedies of which one needs unceasingly to be reminded turns out to be a characteristic device in the construction of national genealogies" (Benedict Anderson, *Imagined Communities* [1983], rev. ed. [London: Verso, 2006], 201). For this purpose, the triumph of the revolution worked as well as a tragedy. For his American example, Anderson himself provides a scene from *Moby-Dick*, in which Ishmael is reminded by Queequeg's head of George Washington (Anderson, *Imagined Communities*, 203). Renan's essay "What is a Nation?" is included in *Nation and Narration*, ed. Homi K. Bhabha (New York: Routledge, 1990), 8–22.

44. Compare also the version of this sentence included in "Fate" (*CW*, vol. 6, 7).

45. On May 13, 1852, Thoreau noted in his journal: "The best men that I know are not serene—a world in themselves. They dwell in form. They flatter & study effect—only more finely than the rest. . . . I accuse my finest acquaintances—of an immense frivolity" (Henry D. Thoreau, *Journal 5: 1852–1853*, ed. Patrick F. O'Connell [Princeton, NJ: Princeton University Press, 1997], 51).

BIBLIOGRAPHY

Aarsleff, Hans. *From Locke to Saussure: Essays on the Study of Language and Intellectual History*. Minneapolis: University of Minnesota Press, 1982.

Adorno, Theodor W., and Max Horkheimer. *Dialectic of Enlightenment*. 1947. London: Verso, 1997.

Albee, John. *Remembrances of Emerson*. New York: Robert Grier Cooke, 1901.

Albrecht, James M. "What's the Use of Reading Emerson Pragmatically? The Example of William James." *Nineteenth-Century Prose* 30, nos. 1–2 (Spring/Fall 2003): 388–432.

Althusser, Louis. *Lenin and Philosophy and Other Essays*. Translated by Ben Brewster. New York: Monthly Review Press, 1971.

Anderson, Amanda. "Cosmopolitanism, Universalism, and the Divided Legacies of Modernity." In Cheah and Robbins, *Cosmopolitics*, 265–89.

Anderson, Benedict. *Imagined Communities*. 1983. rev. ed. London: Verso, 2006.

Anonymous. "Illustrated Criticism." *New-York Daily Tribune*, February 6, 1849, 2.

———. "Illustrated Criticism." *Boston Evening Transcript*, February 8, 1849, 2.

———. *Kossuth in New England: A Full Account of the Hungarian Governor's Visit to Massachusetts*. Boston: John P. Jewett, 1852.

———. "Mr Emerson's Lecture." *Boston Evening Transcript*, February 9, 1844, 2.

———. "Ralph Waldo Emerson's First Lecture on 'the Times.'" *New York Weekly Herald*, March 5, 1842, 189.

———. "Unity of the Human Race." *American Whig Review* 12, no. 36 (December 1850): 567–87.

Appiah, Kwame Anthony. *The Ethics of Identity*. Princeton, NJ: Princeton University Press, 2005.

———. "Identity, Authenticity, Survival: Multicultural Societies and Social Reproduction." In Taylor and Gutman, *Multiculturalism*, 149–63.

Arac, Jonathan. "Global and Babel: Two Perspectives on Language in American Literature." *ESQ* 50, nos. 1–3 (2004): 95–119.

Aristotle. *Nicomachean Ethics*. Translated by Terence Irwin. 2nd ed. Indianapolis: Hackett, 1999.

Aronowitz, Stanley. "Reflections on Identity." In Rajchman, *Identity in Question*, 111–27.

Augst, Thomas. *The Clerk's Tale: Young Men and Moral Life in Nineteenth-Century America*. Chicago: University of Chicago Press, 2003.

Bai, Matt. "The Crusader." *New York Times Magazine*, September 9, 2007, 46–53, 116–19.

Barish, Evelyn. *Emerson: The Roots of Prophecy*. Princeton, NJ: Princeton University Press, 1989.

Baym, Nina. "Melodramas of Beset Manhood: How Theories of American Fiction Exclude Women Authors." *American Quarterly* 33, no. 2 (Summer 1981): 123–39.

———. [Review of Myra Jehlen: *American Incarnation*]. *American Literature* 59, no. 2 (Summer 1987): 287–88.

Beck, Ulrich, and Elisabeth Beck-Gernsheim. *Individualization: Institutionalized Individualism and its Social and Political Consequences*. London: Sage, 2002.

Beecher, Henry Ward. *Eyes and Ears*. Boston: Ticknor and Fields, 1863.

Bercovitch, Sacvan. "The Problem of Ideology in American Literary History." *Critical Inquiry* 12, no. 4 (Summer 1986): 631–53.

———. *The Rites of Assent: Transformations in the Symbolic Construction of America*. New York: Routledge, 1993.

Bercovitch, Sacvan, and Myra Jehlen, eds. *Ideology and Classic American Literature*. Cambridge: Cambridge University Press, 1986.

Berlin, Isaiah. *Four Essays on Liberty*. London: Oxford University Press, 1969.

Bhabha, Homi K. *The Location of Culture*. New York: Routledge, 1994.

Bhabha, Homi K., ed. *Nation and Narration*. New York: Routledge, 1990.

Bishop, Jonathan. *Emerson On the Soul*. Cambridge, MA: Harvard University Press, 1964.

Bode, Carl. *The American Lyceum: Town Meeting of the Mind*. New York: Oxford University Press, 1956.

Booth, Wayne C. *The Company We Keep: An Ethics of Fiction*. Berkeley: University of California Press, 1988.

Boyden, Michael. *Predicting the Past: The Paradoxes of American Literary History*. Leuven: Leuven University Press, 2009.

Broaddus, Dottie. "Authoring Elitism: Francis Hutcheson and Hugh Blair in Scotland and America." *Rhetoric Society Quarterly* 24, nos. 3–4 (Summer/Fall 1994): 39–52.

Brown, Wendy. *States of Injury: Power and Freedom in Late Modernity*. Princeton, NJ: Princeton University Press, 1995.

Buell, Lawrence. [Commentary on Henry Nash Smith, "Can 'American Studies' Develop a Method?"]. In *Locating American Studies: The Evolution of a Discipline*, edited by Lucy Maddox, 13–16. Baltimore: Johns Hopkins University Press, 1999.

———. *Emerson*. Cambridge, MA: Harvard University Press, 2003.

———. "The Emerson Industry in the 1980's: A Survey of Trends and Achievements." *ESQ* 30, no. 2 (1984): 117–36.

———. *The Future of Environmental Criticism: Environmental Crisis and Literary Imagination*. Malden, MA: Blackwell, 2005.

———. *Literary Transcendentalism*. Ithaca, NY: Cornell University Press, 1973.

———. *New England Literary Culture*. New York: Cambridge University Press, 1986.

Butler, Judith. *The Psychic Life of Power: Theories in Subjection*. Stanford, CA: Stanford University Press, 1997.

Cadava, Eduardo. *Emerson and the Climates of History*. Stanford, CA: Stanford University Press, 1997.

Cameron, Sharon. "The Way of Life by Abandonment: Emerson's Impersonal." *Critical Inquiry.* 25 (Autumn 1998): 1–31.

Carpenter, Frederic I. "Charles Sanders Peirce: Pragmatic Transcendentalist." *New England Quarterly* 14, no. 1 (March 1941): 34–48.

Castillo, Susan. "'The Best of Nations'? Race and Imperial Destinies in Emerson's *English Traits.*" *Yearbook of English Studies* 34 (2004): 100–11.

Castronovo, Russ. *Necro Citizenship: Death, Eroticism, and the Public Sphere in the Nineteenth-Century United States.* Durham, NC: Duke University Press, 2001.

Castronovo, Russ, and Dana D. Nelson, eds. *Materializing Democracy: Toward a Revitalized Cultural Politics.* Durham, NC: Duke University Press, 2002.

Cavell, Stanley. *Conditions Handsome and Unhandsome: The Constitution of Emersonian Perfectionism.* Chicago: University of Chicago Press, 1990.

———. *Emerson's Transcendental Etudes.* Edited by David Justin Hodge. Stanford, CA: Stanford University Press, 2003.

Cayton, Mary Kupiec. *Emerson's Emergence: Self and Society in the Transformation of New England, 1800–1845.* Chapel Hill: University of North Carolina Press, 1989.

———. "The Making of an American Prophet: Emerson, His Audiences, and the Rise of the Culture Industry in Nineteenth-Century America." *American Historical Review* 92, no. 3 (June 1987): 597–620.

Chambers, Robert. *Vestiges of the Natural History of Creation.* London: John Churchill, 1844.

Channing, Edward T. *Lectures Read to the Seniors at Harvard College.* Boston: Ticknor and Fields, 1856.

Cheah, Pheng. "Given Culture: Rethinking Cosmopolitical Freedom in Transnationalism." In Cheah and Robbins, *Cosmopolitics,* 290–328.

———. *Inhuman Conditions: On Cosmopolitanism and Human Rights.* Cambridge, MA: Harvard University Press, 2007.

———. "Spectral Nationality: The Living On [*sur-vie*] of the Postcolonial Nation in Neocolonial Globalization." *boundary 2* 26, no. 3 (Autumn 1999): 225–52.

———. *Spectral Nationality: Passages of Freedom from Kant to Postcolonial Literatures of Liberation.* New York: Columbia University Press, 2003.

Cheah, Pheng, and Bruce Robbins, eds. *Cosmopolitics: Thinking and Feeling Beyond the Nation.* Minneapolis: University of Minnesota Press, 1998.

Cheyfitz, Eric. "A Common Emerson: Ralph Waldo Emerson in an Ethnohistorical Context." *Nineteenth-Century Prose* 30, nos. 1–2 (Spring/Fall 2003): 250–81.

Clark, Gregory, and S. Michael Halloran. "Introduction: Transformations of Public Discourse in Nineteenth-Century America." In *Oratorical Culture in Nineteenth-Century America,* edited by Gregory Clark and S. Michael Halloran, 1–26. Carbondale: Southern Illinois University Press, 1993.

Cmiel, Kenneth. *Democratic Eloquence: The Fight Over Popular Speech in Nineteenth-Century America.* New York: William Morrow, 1990.

Colapietro, Vincent. "The Question of Voice and the Limits of Pragmatism: Emerson, Dewey, and Cavell." In *The Range of Pragmatism and the Limits of Philosophy,* edited by Richard Shusterman, 174–96. Malden, MA: Blackwell, 2004.

Cole, Phyllis. "Emerson, England, and Fate." In Levin, *Emerson,* 83–106.

———. "The New Movement's Tide: Emerson and Women's Rights." In *Emerson Bicentennial Essays*, edited by Ronald A. Bosco and Joel Myerson, 117–52. Boston: Massachusetts Historical Society; Charlottesville: Distributed by the University of Virginia Press, 2006.

Connolly, William E. *The Ethos of Pluralization*. Minneapolis: University of Minnesota Press, 1995.

Cousin, Victor. *Introduction to the Philosophy of History*. Boston: Hilliard, Gray, Little, and Wilkins, 1832.

Cox, James M. "R. W. Emerson: The Circles of the Eye." In Levin, *Emerson*, 57–81.

Crain, Caleb. *American Sympathy: Men, Friendship, and Literature in the New Nation*. New Haven, CT: Yale University Press, 2001.

Crane, Gregg D. *Race, Citizenship, and Law in American Literature*. New York: Cambridge University Press, 2002.

Crews, Frederick C. *The Critics Bear it Away: American Fiction and the Academy*. New York: Random House, 1992.

———. "Melville the Great." *New York Review of Books* 52, no. 19 (December 1, 2005): 6–12.

———. "The New Americanists." *New York Review of Books* 39, no. 15 (September 24, 1992): 32–34.

———. "Whose American Renaissance?" *New York Review of Books* 35, no. 16 (October 27, 1988): 61–81.

Curti, Merle E. "The Impact of the Revolutions of 1848 on American Thought." *Proceedings of the American Philosophical Society* 93, no. 3 (June 1949): 209–15.

———. "Young America." *American Historical Review* 32, no. 1 (Autumn 1926): 34–55.

Dallal, Jenine Abboushi. "American Imperialism UnManifest: Emerson's 'Inquest' and Cultural Regeneration." *American Literature* 73, no. 1 (Spring 2001): 47–83.

Dauber, Kenneth. "On Not Being Able to Read Emerson, or 'Representative Men.'" *boundary 2* 21, no. 2 (Summer 1994): 220–42.

Delbanco, Andrew. "Melville in the '80s." *American Literary History* 4, no. 4 (Winter 1992): 709–25.

Derrida, Jacques. *The Politics of Friendship*. London: Verso, 1997.

———. *Specters of Marx*. New York: Routledge, 1994.

Dillon, Elizabeth M. "Fear of Formalism: Kant, Twain, and Cultural Studies in American Literature." *Diacritics* 27, no. 4 (Winter 1997): 46–69.

Dimock, Wai Chee. "Introduction: Planet and America, Set and Subset." In Dimock and Buell, *Shades of the Planet*, 1–16.

———. "Scarcity, Subjectivity, and Emerson." *boundary 2* 17, no. 1 (Spring 1990): 83–99.

———. *Through Other Continents: American Literature across Deep Time*. Princeton, NJ: Princeton University Press, 2006.

Dimock, Wai Chee, and Lawrence Buell, eds. *Shades of the Planet: American Literature as World Literature*. Princeton, NJ: Princeton University Press, 2007.

Dolan, Neal. *Emerson's Liberalism*. Madison: University of Wisconsin Press, 2009.

Easthope, Anthony. *Literary into Cultural Studies*. London: Routledge, 1991.

Elliott, Emory. "Diversity in the United States and Abroad: What Does it Mean When American Studies is Transnational?" *American Quarterly* 59, no. 1 (Spring 2007): 1–22.

Ellis, Joseph J. *American Sphinx: The Character of Thomas Jefferson.* New York: Alfred A. Knopf, 1997.

Ellison, Julie. "Aggressive Allegory." *Raritan* 3, no. 3 (Winter 1984): 100–15.

———. "The Edge of Urbanity: Emerson's *English Traits.*" *ESQ* 32, no. 2 (Summer 1986): 96–108.

———. *Emerson's Romantic Style.* Princeton, NJ: Princeton University Press, 1984.

———. "The Gender of Transparency: Masculinity and the Conduct of Life." *American Literary History* 4, no. 4 (Winter 1992): 584–606.

———. "The Laws of Ice: Emerson's Irony and 'The Comic.'" *ESQ* 30, no. 2 (Summer 1984): 73–82.

Ferry, Luc, and Alain Renaut. *French Philosophy of the Sixties.* Translated by Mary Cattani. Amherst: University of Massachusetts Press, 1990.

Field, Peter S. "'The Transformation of Genius into Practical Power': Emerson and the Public Lecture." *Journal of the Early Republic* 21, no. 3 (Autumn 2001): 467–93.

Fisher, Philip. *Hard Facts: Setting and Form in the American Novel.* New York: Oxford University Press, 1985.

———. "Introduction: The New American Studies." In *The New American Studies: Essays from Representations*, edited by Philip Fisher, vii–xxii. Berkeley: University of California Press, 1991.

Fisher, Philip, ed. *The New American Studies: Essays from Representations.* Berkeley: University of California Press, 1991.

Fishkin, Shelley Fisher: "Crossroads of Cultures: The Transnational Turn in American Studies—Presidential Address to the American Studies Association, November 12, 2004." *American Quarterly* 57, no. 1 (March 2005): 17–55.

Fluck, Winfried. "Die 'Amerikanisierung' der Geschichte im *New Historicism.*" In *New Historicism. Literaturgeschichte als Poetik der Kultur*, edited by Moritz Bassler, 229–50. Frankfurt/Main: Fischer, 1995. (English version: "The Activist and the Actor: The Re-Authorization of Historical Criticism in New Historicism." In Fluck, *Romance with America?* 39–48.)

———. "Das ästhetische Vorverständnis der 'American Studies.'" *Jahrbuch für Amerikastudien* 18 (1973): 110–29. (English version: "Aesthetic Premises in American Studies." In Fluck, *Romance with America?* 15–38.)

———. "The Humanities in the Age of Expressive Individualism and Cultural Radicalism." In *The Futures of American Studies*, edited by Donald E. Pease and Robyn Wiegman, 211–30. Durham, NC: Duke University Press, 2002.

———. *Romance with America? Essays on Culture, Literature, and American Studies.* Edited by Laura Bieger and Johannes Voelz. Heidelberg: Winter, 2009.

———. "Theories of American Culture (and the Transnational Turn in American Studies)." *REAL* 23 (2007): 59–77.

———. "Die Wissenschaft vom systemischen Effekt: Von der Counter-Culture zu den Race, Class, and Gender Studies." In *Der Geist der Unruhe. 1968 im Vergleich. Wissenschaft—Literatur—Medien*, edited by Rainer Rosenberg, Inge Münz-Koenen, and Petra Boden, 111–24. Berlin: Akademie-Verlag, 2000.

Fraser, Nancy. "Recognition Without Ethics." In *Recognition and Difference: Politics, Identity, Multiculture*, edited by Scott Lash and Mike Featherstone, 21–42. London: Sage, 2002.

Freud, Sigmund. "Das ökonomische Problem des Masochismus." 1924. *Gesammelte Werke*. Frankfurt/Main: Fischer, 1999 [London: Imago, 1940], vol. 13, 369–84.

Friedl, Herwig. "Thinking America: Emerson and Dewey." In *Negotiations of America's National Identity*, edited by Roland Hagenbüchle and Josef Raab, 2 vols., 2:131–57. Tübingen: Stauffenberg Verlag, 2000.

Fuller, Randall. *Emerson's Ghosts: Literature, Politics, and the Making of Americanists*. New York: Oxford University Press, 2007.

Garvey, Gregory, ed. *The Emerson Dilemma: Essays on Emerson and Social Reform*. Athens: University of Georgia Press, 2001.

Giles, Paul. "Commentary: Hemispheric Partiality." *American Literary History* 18, no. 3 (Fall 2006): 648–55.

———. "The Deterritorialization of American Literature." In Dimock and Buell, *Shades of the Planet*, 39–61.

Goodman, Russell B. "East-West Philosophy in Nineteenth-Century America: Emerson and Hinduism." *Journal of the History of Ideas* 51, no. 4 (October 1990): 625–45.

Gorlier, Claudio. "Listening to the Master: William James and the 'Making of the New' in Italian Culture." In *The Sweetest Impression of Life: The James Family and Italy*, edited by James W. Tuttleton and Agostino Lombardo, 182–96. New York: New York University Press, 1990.

Gougeon, Len. "Emerson and the British: Challenging the Limits of Liberty." *REAL* 22 (2006): 179–213.

———. *Virtue's Hero*. Athens: University of Georgia Press, 1990.

Graff, Gerald. *Professing Literature: An Institutional History*. Chicago: University of Chicago Press, 1987.

Gramsci, Antonio. *Selections from Cultural Writings*. London: Lawrence and Wishart, 1985.

———. *Selections from the Prison Notebooks*. London: Lawrence and Wishart, 1971.

Grossman, Jay. *Reconstituting the American Renaissance: Emerson, Whitman, and the Politics of Representation*. Durham, NC: Duke University Press, 2003.

Grusin, Richard. "Revisionism and the Structure of Emersonian Action." *American Literary History* 1, no. 2 (Summer 1989): 404–31.

Gura, Philip. *American Transcendentalism: A History*. New York: Hill and Wang, 2007.

Guthrie, James R. *Above Time: Emerson's and Thoreau's Temporal Revolutions*. Columbia: University of Missouri Press, 2001.

Habermas, Jürgen. "Struggles for Recognition in the Democratic Constitutional State." In Taylor and Gutman, *Multiculturalism*, 107–48.

———. "Three Normative Models of Democracy." In *Democracy and Difference: Contesting the Boundaries of the Political*, edited by Seyla Benhabib, 21–30. Princeton, NJ: Princeton University Press, 1996.

Hall, Stuart. "The Work of Representation." In *Representation: Cultural Representations and Signifying Practices*, edited by Stuart Hall, 13–74. London: Sage in association with the Open University, 1997.

Halttunen, Karen. *Confidence Men and Painted Women*. New Haven, CT: Yale University Press, 1982.

Hansen, Olaf. *Aesthetic Individualism and Practical Intellect.* Princeton, NJ: Princeton University Press, 1990.

Haselstein, Ulla. "Seen from a Distance: Moments of Negativity in the American Sublime: Tocqueville, Bryant, Emerson." *Amerikastudien/American Studies* 43 (1998): 405–21.

Higginson, Thomas Wentworth. "The American Lecture-System." *Macmillan's Magazine* 18 (May 1868): 48–56.

Holub, Renate. *Antonio Gramsci: Beyond Marxism and Postmodernism.* London: Routledge, 1992.

Honneth, Axel. "Recognition or Redistribution? Changing Perspectives on the Moral Order of Society." In *Recognition and Difference: Politics, Identity, Multiculture,* edited by Scott Lash and Mike Featherstone, 43–56. London: Sage, 2002.

———. *Verdinglichung: Eine Anerkennungstheoretische Studie.* Frankfurt/Main: Suhrkamp, 2006.

Horsman, Reginald. "Origins of Racial Anglo-Saxonism in Great Britain before 1850." *Journal of the History of Ideas* 37, no. 3 (Summer 1976): 387–410.

———. *Race and Manifest Destiny: The Origins of American Racial Anglo-Saxonism.* Cambridge, MA: Harvard University Press, 1981.

Howe, Daniel Walker. *What Hath God Wrought: The Transformation of America, 1815–1848.* New York: Oxford University Press, 2007.

Hutcheson, Francis. *Inquiry into the Origins of Our Ideas of Beauty and Virtue.* 1725. London: Darby, Bettesworth, et al., 1726.

Ickstadt, Heinz. "American Studies in an Age of Globalization." *American Quarterly* 54, no. 4 (December 2002): 543–62.

Innis, Robert E. "Pragmatism and the Analysis of Meaning in the Philosophy of Giovanni Vailati." *Differentia: Review of Italian Thought,* nos. 3–4 (Spring/Autumn 1989): 177–98.

Jameson, Frederic. *The Political Unconscious: Narrative as a Socially Symbolic Act.* Ithaca, NY: Cornell University Press, 1981.

Jay, Martin. *Marxism and Totality: The Adventures of a Concept from Lukács to Habermas.* Berkeley: University of California Press, 1984.

Jehlen, Myra. *American Incarnation: The Individual, the Nation, and the Continent.* Cambridge, MA: Harvard University Press, 1986.

———. "Why Did the Europeans Cross the Ocean? A Seventeenth-Century Riddle." In Kaplan and Pease, *Cultures of United States Imperialism,* 41–58.

Joas, Hans. "Ein Pragmatist wider Willen?" *Deutsche Zeitschrift für Philosophie* 44, no. 4 (1996): 661–70.

Kalinevitch, Karen. "Emerson on Friendship: An Unpublished Manuscript." *Studies in the American Renaissance* 9 (1985): 47–61.

Kaplan, Amy. *The Anarchy of Empire in the Making of U.S. Culture.* Cambridge, MA: Harvard University Press, 2002.

———. "'Left Alone with America': The Absence of Empire in the Study of American Culture." In Kaplan and Pease, *Cultures of United States Imperialism,* 3–21.

———. "Violent Belongings and the Question of Empire Today. Presidential Address to the American Studies Association. October 17, 2003." *American Quarterly* 56, no. 1 (Spring 2004): 1–18.

Kaplan, Amy, and Donald E. Pease, eds. *Cultures of United States Imperialism*. Durham, NC: Duke University Press, 1993.

Kateb, George. *Emerson and Self-Reliance*. Thousand Oaks, CA: Sage, 1995.

Kater, Michael H. "Forbidden Fruit? Jazz in the Third Reich." *American Historical Review* 94, no. 1 (Spring 1989): 11–43.

Kelly, R. Gordon. "Literature and the Historian." *American Quarterly* 26, no. 2 (Summer 1974): 141–59.

Kliger, Samuel. "Emerson and the Usable Anglo-Saxon Past." *Journal of the History of Ideas* 16, no. 4 (October 1955): 476–93.

Kohl, Lawrence. *The Politics of Individualism*. New York: Oxford University Press, 1989.

Korhonen, Kuisma. *Textual Friendship: The Essay as Impossible Encounter*. New York: Humanity Books, 2006.

Kramer, Michael P. "Imagining Authorship in America: 'Whose American Renaissance?' Revisited." *American Literary History* 13, no. 1 (Spring 2001): 108–25.

Kuhn, Thomas S. *The Structure of Scientific Revolutions*. Chicago: University of Chicago Press, 1962.

Kuklick, Bruce. "Myth and Symbol in American Studies." *American Quarterly* 24, no. 4 (Autumn 1972): 435–50.

Laclau, Ernesto, and Chantal Mouffe. *Hegemony and Socialist Strategy*. 1985. 2nd ed. London: Verso, 2001.

Larson, Kerry. "Emerson's Strange Equality." *Nineteenth-Century Literature* 59, no. 3 (Autumn 2004): 315–39.

Lash, Scott. "Preface." In Beck and Beck-Gernsheim, *Individualization*, vii–xiii.

Lee, Maurice S. *Slavery, Philosophy, and American Literature, 1830–1860*. New York: Cambridge University Press, 2005.

LeMenager, Stephanie. *Manifest and Other Destinies*. Lincoln: University of Nebraska Press, 2004.

Lennon, Thomas M. "Locke on Ideas and Representation." In *The Cambridge Companion to Locke's "Essay Concerning Human Understanding,"* edited by Lex Newman, 231–57. Cambridge: Cambridge University Press, 2007.

Levin, Jonathan. *The Poetics of Transition: Emerson, Pragmatism, and American Literary Modernism*. Durham, NC: Duke University Press, 1999.

Liebman, Sheldon W. "The Origins of Emerson's Early Poetics: His Reading in the Scottish Common Sense Critics." *American Literature* 45, no. 1 (March 1973): 23–33.

Losonsky, Michael. "Language, Meaning, and Mind in Locke's *Essay*." In *The Cambridge Companion to Locke's "Essay Concerning Human Understanding,"* edited by Lex Newman, 286–312. Cambridge: Cambridge University Press, 2007.

Lowell, James Russell. "Emerson the Lecturer." In *My Study Windows*. Boston: Houghton, Mifflin, 1871, 375–84.

Lukács, Georg. "Reification and the Consciousness of the Proletariat." In *History and Class Consciousness: Studies in Marxist Dialectics*, translated by Rodney Livingstone, 83–222. Cambridge, MA: MIT Press, 1971.

Macdonell, Diane. *Theories of Discourse: An Introduction*. Oxford: Basil Blackwell, 1986.

Marsh, James. "Preliminary Essay." In Samuel Taylor Coleridge, *Aids to Reflection*, 1st American ed., vii–liii. Burlington, VT, 1829.

Marx, Leo. "American Studies: A Defense of an Unscientific Method." *New Literary History* 1, no. 1 (Autumn 1969): 75–90.

———. "On Recovering the 'Ur' Theory of American Studies." *American Literary History* 17, no. 1 (Spring 2005): 118–34.

Matthiessen, F. O. *American Renaissance: Art and Expression in the Age of Emerson and Whitman*. New York: Oxford University Press, 1941.

McBath, James H. "The Platform and Public Thought." In *The Rhetoric of Protest and Reform 1878–1898*, edited by Paul H. Boase, 320–41. Athens: Ohio University Press, 1980.

Mead, David. *Yankee Eloquence in the Middle West*. East Lansing: Michigan State College Press, 1951.

Mead, George Herbert. *Mind, Self, and Society*. 1934. Chicago: University of Chicago Press, 1955.

———. *The Philosophy of the Present*. 1932. New York: Prometheus Books, 2002.

———. *Selected Writings*. Edited by Andrew J. Reck. Chicago: University of Chicago Press, 1964.

Menand, Louis. "Missionary: Edmund Wilson and American Culture." *New Yorker* 81, no. 23 (August 8 and 15, 2005): 82–88.

Michael, John. "Democracy, Aesthetics, Individualism: Emerson as Public Intellectual." *Nineteenth-Century Prose* 30, nos. 1–2 (Spring/Fall 2003): 195–226.

Michaels, Walter Benn. "The Shape of the Signifier." *Critical Inquiry* 27, no. 2 (Winter 2001): 266–83.

Michaels, Walter Benn, and Donald E. Pease, eds. *The American Renaissance Reconsidered: Selected Papers from the English Institute, 1982–83*. Baltimore: Johns Hopkins University Press, 1985.

Mouffe, Chantal. "Democratic Citizenship and the Political Community," In *Dimensions of Radical Democracy: Pluralism, Citizenship, Community*, edited by Chantal Mouffe, 225–239. London: Verso 1992.

Myers, Gerald. "The Influence of William James's Pragmatism in Italy." In *The Sweetest Impression of Life: The James Family and Italy*, edited by James W. Tuttleton and Agostino Lombardo, 162–81. New York: New York University Press, 1990.

Nelson, Dana D. "Representative/Democracy: The Political Work of Countersymbolic Representation." In Castronovo and Nelson, *Materializing Democracy*, 218–47.

Newfield, Christopher. "Democratic Passions: Reconstructing Individual Agency." In Castronovo and Nelson, *Materializing Democracy*, 314–44.

———. *The Emerson Effect: Individualism and Submission in America*. Chicago: University of Chicago Press, 1996.

Nicoloff, Philip L. *Emerson on Race and History*. New York: Columbia University Press, 1961.

Nietzsche, Friedrich. *The Gay Science: With a Prelude in German Rhymes and an Appendix of Songs*. Cambridge: Cambridge University Press, 2001.

O'Sullivan, John. "The Great Nation of Futurity." *United States Democratic Review* 6, no. 23 (November 1839): 426–30.

Packer, Barbara. *Emerson's Fall*. New York: Continuum, 1982.

———. "Historical Introduction." In *The Collected Works of Ralph Waldo Emerson. Volume VI: The Conduct of Life*, xv–lxvii. Cambridge, MA: Harvard University Press, 2003.

———. "History and Form in Emerson's 'Fate.'" In *Emerson Bicentennial Essays*, edited by Ronald A. Bosco and Joel Myerson, 432–52. Boston: Massachusetts Historical Society; Charlottesville: Distributed by the University of Virginia Press, 2006.

———. "The Transcendentalists." In *The Cambridge History of American Literature*. Vol. 2. Edited by Sacvan Bercovitch. New York: Cambridge University Press, 1995, 331–604.

Parekh, Bhikhu. *Rethinking Multiculturalism: Cultural Diversity and Political Theory*. 2nd ed. New York: Palgrave Macmillan, 2006.

Parrington, Vernon Louis. *Main Currents in American Thought: An Interpretation of American Literature From the Beginnings to 1920*. New York: Harcourt, Brace, 1927–1930.

Patterson, Anita Haya. *From Emerson to King*. New York: Oxford University Press, 1997.

Patterson, Orlando. *Slavery and Social Death*. Cambridge, MA: Harvard University Press, 1982.

Paulson, William. *Literary Culture in a World Transformed*. Ithaca, NY: Cornell University Press, 2001.

Pease, Donald E. "American Studies: An Interview with Donald Pease. Interview by John Eperjesi." *Minnesota Review*, nos. 65–66 (Spring 2006): unpaged. http://www.theminnesotareview.org/journal/ns6566/iae_ns6566_americanstudies.shtml (accessed July 7, 2007).

———. "C. L. R. James, *Moby-Dick*, and the Emergence of Transnational American Studies." In *The Futures of American Studies*, edited by Donald E. Pease and Robyn Wiegman, 135–63. Durham, NC: Duke University Press, 2002.

———. "Emerson, *Nature*, and the Sovereignty of Influence." *boundary 2* 8, no. 3 (Spring 1980): 43–74.

———. "'Experience,' Antislavery, and the Crisis of Emersonianism." *boundary 2* 34, no. 2 (Summer 2007): 71–103.

———. "The Extraterritoriality of the Literature of Our Planet." *ESQ* 50, nos. 1–3 (2004; published 2006): 177–222.

———. "National Identities, Postmodern Artifacts, and Postnational Narratives." *boundary 2* 19, no. 1 (Spring 1992): 1–13.

———. "Negative Interpellations: From Oklahoma City to the Trilling-Matthiessen Transmission." *boundary 2* 23, no. 1 (Spring 1996): 1–33.

———. "New Americanists: Revisionist Interventions into the Canon." *boundary 2* 17, no. 1 (Spring 1990): 1–37.

———. "9/11: When was 'American Studies after the New Americanists'?" *boundary 2* 33, no. 3 (Fall 2006): 73–101.

———. "Preface." In *Revisionist Interventions into the Americanist Canon*, edited by Donald E. Pease, vii–viii. Durham, NC: Duke University Press, 1994.

———. *Visionary Compacts: American Renaissance Writings in Cultural Context*. Madison: University of Wisconsin Press, 1987.

Pease, Donald E., ed. *Revisionist Interventions into the Americanist Canon.* Durham, NC: Duke University Press, 1994.

Pease, Donald. E., and Robyn Wiegman. "Futures." In *The Futures of American Studies,* edited by Donald E. Pease and Robyn Wiegman, 1–42. Durham, NC: Duke University Press, 2002.

Perry, Bliss. *Emerson Today.* Princeton, NJ: Princeton University Press, 1931.

Peukert, Detlev. *Volksgenossen und Gemeinschaftsfremde. Anpassung, Ausmerze und Aufbegehren unter dem Nationalsozialismus.* Cologne: Bund Verlag, 1982. (English version: *Inside Nazi Germany: Conformity, Opposition, and Racism in Everyday Life.* New Haven, CT: Yale University Press, 1987.)

Plato. *Cratylus.* Translated by C. D. C. Reeve. In *Plato: Complete Works,* edited by John M. Cooper, 101–56. Indianapolis: Hackett, 1997.

Poirier, Richard. *Poetry and Pragmatism.* Cambridge, MA: Harvard University Press, 1992.

———. *A World Elsewhere: The Place of Style in American Literature.* New York: Oxford University Press, 1966.

Porter, Carolyn. "Reification and American Literature." In *Ideology and Classic American Literature,* edited by Sacvan Bercovitch and Myra Jehlen, 188–217. Cambridge: Cambridge University Press, 1986.

———. *Seeing and Being: The Plight of the Participant Observer in Emerson, James, Adams, and Faulkner.* Middletown, CT: Wesleyan University Press, 1981.

Radway, Janice. "What's in a Name? Presidential Address to the American Studies Association, November 20, 1998." *American Quarterly* 51, no. 1 (Spring 1999): 1–32.

Rajchman, John, ed. *The Identity in Question.* New York: Routledge, 1995.

Rawls, John. *A Theory of Justice.* Cambridge, MA: Harvard University Press, 1971.

Ray, Angela G. *The Lyceum and Public Culture in the Nineteenth-Century United States.* East Lansing: Michigan State University Press, 2005.

Readings, Bill. *The University in Ruins.* Cambridge, MA: Harvard University Press, 1996.

Reed, Sampson. *Observations on the Growth of the Mind.* 1826. Boston: Otis Clapp, 1838.

Reising, Russell J. *The Unusable Past: Theory and the Study of American Literature.* New York: Methuen, 1986.

Renan, Ernest. "What is a Nation?" 1882. In Bhabha, *Nation and Narration,* 8–22.

Reynolds, David S. *Beneath the American Renaissance: The Subversive Imagination in the Age of Emerson and Melville.* New York: Alfred A. Knopf, 1988.

Reynolds, Larry J. *European Revolutions and the American Literary Renaissance.* New Haven, CT: Yale University Press, 1988.

Richardson, Joan. *A Natural History of Pragmatism.* New York: Cambridge University Press, 2007.

Richardson, Robert D. Jr. *Emerson: The Mind on Fire.* Berkeley: University of California Press, 1995.

———. "Schleiermacher and the Transcendentalists." In *Transient and Permanent: The Transcendentalist Movement and Its Contexts,* edited by Charles Capper and Conrad E. Wright, 121–47. Boston: Massachusetts Historical Society, 1999. Distributed by Northeastern University Press.

Riss, Arthur. *Race, Slavery, and Liberalism in Nineteenth-Century American Literature.* New York: Cambridge University Press, 2006.

Robinson, David M. *Apostle of Culture: Emerson as Preacher and Lecturer.* Philadelphia: University of Pennsylvania Press, 1982.

———. *Emerson and the Conduct of Life: Pragmatism and Ethical Purpose in the Later Work.* New York: Cambridge University Press, 1993.

Rohr, Susanne. *Über die Schönheit des Findens: Die Binnenstruktur Menschlichen Verstehens nach Charles S. Peirce: Abduktionslogik und Kreativität.* Stuttgart: M&P, Verlag für Wissenschaft und Forschung, 1993.

Rowe, John Carlos. *At Emerson's Tomb: The Politics of Classic American Literature.* New York: Columbia University Press, 1997.

———. "Deconstructing America: Recent Approaches to Nineteenth-Century Literature and Culture." *ESQ* 31, no. 1 (Spring 1985): 49–63.

———. *Literary Culture and U.S. Imperialism: From the Revolution to World War II.* Oxford: Oxford University Press, 2000.

———. *The New American Studies.* Minneapolis: University of Minnesota Press, 2002.

———. "Nineteenth-Century United States Literary Culture and Transnationality." *PMLA* 118, no. 1 (2003): 78–89.

———. "Surplus Economies: Deconstruction, Ideology, and the Humanities." In *The Aims of Representation: Subject/Text/History,* edited by Murray Krieger, 131–58. Stanford, CA: Stanford University Press, 1987.

———. "'To Live outside the Law, You Must Be Honest': The Authority of the Margin in Contemporary Theory." *Cultural Critique,* no. 2 (Winter 1985): 35–68.

Rowe, John Carlos, ed. *Post-Nationalist American Studies.* Berkeley: University of California Press, 2000.

Ryan, Susan M. *The Grammar of Good Intentions.* Ithaca, NY: Cornell University Press, 2003.

Said, Edward. *Culture and Imperialism.* New York: Alfred A. Knopf, 1993.

Saito, Naoko. *The Gleam of Light: Moral Perfectionism and Education in Dewey and Emerson.* New York: Fordham University Press, 2005.

Sandel, Michael. "The Procedural Republic and the Unencumbered Self." *Political Theory* 12, no. 1 (Spring 1984): 81–96.

Santayana, George. *Interpretations of Poetry and Religion.* New York: Scribner's Sons, 1900.

Sassen, Saskia. *Territory, Authority, Rights.* Princeton, NJ: Princeton University Press, 2006.

Scorza, Jason A. "Liberal Citizenship and Civic Friendship." *Political Theory* 32, no. 1 (February 2004): 85–108.

Scott, Donald M. "The Profession that Vanished: Public Lecturing in Mid-Nineteenth-Century America." In *Professions and Professional Ideologies in America,* edited by Gerald L. Geison, 12–28. Chapel Hill: University of North Carolina Press, 1983.

———. "The Popular Lecture and the Creation of a Public in Mid-Nineteenth-Century America." *Journal of American History* 66, no. 4 (March 1980): 791–809.

Schueller, Malini Johar. *U.S. Orientalisms: Race, Nation, and Gender in Literature, 1790–1890.* Ann Arbor: University of Michigan Press, 1998.

Scott, Walter. *Ivanhoe.* 1817. New York: Modern Library, 2001.

Sebouhian, George. "A Dialogue with Death: An Examination of Emerson's 'Friendship.'" *Studies in the American Renaissance* 13 (1989): 219–39.

Sellers, Charles. *The Market Revolution: Jacksonian America, 1815–1846.* New York: Oxford University Press, 1991.

Sen, Amartya. *Identity and Violence: The Illusion of Destiny.* New York: Norton, 2006.

Simmons, Nancy Craig. "Emerson and his Audiences: The New England Lectures, 1843–44." In *Emerson Bicentennial Essays,* edited by Ronald A. Bosco and Joel Myerson, 51–85. Boston: Massachusetts Historical Society; Charlottesville: Distributed by the University of Virginia Press, 2006.

Sklar, Robert. "American Studies and the Realities of America." *American Quarterly* 22, no. 2, part 2 (Summer 1970): 597–605.

Smith, Henry Nash. "Can 'American Studies' Develop a Method?" *American Quarterly* 9, no. 2, part 2 (Summer 1957): 197–208.

Spencer, Donald S. *Louis Kossuth and Young America: A Study of Sectionalism and Foreign Policy, 1848–1852.* Columbia: University of Missouri Press, 1977.

Stallo, John Bernard. *General Principles of the Philosophy of Nature.* Boston: Crosby and Nichols, 1848.

Sumida, Stephen. "Where in the World is American Studies? Presidential Address to the American Studies Association. November 15, 2002." *American Quarterly* 55, no. 3 (Fall 2003): 333–52.

Swedenborg, Emanuel. *Concerning Heaven, and its Wonders, and Concerning Hell; From Things Heard and Seen.* 1758. Boston: Boston New Church Printing Society, 1837.

Taylor, Andrew. "'Mixture is a Secret of the English Island.' Transatlantic Emerson and the Location of the Intellectual." *Atlantic Studies* 1, no. 2 (Summer 2004): 158–77.

Taylor, Charles. "The Politics of Recognition." In Taylor and Gutman, *Multiculturalism,* 25–73.

Taylor, Charles, and Amy Gutman, eds. *Multiculturalism: Examining the Politics of Recognition.* Princeton, NJ: Princeton University Press, 1994.

Taylor, George Rogers. *The Transportation Revolution, 1815–1860.* New York: Rinehart, 1951.

Teichgraeber, Richard F. III. *Sublime Thoughts/Penny Wisdom: Situating Emerson and Thoreau in the American Market.* Baltimore: Johns Hopkins University Press, 1995.

Thomas, Joseph M. "Poverty and Power: Revisiting Emerson's Poetics." In *Emerson Bicentennial Essays,* edited by Ronald A. Bosco and Joel Myerson, 213–46. Boston: Massachusetts Historical Society; Charlottesville: Distributed by the University of Virginia Press, 2006.

Thoreau, Henry D. *Journal 5: 1852–1853.* Edited by Patrick F. O'Connell. Princeton, NJ: Princeton University Press, 1997.

Tilton, Eleanor. "The True Romance of Anna Hazard Barker and Samuel Gray Ward." *Studies in the American Renaissance* 11 (1987): 53–72.

Tocqueville, Alexis de. *Democracy in America* and *Two Essays on America.* Translated by Gerald E. Bevan. New York: Penguin Classics, 2003.

Todorov, Tzvetan. *Theories of the Symbol.* Translated by Catherine Porter. Oxford: Basil Blackwell, 1982.

Tompkins, Jane. *Sensational Designs: The Cultural Work of American Fiction, 1790–1860.* New York: Oxford University Press, 1986.

Trachtenberg, Alan. *Brooklyn Bridge: Fact and Symbol.* New York: Oxford University Press, 1965.

Trilling, Lionel. *The Liberal Imagination.* New York: Viking, 1950.

———. *Sincerity and Authenticity.* Cambridge, MA: Harvard University Press, 1971.

Turner, Sharon. *The History of the Anglo-Saxons.* 3 vols. 1799–1805. Paris: Baudry's European Library, 1840.

Turner, Victor. "Social Dramas and Stories about Them." *Critical Inquiry* 7, no. 1 (Autumn 1980): 141–68.

Wald, Priscilla. "Fabulous Shadows: Rethinking the Emersonian Tradition." [Review of Rowe, *At Emerson's Tomb*]. *American Quarterly* 50, no. 4 (December 1998): 831–39.

Walls, Laura Dassow. *Emerson's Life in Science: The Culture of Truth.* Ithaca, NY: Cornell University Press, 2003.

Warren, James P. *Culture of Eloquence: Oratory and Reform in Antebellum America.* University Park: Pennsylvania State University Press, 1999.

Washington, George. *Washington's Farewell Address to the People of the United States and Webster's First Bunker Hill Oration.* Boston: Houghton Mifflin, 1909.

Watson, Harry L. *Liberty and Power: The Politics of Jacksonian America.* New York: Hill and Wang, 1990.

Widmer, Edward L. *Young America: The Flowering of Democracy in New York City.* New York: Oxford University Press, 1999.

Williams, Raymond. *Culture and Society 1780–1950.* New York: Columbia University Press, 1958.

———. *Marxism and Literature.* Oxford: Oxford University Press, 1977.

Wilson, Edmund. *The Cold War and the Income Tax: A Protest.* New York: Farrar, Straus, 1963.

Wilson, R. Jackson. "Emerson as Lecturer: Man Thinking, Man Saying." In *The Cambridge Companion to Ralph Waldo Emerson*, edited by Joel Porte and Saundra Morris, 76–96. New York: Cambridge University Press, 1999.

Wise, Gene. "'Paradigm Dramas' in American Studies: A Cultural and Institutional History of the Movement." *American Quarterly* 31, no. 3 (1979): 293–337.

Wood, Allen W. "Kant's Project for Perpetual Peace." In Cheah and Robbins, *Cosmopolitics*, 59–76.

Wyatt, David M. "Spelling Time: The Reader in Emerson's 'Circles.'" *American Literature* 48, no. 2 (May 1976): 140–51.

INDEX

abolitionism. *See* Emerson, Ralph Waldo: and (anti-)slavery

Adams, John Quincy, 236

Adams, John, 291n5

Adorno, Theodor W.: *Dialectic of Enlightenment*, 196, 289–90n34

aesthetic experience: and correspondence (Emerson), 83–85; and recognition in literature, 121; of sincerity and self-culture, 72, 75. *See also* reception aesthetics

Albee, John, 66, 262nn18, 19

Althusser, Louis: and Jacques Lacan, 37–39; "Ideology and Ideological State Apparatuses," 36–37; and interpellation, 6, 41, 50, 54, 57–58, 107–8, 114–15, 126, 257n52; and structuralism, 36, 49

American exceptionalism, 1, 3, 175, 180, 189; and Emerson's rhetoric during Civil War, 242

American Renaissance, 2, 3, 55, 108

American Studies: function of critical theory for, 24–25; historical development of, 19–27; Myth and Symbol School of, 19–24, 108, 248n10, 249n3, 249–50n6; and the nation, 8, 247n5. *See also* New Americanists; transnational American Studies; empire criticism

American Studies Association (ASA): presidential addresses, 189–94, 287n23

American Whig Review, 223

Anderson, Benedict, 297n43

Anglo-Saxonism: and anti-French sentiment, 210–11; and Emerson's nationalism, 201–12; and Gothic myth, 210; racialization of, 211

Appiah, Kwame Anthony, 110, 118; and narrative identity, 132–33

Arac, Jonathan, 8; "Global and Babel," 186–88, 201–2

Aristotle, 97, 137, 161, 279n17

Arnim, Bettina von: *Goethe's Correspondence with a Child*, 146–47

Aronowitz, Stanley, 274–75nn35, 36

ASA. *See* American Studies Association

Associated Western Literary Societies, 71

Augst, Thomas: *The Clerk's Tale*, 64–65; on Emerson's philosophical style, 259n1

authorial intention, 14–15; 207

AWLS. *See* Associated Western Literary Societies

Bai, Matt, 283–84n5

Bakhtin, Mikhail, 39, 275n36

Barker, Anna, 145–47, 152, 278n10

Barnum, P. T., 262n16

Barthes, Roland, 39

Baym, Nina, 34, 286n15,

Beck, Ulrich, 248n8

Beecher, Henry Ward, 261–62n16

Bercovitch, Sacvan, 52, 274n30; on American ideology, 13–14, 251–52n17; associated with New Americanists, 252n17; and *The Cambridge History*